STUDIES IN UK LAW

STUDIES IN UK LAW 2002

Edited by
JOHN BELL

UKNCCL
2002

Published by
The United Kingdom National Committee of Comparative Law
<http://www.ukncel.bham.ac.uk>

British Library Cataloguing in Publication Data
A Catalogue record of this book is available from the British Library

ISBN 0–904281–17–5

Distributed by the British Institute of International and Comparative Law
Charles Clore House, 17 Russell Square, London WC1B 5DR
<http://www.biicl.org>

Typeset by Cambrian Typesetters
Frimley, Surrey
Printed in Great Britain by Biddles Ltd,
Guildford and King's Lynn

CONTENTS

Note: The reference numbers relate to the Sections of the XVI Congress of Comparative Law to which the reports relate

PART FOUR: COMMERCIAL LAW

PART FIVE: CRIMINAL PROCEDURE

LIST OF CONTRIBUTORS

STATHIS BANAKAS, University of East Anglia

DOUGLAS BRODIE, University of Edinburgh

DAVID L CAREY MILLER, Professor of Property Law, School of Law, University of Aberdeen

JANET DINE, Professor of Law, University of Essex

LILIAN EDWARDS, Senior Lecturer, Faculty of Law, University of Edinburgh

JOËLLE GODARD, Lecturer, Faculty of Law, University of Edinburgh

KAY GOODALL, School of Law, University of Glasgow

GERALD MCCORMACK, Professor of Law, University of Manchester

LOUKAS A MISTELIS, Clive M Schmitthoff Senior Lecturer in International Commercial Law, School of International Arbitration, Centre for Commercial Law Studies, Queen Mary, University of London

ESIN ÖRÜCÜ, Professor of Law, University of Glasgow

MARGARET ROSS, University of Aberdeen

CHARLOTTE WAELDE, Co-Director AHRB Research Centre for Studies in Intellectual Property and Technology Law, University of Edinburgh

INTRODUCTION

The papers included in this volume were prepared as the UK contributions to the *XVIth Congress of the International Academy of Comparative Law* held in Brisbane, Australia, on 14–20 July 2002. The papers were prepared in the light of a questionnaire produced by the General Reporter for each topic. These general reports will be published separately, including the reports of the four UK general reporters: Michael Addo, Andrew Ashworth, John Bridge, and Christopher Rodgers. The Table of Contents indicates the Congress topic area to which paper relates. This volume presents the papers as self-standing chapters that can be read in their own right. They give detailed and up-to-date insights into current issues in the law of the United Kingdom. Readers will be aware that the United Kingdom has three jurisdictions—Scotland, England and Wales, and Northern Ireland. It was not considered fruitful to have three chapters on each topic, since this might lead to much overlap. Rather, the chapters present either the position in the lead jurisdiction or that in a jurisdiction that has an interesting and distinctive position, which is not well covered in the existing literature.

The United Kingdom National Committee of Comparative Law has brought these papers together. It is grateful to the British Academy for an Overseas Conference Grant, which enabled so many colleagues to participate in this Congress.

Because of the timescale for submitting reports to the General Reporters, the law is stated in the papers as at 1 January 2002.

JOHN BELL
Chair, UKNCCL

PART ONE: GENERAL

Chapter 1

Teaching Comparative Law and Comparative Law Teaching in the UK

*Esin Örücü**

I. INTRODUCTION

This Rapport follows the guidelines provided in the questionnaire circulated by the General Rapporteur to the National Rapporteurs for the topic IC. Most of the issues raised have been addressed. Other items regarded as worthy of consideration have been added. In order to answer some of the questions, the empirical method has been preferred and to this end a list of fifteen questions covering issues posed by the General Rapporteur was sent to a hundred Law Schools and Law teaching institutions in the UK which might be teaching comparative law in any of its forms.[1] Forty responses have been received (40 per cent response rate). Sixteen of these were to the effect that in these institutions comparative law is not taught (41 per cent of the responses). Of these, two were about to introduce comparative law teaching in the form of, in one case a half option in Comparative Law of Obligations, and in the other, a module on Comparative Law and the European Union as part of a new LL M degree in European Union Law. Five responses (12 per cent of the responses) were to the effect that, though there is no comparative law course on offer, comparative law is an integral part of many of the 'substantive law' modules (two responses) or, that though comparative law is not on offer, the institution is part of the SOCRATES exchange or TEMPUS Programmes (three responses). Of these five, one stated that some final year dissertations are written comparatively. Eighteen of the respondent institutions do teach comparative law offering courses called 'Comparative Law' and/or courses that would qualify as teaching comparative law or teaching law comparatively (47 per cent of responses). The following therefore relies on the replies from these eighteen

* Professor of Law at the University of Glasgow.

1 Although there are eighty-seven Law Schools in the UK, the questionnaire was sent to all law teaching institutions in the SPTL Directory for 2001. Since all the positive responses were returned from Law Schools however, the positive response rate could be regarded as 21.7 per cent of all Law Schools.

institutions—in fact nineteen, with my own response included—and my personal assessment of teaching of comparative law and comparative law teaching in the UK.[2] This therefore, cannot be regarded as a complete survey, but the information provided by the respondents warrants generalisation.

Although there appears to be 'a discernible trend in law schools around the world to improve the teaching of law in general, and comparative law in particular',[3] and although academics and practitioners may be 'aware that solutions to transnational problems often require the application of international laws and harmonized national legislation', these general observations by the General Rapporteur cannot be easily substantiated as regards the UK. It is 'increasingly important that law students as well as legal practitioners receive education tailored to match the challenges of the modern world', but they still find the unknown intimidating and sometimes think it unnecessary to spend time on this subject, and in the law teaching institutions the number of students taking such courses when on offer is rather small. It is certainly true that legal professionals are today more closely involved with foreign law, foreign lawyers and foreign clients. Therefore how foreign law is known and taught is becoming more important.[4]

This study is concerned with the two major topics: *Teaching comparative law*, and *comparative law teaching*. The General Rapporteur defined the topics thus:

> The first topic deals with the actual teaching of comparative law in universities and comparative law institutes. In particular, this topic examines the teaching methods used . . . in the comparative law discipline. . . . . The second topic deals with the impact of current global developments on the teaching of comparative law. In particular, it focuses on the influences of globalisation and multi-culturalism on the teaching of comparative law.

II. COMPARATIVE LAW IN BRITISH UNIVERSITIES

A. Teaching Comparative Law

1. Traditional Teaching Methods and Teaching Comparative Law

The traditional teaching methods, such as lectures and tutorials, do not provide adequate legal education for students and practitioners in any area

[2] See the Appendix for a summary of responses.

[3] Unless otherwise indicated all remarks in quotation marks are from the Note sent to National Rapporteurs by the General Rapporteur, Professor Gabriel Moens, Australia.

[4] See DJ Gerber, 'Globalization and Legal Knowledge: Implications for Comparative Law' (2001) 75 *Tul.L.Rev.* 949 at 975.

of law, but limits of time and financial restraints in the universities tend to encourage such methods, especially in the first two years of legal study.

In the teaching of comparative law to students or practitioners, traditional teaching methods, including the lecture and seminar methods, backed up by problem-focused examinations and essays, are considered to be appropriate, especially if the legal systems covered are from the same or similar socio-legal traditions. This is the case in most institutions in the UK.

It must be pointed out that teaching methods generally used in the UK in the teaching of comparative law are in no way different to the teaching methods used in most other areas of law. If the course is offered as a final year or an LL M course, then the students are expected to analyse areas of law and/or systems of law chosen by them and, in this context, to provide their own bibliography.

2. The Use of Electronic Technology in Teaching Comparative Law

Electronic technology such as the Internet, especially Westlaw and Lexis-Nexis, is actively used as a teaching aid in the teaching of comparative law, and as a general research tool. Most University courses, including comparative law, now require students to be conversant with internet sources and more and more material on foreign legal systems, both legislative material and court decisions, is included in reading lists. However, this is in no way different to the teaching of other law subjects. The main point here is that intelligent use must be made of these sources and the student should be equipped with the capacity to sift through the bulk of available information and transform it into knowledge. Here the task of the teacher of comparative law may be more onerous than that of the teacher of domestic law as the sheer volume of information may lead the student to incorrect conclusions. The toughest challenge is how to handle the sheer mass of ever changing and increasing law on-line.

B. What Does Comparative Law Encourage: Thinking Within the Law or Thinking Upon the Law?

This question highlights a difference in emphasis in the two approaches to Comparative Law that we see today among comparatists: the normative inquiry and the contextual or jurisprudential inquiry. Some comparative law teaching concentrates on an examination of statutory regimes adopted in different legal systems and some focuses on an exploration of the historical, jurisprudential and cultural backgrounds of studied legal systems. It is true that most law teachers are skeptical of cultural analysis and prefer normative inquiry, but a number of colleagues, and therefore, institutions, do try to focus the students' minds on social, historical, cultural, and economic contexts.[5]

The historical legacy of a largely vocational training persists in Britain with little contact between lawyers and social scientists. The reasons for the lack of interest and confidence in theory and the relative lack of methodological debate are partly cultural and partly institutional. Except in jurisprudence courses, undergraduate students are often not exposed to these concerns. Comparative law should provide a good opportunity for developing these interests and skills, but on the whole comparative law courses remain either simply descriptive or, at best, functionally oriented. The approach is either an anatomical survey of the rules, or oriented around legal problems by laying down rules with similar functions side-by-side thus exposing students to variations on a larger general theme.

As becomes evident from the responses, many of the law teaching institutions offer purely vocational courses and not comparative law in any of its forms. In the undergraduate programmes, comparative law, where it is taught, is on an individualistic and idiosyncratic basis, its flair depending entirely on the teacher. There is no programmed approach to comparative law in the curriculum. Individual academics are left to fend for themselves. For both students and young members of staff there is a danger of being left in relative ignorance. Rather than being fundamental to the education of lawyers of tomorrow, comparative law is envisaged at best, as a 'add-on'.

There is a place for the comparison of 'decontextualised facts' as there is a place for the appreciation of the 'big questions'. It is true that one cannot study formal legal texts alone. 'Comparative law loses some of its utility, and most of its charm, if it reduces itself to a level of dry, formalistic, historical introduction to foreign legal systems, and comparison of legal rules and institutions.'[6] 'Comparative law must come to life and help us confront the major choices of the times, . . . policy analysis . . . must be integrated into comparative law.'[7] As a matter of fact it is possible to combine the two approaches in one comparative law course. The aims of the course and the inclinations of the lecturer determine this choice. As long as students are aware of the options and different trends in comparative law scholarship,

[5] See generally, G Samuel, 'Comparative law as a core subject' (2001) 21 *Legal Studies*, 444; id, 'Comparative Law and Jurisprudence' (1998) 47 *ICLQ*, 817; J Gordley, 'Is Comparative Law a Distinct Discipline?' (1998) 46 *Am J Comp L*, 607; GP Fletcher, 'Comparative Law as a Subversive Discipline' (1998) 46 *Am J Comp L*, 683; RB Schlesinger, 'The Past and Future of Comparative Law' (1995) 43 *Am J Comp L*, 477; VG Curran, 'Dealing in Difference: Comparative Law's Potential for Broadening Legal Perspective' (1998) 46 *Am J Comp L*, 657; NV Demleitner, 'Challenge, Opportunity and Risk: An Era of Change in Comparative Law' (1998) 46 *Am J Comp L*, 647; and, PG Kozyris, 'Comparative Law for the Twenty-First Century: New Horizons and New Technologies' (1994), 69 *Tulane LR*. 165.

[6] Kozyris, op cit, above n 5, 175.

[7] Ibid.

there can be nothing wrong with 'the fragmentation of comparative law'. Both thinking within the law and thinking upon the law are fundamental to legal education and it may not be possible to do one well without the other.

It must be observed however, that in the UK the emphasis in law teaching being on 'thinking within the law', comparative law teaching on the whole reflects this approach. It is a truism that teaching and scholarship agendas reinforce each other.

1. Alternative Teaching Methods

One of the alternative teaching methods, the art of mooting, which is used as part of domestic law teaching, is not used extensively in the teaching of comparative law in the UK, although more and more British law students enter international moots and competitions. Mooting competitions, especially international competitions such as the Telder's International Moot, are popular. Whether these competitions are helpful in teaching comparative law is doubtful, as they are not geared towards comparative law but rather towards mooting and competition. Enhancing an interest in comparative law however, could be a by-product, though the main emphasis remains on international law.

Law Schools have two options: to have their students study foreign law under foreign professors in programmes such as summer programmes abroad, ERASMUS programmes, in foreign universities long enough to obtain a foreign law degree along with their own, or, to bring professors from abroad to teach students who remain at home.

Visits by students to law schools and comparative law institutes in other countries are valuable in the teaching of comparative law. Such visits are on the whole possible only through Programmes such as ERASMUS, SOCRATES, and TEMPUS. These Programmes can be beneficial for future practitioners, depending on how they are run, and how much is done for purely educational reasons and how much for the prestige of the institutions concerned. If well run, they introduce students to different socio-legal cultures, help in overcoming barriers between peoples of different traditions and help to create broader minds. However, the courses offered are mostly in English, thus the students do not get the real taste of the foreign legal system, do not study the primary sources and do not mix well with the host student body, tending to stay with their own group.[8] At present, these Programmes remain at the level of interesting experiences for both teachers and students, although, those students who do participate in such Programmes are reported to be more interested in comparative law upon their return and do better on the whole than those who stay at home.

8 They are also more interested in things other than the law environment.

For teachers of comparative law, 'teaching tourism' is fashionable and can be a beneficial experience. Whether 'teaching tourism' is really beneficial to teachers and students alike, depends to a large extent on the integrity of the individual researcher and teacher. 'Teaching tourism' can of course be 'disguised imperialism of legal systems'. To generalise on this point however, is extremely dangerous and puts individuals and institutions as well as legal systems in straight jackets. When carried out within the European Union for example, the purpose of 'teaching tourism' is more to facilitate legal integration than to establish the hegemony of one legal system over another. If, however, it is an American or a German scholar on a teaching visit to Ukraine or Turkmenistan, this could be regarded as a step to facilitate the export of his/her legal system.

Teaching comparative law can be regarded as directly related to the import/export market in law, since one of the functions of comparative law is to provide a pool of models to be used in law reform. Legal transpositions are much in evidence today and comparatists are being asked to aid in the smooth import/export of legal institutions.

Comparative law research projects and conferences are invaluable in the teaching of comparative law. As teaching and research must go hand in hand, the experience gained, the contacts formed and the ideas exchanged, essentially benefit teachers and postgraduate students, and indirectly, undergraduate students. It is important and desirable to secure the participation of law students in research projects and conferences. However, in the real world, the restraints of time and money preclude this. Students often participate as ushers and usherettes to make money rather than to take part in the proceedings. Postgraduate students on the other hand give, and should be encouraged to give papers and to overcome their methodological deficiencies in comparative research through attending such gatherings.

It must be admitted however that in the UK, the degree of specialisation required in order to offer comparative law courses proper and sufficient funding for significant comparative law studies do not exist. There are no special funding bodies such as for example, those for socio-legal studies, dedicated to comparative law research.

C. Assessing the Quality of Comparative Law Teaching

In the UK no special techniques, modern or otherwise, are used in the evaluation of comparative law teaching different to the evaluation of the teaching of other topics. There is no special input by comparatists in quality assurance committees, for example. Concepts of assessment are the same as for other law disciplines and courses. If there were recognised methods of good practice and if there were sufficient demand for, and offer of, comparative law courses, Law Schools could set up quality assessment programmes to identify, recognise and encourage better teaching of comparative law. Substantive law courses that pay lip service to comparative law by cursory reference to practices in other legal systems, should be assessed by comparatists on the teams of quality assessors. The question can become, 'Are there enough experienced comparatists to serve on such assessment programmes?' Similar to the US, 'oftentimes those listed as comparativists have a tenuous connection to the discipline',[9] typical comparatists teaching and researching in a number of unrelated areas. So, who should be considered full-time comparatists?

III. COMPARATIVE LAW TEACHING

A. *Comparative Law Teaching and Multiplicity of Cultures*

Comparative law teaching can contribute to an evaluation of one's own culture and the culture of others if taught in context. In context, comparative law teaching creates a synergetic interrelationship between two or more cultures. However, the dominant normative approach may not only inhibit this but lead to self-satisfaction. Instead of widening horizons, it could lead to a re-assertion of the superiority of one's own legal culture and ready criticism of others. There is a danger that the teaching of comparative law can result in the exposition of the weaknesses of other legal systems and an overemphasis of the merits of one's own. Much depends on the teacher and the systems chosen for study.

Comparative law teaching can result in cultural criticism or it can become a genuine attempt to understand the thinking of other lawyers. In most cases, it does neither, merely serving as a source of information, which unfortunately students do not always fully use.

A cross-cultural approach to, and an understanding of, different cultures can become the key to successful comparative law teaching. However, most courses on comparative law do not approach the subject in this manner. As this author has said on many earlier occasions, comparative law training must create an awareness of differences between the similar and similarities between the different. 'The value of studying foreign law alongside one's own is even greater when they do differ',[10] as the student is encouraged to think when he sees two answers.

General comparative law courses, after a cursory introduction to methodology and the aims and purposes of comparative law, follow the traditional path of getting the students to observe rather than to appreciate

[9] VV Palmer, 'Insularity and Leadership in American Comparative Law: The Past One Hundred Years' (2001) 75 *Tul L Rev*, 1093, at 1099.

[10] Gordley, 'Comparative Law and Legal Education', 1003 at 1008.

the major legal families of the world in a century-old fashion. Specific autonomous comparative law courses and integrated courses often merely expose the student to only one or two examples of how a foreign legal system deals with the same problem, and in the UK these are mostly systems in the EU or the more prominent systems of the Commonwealth. Asian and African literature is growing, so is literature on former communist nations, but even then the discourse is conducted mostly with the traditional tools of the Western legal tradition and the teaching is from the point of view of the law of the country where the course is offered. Moving from the Eurocentric to the global is difficult and there are additional and serious linguistic and cultural obstacles. Even if these obstacles are removed for those engaged in comparative law research, how could this be done for students taking comparative law courses?

Some comparatists who put the emphasis on legal theory do include the cultural and contextual approach in their teaching,[11] but on the whole, many comparatists teaching comparative law to undergraduate students would not regard studying and then teaching the legal thinking of a foreign culture as their primary concern and would not necessarily consider that comparative law should aim at understanding ideas at work in foreign legal systems. 'Theory has seldom been an important part of comparative law scholarship because it has been perceived to have little value for existing objectives.'[12] However, theory is necessary for developing effective tools for interpreting legal information in on-line studies and better understanding the process by which we acquire, process, and transmit legal knowledge; a language of comparative law needs to be created.[13]

In Scotland, traditionally comparative law has been thought of in connection with Jurisprudence and Legal History, but in England and Northern Ireland it takes on a more practical character and remains, maybe out of necessity and being a marginal subject, normative in nature. The only institution to take a cultural slant throughout legal education including comparative law education is SOAS (School of Oriental and African Studies, London University) School of Law.[14]

When a survey was carried out on the place of legal history in the teaching of comparative law in the UK for the XVth International Congress of Comparative Law in Bristol in 1998, the UK Rapporteur thought that first a distinction should be made

> between those universities in which courses dealing with other legal systems are explicitly courses on comparative law and those in which other legal systems are

[11] See, eg, the Appendix for Kent.

[12] Gerber, op cit, above n 4, 969.

[13] Ibid, 972.

[14] See the summary of the response received from SOAS in the Appendix.

taught but in the relevant courses where any comparison is more implicit than explicit.[15]

In the latter case, foreign legal systems are taught but not in designated comparative law courses, and in these there may be incidental comparisons but

> no sustained attempt to draw comparisons between the two systems as comparative lawyers seek to do for the various reasons which draw them into the field of comparative law.[16]

The present study therefore includes, as indicated, an Appendix by which the reader can see which universities offer which kind of teaching of comparative law.

The historical approach was found to be the mainstream approach to the teaching of comparative law in the UK, at least as a starting point,[17] followed by the functional approach. Generally in the UK, courses in comparative law deal with private law and recently with public law, constitutionalism and human rights. Most courses, with the exception of those at SOAS, deal mainly with systems in the Western legal tradition, and mainstream comparative law narrowly focuses on national legal systems.

B. Comparative Law and Globalisation

Global players and/or multinational law firms do not necessarily have an impact on comparative law teaching. It is possible that 'the needs of multinational companies are met by the expertise of multinational law firms which promote the harmonisation of legal systems and the globalisation of law better than law schools ever could'. It must be stressed here that the necessity perceived by multi-national law firms is not that perceived by the Universities. In addition, the knowledge gained through multinational companies and law firms offering such training to their staff will on the whole remain practical but superficial, enough to cope with the specific problems as seen by the companies and firms. In-house training is always purposive, thus narrow. It might be useful however, to undertake such comparative law teaching in a practical environment (for example, in law firms) rather than exclusively in Law Schools.

Comparative law teaching in the UK does not purport to have the mission of helping students to 'make informed legal decisions with respect to problems arising out of globalisation', or 'equip them with academic

[15] WM Gordon, 'The Place of Legal History in the Teaching of Comparative Law and in the Education of Comparative Lawyers', in JW Bridge (ed), *UK Law For the Millennium*, United Kingdom Comparative Law Series 19, 2nd edn (London: UKNCCL, 2000), 286–97, at 286.

[16] Ibid, 287.

[17] Ibid, 288.

tools sharp enough to model the future of global societies'. These visions do not even appear in the course-outlines informing students of the aims and purposes of the comparative law courses on offer. The courses are too short and they remain mostly theoretical and superficial. If the importance attributed to teaching comparative law were to increase and more time and space were allocated to it, then one could think of ways in which this aspect of comparative law could also be considered. In the UK this is not on the agenda yet.

Have the potential effects and implications of globalisation for teaching law been fully assessed? Is comparative law regarded to be among the tools needed to equip students to penetrate and deal with the density of information? Students have little time, little background knowledge about foreign systems, and few resources to invest in learning about them. How should they be taught how foreign systems operate? Should not the pedagogical focus be on developing abilities so that students can orient themselves within a foreign institution, interpret information, decide what kinds of questions to ask and where to look for information, rather than on transmitting data?[18]

A 'Global Law Faculty' could enhance comparative law teaching in order to deal efficiently with changes caused by globalisation and trade liberalisation, though this is regarded, especially at the undergraduate level, as too ambitious according to the comparative law teachers in the UK who answered the questionnaire sent out. At a more regional and therefore, practical level, in the European Union there are plans to set up European Law Schools; and since 1995, Maastricht Law Faculty in the Netherlands is the first such. The project of integration in Europe has definitely had a positive impact on such developments and created enhanced interest in comparative law. Whether the efforts are effective or practical is yet to be seen.

The Global Law School Programme launched in 1995 in New York University, where fifty-eight foreign professors belonging to various foreign jurisdictions form the Global Law Faculty and teach a variety of courses, is an ambitious project.[19] However, these courses do not systematically integrate the study of foreign and domestic law, there are no full-time comparatists on the Faculty, and there are no autonomous comparative law courses involved in systematic comparison of the doctrines of different legal systems in some basic field of law.[20] This is not the kind of project under discussion in the UK at present.

[18] See Gerber, op cit, above n 4, 973.

[19] See Gordley, op cit, above n. 10, 1004. For further information and discussion related to Global Law Schools, see DS Clark, 'Transnational Legal Practice: The Need for Global Law Schools', in GA Bermann and SC Symeonides, *American Law at the End of the 20th Century: US National Reports to the XVth International Congress of Comparative Law* (1998) 46 *Am J Com L* (Supplement).

[20] Ibid.

At the postgraduate level and at the level of comparative law research 'Global Law Faculties' could be of great value to facilitate the teaching of comparative law, but at the undergraduate level there would be no place for such a venture.

In the UK, 'traditional' law schools are the norm and these are not seen as 'a species on the verge of extinction if they do not convert from national-centred teaching to international-centred teaching'. Law is still perceived as a parochial subject. This position is also reflected in comparative law teaching. Much depends on the predominant legal vision. Although many would regard international-centred teaching as interesting, the majority of lawyers, both academics and practitioners, believe in the value of national-centred teaching of law, with any appropriate reference to the international or foreign. There are no specific transnational courses on offer at the undergraduate level. Traditional comparative law works on the horizontal plane, whereas, national and transnational systems work vertically.[21] If, 'comparative law must also provide the students with a map of the legal universe in which they will have to work',[22] then, not to present law in a comparative and transnational perspective would mislead the student and foster over-simplistic thinking. So, it may be appropriate to ask not only what is the purpose of the autonomous comparative law course, but also whether the autonomous comparative law course is serving its purpose, in spite of the numbers teaching and writing in the area of comparative law being probably at an all-time high?[23]

C. What Can Comparative Law Teaching Achieve?

Comparative law teaching can have practical applications or it can remain primarily an academic discipline depending on how it is taught, what is taught, and what is expected of it. Comparative law in the UK is not regarded as a distinct category within the law. It is usually regarded as a method, a way of looking at the law, with a number of purposes. It is not a 'above law' intertwined with other legal disciplines. It can be used to highlight international aspects of every legal subject, but very few institutions undertaking comparative law teaching approach the subject in this way. At this moment its use is fashionable and decorative rather than real and practical. Comparative law teaching has had little impact on national jurisdictions in the UK. This state of affairs could of course be due to the crisis comparative law finds itself in. Today, its working assumptions and methodology are challenged, and the need to build a theoretical base is

[21] M Reimann, 'Beyond National Systems: A Comparative Law for the International Age' (2001) 75 *Tul L Rev*, 1103, at 1113.

[22] Ibid, 1116.

[23] See Palmer, op cit, above n. 9, 1097–8.

stressed. As its importance increases in the globalising world with increasing interest in the peculiarities of localisms, in appreciating cultural differences and the particular, and yet working towards commonality and the universal, comparatists are busy rethinking their subject.[24]

Law Schools are changing their curriculum at undergraduate and postgraduate levels in order to establish an infrastructure of skills to help students to become more effective lawyers. In this context, comparative law teaching may help to create the 'Global Lawyer'. This depends very much on how it is taught and what is taught however. It must also be remembered that 'global lawyers' are not necessarily more effective lawyers and they may well merely be filling a convenient niche.

Globalisation may 'force lawyers to be familiar with, and to operate smoothly in, other jurisdictions', but the realisation of this has not sunk into the Law Schools as yet. This would require a rethink of the basic core curriculum of Law Schools. If what should be taught is insight into comparative legal traditions, comparative legal reasoning and major legal systems, in the belief that comparison lends perspective, then this cannot meet the needs of multinational companies. The generalist approach might 'broaden the minds or help students to better understand their own systems'. What about the needs of the multinational companies and the multinational law firms? Can Law Schools help here? What sort of comparative law is needed for those who are 'just interested in doing business abroad'?[25] Should we be in the business of providing help for them?

Other questions have also been asked:

> Should comparative law be taught as a distinct subject or should it be integrated into the teaching of domestic law? What means could be used to increase the international exchange of scholars and students, develop joint degree programmes and improve the training of professors? What is the best way to foster research projects?[26]

How can comparative law move from being 'learned law' to 'practical law'? If this process were to materialise how could teachers of comparative law combat the risk of superficial knowledge or insufficient understanding of foreign law, a 'legal polyglottism'?[27]

The 'pure' academic comparative lawyer may not be in much demand, but increasingly, as interest in foreign law 'secundum comparatum' mounts and literature of foreign legal systems abounds, experts in foreign law are

[24] Witness the large number of Comparative Law Congresses and Conferences in the years 2000 and 2001.

[25] X Blanc-Jouvan, 'Centennial World Congress on Comparative Law: Closing Remarks' (2001) 75 *Tul L Rev*, 1235, at 1244.

[26] Ibid, 1243–4.

[27] R Sacco, 'One Hundred Years of Comparative Law' (2001) 75 *Tul L Rev*, 1159, 1169–70.

in high demand to aid the courts in transnational cases. It is vital that practitioners also become masters of 'secundum comparatum'. These developments may have an impact on the numbers of students wishing to take the integrated comparative law courses or courses on particular legal systems such as the French or German, if not general autonomous and theoretical comparative law courses.

Although the time may have come for replacing the traditional 'national' curriculum with a more 'international-centred' curriculum, in the UK this is not regarded as really necessary, desirable or feasible as yet. Most UK Law Schools are national-centred institutions and seem set to remain so for the foreseeable future. The international-centred curriculum falls within the remit of a small number of Centres within Law Schools, which are also seen as catering for the needs of international lawyers and researchers. The postgraduate level is seen as more appropriate for this. Moreover, the mere introduction of an 'international-centred' curriculum is no short cut to the goal of educating 'more effective' lawyers.

D. Where Do We Stand?

Academics, lawyers and judges in Britain have always been aware that there is 'a world elsewhere'.[28] This 'elsewhere', which is captive to the fact that law is a parochial and vocational subject, was in the past mostly the Commonwealth and the legal systems that derived their laws from the common law tradition. This is largely due to the language factor. As this Rapporteur found out, such comparative law is extensively used in one form or another by judges and by counsel, in both English and Scottish courts.[29] Recently, we have also seen a growing interest in systems within the European Union, though those looked at are usually France and Germany.[30]

Comparative law has been heralded as the science of this century. Judges and academics have given impressive papers on the role and importance of comparative law, and the years 2000 and 2001 have witnessed a number of significant seminars and conferences on comparative law and comparative legal studies, not only in the UK, but elsewhere. Yet, comparative law teaching has remained a marginal activity, courses being taken by a small number of enthusiastic and dedicated students. Full-time teachers of comparative

[28] J Bingham, 'There is a World Elsewhere: The Changing Perspectives of English Law' (1992) 41 *ICLQ*, 527.

[29] E Örücü 'Comparative Law in British Courts', in U Drobnig and S van Erp (eds), *The Use of Comparative Law by Courts* (The Hague: Kluwer Law International, 1999), 253–95; Örücü, 'Comparative Law as a Tool of Construction in Scottish Courts' (2000) *The Juridical Review*, 27.

[30] See, eg, *White and Another v Jones and others* [1995] 1 All ER, 691 at 705 (HL).

law also belong to the outer circle of academia. They themselves see their work as vital but others often do not. They may be considered an élite clique with a cloistered subject. Even if it is true that comparative law academics are clustered around the United Kingdom National Committee of Comparative Law, with Law Schools where comparative law is taught being members, and the British Institute of International and Comparative Law, their influence on the general UK scene has remained marginal. In recent years the Society of Public Teachers of Law (now Society of Legal Scholars) also set up a Comparative Law Subject Section, but the membership remains small. The value of comparative law research for academics, researchers, the Law Commissions, law-makers and even courts is more easily granted, but for law students, it is still regarded as mainly a tool for 'providing a better understanding of one's own law' and for 'broadening the mind'.

Our main questions must be, 'Has anything changed?' and, 'Is the legal education law students now receive, especially through comparative law teaching, tailored to meet the challenges of the modern world?' In the UK, one rather pessimistic answer to both questions is, 'No'. Topics covered in comparative law courses are the same as they were twenty years ago, the methods of teaching and assessing remain on the whole unchanged and comparative law courses are evaluated in exactly the same way as all other law courses. Concepts and aims changed so little over the past century, that it was said, 'there is nothing new in 2000'.[31]

A more optimistic answer is, 'Yes, there are glimmers of hope'. Innovative approaches are emerging, many substantive law courses do now contain comparative elements and many dissertations show signs of such curiosity. The number of academics and legal professionals aware of the important role of comparative law in enabling the law graduate to live up to the present and future challenges is on the increase. The number of students going abroad to study is also rising. When and how this glimmer becomes a beacon however, is not easy to predict.

The legal curriculum in the UK tends to concentrate on the native system, now including the EU, and comparative law is perceived to be on the periphery of this curriculum.

The constraints of time and financial resources are also growing. Unless comparative law is taught more extensively and only in certain centres of excellence, it will remain as an interesting but ornamental addition to a crammed curriculum. In the UK where university education is seen as more and more relevant to employment, interest in comparative law will only increase when law firms see the benefits of employing lawyers who have

[31] DC Clark, 'Nothing New in 2000: Comparative Law in 1900 and Today' (2001) 75 *Tul L Rev*, 871 at 911.

received some training in comparative law and foreign legal systems.[32] However, if this were to happen, the approach to teaching comparative law and comparative law teaching would have to change.

Should comparative law rethink itself in the light of critical legal studies, law and economics, feminism and critical race theory, acknowledge and integrate cultural diversity and avoid Western hegemony? If so, should this be reflected in comparative law teaching? The answers to these questions become crucial considering that nothing much has changed recently in the practice of the law in the UK. The next issue to be addressed in comparative law teaching in the UK is the continued emphasis on common law/civil law comparisons. So, the question becomes, 'What of interdisciplinary comparative jurisprudence and a change of emphasis towards cultures other than common law/civil law?' But then we may also ask whether in the market of students and lawyers studying and practicing law with its parochial and nationalistic vision, there is enough of an interest in this novel direction. Should the mission of comparatists be the cultivation of a new interest in moving the clash between law as a science and law as a practical tool into a dialogue and beyond? Do comparatists have a common agenda? Even if the answer is a partial 'Yes', should this agenda be moved into comparative law teaching? Today, there is a higher awareness of theory and method in comparative law rather than regarding or teaching it only as an aid to the practicing lawyer.[33]

If we are expected as comparative law teachers and researchers to promote globalised teaching in, and denationalised understanding of law, positivism and localism have to be overcome with a 'multinational body of law teachers devoted as much as possible to an interdisciplinary approach to law'.[34] How is this is to be achieved? Is this vision on the agenda for Law School curricula in the UK? The answer at present is 'No'.

The curriculum is already overcrowded, new topics come into existence, gain importance but cannot all be added to the undergraduate curriculum. The volume of changes introduced into higher education as to content and structure as well as techniques and facilities defies imagination. Yet, teaching comparative law has not greatly benefited from this, although comparative law research has. The impact of the changes on comparative law teaching however, has been of great benefit to some comparative law teachers who want to use the new challenges to enhance their research and, as a by-product, their teaching. The burden falls on the student to take advan-

[32] See Lord Goff of Chieveley, 'The Future of the Common Law' (1997) 46 *ICLQ*, 745, for the claim that the value of comparative law is on the increase in the UK.

[33] However, see B Markesinis, 'Comparative Law: A Subject in Search of an Audience' (1990) 53 *MLR*, 1.

[34] F Werro, 'Notes on the Purpose and Aims of Comparative Law' (2001) 75 *Tul L Rev,* 1225, at 1233.

tage of these developments. Unless students are innovative, curious and enthusiastic, efforts can remain one-sided. The number of students at the undergraduate level interested in comparative law studies is not promising. It may be that the real place for comparative law studies is at the postgraduate level. But this could be a chicken and egg situation in that if students in the early part of their education do not come into contact with 'the world elsewhere' why should they later find this kind of education and research desirable? In any case, the number of students entering postgraduate studies in law is also rather small.

On the one hand, there has not been much change in the teaching of comparative law over the years apart from new methods of teaching and learning, which affect the whole law curriculum. New electronic facilities are among these changes: Lexis-Nexis, Westlaw and other Internet sources are now freely available to students. Comparative law teaching on the other hand, has been influenced by new developments considerably. With awareness of the importance of comparative law and as a result of instant and easy access to foreign sources such as court decisions on the electronic facilities, electronic comparative law journals, comparative law discussion fora and electronically published draft research papers, more material has become available and is used to enhance research. The academic is now in a much better position to be fully informed of foreign law developments without having to travel to foreign countries or even go to libraries to access sources. The danger is that one may not anymore be making an effort to live in the real world but live in virtual reality. For the student another danger is that this information might remain superficial, be imperfectly selected and might not get transferred into knowledge.

Many more courses now contain scattered comparative elements, but this does not mean that all academics have become comparatists, nor that all courses have become replacement courses for comparative law courses proper. Actually, the problem in this development might be that comparative lawyers will be regarded as redundant and general comparative law courses be replaced by what is sometimes called 'mezza' courses. Many comparatists believe that the theory and methodology of comparative law need to be strengthened, and this is the field in which they should concentrate their efforts now in order to countenance the challenge from other colleagues. The changes in the globalised world related to integration and to specific system analysis are catching up with comparatists as more and more systems in transition seek their help. Comparative law, its role, value, and relevance is changing and the hope is that this will impact on the teaching of comparative law and comparative law teaching now and in the coming decades.

In 1983 it was said that in the US, a typical and perennial complaint of the academic teacher of comparative law was: 'Colleagues are not interested in foreign law; students are ethnocentric boors; the bar consists of monolingual hicks; deans won't finance foreign travel; nobody will take Comparative Law.'[35] The writer then went on to say that all this was true somewhere but none was true everywhere, and that the picture was changing. On that rather pessimistic note a similar complaint might be made in the UK. The optimistic message is that things can only get better.

Teaching comparative law has always been attractive for a certain kind of academic. Such academics do well and are appreciated by their students and other comparatists. However, in the UK nothing much has changed. Teaching and research have benefited from the electronic information age, but the tools to translate this information into usable knowledge, and especially the use of these tools, is very much dependent on the human factor and this is not just the researcher or the teacher, but also, more important, the student. Creative, imaginative, innovative, and enthusiastic academics and students can benefit from this new world and themselves bring benefit to it. The tools are there. We need informed and discerning users and maybe also a new vision for comparative law.

V. APPENDIX

Some of the nineteen positive responses were brief, whereas others offered not only the information asked for, but gave further insight into, and opinion on, the teaching of comparative law and comparative law teaching. Below is a summary of the more elaborate responses in alphabetical order.

The University of Aberdeen: Here one Honours 'Comparative Law' course is offered with specialised coverage. The course starts with a preliminary survey of the role and limitations of the comparative method in the context of western legal traditions with particular reference to Scotland and South Africa leading to a comparison of selected aspects of Scots and South African property law and the protection of privacy in England, Scotland, Germany, and the USA. One aim is to engage with the comparative method and carry out critical comparative work on selected topics with a view to better understanding of the solutions reached by certain foreign systems. Another aim is to consider to what extent the foreign approach and solutions in the topics covered may be relevant to the Scottish position. The course also aims to give insight into the general nature and modes of operation of the foreign systems concerned and to raise basic issues as to the role and utility of a comparative approach. There is no direct practical aspect to

[35] HW Baade, 'Comparative Law and the Practitioner' (1983) 31 *Am J Comp L*, 499 at 508.

the course. It is not meant to prepare students for work in global markets or in multinational companies. The teaching method is by seminar. Students prepare papers for presentation in class. Only 15 to 20 students out of 150 take the course. Techniques used in the evaluation of the course are the same as in other courses. Electronic technology is not used. SOCRATES Programmes are regarded as being very useful. The respondent (D Carey-Miller) says that 'better informed and more critical' must mean more efficient, and that as to a Global Law Faculty, 'the US model is the closest we have got to it'. Aberdeen also offers two ordinary courses, one on French Law, the other on German Law.

The University of Birmingham: This university does not offer a general comparative law course, but does offer a number of specialised courses, though these have no practical slant. Substantive courses are offered such as 'Comparative Common Law', 'Comparative Constitutional Law', and 'Law of Personal Liberty', with the legal systems normally covered being the Commonwealth, Canada, Australia, the USA, Malawi, South Africa, Germany, France, Portugal, and Eastern Europe. Cultural criticism is not a high priority, nor do current global developments have a prominent place in comparative law teaching. The method of teaching is lectures and small group seminars.[36] A few students opt for comparative law projects. No special techniques are used in evaluating comparative law teaching and electronic technology is used to the same extent as in other courses. It is assumed that comparative law teaching does help students to make more informed decisions in a globalising world. Around 20 per cent of the students per year are interested in comparative law.

The University of Bristol: This respondent university offers a general comparative law course in 'Constitutional Law' and the 'Law of Obligations', covering France and Germany as comparators with reference to other European legal systems where material is available. The course has no practical slant. The focus is on substantive law with some consideration given to the historical background of European legal systems. If from 'cultural criticism' one understands consideration of the advantages and disadvantages of different approaches to similar problems, then we can say that it is undertaken. The courses are run on a seminar basis. There are no mooting competitions. All students taking the 'Introduction to Comparative Law' unit in the second year are preparing to go to another European country under the SOCRATES Programme and are introduced to the basic features of the legal system into which they will be going. Staff, with the help of a few students, undertake comparative law research

[36] Information supplied by Evelyn Ellis.

projects. Some of the students returning from abroad in the third year, do write dissertations in their final year with a comparative element. This applies equally to students from abroad. The courses are evaluated in exactly the same way as all other law courses, but, electronic technology is less used in this area than in others at present. The respondent (J Rivers) says that the courses offered are not significant enough to help students to make more informed decisions related to globalisation. It is felt that at most the courses introduce them to different legal traditions in the world and broaden perspectives as to the variety of possible legal techniques involved in solving typical social problems. It is thought that if a 'Global Law Faculty' involved distance learning, then it would never be as effective as personal experience, since successful comparative lawyers are formed through substantial exposure to foreign legal systems and this can only be achieved by spending a sustained period of time in the country in question. Rather than producing 'efficient lawyers' comparative law contributes to the education of 'better educated' lawyers, by primarily enhancing the students' understanding of the range of choices which a legal system has to make and it thus gives the students a deeper understanding of the characteristic features of their own legal system. Around 15 to 20 per cent of home students go on the ERASMUS Programmes. The second year 'Introduction to Comparative Law' unit is a compulsory part of those programmes, therefore, the student interest in comparative law is related to a general interest in studying abroad, since comparative law is envisaged by the students as a useful form of preparation.

The University of Cardiff: The response from Cardiff Law School, where they do not offer a general comparative law course, but where they have courses in French, Italian, Spanish, and German legal systems for students going to study in these countries, stresses the importance of 'legal translation' and therefore the need for fluency in general legal languages and cultures as one of the outcomes of current global development.

University of Dundee: This is the only university in the UK which offers a full qualifying English Law Degree as well as a Scots Law LL B.[37] The teaching necessarily has a strong comparative dimension. The only explicitly described comparative course is 'Comparative Charity Law'. The main comparator is obviously England and Wales with limited reference to Continental Europe.

The University of Edinburgh: There is a 'Comparative Law' Honours course (a general comparative law course) and a 'Comparative Criminal

[37] Information supplied by S Moody, Erasmus Contact.

Procedure' course on offer. The general course studies the distinguishing features of legal families and a range of specific jurisdictions in the first half. In the second half, it considers various broad based topics such as succession law, privacy, etc, from a comparative perspective. It concludes with a survey of theories of comparative law. A range of practical subjects is covered in this course. Both the substantive law and the historical and cultural background of legal systems are covered in some detail and it is hoped that the courses encourage cultural criticism and cultural curiosity and tolerance. The respondent (E Reid) says that she has 'attempted, in so far as material is available, to move a little away from the traditional Euro-American perspective of comparative law and focus on the development of new legal families, and the consequences this has for existing comparative law theories'. The course is seminar based. It covers a range of common law, civil law and mixed jurisdictions, looks at Islamic law, and also at the new legal systems of the former Soviet Union. There is no direct involvement in mooting events. The presence of SOCRATES exchange students enriches seminar discussions. The respondent says that in teaching the class, she draws upon her experience of common core research projects and various research projects with the FSU. The course is examined in the same way as other Honours courses in the Law School, part by essay and part by unseen written examination. Electronic technology is used constantly as students are referred to electronic sources in most reading lists on the Internet or held within the Faculty network. All handouts are available electronically with hypertext links. The respondent says in relation to 'informed legal decisions' on problems arising out of globalisation, that, 'while it would be unrealistic to suggest that the course provides the solutions to problems at that level, I hope it helps students to find their bearings when confronting such issues—so that they know where to look to find the answer'. 'Global Law Faculty' is thought to be highly desirable, and, if efficiently organisd, would enhance comparative law teaching, but how and when it could be set up is unclear. Comparative law is seen to contribute to producing more 'efficient lawyers' in various ways. It is suggested that at the practical level, it helps lawyers to find solutions to problems which have a dimension outwith their own jurisdiction. At an academic level, the study of comparative law can help to develop a sharper focus on the issues within one's own system. Honours courses have a quota of 25 and the Comparative Honours course is regularly full. 15–20 per cent of students in any given year take this course. It is well eceived as indicated by course questionnaires. The respondent suspects however, that there is a perception that large solicitors' firms prefer to see 'black-letter' Honours options on applicants' CVs. The 'Comparative Criminal Procedure' course (J Godard) is a substantive law course with a practical approach, and the legal systems covered are Scotland, England, and France. There are no mooting competitions, the method of teaching is by handouts and student presentations and the assessment is by essay and examination.

The University of Glasgow: This is the home institution of this National Rapportuer. Until 1998 the School of Law of the University of Glasgow offered named Honours degrees (LL B Honours) together with an ordinary LL B. An Honours Programme in Comparative Law was on offer among other Honours Programmes. This Programme attracted around 5–10 per cent of the students who took over two years a general introductory course 'Comparative Law', 'Comparative Institutions' (Public, Private, Criminal Law topics), 'Reception of Laws and Mixed Jurisdictions', and 'French Law', with an additional special subject 'Harmonisation of Laws'. None of the courses were practically oriented. For the General Paper students covered specific topics chosen by themselves, using comparative law methodology. This Programme was seen by external examiners, as equivalent to an LLM in Comparative Law offered in English universities. With this undergraduate Honours Programme, Glasgow School of Law was the only Law School in the UK offering such an extensive treatment of the subject. Since 1998 however, within a 'pick and mix' Honours system, only two of the courses have been available, Honours 'Comparative Law' and 'Reception of Laws and Mixed Jurisdictions', with an Advanced Subject, 'Introduction to Comparative Law', in the ordinary degree. In the ordinary 'Jurisprudence' course there is also a component, 'Comparative Jurisprudence'. There is still one designated Professor of Comparative Law (E Örücü), who undertakes the teaching of these courses. The Honours courses have a quota of twenty and the 'Comparative Law' course is always filled, whereas the 'Reception of Laws and Mixed Jurisdictions' has around eight students yearly. The teaching method is by seminars with area case studies prepared by the students, which then form the bases of some of the exam questions. The students are encouraged to use electronic technology, especially in the preparation of their case studies. The case studies cover countries and topics chosen by students. Some final year Honours dissertations also have a comparative element. The systems covered are common law and civilian jurisdictions based on student interest. Mixed systems and systems in transition are given prominence. The School of Law also offers combinations such as Law with Language (one of French, German, Spanish, or Italian), and Law with European Legal Studies, the available legal systems being the Belgian, French, German, Italian, and Spanish. Two international moot options are also available to students: Telder's International Moot and the European Human Rights (Strasbourg) Project. These do not have comparative law slants however. A Global Law School is thought to be unrealistic at undergraduate level. At the LL M level, one comparative law course Legal Cultures in Europe is offered as part of the

LL M in European Legal Studies. This is a course where the approach is critical and cultural context is uppermost in the minds of the students, who choose and prepare their own case studies.

University of Kent: One of the most progressive comparatists in the UK (G Samuel) teaching in this institution, says that the demand for comparative law is not great and students taking the course at the LL B level are mainly incoming ERASMUS students. Demand for the several courses offered at the LL M level is not high either. One of the LL M courses is Comparative Law of Obligations and another, European Contract Law. The LL B course titled 'European Legal Systems' (European Comparative Law) designed primarily for the outgoing ERASMUS students, has this to tell us in the Course outline:

> The purpose of this module is to provide a basic introduction to the theoretical and practical considerations surrounding comparison in law within the context of European legal systems. The general focal points are twofold: comparative law as a discipline in itself (aims, functions, merits, dangers, methodology and theory) and comparative law as a means of access to the two principal European legal mentalities (common law and civil law traditions). Part I of the course will be concerned with the main debates, issues, methods and critical approaches to the subject together with an introduction to the common law and the codes. Part II will investigate the classification, institutional and reasoning structures of the common law and civil law traditions, with the aim of identifying similarity and difference at the legal knowledge level. Contextual topics will include legal imperialism, legal cultures, legal harmonization and theoretical poverty.

This is a comprehensive outline of a typical general comparative law course on offer in British universities. However, many such courses would be minus the contextual part portrayed in the last sentence of the outline as well as the 'comparative legal reasoning and legal methods' section. Teaching here is by seminar (one two-hour seminar per week), and assessment is by coursework and written examination. A replacement dissertation is an option. This is a typical scheme. The course offered by this Rapporteur at Honours level in Glasgow would have a similar course outline, with additional emphasis on 'transposition of laws, legal migrations and their consequences', a pet subject on which I carry out research. The reading list also looks familiar in including both traditional and more recent and controversial reading to enhance debate.

The University of Kingston-upon-Thames, Surrey: This institution offers two courses, 'Legal Systems and Constitutions' in the first semester and 'Aspects of Civil Law' in the second, both of which cover French and Russian Law. German Law is also taught as a separate subject. There is no practical slant to these courses. The focus is on both substantive law and the historical and the cultural background of the systems. If by cultural criticism one understands analysis of culture the answer is then, this is done in the courses. Electronic technology is not used to a great extent. The method of teaching is by lectures and tutorials. Evaluation of courses is by student questionnaires as in other courses. To a certain extent these courses help students to make informed decisions, and they may become more 'efficient lawyers' as they gain an awareness of other legal solutions and potential legal solutions, and improve their inter/transnational negotiating skills. 20–25 per cent of students are interested in these courses. As for the impact of current global developments on comparative law, it was felt that the collapse of communism and its consequences for Central and Eastern Europe and beyond, the developments in European law and the increased confidence of Islam mean that comparative law has to look at issues other than the traditional alone.

King's College London: Here a general comparative law course is on offer, covering constitutional law (institutions, general principles and human rights) and civil law (contracts and tort). There is no practical slant to this course. It is reported (A Tuerk) that though the focus is on the study of substantive law, historical and cultural background is also considered important in explaining substantive law. The cultural background is subject to scrutiny, but understanding is deemed more important than criticism and therefore each student is free to draw his or her own conclusions. The legal systems normally covered are the British, French and German and occasionally the EU system. This College has a wide range of SOCRATES partners, and experience shows that exchange students are better motivated on their return, show a better understanding of foreign jurisdictions and express a greater willingness to learn more about them. Comparative research is regarded as essential by the respondent for any meaningful understanding of the EU legal system. The evaluation methods for the course are the same as for other law courses. Electronic technology is not specifically used in comparative law teaching. As comparative law cannot enable students to know other legal systems as fully as they do their own, problems arising out of globalisation and in multi-national companies could only receive a limited answer from them. The respondent feels that some courses could be taught in a 'Global Law Faculty'. However, the major part of legal study is still dominated by national law, knowledge of which is indispensable; a Global Law Faculty could serve postgraduates but would not be of great assistance to undergraduates. As comparative law teaching provides the opportunity to search for solutions beyond national boundaries, advice given by lawyers conversant with comparative law must be better the more solutions they can offer to their clients. Only 2 per cent of students opt for the comparative law course. However, there are other courses offering some comparative elements, such as LL B with German Law (2 per cent), LL B with French Law (10 per cent), LL B with European Legal Studies (2 per cent), and many LL M courses have a comparative element. The respondent feels that since students in this country are reluctant to take up foreign languages, there is a major inhibition for any comparative law study. The few students who have taken the above courses however, are genuinely enthusiastic about them.

Lancaster University: In this Law School a number of comparative law courses are on offer in the European Legal Studies Programme and extensive information is provided on their website.[38] The respondent (R O'Connell) provided the following information. The courses on offer are 'Introduction to Comparative Law I' and 'Introduction to Comparative Law II', 'Comparative Constitutional Law', 'Advanced Comparative Law', and Fourth Year ELS Dissertations. The 'Introduction to Comparative Law' courses aim to provide for a comparative analysis of legal phenomena. The emphasis is on European civil law, especially in France and Germany. 'Comparative Constitutional Law' is interdisciplinary and comparative, studying the notions of constitutionalism, and different mechanisms of enforcing constitutional legality. The course examines political, moral and other aspects in the constitutional regulation of political issues, by focusing on a specific topic for detailed scrutiny in comparative perspective. The aim is to appreciate how each country solves the same problem in the light of its own politics, history, and culture. The 'Advanced Comparative Law' course, in which students apply what they have learnt on comparative methodology to certain specific legal issues, builds upon the legal experience that ELS students have had during their third year at a partner university and is compulsory for LLB (ELS) students. These same students are also required to write a 7,500 word dissertation for their degree. The aim of the dissertation is to equip students to deal with a more international (and specifically European) legal experience (practical and academic). Issues accepted for dissertation are comparative case studies, topics dealing with the theory or practice of comparative law, questions relating broadly to the legal aspects of the 'European project', and issues concerning 'globalisation'/'trans-national legal phenomena'. Some of the courses are more substantive, some more historical and some concern methodology. The courses encourage cultural criticism. The seminar approach is used with all material posted on the dedicated website. The systems covered are the US, Germany, and France with some reference to Italy, Spain, Canada and South Africa. The popular 'Comparative Constitutional Law' course is partly assessed by a moot court, and in 'Introduction to Comparative Law

[38] <http://www.lanc.ac.uk/staff/oconnelr/ug/htm>.

II' there is continuous assessment and teamwork. Electronic technology is widely used. Only about 5–10 per cent of students take these courses, though students who take them enjoy them.

The University of Leicester: The Faculty of Law offers LL B with French Law, LL B (European Union) and LL B (International). In the latter Programme the students spend their third year at either the National University of Singapore or Rhodes University in South Africa. These arrangements are being extended to Universities in Australia and North America. The Faculty does not offer a general comparative law course, but many of the substantive law courses cover elements of foreign law discussed in a comparative context. Courses are practical, covering mainly commercial subjects: the Law with French Programme and the Intellectual Property course are such examples. The systems covered are the French, other member states of the EU and the USA. The focus is on substantive law with a background of these rules whenever there is a difference or where historical background has had a significant impact on the development of substantive rules. Cultural criticism is understood to be critical analysis of the current justification of the historical rationale behind the substantive rules. Globalisation of commercial law issues is presented as the main reason for the incorporation of comparative elements in the courses, and therefore its impact on comparative law teaching has been strong. The courses are offered as standard lectures and tutorials, and electronic technology is not used. It is felt that having students from different jurisdictions under ERASMUS exchanges stimulates the discussions. At the postgraduate level, the teaching is research based and most of the research is comparative in nature. As the comparative law component forms an integral part of each course standard techniques are used for evaluation. In the field of commercial law, the comparative component certainly helps students to make more informed legal decisions. As for a Global Law Faculty, it is felt that it is not form but substance that is of value and that a strong integration into the curricula would be needed. It was put forward (P Torremans) that comparative law obliges students to take nothing for granted and to ask questions about the most fundamental points of their own legal systems. Looking at things from a new angle greatly improves the quality of the final analysis. It is reported that most of the courses are very popular, but that it is hard to say whether the comparative component is the reason.

School of Oriental and African Studies: SOAS is the only university Law School in the UK where most courses are comparative law courses and where regional studies are undertaken. In terms of general comparative law theory there is a compulsory first year course 'Legal Systems of Asia and Africa' and an optional course 'Comparative Legal Theory'. The focus is on the historical and cultural background. Comparative law courses that offer a practical slant are 'Comparative Company Law' at the undergraduate level and 'Comparative Commercial Law' at the postgraduate level. Cultural criticism is always encouraged. All teaching of regional laws, which is the main emphasis in this Programme, is influenced by globalisation and in this context, international law has become more important. The methods used in teaching at the undergraduate level are lectures and tutorials and at the postgraduate level seminars. Systems normally covered are the legal systems of Asia and Africa and English and EU law. Almost all research, both individual and collective, is in comparative law and that includes undergraduate and postgraduate dissertations and PhD theses. Electronic technology is used in teaching, but this is not peculiar to comparative law teaching. The response (A Harding) specifically emphasizes the point that this School's graduates are much sought after by multinational companies as the markets believe that they can make informed decisions with respect to problems related to globalisation. More than 90 per cent of the students here are interested in comparative law and students come to SOAS mainly for comparative law, though sometimes for international law only. In 1994 a teaching assessment was carried out which indicated a highly positive response to comparative law teaching, with students responding more positively to comparative law than to English law subjects. The possibility of having a Global Law Faculty was considered by the respondent to be, though desirable, an impossible dream. Professor Harding is of the opinion that comparative law teaching can contribute to the production of more 'efficient lawyers' in that a comparative lawyer is able to cope with the demands of international practice better than one educated solely in the law of one jurisdiction. Gaining more knowledge of how other legal systems think and practice, and developing a more flexible and imaginative approach to dealing with problems must contribute to the 'efficiency' of the lawyer. Harding points out that a lawyer without any knowledge of comparative law is legally illiterate (Twining).

The University of Oxford: The Institute of European and Comparative Law offers a number of options.[39] A four-year Bachelor of Arts Degree can be taken as English Law with either French Law, German Law, or European Law. There is also a degree in English Law with Italian. Students follow the same syllabus as those who do the three-year course, and they also attend special language courses in their first year of study followed by a specially designed introductory course in French or German law. In their third year these students attend prescribed courses at a university in a member state of

[39] This information was not provided by the institution concerned but downloaded by the Rapporteur from <http://www.iuscomp.org/iecl/anrep/e&cteach.htm>.

the EU. They spend their fourth year in Oxford. The University of Oxford also offers a Magister Juris in European and Comparative Law. This is a one-year course with four written examinations or three written examinations and a dissertation. There are approximately thirty-six options, including some with a particularly European emphasis. Each year there is a cosmopolitan intake of forty students. The website from where this information has been downloaded says:

> Oxford graduates occupy the highest positions in the legal profession throughout the world. They become lawyers, judges and legislators and pursue successful careers in the UK, the Commonwealth, and the US. More recently, they have turned to the Continent of Europe; the three members of the Courts in Luxembourg are Oxonians.

University of Southampton: R Asariotis offers a general course in comparative law named 'Comparative European Law', which provides an introduction to the study of comparative law where the relevance of comparative legal studies is discussed. Two major legal systems, the German and the French are covered. Written sources of law and the relevant social, political and economic context are considered. The specific area of inquiry is contract law. The comparative study of contract law also provides a practical slant. Both the substantive rules and the historical and cultural background are examined as far as is possible in a one semester course. The intention is to encourage cultural criticism. Comparative law is deemed to be gaining in relevance as a result of globalisation and European integration. The method of teaching is by seminars, some student-led. Domestic SOCRATES students choose this subject either before or after their year abroad. The techniques used in evaluating the course are the same as in other courses and include peer-observation and questionnaires. Electronic material is accessible but not specifically used in the course. The respondent feels that comparative law teaching contributes to lawyers' ability to make informed choices in 'choice of law' and 'forum in commercial contracts', and to their understanding of international conventions. 5–10 per cent of the students take this course. They are all enthusiastic, dedicated and satisfied. Foreign students on SOCRATES exchange usually choose this option.

University of Sussex: The Graduate Research Centre in Legal Studies offers 'Comparative Criminal Justice Systems' as a 'core course' on the LL M International Criminal Law Programme. This course is intended to assist law professionals working in different jurisdictions, thus it has a practical as well as a theoretical slant. Very little substantive law is covered, the emphasis being on historical and theoretical issues and procedural law. The teaching involves cultural criticism. The respondent (R Vogler) says that he has problems with the current theoretical perspective of comparative law which, in his view, is too much focused on private law, on substantive law and on Europe/North America. He hopes that globalisation will open up the discipline. The methods used are lectures, seminars and study visits. The focus is on Europe, the USA, Russia, Japan, Latin America, China, Africa, and the Middle East and specific countries are chosen in response to student interest. There are mooting competitions and programmes such as SOCRATES, which are seen as furthering the teaching of comparative law. The role of the comparative law projects is seen to be crucial but it is admitted that using the comparative law method is not easy even for postgraduates. The technique used for assessing is examination as for other law courses. Electronic technology is used extensively as a source of information. Comparative law teaching is seen by the respondent to help students to make informed legal decisions but the question asked is: Why is the emphasis on 'multinational companies?' A 'Global Law Faculty' is regarded as extremely desirable. The aim of comparative law teaching is not specifically to contribute to the education of the more 'efficient lawyer' but this may happen as a by-product. As this is a specialist programme, most of the students are interested in comparative law studies.

Chapter 2

The Legitimacy of the Judge in the United Kingdom

*Kay Goodall**

In this paper I will take a jurisprudential look at the concept of judicial legitimacy in the UK. My aim is to draw out connections. There is an interesting relationship between lawyers' understanding of what makes a judge legitimate and the underlying principles of law and democracy that this understanding enshrines. I hope in this paper to throw a little light on that.

In the first part of the paper, I will examine the legitimacy of the judiciary as an institution. In the second part, I will consider the conditions that must be met by individual judges.

I. A BRIEF INTRODUCTION TO JUDICIAL ROLES IN THE UK

Before I begin examining the main subject of this chapter, it is worth making a few preliminary observations on the judiciary in the UK.

Throughout the UK, the middle-ranking and senior judiciary is largely composed of professional judges[1] who are not trained for that career from an early stage. Instead, they are appointed after a substantial period practising as barristers or solicitors or their equivalent. Not all work as judges full-time: a significant proportion of the middle-ranking posts are occupied part-time by professional lawyers who continue to practise in their own fields alongside their judicial employment.

It is the professional judiciary (full-time and part-time) on whom I focus in this paper. I have excluded lay judges from the discussion, because very different issues of legitimacy arise in their case. Much as I would like to find the space to examine these other issues, it is not possible to cover both areas

* School of Law, University of Glasgow. Thanks to John Bell for his helpful comments on the first draft. The introductory notes and the later paragraph on the Kilmuir Rules are substantially his. Thanks also to Noreen Burrows for kindly agreeing to carry out an eleventh-hour reading of the final draft. As ever, any errors in this chapter are mine.

[1] This is particularly so in Scotland, where professional judges are responsible for a greater range of casework and where the lay Justices of the Peace in the local district courts have a more limited jurisdiction than their English, Welsh and Northern Irish counterparts.

of judicial legitimacy adequately. Nevertheless, although relatively little attention has been paid by academic and media commentators to this branch of the judiciary in the UK in the past,[2] it is worth noting that the role of lay judges is increasing in importance. Even though they are mainly restricted to the most minor cases, the number of cases in which they now adjudicate makes their role significant. Also, within the tribunal system in particular, they may participate up to a relatively senior level of decision-making at first instance and at appeal. The seniority of their role is particularly marked in the asylum and immigration appeals system following recent changes.[3]

It is likely that the elevation of these lay judges (which has sometimes been accompanied by disquieting alterations in traditional court procedures) will sooner or later be met with accusations of 'court-stripping'.[4] 'Court-stripping' is a term which originates from North American jurisprudence. It refers to the process by which inferior courts are given the status of higher courts, even though they are partially staffed by judges who are not trained lawyers and even though their procedures provide a weakened protection of the rights of vulnerable participants. The debate around whether these developments are justified has not yet taken off but it is to be hoped that it will soon begin.

Both lay and professional judges in the UK are more limited in their powers than those of many of their counterparts in other legal systems. In particular, judges in the criminal justice system are not involved in the investigation of crimes, except in the role of a kind of 'judge of liberties': they authorise detention and searches but do not control the collection of evidence and the interviewing of suspects and witnesses.

The judiciary also has a relatively limited role in constitutional review. As Bell, Ockelton, and Seago put it:

> [British judges] have a limited function in ensuring compliance with the hierarchy of norms, and so may apply Community law which contradicts a national statute. But they have no power to annul statutes either for procedural defects or for breach of fundamental freedoms. This role is performed by the legislature itself.[5]

Since that paper was written, the function of ensuring compliance with the

[2] An interesting exception can be found in the work of Z Bankowski, N Hutton, and J McManus, *Lay Justice* (Edinburgh: T&T Clark, 1987).

[3] See, for instance, the enhancement of their responsibilities in certain areas of asylum law under the Anti-Terrorism, Crime and Security Act 2001, a change that was not adequately made clear by the UK government to the UK Parliament during the debate on the Bill. The time allocated to the debate on that aspect of the Bill was also truncated by the government to a matter of minutes, rather than a matter of days as would have been more appropriate.

[4] Thanks to Conor Gearty for introducing me to this term.

[5] J Bell, M Ockelton, and P Seago, 'The Legal Cultures of British Judges', conference paper 1994.

hierarchy of norms has been extended in the areas of devolution and human rights. It enables certain courts to strike down statutes made by the devolved legislatures when these are incompatible with the devolution and human rights legislation. Nevertheless the judiciary still does not possess the power to strike down primary legislation of the UK Parliament.[6]

Another interesting aspect of the roles of the judiciary in the UK is the limitations imposed on their freedom to appear in the media and to take part in public debate. Until relatively recently, a set of rules known as the 'Kilmuir Rules' restricted them from making statements to the media. These were relaxed from the late 1980s onwards, but it is still rare for judges to give any interviews on the system of justice in general. Judges do however participate in prestigious lecture series such as the annual Reith lectures and it is now not uncommon for judges to write for legal journals and to give formal addresses at law schools and conferences which are later published in legal journals. These addresses are sometimes reported in the more serious newspapers. The Lord Chief Justice also gives an annual press conference.

The style of presentation is however usually quasi-academic, and criticism of the justice system will tend to be either restrained or carefully worded. Where judges have been more outspoken, the response of other judges has been harsh. The senior Scottish judge Lord McCluskey made a fiery attack in a newspaper article on what he regarded as the likely deleterious consequences of enacting the Human Rights Act 1998. These frank comments were met by much discreet muttering among his judicial colleagues. Later, the Scottish Court of Session effectively disciplined him when they held that there was a risk of a 'legitimate apprehension' of bias when he adjudicated in a case that raised a point of law under that Act.[7]

As we will see, this distancing of the judiciary from public debate is significant. Their distancing from public debate has not been confined only to media exposure. It is much more radical.

[6] It may also be noted that the Judicial Committee of the Privy Council in the appeal case of *Follen v Lord Advocate* 2001 SLT 774 emphasised that the court had not become a constitutional court for the UK outwith within the (narrowly specified) powers accorded it by devolution statute. JCPC judgments can be found online at <http://www.privy-council.org.uk/judicial-committee/jindex.htm>. For a discussion of related issues, see A O'Neill, 'Judicial Politics and the Judicial Committee' (2001) 64(4) *Modern Law Review*, 608.

[7] *Hoekstra v H. M. Advocate (No. 2)* 2000 SCCR 367. It is interesting to note that part of the criticism of Lord McCluskey was directed at the language in which he expressed his views: the Lord Justice General stated that it would have been 'very different' had Lord McCluskey confined himself to a use of 'moderate' language. Judgments of the Scottish courts can be found online at <http://www.scotcourts.gov.uk/index1.htm>. For a good analysis and critique of the developing common law on extra-judicial pronouncements, as articulated in recent Scots and English case law, see S Tierney, 'Convention Rights and the Scotland Act: redefining judicial roles' [2001] *Public Law* 38.

II. SOURCES OF THE CONCEPTS OF JUDICIAL LEGITIMACY: LEGAL OR SOCIO-POLITICAL?

Having got the introductory points out of the way, our starting point is to enquire into whether the source of the concept of the legitimacy of the judge is a socio-political one or a legal one in the UK.

The immediate answer to this must be that it is always socio-political, whether or not a legal concept exists. The bedrock foundations of law in modern Western societies rest on an ideological discourse of legitimate authority. The matter goes to the heart of politics and government.

The discourse of judicial authority may however at certain periods be more or less successfully removed from the political and social arenas, allowing it to be managed and controlled by the judicial branch of the state. This will give it the appearance of a solely legal nature. Nevertheless, such a status is always potentially unstable. Whenever there is an open struggle to define the boundaries of that authority, the territory of legal legitimacy will become contested. A public debate will centre around claims about the politicisation of the judiciary or the juridification of political disputes. At this point, the legal definition of judicial legitimacy (whether precisely defined or whether contained within a wider claim to authority) becomes particularly significant because it can be used to protect individual judges or the institution of the judiciary against political criticism.

Judicial legitimacy, in the sense of the legitimacy of the judiciary as an institution, was fundamentally uncontested in most of the UK during the twentieth century. There was a remarkably strong ideological separation of the judiciary from what was seen as the arena of politics. Only in Northern Ireland was the legitimate status of the judiciary called seriously into question. There, the judges were seen by a large sector of the community as representatives of an external governing power, the British state. Elsewhere however their role in public life was so cushioned that few members of the public could name even the most senior judges.

The most striking recent example of the ideological separation of judicial legitimacy from the 'political' arena can be found in the Race Relations (Amendment) Act 2000. This statute extended provisions on race relations to most public bodies, but stopped short of imposing upon the judiciary a duty to promote racial equality. The government maintained that this omission was necessary to 'protect . . . the independence of the judiciary'.[8]

[8] *Explanatory Notes to Race Relations (Amendment) Act 2000*, Ch 34, HMSO (2001). Management of this is regarded as falling within the judiciary's own territory. In England, the Lord Chancellor, who is a member of the Cabinet and a senior judge, is in charge of judicial appointments and judicial training. The Lord Chancellor's Department issued guidelines last year on cultural awareness and the Lord Chancellor revealed that since taking office in 1997 he had 'disciplined' several judges for making offensive racial remarks (under guidelines introduced by his predecessor in 1994).

Undoubtedly, this ideological separation is not complete and is probably growing less so by the decade. Public criticism of individual judges has mushroomed since the exposure of several highly publicised miscarriages of justice in the 1980s and 1990s. In the last couple of years we have seen unusually fierce criticism of one very senior Scottish judge by another[9] and a groundbreaking case where a House of Lords decision was set aside because of the undisclosed affiliations of a Law Lord on the original panel.[10] The legitimacy of the judiciary itself as an institution has also been called into question regularly in recent years by media commentators discussing enhanced judicial powers under the Human Rights Act 1998. Indeed, the authoritative status of the entire Scottish appeal system was very recently impugned by the English members of the defence team in the Lockerbie case. One senior English lawyer called the Scottish system 'golf-club justice' and stated that it is not possible to meet the requirements of an independent appeal procedure given the small size of the Scottish bench and bar, coupled with an appeals system in which a larger number of judges at the same level review the decisions of judges at first instance.[11]

All this gives the impression of a political storm. We must ask though whether it is much more than a storm in a media teacup, or perhaps a succession of disposable media teacups. The criticisms have not been followed up by an organised activist campaign or a governmental move towards extensive, fundamental reform. The judiciary survived, with seemingly little lasting damage, the series of miscarriage of justice cases, and the institution appears relatively sanguine today. Judges still possess a sufficiently high status that their presence adds authority to public inquiries[12] and their status affords them, as individuals, considerable public trust.[13]

At an institutional level, there seems to be little perception of a judiciary

[9] Lord Hardie, the Lord Advocate, was severely criticised by the trial judge Lord McCluskey in a high-profile murder and the subsequent issue of whether the second trial was prejudiced by the pre-trial publicity resulted in the human rights appeal case of *Montgomery & Coulter v HMA and Advocate General for Scotland* 2001 SLT 37. Because the relevant legislation had newly introduced the right of appeal from what had previously been a court of final instance, the case was the first to be appealed from a Scottish criminal court to the UK court of the Judicial Committee of the Privy Council. (It is perhaps worth mentioning that the maverick Lord McCluskey, whose name tends to pop up frequently when high judicial controversy surfaces in Scotland, is widely regarded by Scottish legal professionals as accomplished and talented.)

[10] *R v Bow Street Metropolitan Stipendiary Magistrate, ex p. Pinochet (No 2)* [1999] WLR 272. There is a good discussion of the case by Timothy Jones in the 1999 edition of *Public Law* at 391.

[11] *The Herald*, 17 Mar 2002.

[12] See Gavin Drewry 'Judicial inquiries and public reassurance' [1996] *Public Law* 368.

[13] A MORI opinion poll earlier in 2002 found that British judges (in Scotland, England and Wales) were among those most trusted to tell the truth: *The Herald*, 20 Apr 2002. Of course, such sources may be untrustworthy and it is notable that there is not a great deal of academic research in Great Britain on this point.

facing a crisis of legitimacy. Even now the Scottish judicial administration, for instance, has no public relations department.[14] Media enquiries are dealt with on behalf of the Scottish Court Service by the general press office of the Scottish Executive. Enquiries from the general public can now be made to the Scottish Courts Service through a relatively new public website, but it appears to be expected that these will be made by letter or email: telephone enquiries are met with some bafflement. The service presents itself publicly as an administrative body whose external liaison is primarily with persons involved in some way with court actions, rather than with the general public.[15]

This is not simply a stubborn refusal to acknowledge the howls of the mob outside the castle, even though an element of wilful ignorance most probably exists. The social position of the judiciary is genuinely and dramatically different from that of many other state organisations whose role involves some direct contact with the public in the UK. The police service is only one contrasting example: it has had to introduce radical reforms after being in the spotlight of unremitting political criticism and public attention in the UK for decades.[16]

Why is this? What secures the position of the UK judiciary to the extent that the institution repeatedly escapes anything more than passing censure? How can the judiciary maintain its ideological distance from the 'political'? This is a distinctively British phenomenon. While it is not unusual (even in legal systems with an openly activist judiciary) for judges to present themselves as the least dangerous branch, and while senior UK judges are now commenting regularly on the growth of their powers, this particular expression of neutrality still exists to a greater extent in the UK than it does in most other Western legal systems. The cultural ideology that surrounds and downplays this is for me one of the most interesting qualities of law in the UK and I welcome the opportunity to analyse the structures that lie behind it.

In most parts of the UK, the judiciary has had a discursive and institutional invisibility. The two are closely linked. Our relatively formal approach to legal reasoning is a feature of UK institutions which travels hand-in-hand with the discursive minimising of the importance of judicial discretion. This minimisation of the apparent role of the judge was at its height in the late nineteenth century. Even today, however, although the creative and law-making power of the judge has been recognised in higher

[14] Thanks to Cyrus Tata for drawing my attention to this some years ago.

[15] See the Scottish Courts Service website at <http://www.scotcourts.gov.uk/>.

[16] The most famous example of this must be the 1999 Macpherson Report of the inquiry into the murder of a young African-Caribbean man, Stephen Lawrence (London: HMSO): this report and its findings of institutional racism in the Metropolitan police force attracted international coverage.

court discourse for decades,[17] there remains very little formal institutional recognition of that power within law-creating procedures. One feature of this invisibility has been a very underdeveloped understanding in the UK of concepts such as judicial legitimacy. This particular concept has been in practice bound up with the concept of judicial independence, which I will discuss shortly.

Before that it is worth considering what has anchored this invisibility. There are many historical and social factors which have brought about this judicial status. In this paper, I only have space to consider the vision of law which grounds this, but I hope that that will go some way towards explaining what is a quite unusual position for a public body in a modern Western society.

III. NATIONAL VISIONS OF LAW AND DEMOCRACY

As we have seen, we are asking a very broad and political question when we enquire about the legitimacy of the judge in a legal system. To appreciate the particular judicial roles occupied in a particular legal system, and whether or not the judges and their actions are perceived as legitimate, it is essential then to understand the constitutional and political setting of that system's judiciary. What a judge does, what she or he represents and how this is viewed by others depends very much on national conceptions of law and democracy and how these impact on judicial authority. And while there is no space to consider it here, we should not forget that judges play an active part themselves in legitimising through law the activities of the other branches of government. The bigger question for jurists is not only what legitimises judges, but also what they themselves legitimate.

We require a set of tools with which to analyse distinctions between different elements of the judicial role. In particular, when comparing concepts of the legitimacy of the judge among different legal systems, we find ourselves peering at a whole range of odd local phenomena, such as particular approaches to statutory interpretation, or lists of particular tasks, which a judge may or may not carry out without criticism. In themselves these rules may seem apolitical and arcane, even mystificatory. At the very least they may appear arbitrary accidents of history. Understood in

[17] The classic exponent of this was Lord Reid in the 1970s. For more recent examples declaring the purported limits of the judicial power to 'develop' law generally see: *Ex parte Begley* [1997] NI 278 (quote taken from LEXIS transcript), *R v Clegg* [1995] 1 AC 482 at 500, *C v DPP* [1996] 1 AC 1 at 39, *R v Kingston* [1995] 2 AC 355. See also the European Court of Human Rights in *SW* v *United Kingdom* Case 47/1994/494/576, transcript 15. House of Lords judgments can be found online at: <http://www.parliament.the-stationery-office.co.uk/pa/ld199697/ldjudgmt/ldjudgmt.htm>.

their institutional and ideological context, though, they often have a greater significance and we can use them to build up broader analyses of the democratic roles of the judge. We would do well then to begin at the systemic level, using legal theory to analyse what this institutional and ideological context is in the UK.

Patrick Atiyah and Robert Summers envisage two 'visions' of law which lie behind legal and political discourse.[18] These, they maintain, can be used to contrast law in different legal systems. The formal vision at its strongest sees law as deriving its validity from authoritative sources. The act of enactment or authoritative statement becomes the criterion which makes a norm legal. Formal rules and substantive principles are seen as relatively separate and independent. The legislature is expected to provide a comprehensive body of detailed rules and the higher courts are expected to police the application of law.

The substantive vision in contrast adds great weight to the content of a norm. A norm cannot pass the test of legal validity unless it meets substantive standards of justice or rightness. Reasons which decide a case will more often contain, and will more often be transparent to, background substantive principles. Statutes will be interpreted more purposively than literally and precedents will be interpreted more liberally. The legislature lays down relatively broad rules while higher courts evaluate and develop the law, leaving some space to promote particular justice in the instant case. The price of this is some sacrifice of rule of law values. The loss of foreseeability inherent in substantive justice will mean that law will be less accessible to the citizen and less predictable when it is promulgated.

These two visions are ideal types and are best understood at the systemic level. The formal and substantive forms of reasoning around which the visions are built are in practice rarely wholly separable. Formal reasons even in their purest incarnation are legitimated by second-order substantive reasons:[19] it is because formal reasoning is among other things likely to be directive, cost-efficient and predictable that it can be a successful and legitimate alternative to the seemingly ideal legal hearing in which every citizen could hope for a decision which is the most fair and just in his or her particular case. A balance of formal and substantive reasoning enables an affordable and accountable legal system. It is the *prominence* of one or other types which Atiyah and Summers see as creating the different characteristics of various legal systems.

What, then, is the underlying vision of law which typifies the UK legal systems and lays the foundations for our distinctive conception of judicial

[18] PS Atiyah and Robert S Summers, *Form and Substance in Anglo-American Law* (Oxford: Clarendon Press,1987).

[19] Ibid, 23 ff.

legitimacy? Atiyah and Summers attempt to give a partial answer to this (for England) in their comparison of England and the United States. In their view, there is a greater use of formal reasoning by English judges, which reflects not simply a more literal or cautious method of adjudication. Rather, they maintain, 'this difference in methods of reasoning reflects a deep difference in legal style, legal culture, and, more generally, the visions of law which prevail in the two countries'.[20] It tells us something about the judicial mandate: the judge is predominantly given the task of policing the law rather than developing it.

John Bell, although partially in agreement with Atiyah and Summers, argues that English judges are more creative than Atiyah and Summers suggest. It is true, he maintains, that the judges are unwilling to create policies of their own independent of the legislature, but nevertheless they will reason substantively, relying on policies which the legislature has previously expressed.[21] Bell's argument, based on his own extensive research, is convincing[22] and it is unfortunate that Atiyah and Summers perpetuate a misunderstanding about the role of the English judge, particularly in a work of legal theory which is more empirically-informed than many similar works which claim to have a sociological element. It is also worth asking whether Atiyah and Summers' work needs updating today and I will do this shortly.

A final point worth noting is that Atiyah and Summers's methodological framework is essentially a liberal and institutional one rather than a critical one. Their interest is in a largely 'official' picture of how judges reason and what roles they occupy. The picture they paint is one more appropriate to the higher judges in the more prestigious courts in the UK rather than the more junior judges dealing with processes and areas of law which are more marginal and underfunded. Their English 'vision' of law is legitimising, ideological; it should not be regarded as simply a descriptive analysis. An understanding of this legitimisation is however just what I am seeking here, so it suits my purposes well. I will turn now to use this to examine the other constituent legal systems of the UK.

IV. VISIONS OF LAW AND DEMOCRACY IN THE UK

Traditionally in the UK, judges have been seen to possess no (or at least very little) original law-making power within the province which is already

[20] Ibid, 1.

[21] Bell in van Dunné, *Legal Reasoning and Statutory Interpretation: Rotterdam Lectures in Jurisprudence* (1989), 56 and *passim.*

[22] See also the cases I have cited at n.18: these provide more recent support for Bell's argument.

defined by the legislature. While it is now generally accepted in mainstream juristic discourse that judges unavoidably have a law-making function, they are largely denied overt formal powers to make law. Even in the common law, where they have developed legal principles, their role was traditionally seen as 'declaratory' of a pre-existing rule waiting to be given spoken form. It was not seen as creative.

Conventional political ideology in the UK states that the major part of the primary law-making function is given to the elected body of Parliament (regardless of the modern reality of European law, the power of the executive and the quantity of delegated legislation made by ministerial departments).[23] Legislative law-making in controversial moral and political areas has been relatively prompt and effective, for a variety of reasons, so judges have not been placed in the position of gap-filling that their counterparts in other jurisdictions such as Ireland[24] have. And while history suggests that the authority of the UK judiciary is at least as well safeguarded by statute, custom and constitutional convention as is the judiciary of many other states by their constitutions, the judiciary of the UK have traditionally had a delegated rather than an original power, even at the highest level (at least in English constitutional theory). As we saw above, the two highest courts in the UK, the House of Lords[25] and the Privy Council,[26] do not possess a comprehensive power of constitutional review of statutes.[27] Statutes lawfully enacted by the legislature are open to judicial interpretation but enjoy a general constitutional immunity from challenge on the basis of invalidity, outwith areas governed by European courts. The only major power of legislative or constitutional review lies in the area of *vires* in delegated legislation.

At this level of generality, we find that the vision of law varies very little across the UK. The ideology of the judicial role even today paints judges as learned expositors rather than wise innovators: their legitimacy rests on their ability to understand and apply the law 'without fear or favour' rather

[23] Legislation of the Scottish Parliament and Northern Ireland Assembly has the status of secondary, or delegated, legislation.

[24] I refer here not to the whole island of Ireland, which would include Northern Ireland, but to the independent jurisdiction which is sometimes inaccurately described as the Republic of Ireland (its official title today is simply Ireland). The Supreme Court in Ireland was forced to develop law in several controversial and embattled areas over a number of decades in the twentieth century in response to the weaknesses of the legislature.

[25] The proper and more accurate title for the judicial element of the House of Lords is the Appellate Committee of the House of Lords.

[26] The proper and more accurate title for the judicial element of the Privy Council is the Judicial Committee of the Privy Council.

[27] For more information on the work and roles of these two courts, see the thorough and interesting analysis carried out by A Le Sueur and R Cornes *The Future of the United Kingdom's Highest Courts* (London: UCL Constitution Unit, 2001).

than to balance formal against particularistic justice.[28] This is of course true at least to some extent of judges throughout Western legal systems. In the UK however it becomes clear that the ideology of the judge as expositor is notably strong when one compares it to that of many other legal systems in which it is acknowledged that judges have political views and personal backgrounds which affect their social perceptions and which are legitimately a matter for public examination and public debate. Our judges in the UK are expected—and generally assumed—to be 'apolitical', even though a judicial post has not infrequently been a reward for active participation in politics.[29] And while a limited creative role is recognised and expounded by the judiciary themselves, it is nonetheless usually seen to be derived from the formal source of legislation; like the notion of the 'declaratory' statement of common law, it is presented as the exercise of a closely controlled delegated function. Within that apparently restricted territory, though, the UK judge is powerfully protected from outside 'interference' and finds little difficulty in staying within the broad boundaries of what it is legitimate for him to do.

This ideology is dominant but it is increasingly being confronted with strong challenges and it is important to be aware that there is far from a universal consistency of views among the judiciary. Senior judges Sir John Laws and Lord Woolf have for instance argued on a number of occasions that the power of judicial review is not simply subordinate to the legislature but is effectively an original one rather than a delegated one.[30] In presenting an overall vision of law, one risks playing down the extent to which the powerful groups in society are fragmented as part of a whole and the extent to which they are internally fractured and in conflict. Nevertheless, I think it is instructive to examine the dominant vision of law, even though it has powerful competitors, because it illuminates our understanding of what is kept on and what is left off the agenda in shaping debate about law in the UK. Although this view has faded in jurisprudential discourse about law and is under challenge in judicial discourse, it still dominates the UK's

[28] For a wide list of examples of statements of this traditional view, see C Palley, *Public Order* (London: Open University Press, 1972), 58. For a recent incisive critique of its persistence, see D Robertson *Judicial Discretion in the House of Lords* (Oxford: Clarendon Press, 1998)

[29] On this see, for instance, A Paterson, TStJN Bates and M Poustie, *The Legal System of Scotland* 4th edn (Edinburgh: Green, 1999), 225–7.

[30] An ongoing debate on this and related questions of the constitutional distribution of power, contributed to by both judges and academic commentators, has been taking place in the journal *Public Law* for several years now. It has sometimes climbed off the pages of the journals and into case law. Most recently, Sir John Laws insisted in a recent decision that there is a hierarchy of statutes with a set of 'constitutional' statutes occupying a protected place at the top. He argued further that this was a development of the common law, not merely a power delegated by statute. See paras 62–4, *Thoburn v Sunderland City Council*, QBD, 18 Feb 2002.

vision of law at a more general level. An awareness of what is left out of the debate as a result—an awareness of what is forgotten or is seen as immutable—is as important as an understanding of the impassioned but sometimes minor battles which occupy juristic and public attention.

This dominant vision of the law and the legitimate territory of the judge is not restricted only to England. It is largely similar in Scotland and Northern Ireland. It is true that in Scotland, there is (even today) a claim to a distinctive approach to law rooted in that legal system's part-common law and part-civilian origins. Criminal law in Scotland is largely part of a separate legal system and some areas of civil law also diverge even though final appeal lies to the UK House of Lords.[31] Legal reasoning in Scotland was regularly depicted during much of the twentieth century as located in a broad, principle-oriented form of reasoning, contrasted to a precedent-based form of reasoning found in English legal method. Later, however, sceptical voices began to speak out[32] and today the notion is a nebulous one with little factual basis. Typically it is stirred together with various notions of legal (rarely political) nationalism and is more often heard among lawyers in the pub than read in any scholarly writing or expressly used by a senior judge in justifying the binding element of a legal decision. This predominantly nineteenth- and twentieth-century ideology of Scots legal reasoning was like most successful ideologies partly founded in fact and partly a distorted perception of that fact.

There is an apparent distinction in forms of reasoning between Scottish and English/UK higher court judgments but I suspect it is also partly the result of structural factors. Scotland, like Northern Ireland, is a relatively small legal system with a low turnover of appeal cases. Few cases reach the highest Scottish courts each year and in areas of law not governed by precedents from Britain or the UK, existing decisions can stand unchallenged for very many years. One consequence of the much smaller number of higher court cases in Scotland is that the judiciary, particularly in previous centuries, laid down decisions of wide general importance for perhaps a good many years. They would have been unwise to confine themselves to narrow areas of law. English judges in contrast, working within a larger legal system, had to provide precise guidance for particular areas of law. In criminal law, for example, it could be argued that one concern of the English higher judges was very often the provision of clear and unmistakable directions for juries, while Scots judges had a greater freedom to be more concerned with the justice of the justification lying behind any particular rule.

[31] Both criminal and civil cases can now be appealed to the UK courts where they raise a devolution issue or human rights point, and it is possible for a criminal case involving a point of EC law to be appealed in that respect to a UK court.

[32] I Willock (1976) 'The Scottish Legal Heritage Revisited', in J Grant (ed) *Independence and Devolution* (Edinburgh: Lindsay & Co, 1976), 5.

A more complete picture of a vision of Scots law in the twenty-first century would acknowledge that a large part of Scotland's law has for centuries been overseen by ultimate courts of appeal in the much larger parent legal system of the UK. Scotland now shares a large proportion of its law with the rest of Britain or the UK, and the final court of appeal in most civil law lies outwith Scotland. At a fundamental level the distinction between forms of reasoning in the two legal systems is not great. Both possess a predominantly formal vision of law and while there will continue to be separate areas of Scots law which differ significantly from their English counterpart, any separate Scots *vision* of law seems to be withering on the vine. It is reasonable to conclude that the Scottish legal perception of judicial legitimacy is little different from the English.

In Northern Ireland there is even less evidence of a distinctive Northern Irish vision of law at present, at least within the legal profession itself. Northern Ireland as a separate nation in any sense is relatively young[33] and the judiciary there has struggled with the problems of uncertain political and constitutional authority. Increasingly in the West, we have a dominant ideological discourse of governance based on representative democracy. Political authority is ideologically strongest when it is seen to be derived from electoral accountability. Judges throughout the UK are appointed, not elected, so their authority largely derives from the general status of the judiciary and the body of the state responsible for appointing them. The authority of Northern Irish judges has suffered from their institutional association with the British state rather than the local area.[34] Confidence in the Northern Ireland criminal justice system has not been as high as it is in the other UK legal systems.[35] It remains to see whether the creation of a devolved Northern Irish Assembly and the introduction of a Northern

[33] Northern Ireland has never been a separate state and its creation as a separate jurisdiction was very much a legal artifice built for political reasons rather than a recognition of a sense of nationhood among a group of people. It was established as a result of the enactment by the UK government of the Government of Ireland Act 1920, which partitioned the island of Ireland into 'North' and 'South' and set up Parliaments for both in 1921. Uprising in the South very quickly led to the creation of a breakaway Irish Free State which later became an independent republic.

[34] Constitutional changes to the structure of the Scottish judiciary are predominantly a matter reserved to the UK Parliament rather than devolved to the Scottish Parliament, but despite concerns raised by Robert Reed (now a judge of the Scottish Court of Session) in the run-up to devolution, this has not so far led to public criticism. R Reed, 'Devolution and the Judiciary', in *Constitutional Reform in the United Kingdom: Practice and Principles* (Cambridge: University of Cambridge Centre for Public Law, 1998).

[35] *NI Community Attitudes Survey* (4th Report 1997); *British Social Attitudes Survey* (8th Report 1991); G Hogan and C Walker, *Political Violence and the Law in Ireland* (Manchester: Manchester University Press, 1989) 109, citing E Moxon-Browne *Nation, Class and Creed in Northern Ireland* (Aldershot: Gower, 1983), 144. See also S Doran and J Jackson in N Dawson and A Ingram, *One Hundred and Fifty Years of Irish Law* (Belfast: SLS Legal Publications, 1996), 101 for other, similar, findings.

Ireland Human Rights Commission will alter these perceptions. Judicial appointments remain a matter for the Lord Chancellor's Department in London, although the creation of a judicial appointments commissioner for Northern Ireland to oversee this is intended to attach some greater legitimacy to the appointments process.

National sentiment can become a means by which the authority and legitimacy of the judiciary is grounded. In the conflict-ridden setting of Northern Ireland, however, any apparently nationalist stance immediately becomes politicised. In Scotland, images of national character have long been used in legal discourse to legitimise developing or maintaining distinctive elements of Scots law. These 'kailyard' images are successfully portrayed as common to all and historically stable—as qualities of the Scottish character which sit above the grubby world of political disputes. This has rarely been used in recent times to shore up the status of the Scottish judge, but media discussion does sometimes distinguish between 'our' and 'their' judges when comparing Scots judges to their senior UK counterparts in the appeal process (albeit that at least one Scots judge sits by convention in any House of Lords appeal).

Such imagery is not available to found and legitimise the status of the judge in Northern Ireland. This, and the problems of authority discussed above, inhibited the identification of any Northern Irish legal vision and subdued judicial divergence from English precedent. These inhibiting factors have not prevented the development of an independent stance in certain controversial areas of law which dealt with particular Northern Ireland problems, but they may have encouraged the higher judiciary to root activist and creative decisions in tradition or to redefine them as uncontroversial rather than assert them as outcomes of a legitimate lawmaking power. The rare forays of Northern Irish judges into substantive reasoning have been a product of isolated failures in the formal effectiveness of the legal system.[36]

While Scotland has maintained a sense of a national legal identity in its partially separate legal system, it is probably fair to say that neither Scotland nor Northern Ireland have a vision of law significantly different from that of England and Wales at the most general level of understanding. While there are certainly important differences to be found in argumentation style and in the substance of the law in Scotland in particular, there is not a fundamentally different vision of law lying behind any legal concept of judicial legitimacy. We can therefore conclude for now that there appears to be a UK-wide vision of law. We can then proceed to look at how this UK vision has evolved in recent times and examine this to see how it might tend to produce a UK conception of judicial legitimacy.

[36] For an extended discussion of this, see K Goodall, 'Judicial Justification in the Two Irish Legal System', PhD thesis, 1999.

V. A CHANGING VISION OF LAW IN THE UK?

Much scholarly attention has been given in the past few years to the changes brought about by two major legislative events: first, the introduction of ECHR principles directly into judicial decision-making in the UK under the aegis of the Human Rights Act 1998 and second, the creation of devolved legislatures for Scotland and Northern Ireland. It is frequently concluded by commentators that a significantly substantive element of reasoning has been introduced by both, but in particular by the enactment of the Human Rights Act. This statute formally brings the rights jurisprudence of the European Court of Human Rights into judicial decision-making, by making it a source with which to interpret legislation. Might we then be witnessing a substantial move from a formal to a substantive vision of law in the UK?

It is too early to say, but I would argue that this is not necessarily the case. Certainly, devolution and the formal instantiation of Convention rights as criteria of reference have founded a system where legislative rules which are potentially and explicitly 'transparent' to the background justifications contained in the devolution and human rights statutes. The UK had already taken decades even to begin to adapt to the notion that European Community law had supremacy over primary legislation. It caused considerable discomfort among judges unused to this degree of vulnerability in legal norms. It is true too that these legislative developments delegate additional power to the judiciary. What is often assumed wrongly, though, is that this is therefore straightforwardly a novel form of substantive decision-making.

These new powers are drawn not from unenumerated constitutional principles but instead from formal documents enshrined as legislation. As was noted above regarding John Bell's analysis, it is not a new thing for the judiciary in the UK to reason substantively under the aegis of legislative statements. It is also significant that the judiciary are required to read legislation in conformity with the Human Rights Act where possible. This involves searching for an appropriate possible interpretation of the legislation[37] and does not empower the judiciary to strike it down[38] or adopt a 'perverse' interpretation of the language of the provision, as Lord Lester has

[37] 'Reading down' involves adopting what may be a strained interpretation of the words of the statute to ensure it is compatible with the ECHR. It excludes reading in words that are not actually there.
On 'reading down', see for instance Lord Steyn's comments in *R v A* (2001) HRLR 48. For an earlier but helpful discussion of the concept, see R Edwards, 'Reading down legislation under the Human Rights Act' (2000) 20(3) *Legal Studies* 353.

[38] A Scottish court can strike down a statute of the Scottish Parliament as this body is regarded as a creature of UK statute, but when confronted with a statute of the UK Parliament, a judge can go no further than a 'declaration of incompatibility', which is not binding on the other branches of government.

put it.[39] As Richard Edwards has pointed out, this involves reading down, not reading in as would be possible with EC legislation.[40]

Nor is it necessarily the case that groundbreaking human rights decisions will be justified by way of substantive reasoning. Often the fundamental principles alluded to are second-order substantive reasons, formally enshrined in the devolution and human rights statutes themselves: here the decision may well be justified by way of close textual analysis or formal adherence to precedent. The Human Rights Act does sanction considerable discretion in referring to Strasbourg jurisprudence, and lawyers examining appeal judgments in this area will notice a wide range of sources being drawn upon, from Europe and beyond. This however may not be an attempt to broaden discretion in a form of substantive reasoning: it may turn out to be the first stage of a search for sources from which to develop relatively formal techniques of reasoning in the longer run.[41]

There are, then, second-order formal reasons which govern the use of substantive reasoning and at that level there are complex questions raised. How they are answered and interpreted will be crucial to identifying how fundamentally—or not—the vision of law is changing in the UK. It should not be uncritically assumed that the changes in the UK mean a radically more substantive vision of law. Indeed, over recent decades there has been a general change in the character of modern Western legal systems: increasingly we find that legitimacy can no longer derive unproblematically from tradition but must be supervised by a variety of formal methods of review.[42] At the highest level, authority in the legal system no longer derives much strength from traditional hierarchies and must increasingly appeal ultimately to democratic confirmation. In the UK, the judiciary are weak in this respect, being unelected, and the institution has instead been protected and legitimised by an accepted definition of a territory which is their dominion but which they must not (appear to) step beyond. If a fundamental socio-political perception is developing that the legitimacy of the judiciary is

[39] Lord Lester, 'The Art of the Possible' (1999), *European Human Rights Law Review*, 669, as cited in Edwards, op cit.

[40] Ibid.

[41] It is also worth observing that the use of persuasive authority from the civilian jurisdictions was regarded as a significant source of law in judicial reasoning some decades ago and is no recent event: see A McCall Smith, 'Scots Law in Comparative Context', in J Grant (ed), *Independence and Devolution* (Edinburgh: Lindsay & Co, 1976).

[42] In the UK, challenge is increasingly being made to all aspects of the justice system, in some circumstances more successfully than that levelled at the judiciary. Fundamental reform is taking place. See, for instance, the removal of powers of self-regulation from the Law Society (England and Wales) in the Administration of Justice Act 1999, the investigation of institutional racism in the appointments of high sheriffs (who mostly enforce civil writs) in England and Wales (*The Guardian,* 27 June 2000) and the concern over potential intimidation of jury members (*The Guardian,* 21 Apr 2000). See also the comments of S Smith in 'Scottish Public Prosecution, Policy and Practice: Issues of Independence and Accountability' (1999) *Judicial Review* 141.

contestable, it seems likely that the judiciary will attempt to regain their uncontested territory by developing an innovative and increasingly clear definition of what the courts' new authority does *not* permit.[43]

There is an element of historical amnesia, or a brushing-over of past conflicts, to be found in juristic discourse in the UK. Significant changes have taken place in our concepts of law and of judicial roles throughout the twentieth century, as Keith Ewing has eloquently pointed out.[44] In addition, the phenomenon of UK judges reasoning substantively under legislative direction is no great novelty, even though it is now provided for under formal rules to a much greater extent than before. The changes of the last few years may prove to be less fundamental than they appear and whether they will shake the institution of the judiciary to its foundations remains to be seen. What was once a judicial invisibility grounded in a broadly formal vision of law may become a partial visibility grounded in a more detailed set of formal rules and principles of law.[45]

The judges may no longer be permitted to be the éminences grises they have been in the past, but it may be that it will take some time before the discourse and institutions of law recognise them as full-blown éminences rouges. John Griffith has argued that UK judges have less influence on policy-making than they once did, although they remain very powerful figures,[46] and it may be that their more shadowy powers may be declining on one hand even as their formally-recognised powers are increasing on the other. It will be interesting to see how the judges adapt argument forms to root their new human rights powers in the old system.

VI. META-VALUES, JUDICIAL INDEPENDENCE, AND JUDICIAL LEGITIMACY

We have begun by identifying a relatively formal vision of law in the UK, with a powerful and possibly growing substantive element of judicial reasoning, legitimised under the protective umbrella of putative legislative

[43] See, for instance, the preliminary moves by a number of senior judges: among others, one might cite Lord Irvine, the present Lord Chancellor, in his 1999 article 'Activism and restraint: human rights and the interpretative process', EHRLR 350; Lord Lester 'Interpreting statutes under the Human Rights Act' [1999] *Statute Law Review* 214, Lord Bingham, 'The way we live now: human rights in the new millennium' (1998) *1 Web Journal of Current Legal Issues* and Lord Hope, 'The Human Rights Act 1998: the task of the judges' [1999] *Statute Law Review* 185.

[44] K Ewing, 'The Politics of the British Constitution' [2000] *Public Law* 405.

[45] See the comments of Jeffrey Jowell in a 2000 piece, 'Beyond the rule of law: towards constitutional judicial review', *Public Law* 671. See also the decision in *R (Daly) v SSHD* [2001] 2 WLR 1622 on the technique of proportionality, and a discussion of *Daly* and this topic in N Blake 'Importing proportionality: clarification or confusion' (2002) *European Human Rights Law Review* 19.

[46] J Griffith *The Politics of the Judiciary* (London: Fontana, 1997), xvii.

sanction. Our next step is to enquire how the core values of law are expressed within this vision of law and how they relate to the legitimacy of the judiciary as an institution.

Scott Veitch has observed that the legalism of law is centred around rules and principles and that this is 'also an ethical or political attitude' founded on a concept of autonomy in community.[47] A group of 'meta-values' derives from this, in Veitch's view, which may draw the bounds of legal norms but which do not normally provide solutions in the individual case. Veitch cites Roberto Unger's definition of the rule of law by reference to the 'meta-values' of neutrality, uniformity and predictability and Veitch suggests that there are others, but I think that these three are in the UK the primary legal meta-values and are to be found restated in many different ways.[48] Linking these to the broader socio-political culture of the UK, I would argue that we find also 'legal-cultural meta-values' based on rationality, national identity and historical progress.

Looking at the legal meta-values of neutrality, uniformity, and predictability, we find that these take a distinctive form in defining judicial legitimacy in the UK. The value of neutrality in judging is expressed distinctively both through the relative invisibility of the process and through our concepts of judicial independence.[49] Our concepts of uniformity and predictability also take a distinctive form. In devolution case law in particular and in extra-judicial commentary by judges, there has been an emphasis on the common law and the evolution of national law rather than on any embracing of a European constitutional—and by implication political—tradition. Even coherent development of the law, then, is located in a historical and national context rather than in a context of political harmonisation or modernising rationalisation.

I will consider in particular our notion of judicial independence, because it most strongly illuminates an understanding of our conception of the legitimacy of the judge (both institutional and individual). I stated earlier that the legal concept of judicial legitimacy in the UK was bound up within the concept of judicial independence. Neither has been clearly articulated in juristic or political discourse, not least because in recent times they have rarely been called seriously into question until very recently.[50]

[47] S Veitch *Moral Conflict and Legal Reasoning* (Oxford: Hart Publishers, 1999), 138.

[48] See, eg, F Schauer, *Playing by the Rules* (Oxford: Clarendon Press, 1991), ch 7.

[49] For some trenchant comments by critical public lawyers on 'neutrality', see John Griffith, op cit, and Ian Loveland's and Keith Ewing's articles in [2000] *Public Law*, 374 and 405.

[50] For comment on a number of recent instances in the UK and a jurisprudential examination of the developments, see Goodall 'Judicial Independence' (2000) *Juridical Review*, 383–90. In particular, see:

- *Starrs v Ruxton*, 2000 SLT 42 and the Scottish Executive's response in abolishing and replacing temporary sheriffs under the Bail, Judicial Appointments etc. (Scotland) Act 2001
- *Clancy v Caird*, 2000 SLT 546
- The Scottish Executive consultation on judicial appointments (1999)

The concept of judicial independence in the UK is somewhat incomprehensible to non-UK lawyers. The separation of powers in the UK is traditionally partial: the senior English and Scottish law officers, the Lord Chancellor and the Lord Advocate, are members of the executive and are political appointees. The executive wields considerable power over the domestic legislature (directly and indirectly), and Law Lords sit both as judiciary and as members of the second chamber of the domestic legislature (although by convention they abstain from participation in debate on topics which might draw criticism of their role). The Lord Chancellor and Lord Advocate, who are politicians, have extensive involvement in judicial appointments, and many senior judges were politically active before elevation to the bench, yet our judges are portrayed as apolitical. The Lord Chancellor also has responsibility for selecting which judges hear which cases and can exercise this to the advantage of the current administration.

At the level of personal impartiality, it is no threat to the judicial reputation for independence should a niece appear on behalf of one party before her aunt who sits as the judge, [51] despite the adversarial nature of our legal systems. In contrast, however, there will be automatically be a retrial on grounds of a 'reasonable apprehension of bias' if one Law Lord on a panel of five examining the deportation of a dictator happens to belong to the charitable arm of a campaign organisation whose work includes supporting political prisoners and which makes a minor statement to the court in that case .[52]

- Press accusations of professional influence in shrieval appointments in Scotland (*The Scotsman*, 20 Jan 2000) and widespread criticism of the power of Lord Advocates, senior Scottish law officers, effectively to appoint themselves to the Scottish bench (*The Scotsman*, 17 Feb 2000)
- findings of discrimination in the judicial appointments system in England and Wales (Malleson and Banda, *Factors affecting the decision to apply for Silk/Judicial Office* (2000))
- recommendations of the Criminal Justice Review on establishing an independent judicial appointments body in Northern Ireland (*The Belfast Telegraph*, 18 Feb 2000), which have been answered with the creation of an independent monitor and auditor (as in England and Wales) but not a fully independent appointments system.
- case law on judicial impartiality and disclosure of interests in England and Wales (See eg *R v Bow Street Metropolitan Stipendiary Magistrate, ex p Pinochet (No 2)* [2000] 1 AC 119 and *Locabail (UK) Ltd v Bayfield Properties Ltd* [2000] 1 All ER 65)
- the Lord Chancellor's revised guidelines for judges on political, professional and financial connections (*The Times*, 20 June 2000)
- appeal decisions on the topics of impartiality and the direct involvement of judges in Guernsey in the passage of legislation or executive rules (*McGonnell v United Kingdom* (Application No 28488/95), European Court of Human Rights, 8 Feb 2000, *The Times* 22 February 2000) and extra-judicial comment on legal developments in Scotland (*Hoekstra v HMA (No 2)*, op cit)
- the statement by the senior Law Lord of the House of Lords attempting partially to separate the Law Lords' legislative and judicial activities (*The Guardian*, 26 June 2000)

[51] As in an English case adjudicated recently by Lady Hale.

[52] *R v Bow Street Metropolitan Stipendiary Magistrate, ex p Pinochet (No 2)* [2000] 1 AC 119.

Even among UK lawyers an understanding of the principles underlying the concept of judicial independence tends to be hazy, as it has not been extensively debated and articulated. Where the concept of judicial independence has been articulated, though, it appears to centre around relatively passive notions of bias rather than the active exercise of institutional power. We see here the linking of legitimacy and independence within the meta-value of neutrality, neutrality being conceived of as a matter of impartiality. This was clearly evident in the case of *Clancy v Caird* where Lords Coulsfield and Penrose rejected elements of Canadian constitutional doctrine and observed that extensive control of the administration of the courts [institutional independence] was not an essential element of judicial independence in Scots or ECHR jurisprudence.[53]

In addition, where the concept has been analysed in the UK, we tend to find that this is restricted to distinguishing between the personal impartiality of the individual judge (or panel) and the collective independence of the judiciary as a branch of government.[54] The analysis typically oversimplifies the distinction between the individual judge and the judiciary as an institution. It also typically reproduces the ideological portrayal of the judicial function as a straightforward one of social service, without examining the many structural conflicts inherent in this role.

This is reflected in wider socio-political debate. While there are intermittent queries raised about the legitimacy of the actions of a particular judge or the judiciary as an institution, this discussion rarely reaches the level of an analysis which considers whether or not there might be a need for immediate serious change. There are certainly regular calls for independent judicial appointments commissions and it is regularly noted that the composition of the judiciary does not reflect that of wider society. The debate however almost invariably centres around the failings of the judicial appointments process, omitting a deeper analysis of the process of selection which begins at a much earlier stage.

Composition is, furthermore, regarded as the most significant factor contributing to legitimacy: we hear little about other potential components of the legitimacy debate. Accountability has barely been explored (other than as regards transparency during the appointments process). Political bias, despite a seminal analysis by English professor John Griffith,[55] is

[53] *Clancy v Caird* 2000 SLT 546 at 562 and 569–70. This is an interesting denial given the reality in the UK of the court services' growing involvement in resource management (on which, see Gavin Drewry's comment in [2000] *Public Law* 545).

[54] See, eg, Lord Cullen, 'The Judge and the Public' 1999 SLT 261; K Malleson, 'Judicial Training and Performance Appraisal: the Problem of Judicial Independence' (1997) 60 *Modern Law Review*, 655 at 658–9 and S Shetreet in Shetreet and Deschênes, *Judicial Independence: The Contemporary Debate* (Dordrecht: Martinus Nijhof, 1985), 598–9. See also the comments of the European Court of Human Rights in *Findlay v UK* (1997) 24 EHRR 221 at 244–5.

[55] J Griffith *The Politics of the Judiciary* (London: Fontana, 1997).

usually overlooked in the debate simply because judges are (with some exceptions such as government law officers) not permitted to exhibit overt political affiliations. Accessibility, in the form of a duty to make judicial decisions comprehensible to the parties to the case so that they understand the significance of what the judge has decided, is a matter largely left to solicitors and counsel.

Even composition tends to be analysed in a relatively superficial way, focusing almost exclusively on numerical representation. Now, it is certainly in my view a matter for disquiet that there are no women or non-white minority ethnic judges at the highest level in the UK judiciary. In fact, of the top 736 judges in England and Wales (a list which includes the House of Lords), only fifty-six are women and only six belong to non-white minority ethnic groups. What representation there is at higher levels is astonishingly recent. In England, only since 1999 has there been a woman judge at the second level (the Court of Appeal). There are no non-white minority ethnic judges at or above High Court level at all. In Scotland, only since 1996 has there been a woman member of the Court of Session, Scotland's highest domestic court (although women now amount to three out of the thirty-two). The first non-white minority ethnic judge in Scotland was appointed in 1999. In Northern Ireland, there are no women or non-white minority ethnic judges at the higher levels of the courts. This problem is endemic in the legal profession. Even where it has high representation from a particular group, such as women, this is not evenly spread through the hierarchy and barely infiltrates the judiciary. As an EOC report of last year stated, 'women remain concentrated in the lower levels of the profession'.[56]

Ethnicity and sex are not the only areas of imbalance in representation. Issues of disability and age have also been raised from time to time in the representativeness debate. Religious orientation has been a particular concern in Northern Ireland. As in England, attorneys general in Northern Ireland have regularly been elevated to the highest court. This method of appointment has not caused widespread concern in England but it has led to some discomfiture about the spread of political representation within the Northern Ireland judiciary at all levels. Throughout the period of devolved government the Unionist parties controlled the legislature and their power was reflected to some degree in appointments to the bench. In a 1973 report Tom Hadden and Paddy Hillyard remarked that it 'is incontrovertible that the majority of judicial appointments in Northern Ireland have been made from the ranks of Unionism'[57] and in 1990 Hadden pointed to the continuing small proportion of Catholic judges as evidence that both the judiciary

[56] *Women and Men in Britain* (London: Equal Opportunities Commission, 2001). Figures as of Feb 2001.

[57] T Hadden and P Hillyard, *Justice in Northern Ireland: A Study in Social Confidence* (London: Cobden Trust, 1973), 11.

and the magistracy 'remain firmly rooted in Unionism'.[58] To be fair, not all were Unionist candidates or campaigning party members, but if there is significance in the fact that others were for instance ex-Attorney Generals (and relatives of theirs) appointed by Unionist governments,[59] then at least on the face of it their political affiliation is open to question. Hadden and Hillyard added:

> It does not follow from the preponderance of 'Unionists' on the bench in Northern Ireland that a challenge to the Unionist administration at central or local government level would necessarily fail. . . . There have been a number of cases in Northern Ireland in which ex-Unionist judges have taken a strong line against the executive. . . . Nonetheless it can hardly be doubted that the composition of the judiciary did have an adverse effect on the confidence of the minority in the prospects of mounting a successful civil rights challenge in the courts.[60]

In such a divided country the over-representation of one section of the political community must have evoked the spectre not just of party political bias but cultural too and it would not be surprising if this failed to encourage confidence in the Northern Ireland judiciary, however deserved or undeserved any criticism may have been. It is less easy to divine the political affiliations of the higher judiciary today following the demise of the Stormont government. Hogan and Walker argued in 1989, with regard to the judicial management of emergency powers:

> Changes in judicial personnel (a third were appointed since 1983) may . . . have produced a more permanent improvement through the introduction of candidates with more legalistic and less political backgrounds.[61]

Hogan and Walker however appear content to provide rather slight evidence for this argument, in the form of a brief citation of a Belfast Bulletin report.[62] Nevertheless, the issue has been part of a significant socio-political challenge, albeit an unfocused challenge, to the legitimacy of the Northern Irish judiciary as an institution.

Class—which was once the primary category by which representativeness was analysed—has become the socialist poor cousin in recent discussions, as the content of such discussions moves increasingly towards a US race-and-sex model in analysing discrimination. It is however surely a significant element of the debate, given that until very recently the sole route to senior judicial office in all three UK legal systems was through

[58] Hadden, in I Jennings *Justice Under Fire*, 2nd edn (London: Pluto, 1990), 200.

[59] As was Lord Chief Justice Lowry, who remained in post until 1989 thus carrying this political legacy well beyond the lifetime of the Stormont administration.

[60] Hadden and Hillyard , op cit, 11.

[61] G Hogan and C Walker *Political Violence and the Law in Ireland* (Manchester: Manchester University Press, 1989), 103.

[62] Ibid, 33: Belfast Bulletin (Belfast, 1982), no10 (Rough Justice), 35–7.

success as a barrister or an advocate. In Scotland and Northern Ireland it is still difficult to enter this branch of the profession without independent funding: the training process is long and financial support during apprenticeship is far from guaranteed.

The question of proportionate representation is therefore a significant one in the UK. Proposed solutions to this problem of 'lack of representation' do not however typically ask what the importance of representative composition actually is. Is it presumed that a few more Asian judges would significantly increase judicial understanding of the implications of the social deprivation and political exclusion experienced by the majority of persons of Bangladeshi origin, say? If not that, then is it hoped that some greater understanding of the experiences of middle-class British Asians would be a start? Or, is it rather less ambitiously presumed that wider representation of women and minority groups will give the judiciary a veneer of socio-political legitimacy which will decrease the pressure for institutional change? These and other possibilities are valid candidates for inclusion in a concept of legitimacy, but they need to be debated, supported with evidence and justified rather than presumed.

Nor do proponents of the 'representation' argument typically ask whether there should be wider social reforms beyond simply having a more open judicial appointments process (which is only the very endpoint of a process marked throughout by covert selection and indirect discrimination). Some do argue that there should be greater widening of the career ladder which leads qualified lawyers to judicial office,[63] and this is gradually taking place. There is little attempt however to make an analytical connection between lifelong problems of discrimination and unequal access to education and the final product of an unrepresentative judiciary.[64] Where such debates about broader exclusion have taken place, further down the legal ladder, they tend to focus on attempting to adjust the supposedly erroneous and under-ambitious perceptions of the excluded. This risks being a form of victim-blaming and a distraction from the structural factors which lead to exclusion.

The broader debate about judicial independence largely sets the parameters of presumptions about judicial legitimacy. A representative judiciary is for instance frequently portrayed as a key element in ensuring lack of bias in judicial decision-making. Why a set number of minority candidates, or women, should result in more unbiased decision-making, and what proportion of these

[63] K Malleson and F Banda, 'Factors Affecting the Decision to Apply for Silk and Judicial Office' (Lord Chancellor's Department Research Series No. 2/00, 2000).

[64] Notable exceptions can be found, such as John Griffith's *The Politics of the Judiciary*, the 1992 report by campaign group Justice, *The Judiciary in England and Wales*, and Colette Blair's 2000 report for the Northern Ireland Office, *Judicial Appointments*; but they are the exception rather than the rule.

candidates would be necessary to achieve this change, is given little thought. Institutional discrimination, as opposed to discrimination by individuals, is regularly debated but rarely fully understood: the debate almost invariably returns to playing with numbers. This individualistic focus impoverishes popular and juristic debate about legitimacy and subsumes it within the independence and representation debates.

Just as the popular debate about legitimacy in the UK has been restricted in its scope, so has the popular debate about judicial independence in general. The focus has largely been on the constitutional aspect of independence, in which the judiciary is portrayed straightforwardly as a branch of the UK government which occupies a protected sphere of powers and responsibilities. This statist conception is somewhat simplistic in the twenty-first century, both because of the move to devolution and the move away from government to governance. State responsibility for social planning and economic management, is being shared with quasi-governmental and non-governmental agencies, both domestic and international. Formal sovereignty and substantive control over legal decision-making is increasingly being dispersed among regional, national and intergovernmental (even supranational) political agencies which possess legal functions. As I have stated in an extended discussion of judicial independence:

> When examining the concept of judicial independence we must give due recognition to the ways in which the constitutional roles of the judiciary are now formally regulated at European levels and substantively influenced by developments at a global level, while also emerging from changing interactions with government agencies at a subnational level. Our understanding of the background to principles of judicial independence needs to be as much a political one as a legal one.
>
> Equally, those examining the changing nature of the context of judicial roles must also recognise the change in political from government to governance. Where once the state took direct responsibility for social planning and economic management, increasingly now such work is shared with quasi-governmental and non-governmental agencies, both domestic and international. In some instances the privatisation of executive functions disempowers the judiciary, as where the right of appeal to an independent tribunal is removed from the decision-making process. In other circumstances judicial powers are strengthened, where the judiciary of the UK seizes the opportunity to share control of aspects of the justice system and the consultative process which were once under the direct management of government departments and ministers. What is significant here for doctrinal analysts and legal theorists is the growing fluidity of the concept of government.[65]

Popular debates on judicial independence tend to vacillate between a description of the present and an analysis based on the past, sometimes recognising some of the changing roles and changing responsibilities of the

[65] Goodall 'Judicial independence' (2000) *Juridical Review*, 383.

judiciary, while frequently failing to locate these in an updated analysis of the constitutional aspect of the UK conception of judicial independence.

XI. LEGITIMACY AND THE INDIVIDUAL JUDGE

As I have explained, the concept of judicial legitimacy has not been the subject of widespread analysis in the UK. We do of course have regulation of the appointment process; we set requirements by which individual judges must abide; and mechanisms exist for the dismissal of judges should they fail to comply. Given that these are an implicit set of standards of legitimacy within the legal system, it is worth spending a little time examining them.

Judges in the UK are appointed, not elected. The method of selection varies, but it is only very recently that vacancies at the senior level have been advertised[66] and we have yet to see independent appointment commissions for senior judges in the UK, although consultation on this possibility has taken place in Scotland over the last year.[67] Finally in the twenty-first century we acquired advisory commissions in England and Northern Ireland, but independent appointment commissions have yet to appear. At present, senior judges are appointed by the Prime Minister or other senior figure such as the First Minister of Scotland, on the basis of the advice of senior members of the judiciary and a Law Officer who has taken discreet 'soundings' as to suitable candidates. Indeed, in Scotland there has been widespread criticism of the considerable power of the Lord Advocate (the most senior Scottish law officer) to promote himself to the bench.[68] A similar process takes place at the level of appointment which has traditionally preceded elevation to the bench, that of promotion to senior counsel, or QC.[69] The extent of secrecy and confidentiality in the process is much greater than that involved in most other public appointments.

Because of the secrecy of the process at senior levels, it is not possible to outline with certainty what is expected by those who carry out appointments. Recent research found that there is a widespread perception within the legal profession of indirect discrimination in the process.[70]

Some basic elements can however be outlined. There is no separate

[66] The senior post of High Court judge in England was first advertised in 1998.

[67] The pilot version of the proposed commission have not met with universal approval; one senior lawyer writing in the Mar 2002 edition of the *Journal of the Law Society of Scotland*, described the proposed system as 'hand-knitted' and questioned whether pilot versions had proved to be either fair or open (J Gilmour 'Judicial appointments system still opaque' (2002) *JLSS* 19).

[68] *The Guardian*, 20 Feb 2000; Oracle Law: <http://www.oraclelaw.co.uk/Scotland/Courts/high_court.htm>.

[69] For the most recent criticisms, see *The Guardian*, 27 Mar 2002.

[70] Malleson and Banda, op cit.

career judiciary in the UK, so senior judges are appointed from senior candidates in the legal profession. Candidates must be citizens of the UK, the Commonwealth or Ireland.[71] For some posts, a significant period of time served in the legal profession is a mandatory requirement of appointment.[72]

At more junior levels and outwith the traditional court process, such as appointments to the panels of tribunals or as justices of the peace in Scotland, a legal qualification is not necessary. Criteria for appointment tend to be more readily available at more junior levels (and even these are a very recent innovation, having first appeared in 1999). The Lord Chancellor's Department has published criteria for the appointment of certain junior judicial posts and these include

> legal knowledge and experience, intellectual and analytical ability, sound judgment, decisiveness, communication skills, authority, integrity, fairness, understanding of people and society, maturity and sound temperament, courtesy and humanity, and commitment to public service.

At senior posts, the description is less detailed and refers simply to the need for 'lawyers of great distinction who have proved themselves capable of handling the most important and complex issues which arise in appeals'.

The focus is as one might expect, given the previous discussion of the UK conception of the judicial role. The requirements centre on an apparently non-political command of legal issues and social and decision-making skills: the risk of partiality or lack of independence is implicitly assumed to be controlled by this method of selection. There is no affirmative action procedure in force in the UK: appointment is on the basis of selecting 'those that appear to be the best regardless of gender, ethnic origin, marital status, sexual orientation, political affiliation, religion or disability, except where the disability prevents fulfilment of the physical requirements of the office'.[73]

While judges may be required to demonstrate these qualities before appointment, they cannot be removed merely for the lack of one or more of them. There is no judicial standards commission or system of disciplinary tribunals and it is exceptionally difficult to remove a senior judge from post in the UK. In England, Wales and Northern Ireland, a judge at the level of the High Court or above can only be removed by a resolution of both Houses of the Westminster Parliament: this has never happened. Following devolution in Scotland, all senior judges can be removed by a complicated

[71] S 3, Act of Settlement 1700.

[72] eg, an appointee to the post of Sheriff in Scotland must have been an advocate or solicitor for at least five years. An appointee to the House of Lords must have held high judicial office for at least two years or had the right of hearing before a court for at least fifteen years (s 6 of the Appellate Jurisdiction Act 1876, as amended by Sch10 to the Courts and Legal Services Act 1990).

[73] <http://www.lcd.gov.uk/judicial/appointments/jappsen.htm>.

procedure which is essentially the same for all levels and revolves around a recommendation for removal by the First Minister followed by a removal resolution by at least two-thirds of the members of the Scottish Parliament, based on the recommendations of an independent committee (to be created by an Act of the Scottish Parliament) who have found evidence of 'inability, neglect of duty or misbehaviour'.[74]

Throughout the UK it has been very rare for a judge to be removed from post.[75] The entertaining collection of tales contained in David Pannick's *Judges*[76] clearly indicate that this is not because of any lack of suitable candidates for immediate sacking. In addition, judges are immune in their judicial function from civil suit.

As mentioned above, popular and media criticism seems to have been insufficiently potent to cause serious wounds to the institution, although public criticism does occasionally result in individual judges taking retirement somewhat sooner than they might have. This influence however is essentially informal. Where a case has gone to appeal, a sharp rebuke from a higher court has in the past herded aberrant judges back into line, but the most successful method of control is most probably internal to the system and administered informally. One can only speculate on how it has been exercised, although it seems likely that the need for it is reduced by the homogeneity of the intake to the bench.

There is no entrenched protection of judicial salaries in the UK but, as with other elements of the institution of the judiciary, it has been centuries since there have been serious allegations of 'political interference' in the exercise of decision-making in this respect. Open threats against the protection of judicial tenure or salaries do not appear to have been used against intransigent judges.

Permanent judges remain in post until retirement age, unless removed by the procedure above. Temporary judges have enjoyed less protection, and the Scottish system of using temporary sheriffs and temporary judges of the Court of Session and High Court was recently the subject of litigation. The lack of security of tenure available to the temporary sheriffs was held to be unacceptable: these posts have now been removed.[77]

[74] S 95 Scotland Act 1998 and s 12 Sheriff Courts (Scotland) Act 1971.

[75] Two Scottish sheriffs have been removed from post: one was in 1977 was removed following his public and close association with a political campaign; the other was removed in 1992 after repeatedly interrupting counsel and making offensive comments during the hearing of cases. Both cases involved extensive review at senior political and legal levels before the decisions were reached. Those individuals were however in permanent posts and Paterson, StJN Bates and Poustie (op cit, at 234) note that in the past, before the post was abolished, temporary sheriffs sometimes did not have their appointments reviewed.

[76] D Pannick *Judges* (Oxford: Oxford University Press, 1987).

[77] *Starrs v Ruxton*, 2000 SLT 42. The matter may not end there: Aidan O'Neill has contended that one of the UK's two Supreme Courts, the Judicial Committee of the Privy

Compliance with judicial orders and respect for judicial authority from other organs of the state seem standard in the UK. I have come across no reports of state bodies refusing to comply with orders made by the judiciary in a court decision. It would be attempting too much to speculate on the covert influence exercised by economic and social elites in the UK. There however is little sign of overt interference, despite intense criticism of judicial powers by the current Home Secretary in the government. In addition, as Bell, Ockelton, and Seago have noted: '[the] protection of judges against corrupt influence and venality has traditionally been through a high salary.'[78]

We may however note some other, more explicit forms of interference by powerful groupings, at least in Northern Ireland. Even today, the continuing threat of violence in Northern Ireland[79] must encourage the judiciary to be circumspect in voicing any opinion which might indirectly give support to one or other of the warring communities. Five members of the Northern Ireland judiciary were been murdered by the IRA, the last of whom was a (relatively) outspoken judge, Lord Justice Gibson, in 1987. In 1997 the RUC confirmed that personal details of Lord Hutton, the then Lord Chief Justice, had been found in a suspected IRA intelligence cell and the judiciary were warned that they were the object of renewed surveillance at that time in the wake of failing peace talks. Threats made against RUC officers may indicate that the judiciary are not immune from loyalist threats either. Judges at all levels and their families remain under heavy guard.[80] The recent (selective) ceasefires and political settlement are undoubtedly too recent and insufficiently stable for anyone to be certain that this type of threat to judicial independence has declined.

Council, is itself unable to meet the requirements of judicial independence because there is no protection against removal of Privy Councillors from their posts: 'Judicial politics and the Judicial Committee' (2001) 64 *Modern Law Review*, 617.

[78] Bell, Ockelton, and Seago, op cit. The setting of rates for judicial salaries is administered by an independent body, the Senior Salaries Review Board. They can be increased, but not reduced. Judicial salaries and pensions are a reserved matter kept out of the hands of the devolved administrations. Against Bell *et al*'s claim, there is the contrary argument put forward by John Griffith, that the drop in income on leaving the bar, coupled with recent chipping by the executive at the generous conditions of judicial pay, may lead to some good candidates refusing to apply for judicial posts: Griffith *The Politics of the Judiciary* (London: Fontana, 1997), xv.

[79] During the 1990s deaths and injuries directly attributed to the security situation ran at slightly under a thousand per year, with a total of over 37,000 between 1969 and 1995 (*NI Annual Abstract of* Statistics, 1997). This has reduced since the Belfast Agreement and ceasefires, but the society remains riven by sectarian division and a degree of caution remains.

[80] See also S Doran and J Jackson, in N Dawson and A Ingram, *One Hundred and Fifty Years of Irish Law* (Belfast: SLS Legal Publications, 1996), 77.

VII. CONCLUSIONS

In general, then, the position of the individual judge in the UK is strong. His or her position and status are both largely assured by the continuing institutional and discursive insulation of the judge from legal and socio-political debates about legitimacy. Discussion of judicial legitimacy has tended to be confined to individual components of this concept, such as representation or separation of powers, rather than extending to a more general analysis. These circumstances are not a historical accident but can instead be related to an invisibility of the judge secured by a relatively formal vision of law which is accompanied by an ideological minimisation of the judicial role in decision-making.

While this may well have been beneficial in ensuring the stability of the judiciary as an institution of government, it has been accompanied by an atrophied understanding of the constitutional and political principles which lie behind judicial roles. Whether one sees it as largely advantageous or disadvantageous depends, perhaps, on how fundamentally one believes the institution of the judiciary requires to be reformed.

PART TWO: CIVIL LAW

Chapter 3

'What Family for the 21st Century?': Scotland

*Lilian Edwards**

I. INTRODUCTION: BRIEF NOTE ON SCOTS FAMILY LAW

Although Scotland is politically part of the United Kingdom, it has its own legal system and hierarchy of courts, and in particular, as guaranteed by the Act of Union, its own system of family law. Scots law is a mixed jurisdiction, combining Roman law origins with a history (and present) of extensive borrowing from English law. Since Scotland is and always has been a small jurisdiction, its case law is not comprehensive and there is a tendency where there is an unfilled gap to assume (perhaps, on occasion, unfortunately) that the law is the same as that in England (hence the frequent reference to English cases in some sections below, although these are technically persuasive rather than authoritative). Until recently, furthermore, all Scots legislation, even dedicated statutes only applying in Scotland, originated from the Westminster Parliament. However since 1999, Scotland has had its own Parliament and this is beginning to impact on its family law as more time is now available to pilot through uniquely Scottish legislation. Due to its mixed heritage, Scots law has never been codified: however it is a noticeable feature of its family law that in modern times (roughly since the late 1960s as marked by the Social Work (Scotland) Act 1968) it has become almost entirely a creature of statute (although then surrounded by an extensive interpretative case law.) Much of this statute law furthermore was drafted by the reform body, the Scottish Law Commission, under the supervision of one person, Dr Eric Clive (now an Honorary Professor at Edinburgh University). Scots family law is thus of interest not just for its hybrid development but for its current status as an almost-codified domain within a common law statutory environment. A new Scots Family Law Bill which will make changes in many significant areas is expected to be passed by the Scottish Parliament before

* Senior Lecturer, Faculty of Law, Edinburgh University: email L.Edwards@ed.ac.uk

summer 2003, implementing numerous recommendations going back as far as 1992; reference may be made to this below as well as to instant law.[1]

II. SEX AS A JURIDICAL TRAIT

Scots law, like UK law in general, operates under a policy of formal equality between the sexes. This means that sex as a juridical trait is not particularly significant except in the arena of marriage. Women and men are considered equal legal persons and there is no longer legislation to the effect that married women are, for example, unable to effect contractual relations, or deal with property without the consent of their husband. Therefore, the main legally significant question in this area affected by how sex is defined is that of capacity to marry (and the associated legal effects of that institution) since marriage, as discussed below, is defined in the UK as only possible between a man and a woman[2].

There have been no cases in Scotland about sex and sex changes. The case law is English and the leading case remains the notorious *Corbett v Corbett*[3]. The test outlined in this case states that the criteria for establishing a person's sex are determined at birth according to certain immutable biological features. These are the person's chromosomal make up; the presence or absence of gonads and the structure of genitals. The test also contains the element of the person's psychological orientation and secondary sexual characteristics but this consideration is of lesser important than the more 'concrete' biological factors.

In English law, and therefore in Scots law, a broad psychological approach based upon gender perceptions has been rejected in favour of a strict biological test.

This is the approach which has been followed in subsequent cases such as *Re P and G (Transsexuals)*[4] where transsexuals were unable to alter their birth certificates to reflect their sex change because the register of births is considered a historical document and therefore cannot be updated except in the case of error. The European Court of Human Rights has also considered UK cases in this area: most cases (such as *Rees v UK*)[5] have condemned the

[1] Leading texts on Scots family law include L Edwards and A Griffiths, *Family Law* (Edinburgh: W Green, 1997) and J Thomson, *Family Law in Scotland*, 3rd edn (London: Butterworths, 1996). Significant policy documents referred to below are: Scottish Law Commission *Report on Family Law*, 1992, SLC No 135, 1992; Scottish Executive Green Paper *Improving Scottish Family Law* (March 1999); Scottish Executive White Paper *Parents and Children* (2000).

[2] *Hyde v Hyde* (1866) LR 1 P&D 130 at 133.

[3] [1970] 2 All ER 33. Upheld most recently in *B v B (Validity of Marriage: Transsexual)* [2001] 1 FLR 389 and *W v W (Nullity: Gender)* [2001] 1 FLR 324.

[4] [1996] 2 FLR 90.

[5] (1987) 9 EHRR 56.

UK's refusal to allow transsexuals to be re-registered as their 'new' sex, while upholding the prevention of transsexuals to marry using arguments such as the substance of marriage including the physical capacity to reproduce. Despite this trend, one of the most recent cases, *X, Y and Z v* UK,[6] declared that the refusal to allow a female to male transsexual to be registered as the father of a child conceived by 'his' partner through AID was in violation of their family life. However, no support was afforded to the couple's contention that the state's refusal to allow them to *marry* was in breach of Article 12 of European Convention of Human Rights. This means that the recent incorporation of the ECHR into UK domestic law by the Human Rights Act 1998 is unlikely to force the UK government to change the marriage laws. However, cases like *B v France*[7] may mean that some provision will have to be made to allow transsexuals to re-register themselves as their 'new' sex (such as the introduction of an Identity Card to display the current information about the holder, as opposed to the historical record).

However, outside of traditional marriage law, transsexuals have been recognised as such to a limited extent in the sphere of employment law (see, eg, *P v S and Cornwall County Council*[8] where the harassment of a transsexual was considered to be discrimination for the purposes of the Equal Treatment Directive 76/207/EEC and therefore actionable). Transsexuals can be considered as a member of their new sex in terms of registering for National Insurance. This does not extend to pensions, and male to female transsexuals do not achieve pensionable age until 65 (although this will become less important when the pensionable age of women in general becomes 65 in 2010).

The 1992 Family Law Report by the Scottish Law Commission made some recommendations in respect of transsexuals, but these findings have not yet been implemented. The most recent Home Office *Report of the Interdepartmental Working Group on Transsexual People* (April 2000) identified two ways to move forward on the problem of identifying transsexuals: first, issue a new birth certificate showing the new name and, possibly, gender; or second, grant full legal recognition of the new gender. Further consultation is likely before any new governmental proposal is advanced.

In summary—in Scotland, one's sex is defined at birth and cannot be changed in a legal sense at a later date. The defining characteristic of sex is biological.

[6] (1997) 24 EHRR 143. [7] (1992) 2 FLR 249.
[8] Case C-13/94, Industrial Tribunal, Truro.

III. MARRIAGE

A. Definitions

The provisions concerning the definition of, and conditions for, a legal marriage under domestic Scots law, which largely evolved via the common law, are now mostly contained in the Marriage (Scotland) Act 1977, as amended. The conditions for marriage are:

- That both parties have reached the age of 16 (s 1, 1977 Act)
- That the parties do not fall within the prohibited degrees of relationship (s 2, 1977 Act and Schedule 1). Scots prohibited degrees restrictions relate mainly now to relationships of consanguinity, and have been reduced from their very broad canon law origins. First cousins are allowed to marry. The relationships of affinity which are barred have been substantially reduced in recent years, but in their place a provision was inserted in 1986 which makes it illegal for marriage to take place between two persons where one or both is under the age of 21, and the younger party at any time before reaching 18 lived in the same household with the elder party as a child of the family. In terms of adoptive relationships, marriage is barred only between adoptive parents and children; remarkably, in view of the conventional social and legal connection, adoptive siblings not related by blood may still marry.
- That the formalities of notice are adhered to as laid down in sections 3 ff (but informality as opposed to essential defect will not invalidate a marriage provided the particulars of the marriage have been entered on the Marriage Schedule—the essential civil piece of documentation—by the appropriate marriage registrar—section 23A of the 1977 Act, as inserted in 1980, and see *Saleh v Saleh* 1987 SLT 633.)
- That the marriage is performed by an authorised person (but section 23A as discussed above may nonetheless protect the marriage from challenge in such circumstances).
- That the parties are of opposite sex (section 5(4)(b) of the 1977 Act, and see the discussion of juridical sex above)
- That the parties have given their effective consent. This requirement, unusually, is defined more widely at common law than it is as a legal impediment to marriage in section 5(4)(d) of the 1977 Act, which applies only where 'one or both of the parties is or are incapable of understanding the nature of a marriage ceremony or of consenting to marriage'. At common law in Scotland, however, it is clear that defects of consent which will invalidate a marriage do not extend merely to incapacity by way of insanity or intoxication, but also will include the voluntary and knowing withholding of true matrimonial consent, eg, where the

marriage is a 'sham' entered into for immigration purposes (contrast England, where on policy grounds the courts have held that such marriages remain valid)—see eg *Orlando v Castelli* 1961 SC 113. Error as to the identity of the other party will also invalidate matrimonial consent at common law, although error as to qualities, for example, eg chastity, pregnancy, will not (*Lang v Lang* 1921 SC 44.

- That neither of the parties is a party to a prior subsisting marriage (*Burke v Burke* 1983 SLT 331)
- In the case of foreign domiciliaries marrying in Scotland, it is also required that there be no legal impediment to their marriage under their ante-nuptial domicile law (s 5(4)(f) of 1977 Act.)

Unusually, Scots law also still recognises a category of *informal* or irregular marriage known as *marriage by cohabitation with habit and repute*. Originally three types of irregular marriage were recognised in Scots common law, but two were repealed by statute (in 1939) and the future of the third remains uncertain: recommendations were made in the Scottish Law Commission *Report on Family Law* (SLC No 135, 1992) that it be abolished but the latest White Paper *Parents and Children* (Scottish Executive, 2000) says there are no plans to implement this as it might disfavour some older couples. There is a reluctance to abolish habit and repute marriage while no adequate legal protection for cohabiting couples has been implemented (see below); yet the very rigid rules as to how 'habit and repute' marriage can be established means as a doctrine it tends to benefit only a few couples, and specifically *not* those great majority of couples who overtly cohabit without holding themselves out as parties to a traditional marriage. In brief, the requirements for habit and repute marriage are: (a) cohabitation together at bed and board as if husband and wife (usually, but not necessarily involving sexual intercourse) for a certain length of time such as to indicate marital commitment *and* (b) a degree of repute as a married couple among their friends and acquaintances which is promoted by the couple behaving towards each other as a married couple would. The underlying theory is that such behaviour indicates that the couple have tacitly exchanged true matrimonial consent; and it is this consent which actually founds the marriage. Establishing that a marriage existed by habit and repute can provide useful remedies for spouses in long-established cohabiting relationships—eg, declarators of marriage by habit and repute are most often sought after the death of one partner, when the other discovers that without being able to claim the status of widow/widower, they have no right to (say) succession, pension or insurance benefits. But habit and repute marriage is largely an unsatisfactory remedy, given (a) that it is so uncertain in many respects how it can be established, for example, the length of cohabitation required; the degree of uniformity of repute required; and (b) given that since it is based on the idea of tacit matrimonial consent, couples who hold themselves out as living together *rather than* married, implicitly exclude themselves from its remit.

It should also be noticed that Scots courts are prepared to recognise, under the rules of international private law (IPL), foreign marriages which are not on all fours with these requirements of domestic law, but only so long as the marriage can be fitted into the Scots/UK conception of what a marriage broadly should look like. The *locus classicus* of this conception of marriage is the statement of Lord Penzance in *Hyde v Hyde*[9] that:

> marriage as understood in Christendom may be defined as the voluntary union for life of one man and one woman to the exclusion of all others.

It is noticeable that the stringency of this conception of marriage, which would on the face of it exclude recognition in the UK of all marriages entered into under traditional Islamic law, has been almost totally relaxed in relation to polygamous marriages which remain *de facto* monogamous, ie marriages to which, although entered into under a law which permits the man to take more than one wife, in fact only one man and one woman are actually party. These can now be given almost full recognition in Scots law by virtue of a chain of legislation which has culminated in the Private International Law (Miscellaneous Provisions) Act 1995.

Interestingly, this legislative relaxation as to the recognition of polygamous marriages has been driven almost entirely by the phenomenon of Asian immigration into the UK from the Commonwealth countries, rather than any wider or more coherent reconsideration of the types of family relationships that the law should recognise. No similar relaxation of attitude has occurred in relation to the two other categories of relationship excluded by *Hyde*, namely the same-sex partnership, and the partnership between heterosexual parties that is non-conform to 'marriage' eg a limited term partnership. In consequence, there is no authority in Scots law (or English law) as to whether, for example, a Dutch registered same sex partnership would be recognised in the Scots courts, with possible consequences for succession and distribution of assets on the breakdown of relationship after the partners had, say, moved to Scotland. This limited recognition in IPL of partnerships not conform to the usual conception of marriage is also unsurprisingly recapitulated in Scots domestic law, where there is still considerable discrimination in terms of the legal recognition given unmarried partners, both heterosexual and same-sex. Noticeably, such legal recognition as has been granted to such unions has been done on a piecemeal basis thus far rather than in any organised programme of reform; by contrast the law relating to regular marriage and divorce has been reformed on a systematic basis in the 1970s, 1980s, and 1990s.

[9] (1866) LR 1 P&D 130 at 133.

B. Heterosexual Cohabiting Couples

Couples who cohabit but who are not married are treated differently from married couples by the law in various significant ways.

1. Property and the Matrimonial Home

Cohabitants have no automatic succession rights as spouses do, both in intestacy (prior rights and legal rights) and where a will is made (legal rights only). In terms of property rights, cohabitants are not considered to have a presumption of equal shares in the household goods (cf section 25 of the Family (Scotland) Act 1985 for spouses). It should be noted however that since in principle there is a rule of separation of property of spouses in Scots law (no matrimonial property regime exists during marriage except for that imposed by section 25 above, or of course, by contract)[10] the differences between unmarried and married couples as to property rights during marriage are rarely that significant. Problems *do* arise however when the relationship breaks down. There is no duty of aliment between cohabitants and in the event of relationship breakdown, crucially, there is no legislation allowing redistribution of the assets of the partnership akin to the rules on financial provision in divorce in the 1985 Act. This can be particularly unfortunate if the title to the home the partners formerly occupied is in the sole name of one partner, as Scotland, unlike England, cannot call on the doctrine of constructive trust to reallocate a share in the home to the un-entitled partner.[11] In relation to the Matrimonial Homes (Family Protection) (Scotland) Act 1981,[12] which seeks to protect partners from domestic violence by giving occupancy rights not necessarily connected to property rights in the home, and allowing the obtaining of exclusion orders, the protection offered to cohabitants is not automatic, and has several major lacunae. Some amelioration of the disadvantages cohabitees suffer under the 1981 Act should be provided in the forthcoming Family Law Bill, which is also likely to include provision for some kind of court based remedy to allow cohabitees to seek an order for financial provision at the end of the relationship.

2. Children

Unmarried fathers (even cohabiting fathers named on the birth certificate) are not automatically in receipt of parental rights and responsibilities unlike

[10] But the use of ante-nuptial marriage contracts in modern Scotland is extremely rare.

[11] Constructive trusts *are* known in Scots law, but since its property law preserves the distinction between real and personal rights, there is considerable hostility to extending the doctrine as has been done in Anglo-American jurisdictions.

[12] Hereafter, 'the 1981 Act'.

their married counterparts (see Children (Scotland) Act 1995, section 3(1)(b)[13]) although they are expected to financially maintain their children in the same way as married biological fathers (see the various stages of child support legislation and the 1985 Act, section 1). If they wish to gain full parental responsibilities and rights currently, they either need to make a costly court application or make a parental rights agreement with the mother which is recorded in a public register (section 4 of the 1995 Act.) This agreement was originally seen as the easy low-cost way for unmarried fathers to become 'full class' parents, but in actuality, the take-up on such agreements since their introduction in 1997 has been minimal—mainly, it seems, because such fathers already think, erroneously, that they have full rights. It has been proposed by the Scottish Executive in their *Improving Scottish Family Law* Green Paper to make the acquisition of parental rights and responsibilities easier for unmarried fathers. The key idea which is likely to be included in the forthcoming legislation is that where a child is jointly registered by mother and unmarried father as parents on the birth certificate, then the father will gain automatic parental rights and responsibilities from birth like a married father (similar reform has been proposed in England for consistency).

3. *Other Aspects*

Unmarried cohabitants are considered to be a family unit or 'household' for the purposes of some social security legislation because they fit the formulation 'living together as husband and wife'. This means that only one partner can claim for benefits such as Jobseeker's Allowance. Where the state saves money by recognising the existence of a *de facto* relationship therefore, it seems it is prepared to take a more liberal view of 'what is family' than is usual in 'traditional' family law (cf also the child support rules for unmarried fathers referred to above.) Cohabitants can claim *solatium* damages under the Damages (Scotland) Act 1976 in the event of the death of a partner, but not damages to represent loss of support. Some pension schemes and insurance policies allow a partner rather than a spouse to be named as the beneficiary, but this depends on the terms of the policy or scheme, and is not controlled by mandatory laws.

The Scottish Executive in *Improving Scottish Family Law* (Scottish Executive, 1999) states that it does not intend to give cohabitation legal protection analogous to marriage because it would entail the removal of choice from couples as to how to organise their affairs. In this writer's opinion, this classically liberal stance is disingenuous as most cohabiting couples have not made an explicit choice between cohabitation and marriage

[13] Hereafter 'the 1995 Act'.

(statistics indicate that stable cohabitation tends to drift into marriage or break up after some indefinite but fairly short period, rather than an initial choice being made between cohabitation and marriage) and many persons furthermore believe that in stable cohabitation, they are part of some kind of 'common law' marriage which in actuality does not exist (cf habit and repute marriage as discussed above.) The belief of fathers that they have rights over their children whether or nor married to the mother is, as mentioned, well entrenched. It is of course possible for some of the disadvantages outlined above to be overcome by a cohabitation contract, or will; but in some areas this is difficult (parental responsibility can only be finally determined by a court, although the natural mother can appoint her cohabitee the testamentary guardian of the child in the event of her death under the 1995 Act); and in any case, the making of cohabitation contracts is still extremely unusual in Scotland. The very legality of such contracts was until recently contested on the grounds that since they encouraged parties not to marry, they might be seen as *contra bonos mores* and hence unenforceable; the modern view is that a court would enforce such a contract as far as it dealt with property rather than parental rights, but this is yet to be tested by any Scottish court.

C. Same Sex Couples

Same sex couples have had virtually no recognition in Scots law,[14] and certainly do not have the same kind of recognition afforded to them as married couples. Like heterosexual unmarried couples, same sex partners have no claim on the property or support of their partner, either during or on the breakdown of, the relationship. The key issue for same sex couples, of course, is that marriage is not an option for them in Scots law (or any kind of registered partnership) and so the discrimination they suffer is arguably even less justified. Again, cohabitation contracts can in theory be made by same sex couples but again there is no clear legal authority in Scotland as to whether a court would enforce them, and the question of whether the contract would be *contra bonos mores* is even more acute.

There has only been one recent Scottish case which has notably stood up for rights to same sex couples. This is *T*, Petitioner,[15] where it was held by the Inner House of the Court of Session that adoption by a single man who lived in a same sex relationship was permissible, and that as in all such cases the deciding factor would be what was in the best interests of the child

[14] However, parenthetically, it is worth noting as Norrie does (in ch 7 of J Scoular (ed), *Family Dynamics* (London: Butterworths, 2001) that the first explicit reference in UK civil law legislation to same-sex partnerships appears in the Adults with Incapacities (Scotland) Act 2001 (an Act of the Scottish Parliament).

[15] 1997 SLT 724.

rather than some particular focus on sexuality as an on-off factor. An English case, *Fitzpatrick v Sterling Housing Association*[16] has also been regarded as influential. This was an English case that allowed a gay man to succeed to a protected tenancy on the death of his partner. The Rents Act 1977 allows succession to this type of tenancy by *inter alia* the spouse of the deceased, where 'spouse' was defined to include partners who had been 'living together as husband and wife'. The man was originally not allowed to succeed, since it was held that the phrase 'living together as husband and wife' did not allow unmarried same sex couples to be included as spouses, as it does unmarried *heterosexual* couples, because a husband and a wife must be a man and a woman. In the end however the claimant was allowed to succeed under another category of possible heirs, as a member of the deceased's family. The case is likely to be followed in Scotland where there is similar legislation.

In the field of social security, same sex couples are not considered to be a couple, and such partners can claim benefit as single people. It seems unlikely therefore that one of a same sex couple could claim pension rights on the strength of their partner's membership of a scheme which gave benefits to partners/spouses, unless partners of the same sex were explicitly mentioned. Employment law also provides an example of much the same scenario: in *Grant v South West Trains*,[17] a lesbian employee sought concessionary fare tickets for her partner as a normal 'perk' of the job but was denied them because her partner was not a man. The European Court of Justice subsequently upheld this English decision.

In more traditional family law areas, Scots cases on applications for residence and contact rights by gay parents have also tended to be treated unfavourably compared with heterosexual spouses/partners. The leading Scots case on gay parenting is still *Early v Early*,[18] in which a gay mother was denied custody of one of her children even though she had been the primary carer before the divorce action, which would normally have guaranteed her a likelihood of being granted custody. The case is confused by its unusual facts, but the decision was clearly made at least partially on the basis that the child would suffer 'unusual difficulties' at school and elsewhere if brought up by two gay women partners—a 'stigmatisation' welfare principle argument which was un-backed by empirical evidence, but accepted by the court. More recent cases have shown a less prejudiced attitude towards gay parenting (eg *Meredith v Meredith*[19] in which a homosexual father was allowed restricted contact with his child, and *T, Petr*, above) and it is thought by some commentators that the incorporation of

[16] [1999] 4 All ER 705 (HL).
[17] Case C-249/96, Industrial Tribunal, Southampton.
[18] 1989 SLT 114, affirmed 1990 SLT 221.
[19] 1994 GWD 19-1150.

the European Convention on Human Rights and its guarantees of respect for the right to family life will have a significant impact on Scots treatment of gay parents.

The Scottish Law Commission in their 1992 report on *Family Law* made the recommendation (45) that it should continue to be a ground of nullity of marriage that both parties are of the same sex. The Scottish Executive have adopted this in *Parents and Children* (2000) and have declared that it is not their policy to introduce same sex marriage to Scotland. Given the hostility to legal recognition of a status of cohabitation for heterosexual unmarried couples, legal recognition of same sex partnerships in Scots law seems a long way off unless there is direct pressure from the Strasbourg court. In England, two Bills have been introduced in the current session of the Westminster Parliament which seeks to introduce a type of registered civil partnership which would be potentially applicable to same sex couples (and indeed to transsexuals denied the right to marry); however their chances of becoming law are regarded as slim.

In summary, it would be fair to say that the dominant regulatory paradigm in Scots family law is still the institution of marriage, as opposed to any alternate model based on a loving or sexual relationships between adults. However this statement is less significant than it might be, as in many ways the focus of Scots law reform has moved to looking at the parent-child relationship, which is permanent and cannot be ended (short of adoption or state care proceedings) as the central fulcrum of the family, rather than the adult-adult sexual relationship, which is of increasing impermanence and multiplicity.

II. NATURAL AND ASSISTED CONCEPTION AND BIRTH: PARENTHOOD AND ORIGINS

A. General

The United Kingdom was the first state in Europe to legislate in relation to the questions raised by assisted reproductive technology in the shape of the Human Fertilisation and Embryology Act 1990 (HFEA90). This Act applies in Scotland as in England. Broadly, the Act set up a Human Fertilisation and Embryology Authority (the HFEA), whose job it is to license all clinics in the UK (whether privately run, or funded by the National Health Service) which *inter alia* provide assistance with reproduction in the form of fertility treatments such as ovum donation, sperm donation or embryo transfer, storage of ova or sperm, artificial insemination by donor (AID, sometimes known as donor insemination or DI), and *in vitro* fertilisation (IVF).

The basic assumption underlying the Act, which was preceded by an extensive ethical enquiry,[20] is that the ways in which children are born with the assistance of technology is a social, public matter, which affects the morals and ethics of the whole community, and not just a private matter for the individual would-be parents. So, for example, there has recently been an extensive debate in the UK as to how far parents seeking to conceive by *in vitro* fertilisation should be allowed to have a say in the genetic make-up of the embryo that is to be re-implanted into the gestational mother, an issue which is becoming known as the 'designer babies' scenario. The latest product of this debate is the reported decision of the HFEA in February 2002,[21] to allow the screening of embryos created by a couple in Leeds, for a certain genetic makeup that will allow the conceived child to donate bone marrow cells to its already-born sibling, who is suffering from the genetically carried disease thallassaemia. This case highlights how the debate has moved on from the issue, controversial enough in itself, of whether parents should be allowed to select for desirable characteristics in their offspring (and abort or discard embryos/foetuses which do not meet their wishes) to the question of whether a child should be conceived solely, or even primarily, to help someone else (a sibling, a parent, or perhaps even an unrelated person).

The HFEA issues a Code of Practice periodically for the clinics it oversees, which deals with ethical, as well as medical, staffing, and technical issues. For example, recent Codes have engaged with whether age limits should be imposed on those attempting to become mothers by IVF, whether egg donors should be paid, and whether eggs taken from white donors should be implanted into non-white women. Since it is a condition of clinics continuing to be licensed that they comply with the guidelines in the Codes of Practice, the HFEA is effectively empowered to provide ethical/moral guidance as to how assisted reproduction should be allowed to operate in the UK. Clinics offering fertility treatments are also encouraged to set up Ethical Committees to consider difficult issues arising out of the cases with which they deal, and judicial review of their decisions can be sought.[22]

There is also one significant piece of primary legislation, section 13(5) of the HFEA90, which provides that a woman shall not be provided with infertility treatment including AID or IVF unless account has been taken of the welfare of any child that may be born as a result of these treatments. Section 13(5) then goes on to declare that the welfare of the child includes its 'need for a father'. The background to this provision was that of an attempt while the Bill was going through Parliament to restrict the availability of assisted

[20] See the Warnock Report (Cmnd 9314) (or 'Report of the Committee of Enquiry into Human Fertilisation and Embryology').

[21] 'Designer baby gets go-ahead', *Guardian*, 23 Feb 2002. This is supposedly the first 'officially sanctioned "designer baby" in British history'.

[22] See *R v Ethical Committee of St Mary's Hospital ex p. Harriott* (1988) 18 Fam Law 165.

reproductive techniques to single women, and, especially, lesbians. Although section 13(5) could thus have been interpreted to further the conservative goals of reserving artificial reproduction to the heterosexual unit, the Code of Practice[23] now in fact simply states : 'The HFE Act does not exclude any category of woman from being considered for treatment. Centres should take note in their procedures of the importance of a stable and supportive environment for any child produced as a result of treatment.'[24]

As things stand in the 5th HFEA Code of Practice (April 2001), the important factors that fertility clinics must take into account when assessing potential parents are:

a. their commitment to having and bringing up a child or children;
b. their ability to provide a stable and supportive environment for any child produced as a result of treatment;
c. their medical histories and the medical histories of their families;
d. their health and consequent future ability to look after or provide for a child's needs;
e. their ages and likely future ability to look after or provide for a child's needs;
f. their ability to meet the needs of any child or children who may be born as a result of treatment, including the implications of any possible multiple births;
g. any risk of harm to the child or children who may be born, including the risk of inherited disorders or transmissible diseases, problems during pregnancy and of neglect or abuse; and
h. the effect of a new baby or babies upon any existing child of the family.

Where people seek treatment using *donated* gametes, centres should also take the following factors into account:

a. a child's potential need to know about their origins and whether or not the prospective parents are prepared for the questions which may arise while the child is growing up;
b. the possible attitudes of other members of the family towards the child, and towards their status in the family;
c. the implications for the welfare of the child if the person providing the gametes for donation is personally known within the child's family and social circle; and
d. any possibility of a dispute about the legal fatherhood of the child

[23] The 5th Code of Practice appeared Apr 2001 and can be found at <http://www.hfea.gov.uk/frame.htm>.

[24] Ibid, para 3.10.

Significantly, the HFEA also recommends that 'centres should take into account each prospective parent's preferences in relation to the general physical characteristics of the person providing gametes for donation. This *does not allow* the prospective parents to choose, *for social reasons alone*, a donor of different ethnic origin(s) from themselves' [italics added].

As can be seen from the above, the HFEA does take an active interest in regulating 'human procreation', but their remit is limited to where some kind of technological or medical assistance is required to facilitate conception, and their view of their role is as medical supervisors rather than eugenic taskforce. It is noticeable that, wherever possible, the HFEA attempts to limit its ethical guidance to good medical practice, rather than to act as a social arbiter. For example there are guidelines restricting donations of sperm or eggs from persons over respectively, 45 and 35, but no guidelines setting out an age limit for mothers wishing to conceive, merely a requirement for counselling when they are over 35 (paras 4.20 and 3.4 of Code of Practice, 5th edn). This does not however mean no barriers remain to, say, a prospective single 50-year-old mother who wishes to conceive in a UK IVF clinic. A very large degree of discretion has been left to individual clinics to decide who is a suitable donor, and who a suitable parent, and only rarely will the HFEA intervene in the local clinic's decision. This margin of discretion may be seen as undesirable as it means those would-be parents who have the financial resources can shop for the most accommodating clinic (within or outwith the UK), while others will be restricted to their local or designated NHS facilities. In fact it is clear that the factor most pressingly restricting reproductive choice for the infertile person or couple in the UK is economic: as NHS funding is possible but limited, and several attempts at treatment are often necessary before conception is achieved.

One fertility treatment—if it is to be regarded as such at all—which requires particular attention is surrogate motherhood. Surrogacy occupies a strange position between natural childbirth and assisted reproduction in UK law, as it does not necessarily require any technical or medical assistance of any kind. Even if AID is introduced to minimise physical contact between commissioning father and surrogate mother, the process remains relatively simple and can be carried out on an 'amateur' basis. Egg donation to the surrogate would of course require clinical treatment. Because of this ambiguity, surrogacy was not originally *per se* regulated in any way in the UK, just as natural conception was, and is, not. After a media scandal erupted around a surrogate mother called Kim Cotton in the early 1980s, emergency legislation was introduced in the form of the Surrogacy Arrangements Act 1985, which declared commercial surrogacy illegal (although the surrogate mother herself is not criminalised.) Non-commercial surrogacy, eg sister A carrying the baby for sister B, remains legal. Since the 1990 Act, if surrogacy is carried out in an HFEA licensed clinic, eg, where AID or egg or embryo donation *is* used to facilitate the creation of the desired surrogate child, then it falls under HFEA regulation. The Code of Practice, 5th edn, allows such use of HFEA licensed premises in principle, but hedges this permission with numerous caveats. In particular, clinics are instructed that 'the application of assisted conception techniques to initiate a surrogate pregnancy should only be considered where it is *physically impossible or highly undesirable for medical reasons* for the commissioning mother to carry the child' (para 3.16, italics added). The social use of surrogacy to assist a woman who wants to avoid a career break, for example, is therefore outlawed. Problems can also arise with who has parental responsibility in relation to a surrogate child, an issue discussed in question 4 below.

In summary: 'natural' procreation remains entirely a matter of private choice in the UK, and even 'assisted' procreation is, in theory, relatively unregulated by the state or its central quango, the HFEA, with the emphasis on medical best practice rather than 'social' or genetic engineering. In practice rather than in theory, the main factors regulating access to fertility treatment for infertile parents are (a) money and (b) the discretion of the medical community who run the fertility clinics. On the second point in question 3, there is no indication to date that the advent of assisted reproductive techniques has changed the attitude of the state or the public in the UK towards embracing regulation of *natural* conception. The safeguard on abuse of the natural ability to become a parent lies as ever in the state's rights to intervene to take children into its care where their parents fail them (see further below, question 7). If anything, judging from recent media outcries, the possibilities inherent in modern genetic engineering combined with *in vitro* fertilisation seem to have stiffened the British (and Scottish) public's general dislike of eugenic tinkering.

B. Parenthood

Parenthood in Scots law is considered as distinct from *having parental rights and responsibilities*, which are ascribed automatically by law only to certain classes of parents (namely, the mother, and the father who has been married to the mother between conception and birth, or subsequently).[25] Parenthood itself is not defined by statute, but at common law is historically a matter of genetic connection, both for fatherhood and motherhood, and is therefore a matter of fact. If disputed, it can be established on the balance of probabilities, in an action for declarator of paternity or (rather unusually) maternity.[26]

[25] Children (Scotland) Act 1995, section 3. Unmarried fathers can however seek parental rights and responsibilities by court order or by agreement with the mother (see above).

[26] Law Reform (Parent and Child) (Scotland) Act 1986, s 7.

This genetic characterisation of parenthood is however subject to three important caveats. First, as a result of the assisted reproduction techniques discussed above (AID, egg donation, IVF, surrogacy, etc) questions were raised as to who should best be regarded as the legal parent in certain cases, and as a result a new category of persons legally deemed to be parents (by a *fictio iuris*) has been established in the HFEA 1990, sections 27–30. Secondly, it is of course possible for legal parentage to be created without genetic link by means of an adoption order (see questions 7 and 8 below). Thirdly, since prior to reliable DNA testing it was not always easy to ascertain who was the genetic father of a child, certain *evidential* presumptions have historically been adopted in Scots law to make the task of discerning the father easier, in particular the rule that the husband of a married woman is the presumptive father of her child (*pater est quem nuptiae demonstrant* at common law—see now section 5(1)(a) of the Law Reform (Parent and Child)(Scotland) Act 1986.) A similar presumption has been created more recently in section 5(1)(b) of the 1986 Act in relation to a man who, though not *married* to the mother between conception and birth, jointly registers the birth of a child with the mother. Although at common law, such presumption of paternity could only be rebutted by proof beyond reasonable doubt, the standard of proof to rebut is now the ordinary civil one of the balance of probabilities.[27]

Returning to the second category, of 'deemed' parenthood, established by sections 27–30 of the HFEA 1990, section 27 deals with maternity and provides that where a woman carries a child 'as a result of the placing in her of an embryo or of sperm and eggs' then she, and no other woman, is to be treated as the legal mother. This is, in other words, a conclusive presumption, which cannot be rebutted by evidence of the true genetic facts. The intent here, following a heated moral debate, was to prefer the gestational mother to the genetic mother as the legal mother in cases involving egg or embryo donation. In such cases, it was felt the gestational mother was most likely to be the person who wished to act as the social parent, while the donor was likely to be anonymous or, even if known, not the intended parent. Similarly, section 28 attempts to deal with the situation where there has been donation of sperm to impregnate the mother. Section 28(2), a complex provision, provides that the husband of a woman who conceives after the donation of sperm, or sperm and eggs, or an embryo, is to be treated as the father of that child for all purposes, *unless* he proves that he did *not* consent to the insemination or implantation etc. Section 28(6) ties this *fictio iuris* up neatly, by providing that the sperm donor is *not* to be treated as the father of the child. It is thus now quite legitimate, and not perjury, for the husband of the woman seeking to conceive by AID to

[27] Section 5(4) of the 1986 Act.

record her husband's name as the father of her child on the birth certificate. Finally, section 28(3) extends this deeming provision to unmarried partners of women being treated with AID etc, by use of the formula that section 28(2) applies where the woman is not married but is inseminated 'in the course of treatment services provided for her and a man together'. This formula was meant to avoid the difficulty of defining who was an unmarried partner (should cohabitation be required? or a particular length of cohabitation?) but has raised some difficulties in English case law.

Sections 27 and 28 were explicitly designed to provide the 'right' results in the paradigm cases of sperm, egg, or embryo donation, where the couple receiving fertility treatment are the couple who intend to become the social parents. They work rather differently though, when applied to the surrogate mother scenario. If commissioning parents Mr A and Mrs A commission a child from surrogate mother Mrs B (for example, Mr A donates sperm, Mrs A donates an egg, and the resulting embryo is implanted in Mrs B in an IVF clinic), then as Mrs B will carry the baby to term, she will be deemed the legal mother under section 27 (and no other person). Furthermore, Mr A will conclusively *not* be deemed the legal father by virtue of section 28(6) even though he is the genetic father.[28] And to add insult to injury, if Mrs B is married at the time of the treatment to Mr B, and Mr B does not rebut the presumption that he consented to the treatment, then he, not Mr A, will be deemed to be the legal father. To deal with this problem (which was, again, highlighted by a controversial case arising during the course of the passing of the 1990 legislation) section 30 was added to the Act. This provides that in cases of conception and birth involving sperm, egg or embryo donation, the commissioning husband and wife may seek special 'parental orders' deeming them to be the legal parents. (These should not be confused with orders for parental responsibility and rights under section 11 of the Children (Scotland) Act 1995.) There is a detailed list of requirements which must be met before a court can grant such an order: the applying couple must be married, both over 18, the child must have its home with them, application must be made within 6 months of the birth, the surrogate mother (and her husband, if applicable) must consent and perhaps most importantly, no money must have changed hands other than expenses reasonably incurred. This provision, which can be seen as a way to shortcut the need to seek an adoption order, has been much criticised, both for being *ad hoc* legislation, based very much on the facts of the case that inspired it, and for displaying an ambivalence about whether those using surrogacy should be supported by the law or not.

'Acceptance' is not in Scots law something that confers the status of

[28] Assuming the treatment takes place under the auspices of the HFEA licensing scheme. 'DIY' sperm donors may still remain the legal father, though this is untested in law.

parenthood. A father who has accepted a stepchild, say, as his own child, would need to formalise the relationship for the purposes of succession and other legal effects if he so wished, by seeking an adoption order.[29] As a concept, it only really figures in one place in Scots law,[30] namely the Family Law (Scotland) Act 1985, section 1(1)(d) which provides that a person is liable to aliment a child who has been accepted by him or her as a child of the family.[31] Notably, the same concept does not appear in the UK-wide Child Support Act 1991, which restricts the obligation of support to biological parents—so the law in Scotland is wider on this point than in England. Finally, it should be noted that the concept of 'relevant person' rather than 'parent' is widely used in Part II of the Children (Scotland) Act 1995, which deals with the public aspects of child care law, state intervention, taking children into care, etc. A 'relevant person' is defined in section 93 of the 1995 Act to include not only persons with parental rights and responsibilities, but also 'any person who appears to be a person who ordinarily.. has charge of, or control over, the child'. This provision is clearly intended to move from the model of only married parents being interested in a child's welfare to a recognition that many different people care for children in modern families including some but not all unmarried fathers, grandparents, siblings, etc.

The legal effects of parenthood *without* accompanying parental responsibilities and rights are relatively minor in Scots law, at least in the sphere of private law. Most declarators of paternity in the Scottish courts are now raised as a preliminary to a demand for child support, since, as noted above, the requirement of support of each parent for their child subsists both under the Family Law (Scotland) Act 1985, section 1, and the Child Support Act 1991, whether or not the father is married to the mother. Paternity (or maternity) will also give sufficient claim of 'interest' to raise an action for parental rights and/or responsibilities under section 11 of the Children (Scotland) Act 1995[32] (but many other persons who are not parents, will also have such interest, eg, grandparents, aunts). Children have rights of succession in respect of both of their parents whether or not those parents were married to each other. (In general, the Law Reform (Parent and Child)(Sc) Act 1986, section 1 provides that, subject to a few exceptions, the fact that a person's parents are not or have not been married

[29] And indeed around half of all adoption orders made in Scotland are step-parent adoptions of this kind.

[30] Although note also that the Matrimonial Homes (Family Protection) (Scotland) Act 1981 defines a 'child of the family' as including 'any person who has been brought up or treated as a child by either spouse' (s 22).

[31] A child whom a father treated as his own but subsequently discovers was fathered by another has not been 'accepted' for the purpose of aliment—*Watson v Watson* 1994 SCLR 1097.

[32] See s 11(3)(a).

to each other shall be of no legal significance.) Paternity does *not* give a father (married or unmarried) the right to insist that a child takes his surname, this being a matter of 'custom and usage' in Scotland , not law. A child cannot acquire an independent domicile of choice until the age of 16 and so parentage is important till then in establishing what the child's domicile of origin or dependence is.[33] A natural father does not have the right to veto his child's adoption unless he has at least one parental right or responsibility,[34] and even then his consent can be dispensed with if it is in the child's welfare.

In summary—parenthood in Scots law is in principle a matter of genetic connection, but with important exceptions in the 'deeming' provisions of the HFEA 1990 (and of course, in the law of adoption). 'Acceptance' as a concept is not important in Scots family law.

C. Origins

The question of donor anonymity is dealt with in HFEA 1990 in section 31, which provides that a child born as a result of fertility treatment services may on attaining the age of 18, seek disclosure from the HFEA of donor information kept on a register by the HFEA. This age is reduced to 16 if the child is seeking information relevant to a proposed marriage. During the debate prior to the passing of the HFEA 1990, it was agreed that donor anonymity was an important principle, as without such anonymity, it was likely donations would dry up; and furthermore it was felt there would be emotional difficulties for all parties if identities were known. The justification for the disclosure provisions of section 31 is therefore not, primarily, to allow an artificially conceived child to find out who their genetic mother or father was; but rather to enable them to find out if there is any factor in their genetic heritage of which they should be aware, eg hereditary diseases; or if they are related too closely to a person they are about to marry. Indeed, section 31(5) provides that the HFEA cannot be forced to provide information that would identify a donor by name, either now or in the future.

The exact information which the HFEA will keep on donors, and reveal on request, has not yet been formalised by regulations, as no child born of these techniques has yet reached the age of 16 (this will happen in 2008). At the moment, the HFEA website declares that they collect information which 'relates to a donor's appearance, interests and occupation'. Revealing this kind of non-identifying information may strike a reasonable compromise between a child's desire to know its origins and the donor's desire for anonymity.

33 Legitimate children take their domicile from their father; illegitimate children from their mother. This is one of the very few remaining areas of Scots law where legitimacy is relevant.

34 Adoption (Scotland) Act 1978, s 16 (1).

In summary, it should perhaps be noted that one major Scottish commentator on medico-legal matters, Mason,[35] has opined that the parallel frequently drawn between the need of adopted children to know about their origins and a similar need assumed in children born of sperm or egg donation is a false one. Children raised in adopted homes can rarely have the truth of their adopted status hidden, especially given the increasing tendency for adoption to be of older children rather than babies; while children born by assisted reproduction need never know they were not their parents' wholly natural genetic children (and in practical terms, their true origin is not immediately apparent from sight of their birth certificate). This writer feels this point of view should be researched empirically as the first generation of IVF children reach adulthood, before legislative effort is put into meeting more fully what may be an unfelt 'need to know'.

D. Legal Status

As described in question 4 above, where a child is born as a result of the donation of sperm or eggs, or an embryo, or is conceived in conjunction with such donation, as in assisted surrogacy, then the deeming provisions of sections 27–30 of the HFEA 1990 will operate to alter the normal rules of who is the legal father and/or mother. As also noted above, those rules have been tailored to provide what is seen as the optimum solution in the more normal fertility treatments of sperm or egg donation; and section 30 was introduced to alleviate the problems that were experienced by commissioning parents in the surrogacy situation, where sections 27 and 28 (arguably) provided the 'wrong' results in terms of legal parentage.

In summary, then, since in UK law, the matter is addressed at the basic level of legal parentage, there is no difficulty in guaranteeing that children born as a result of fertility techniques are subject to the same laws as those born in the more natural way.

III. THE RIGHTS OF PARENTS, THE WELFARE OF CHILDREN OR THE RIGHTS OF CHILDREN?

A. General

Parents do not have a right to a child in Scots law, nor do they have absolute rights to provide a home for a natural child of their own once it is born.

As we have seen above, in the case of infertile parents, clinics have a

[35] JK Mason and R A McCall-Smith, *Law and Medical Ethics*, 5th edn (London: Butterworths, 1999), 66.

discretion to refuse to supply fertility treatments, and although this discretion can be tested in the courts (*R v Ethical Committee of St Mary's Hospital ex p. Harriot, supra)*[36] such review will only be on the usual grounds of judicial review, ie, that the clinic had acted in a way which no reasonable clinic would have acted. Furthermore, and crucially, there is no right to have fertility treatment funded by the National Health Service—and in practice most fertility treatment is private, and thus restricted to those who are financially well off. As we have seen above, the question of whether a single female would-be mother should have access to assisted reproductive techniques such as AID and IVF was debated in Parliament at the time of passing of the HFEA 1990, with the compromise result being section 13(5), which emphasises the need for a father of a child created by assisted reproduction . However given the liberal interpretation of this provision in the HFEA's Code of Practice, it is fair to say that the main barriers to a single woman who wishes to achieve 'virgin birth' as it has sometimes been known, are her access to funding and the policies of the individual clinic approached. There is no reported UK case in which an unmarried woman (gay or heterosexual) has sought review of a clinic's decision to refuse to treat her, but it is known that some clinics, on medical best-practice grounds, prefer only to treat a would-be mother who is in a supportive relationship.

In relation to children born by natural means, the paramount concern of Scots law in regulating the relationship between parents and child is the best interests of the child. This pervades Scottish child law, but is particularly of note in at least three places:

Section 11 of the Children (Scotland) Act 1995 allows a person with interest to seek orders relating to parental rights and responsibilities in respect of a child. In making such an order, the court's paramount consideration is the welfare of the child.

Section 16 of the 1995 Act applies the same test when a court or children's hearing makes a decision about a child in relation to Part II of the Act (which deal with the public law aspects of child law, for example, when a child should be placed under residential supervision, or taken to a place of safety in an emergency.)

Section 6 of the Adoption (Scotland) Act 1978, as amended by the 1995 Act, now provides that when a court or adoption agency makes any decision relating to a child' adoption, again the welfare of the child shall be the paramount concern.

It can thus be seen that the question is incorrectly phrased for Scots (and English) law. The right of the parent to a child does not exist (whether the would-be parent is married or single), but neither to any great extent is the

[36] (1988) 18 Fam Law 165.

law concerned with the *right* of a child to be raised in a loving home (although such right is guaranteed by the UN Convention on the Rights of the Child, to which the UK is a signatory). Instead the law's central concern is for the *best interests* of the child—a welfare, rather than a rights, paradigm. The preference of the law for the *child's welfare* as opposed to *parental rights* (or child rights) can best be seen in sections 1 and 2 of the 1995 Act. Section 1, for the first time in Scots statutory history, provides a comprehensive list of parental responsibilities. Section 2 then goes on to make it clear that parents still have rights in respect of their children—but only in so far as is necessary to exercise their parental responsibilities. The law also now takes explicit account of the child's views—see especially section 11(7) and section 16 of the 1995 Act – but again they are clearly subordinate as a factor to be taken account of in court decision-making terms to the child's welfare. A child who asked to remain with an unfit parent would nonetheless be removed by a court if his welfare demanded it (though in *determining* his welfare, much might rest on the age and maturity of the child).

In principle, this means that wherever it is not in the child's best interests to live with the natural parent or parents, that child should be removed by the state to a better situation. In order to protect family integrity however, the state will not intervene and remove a child against the wishes of the parents unless the child is considered to be in need of such removal as defined in various sections of the Children (Scotland) Act 1995 Pt II, notably sections 52, 55, 57, and 86. (A child may be removed by a court-made parental responsibilities order, by a supervision order made by a children's hearing, by an adoption or freeing for adoption order[37], or by an emergency protection order.) This means that in practice a child will stay at home unless he or she is experiencing physical, emotional, educational or sexual abuse or neglect. The social work authorities, furthermore, in fulfilling their duty to promote the welfare of children in need, so far as possible, are asked to promote the upbringing of children in need by their families. Removal from the family home is thus seen as a last resort. This provision (section 22(1)(b) of the 1995 Act) was inserted when Scottish child care law was reviewed in the early 1990s, as a direct response to what was seen as the possibly overzealous removal of children by social work services in various mass sexual abuse scandals of the 1970s and 1980s—with Scots law, in particular, reacting to the Orkney crisis of 1991 when nine children were removed from their homes in 'dawn raids' and eventually returned in extremely unsatisfactory circumstances.

Where disputes arise between private individuals rather than between

[37] The test for when an adoption or freeing for adoption order may be made is found in the Adoption (Scotland) Act 1978, s 16.

the parents and the state as to where a child should stay, again the welfare principle will determine the outcome of the dispute rather than the 'rights' of the parents to their natural child. Having said this, however, there is a long tradition of Scottish courts preferring to grant residence rights to the natural parent(s) rather than third parties, as an *aspect of* the welfare principle. Parents (or at least, the mother, and the father who has been married to the mother) also have the advantage of having as one of their automatic parental rights the right 'to have the child living with' them (section 2(1)(a) of the 1995 Act) but only *subject* to the welfare principle. In *Clark v* Clark,[38] for example, a dispute between the grandparents and the natural parent of a child, the court found that the parents had a 'pre-eminent right to custody', with similar comments being made in *Kyle v Stewart*[39]. In the more recent case of *Breingan v Jamieson*[40], however, the court was convinced on the evidence that the daughter of a mother who had died was better placed where she was currently settled, with her mother's relatives, rather than with her natural father, even though she had an ongoing and cordial relationship with him and his new wife. Surrogacy cases present some of the best evidence that the court's concern is genuinely for the welfare of the child rather than the 'right' of the natural parent: in *C v* S,[41] the only Scottish surrogacy case reported to date, the custody of a year old baby was granted to the commissioning parents, rather than the natural mother, on the grounds that the child had been living happily with the commissioning parents almost since birth, and was a near stranger to the gestational (and genetic) mother. If the child had remained living with the natural mother after the birth, the decision would almost certainly have been reversed—but on the grounds of the child's welfare, rather than the mother's 'natural' right.

It should be noted that some judges have personally noted their disquiet that the 'natural link' between parent and child is not being given enough weight in family disputes as a result of the emphasis given the welfare principle, especially in cases where a father who is not married to the mother of his child attempts to remain in contact with that child. Such fathers are technically disadvantaged in Scots law, as it currently stands, since they have no automatic parental rights, including the right of contact, and must seek such from the courts if the mother refuses to cooperate. In *Sanderson v McManus*[42] an unmarried father attempted to persuade the Inner House that contact with him would be beneficial to the child, essentially simply because he *was* the natural father. Lord McCluskey, a senior judge, took his side, stating in a much quoted dissenting judgement that the 'parent: child link' was:

[38] 1987 GWD 35-1240.
[39] 1989 GWD 14-580.
[40] 1993 SLT 186.
[41] 1997 SLT 1387.
[42] 1996 SLT 745.

a natural link, the importance of which is felt instinctively; it is a deep and abiding theme in literature, both sacred and profane, and in social and political history. It is a link which is properly understood to have value quite independently of any supposed 'right' in a parent to obtain from a court of law an order allowing 'access' to his or her child.[43]

In the end however, the Inner House found 2:1 against the father and so he was unable to rely solely on his natural link to the child to prove a positive benefit to the child in a contact order being made. The House of Lords also subsequently upheld this finding.

Finally, it should be noted that the foetus does *not* have a right to be born according to Scots Law. While this has been the law in the UK ever since the (UK wide) Abortion Act 1967 decriminalised abortion, it has been confirmed in the recent Scottish case of *Kelly v Kelly*[44] where the married father of the foetus was not allowed to interdict his wife's (legally grounded) abortion, on the grounds that he had no *locus standi* qua husband, father or guardian of the child's best interests. Indeed, he could not have any standing as the child's guardian as the child itself had no legal status as a person until born. Equally, the foetus has no right to be born under the European Convention of Human Rights as held in *Paton v* UK,[45] so the Human Rights Act 1998 which incorporates the ECHR into domestic UK law is unlikely to have any effect on the domestic position.

In summary—parents do not have an absolute right in Scots law either to bear, or to provide a home for their natural children, but neither to any great extent is the law concerned either with the *right* of a child to be raised in a loving home. The law, both in disputes between private individuals, and in state intervention cases, is concerned paramountly with the best interests of the child—a welfare-based paradigm. Finally it should be noted that, since the Abortion Act 1967, the foetus clearly does not have a right to be born, and the husband or partner of a woman seeking an abortion thus cannot vindicate that 'right'.

B. Adoption

Adoption has always been a process under the control of the state in Scotland. Despite the partial Roman law origins of the legal system, as in England, adoption has existed only as a creature of statute in modern times, in Scotland, since 1930. The current consolidating Act is the Adoption (Scotland) Act 1978 as amended by the Children (Scotland) Act 1995. The former Scottish practice of legitimation of children by the Church bore some resemblance to adoption, but the Scottish courts have never recognised as

[43] 1996 SLT 745, at 752.
[44] 1997 SLT 896.
[45] (1980) 3 EHRR 408.

legitimate private contracts of adoption; and attempts to achieve adoptions in this way have been regarded by the courts as unenforceable.[46]

Given that vulnerable children and young people are the subject of the process of adoption, it seems reasonable that there should be strict controls on who should be able to adopt. More cynically, young healthy babies, the optimum desired subject of the adoption process, are an extremely rare commodity in modern Scotland, given the changes in the social climate towards illegitimate birth and the availability of contraception and abortion, and so a process based on strict vetting of potential parents can be regarded as justified to achieve some kind of fair distribution. In 2000 there were 400 adoption applications in Scotland for which an outcome was reached. The average age of an adopted child was 6 and a half. Over half of these adoptions were 'step-parent' adoptions, where the child adopted is already the natural child of one of the new adoptive parents. It can be seen that the number of 'stranger' adoptions involving very young children is now very small (around one-tenth of all adoptions in 1992), and non-`step-parent' adoption is better seen as an alternative form of permanency planning for children taken out of abusive or unfit homes, than as an alternative way for infertile couples to achieve parenthood. This provides further justification for strict vetting of adoptive parents: since many of the adoptive children will already have suffered from lack of parental care, the state should be doubly careful to make sure they do not suffer from it again in the new adoptive home.

Controversy in recent years has centred, not on the principle of vetting adopters, but on two connected points. First, the adoption legislation provides little in the way of *criteria* for adoptive parents, beyond stating that the welfare of the child is of paramount importance, and as a result there is considerable variation between different adoption agencies, or Scottish local authorities, on adoption policies. Such policies must be made available in writing[47] but are by no means all available on the Web: this is a matter to which attention should be given. Secondly, given that many adoptions now involve older children with a history of difficulties in the natural family, the courts are increasingly faced with situations where a decision must be made whether continuing contact with the natural mother and/or family, even post-adoption, may be desirable. Such 'open adoption' is slowly becoming accepted in Scotland, following in the footsteps of research and legislation in countries such as New Zealand. In Scots law, contact can be provided for by a condition of contact being attached to the adoption order under section 12(6) of the 1978 Act. Such a condition can

[46] *Kerrigan v Hall* (1901) 4 F 10. See further PGB McNeill, *Adoption of Children in Scotland* 3rd edn, (Edinburgh: W Green & Co, 1998).

[47] Adoption Agencies (Scotland) Regulations 1996, SI 1996 No 3266, reg 17A.

only validly be made at the time of the adoption, not later, nor can a variation be sought later; and a natural mother whose child has been the subject of adoption has explicitly no standing to seek an 'ordinary' contact order under section 11(3) of the 1995 Act: this is a clear problem in current Scots adoption law which requires legislation.

In summary—the role of the State, and the courts, in vetting would-be adoptive parents is and always has been accepted in Scots law for so long as adoption has been available.

C. Children's Rights

As we have already seen above, Scots law clearly prefers the welfare of the child to the rights of the parents. The leading Scottish instrument on the law of parent and child, the Children (Scotland) Act 1995, explicitly states that parents only have rights over their children in order to allow them to carry out their parental responsibilities, and parental responsibilities can only be exercised in the interest of the child.[48] The concept of parental authority or *patria potestas*, in the sense of an absolute right to deal with one's children, as objects of property rather than legal subjects, now has little or no place in Scots law.[49] Indeed, section 6 of the 1995 Act now demands that parents, when making a major decision relating to their child, must have regard to the views of that child, depending on his or her age of maturity.[50] Although this provision is basically unenforceable, it was seen by the Scottish Law Commission when it was introduced as being of key rhetorical value (and also an essential part of the implementation of Art 12 of the UN Convention on the Rights of the Child) in extending concern for the wishes of the child from the courts into the domestic sphere[51]. Thus the parent or parents' decision about issues affecting children such as punishment, education, holidays, lifestyle etc, must in theory be influenced by, but is not controlled by the views of the sufficiently mature child; however the real break on parental power is still the best interests of the child. It is theoretically possible, though there is no reported case law as yet, for a child to bring a parental exercise of power to the court for review in terms of the welfare principle, using a specific issue order under section 11(2)(e);[52] in practice, thus far, it has always been the other parent, or a state agent such as the social work department, that has taken action when a parent has

[48] Sections 1 and 2 , 1995 Act.

[49] See further, Edwards and Griffiths, op cit, ch 4.

[50] As in the rest of the 1995 Act, a child is presumed of sufficient maturity to express a view at the age of 12; see s 6(1).

[51] Empirical research is currently being carried out by the Scottish Executive on the actual impact of s 6 on domestic households.

[52] Note also s 1(3) that specifically says that the child has title to sue or defend in any proceedings relating to parental responsibilities.

been seen as acting contrary to the welfare principle. So, for example, in *Finlayson Petr*,[53] a child's parents, who were practicing Jehovah's Witnesses, refused to allow their child, who was haemophiliac, to receive blood transfusions. The social work department intervened and the child was referred to a children's hearing, which made a supervision order, one of the conditions of which was that the local authority could consent to the child receiving medical treatment. Effectively, the *parents'* decision about was right for their child was overturned and a regime where the child's best interests were met was substituted. A similar decision could now be reached if (say) a hospital wished to ask a court to overturn a parent's decision about medical treatment by their applying to the court for a specific issue order (see above), which would be resolved according to the welfare principle.

The area of tension between parental rights and the child's welfare which has caused the most concern and debate in Scotland in recent years has been the issue of corporal punishment. (Religion—which might perhaps be expected to throw up the most cases—has oddly produced very little modern jurisprudence in Scots law beyond the *Finlayson* case, above.) Historically, Scots parents have been recognised as having the right of 'reasonable chastisement'. In modern legal terminology, this has been regarded as the right to chastise the child but only so far as this is in the child's best interests. Many Scots parents however, still tend to regard the right to discipline their children as one of the prerogatives of parenthood. In practice, the right of reasonable chastisement has been supervised by the state in two ways in Scotland. First, if a child is disciplined physically in a way that goes beyond the 'reasonable' then a criminal assault is committed, which may come before the criminal courts[54] Secondly, and more commonly, if a child is so assaulted then they are the victim of a criminal offence and as such may be referred to the children's hearing,[55] which then has powers to make home and residential supervision orders in respect of the child.

Such arrangements have generally been seen as adequately reconciling the state's need to protect children from violence at home, with the rights of parents to discipline their own children. However this balance was recently jeopardised by an English case[56], *A v UK*,[57] which involved a 9-year-old boy who sought redress at Strasbourg because English law had failed adequately to prosecute his stepfather for the savage beatings he had

[53] 1989 SCLR 601.
[54] Children and Young Persons (Scotland) Act 1937, s 12.
[55] See the 1995 Act, s 52(2)(d).
[56] The English law of reasonable chastisement is similar though not identical to the Scots law.
[57] (1999) 27 EHRR 611.

suffered, a jury having upheld the stepfather's defence of 'reasonable chastisement'. Since the child's success at Strasbourg, it has become accepted that UK law will need to be revised. No final decision has yet been implemented in legislation, but it seems likely that further restrictions will be imposed on parents such as a ban on the use of implements for hitting children, and a total ban on any physical punishment in respect of children under 3.[58]

Most recently, there has been considerable debate around what impact the incorporation of the European Convention on Human Rights in the Human Rights Act 1998 may have on the welfare principle basis of Scots family law.[59] Many commentators are concerned that the rights based discourse of Strasbourg judgements, and in particular the jurisprudence around Art 8 of the ECHR which gives parents rights to 'respect for their family life', will set back the progress that has been made in domestic child law away from concepts of parental authority and towards concepts of the child's best interests and children's rights. To date, only one reported private law case has attempted to reconcile the welfare principle with the demands of Art 8 as interpreted by the European Court. In *White v White*,[60] the court refused to grant rights of contact to a divorced father. He appealed to the Inner House, *inter alia* claiming that his Art 8 right to respect for his family life was being infringed. The question for the Inner House was whether the structure of the law on parental rights and responsibilities in the 1995 Act was compliant with Art 8, given that it clearly made the welfare of the child the paramount consideration, not the rights of the natural parents. Lord Rodger giving the lead opinion held firmly that it the 1995 Act was compliant. The European Court had held in *Elsholz v Germany*[61] that a fair balance must be struck between the interests of the child and those of the parent and that

> in doing so particular importance must be attached to the best interests of the child which, depending on their nature and seriousness may over-ride those of the parent. In particular, the parent cannot be entitled under Art 8 . . . to have such measures taken as would harm the child's health and development.

The right of the non-custodial parent to contact by virtue of his Art 8 rights was not absolute and 'the interests, as well as the rights and freedoms of all', must be taken into account. Lord Rodger concluded that even though section 11(7) contained provisions making the welfare of the child paramount, it was

[58] See further *The Physical Punishment of Children: A Consultation* (Scottish Executive Justice Department, Feb 2000); and news release of 6 Sept 2001 that the Scottish Parliament plans to legislate to ban entirely smacking of children under 3.

[59] See further Edwards, 'Incorporation of the ECHR: what will it mean for Scotland's children?', in A Boyle and H MacQueen (eds), *Human Rights and Scots Law*, forthcoming 2002 (Oxford: Hart Publishing, Oxford).

[60] 2001 SLT 485.

[61] [2000] FLR 497 .

thus compliant with Article 8 in principle. In this writer's impression, however, the finding in *White* is over-optimistic: is it really the same to say, as the Strasbourg court occasionally has, that the child's welfare may *infringe on* the ECHR rights of the parents, as to say the child's welfare is *paramount*? Future case law will no doubt find itself grappling with this issue.

In summary therefore, the view of Scots law is that the best interests of the child are paramount and that the rights of parents are given to them in principle only to fulfil their parental responsibilities. Parental rights are not, and should not, be absolute, and increasingly, consultation with mature children as to how parents *should* exercise their parental authority is seen as the way forward, with concern for the welfare of child also beginning to embrace concern for children's *rights*. It is unlikely the incorporation of the ECHR will extensively change this balance.

IV. OLDER PERSONS

There is no specific family law legislation aimed at older persons, *per se*. It is difficult therefore to recount exactly what laws in Scotland or the UK guarantee the rights and interests of older persons (or as the questionnaire puts it, 'persons of the Third Age', a term which is, to this writer's knowledge, not in popular use in the UK). The most recent governmental initiative on treatment of the elderly was the Royal Commission on Long Term Care for the Elderly.[62] It found that personal care for the elderly (defined expressly not to include board and lodging) should always be free, and that a National Care Commission should be set up to look at the whole system in a strategic way, to represent the interests of older people receiving services and provide benchmarks. Pensions and social security, matters that affect the elderly to a great extent, are reserved matters to the UK Parliament so any review of these areas must come from Westminster. Matters of health, family law, succession, mental health and guardianship, elder abuse and community care, all areas key to the protection of the rights and interests of the elderly, are however all areas that are dealt with by specifically Scottish legislation and case law.

Older persons feature in family-specific case law primarily only as grandparents. There has not been many reported cases on grandparental contact or residence orders in Scotland, partly because it is known anecdotally that their chances in a legal battle with natural parents are not good and so they are recommended not to litigate. On the one hand, there is no

[62] Headed by Sir Stewart Sutherland. The Scottish Executive responded to the Royal Commission in Oct 2000.

issue as there is in some jurisdictions about whether persons other than parents have *title* to apply for parental (*sic*) rights: section 11 of the 1995 Act is extremely wide in this regard with title granted to anyone claiming an 'interest'(section 11(3)). However, grandparents (like unmarried fathers) have no automatic rights or responsibilities towards their grandchildren under the present law. These must be applied for. Usually this is unnecessary because informal contact is maintained through family visits. However, especially in post divorce situations, the grandparents may feel that it is necessary to apply for a contact, or even a residence order under section 11 of the Children (Scotland) Act 1995. Where this occurs, the relevant guiding principle would probably be the one contained in *Sanderson v McManus (supra)* in that the grandparent could not just rely on their natural link with the child to found their claim. As noted above, although the welfare principle must be the paramount concern of the courts in any application for parental rights or responsibilities, the courts do tend to regard it as more likely to be in the child's best interests to stay with a natural blood parent than a third party, even a close relative. In some cases however other factors have caused a reversal of this position. In *Smith v Woodhead*[63], for example, a mature 12-year-old boy expressed a strong wish to live with his grandmother rather than his mother, and this was respected by the court. In *Clark v Clark* [64] however, grandparents lost a custody battle with a child's natural parents, even though they had previously been the primary carers of the children for some time, a factor that is often persuasive to the courts (the so-called 'status quo' principle). In general, unless they are in some way deeply unsatisfactory, the natural parents are likely to win any legal residence/contact dispute, not just because grandparents have no automatic rights, but because the court is acutely aware that support by older relatives may not suffice to sustain the whole of a child's dependent lifespan and may prejudice the reinstatement of parental contact (see further *Hastie v Hastie*[65]).[66]

_The status of grandparents has been considered in the European Court of Human Rights, but it is not clear yet whether the incorporation of the ECHR is likely to lead to their having a stronger standing in law in family disputes. The leading case is *Marckx v Belgium*[67] which held that Art 8 'family life' can exist between grandparents and grandchildren providing that the existence of 'real' de facto relations can be proved. This is usually in the form of care being given to the grandchildren by the grandparents. It was further held that states may impose formal rules which do not depend

[63] 1996 GWD 10-533. [64] 1987 GWD 35-1240. [65] 1985 SLT 146.

[66] But see also *Breingan v Jamieson*, above which stands as a helpful precedent for the parties including grandparents (the case actually concerned a maternal aunt and grandparents).

[67] [1980] 2 EHRR 330.

on determination of prior *de facto* relations between parties where it comes to areas such as succession. Even if they can prove the existence of family life, however, the European Court jurisprudence will not uphold grandparents preventing a parent from exercising the right of contact: *Hokkanen v* Finland.[68] It has however been held that a local authority decision to end all contact between grandparents and a grandchild did constitute an interference with family life (*Price v UK*).[69]

Basically, it seems fair to say that Scots family law is beginning to recognise multiple forms of coupling, married, unmarried, and same-sex, but the centrality of some kind of 'nuclear family' is what continues to be emphasised in child law (despite, as noted earlier, its increasingly illusory nature in real life). The child is bonded in law almost exclusively to their parents, and not to the idea of being a member of a wider community or kin network.

Grandparents can benefit however from certain laws which are not restricted in ambit to parents. For example, section 5 of the 1995 Act provides that any person who has care or control of a child under 16 can do what is reasonable in the circumstances to safeguard the child's health, welfare, or development, even if that carer has no parental rights or responsibilities. So a grandparent babysitting, for example, could give consent to the treatment of a child who has an asthma attack during their care, even in the absence of the parents. Grandparents may be nominated by a parent as testamentary guardians (section 7 of the 1995 Act) and can apply to the courts to become legal guardian even against the will of the parents (the test for the courts being the welfare principle)—imaginable, for example, in an extreme situation such as where a parent was dissipating property belonging to young children (section 11(1)(c) of the 1995 Act). Grandparents have however no involvement in or veto over the adoption of their grandchildren, unless they have acquired rights as guardians from a deed or court.[70] Similarly, they also have no right to attend a children's hearing called for a grandchild, unless they have acquired parental responsibility or ordinarily have charge of or control over the child.[71]

The piece of Scottish family law legislation that is probably of most significance to the elderly is the recent Adults with Incapacity (Scotland) Act 2000. The main cause of adult incapacity in Scotland is dementia, with 60,000 people in Scotland suffering from progressive dementia (mainly as a result of Alzheimer's disease). 91 per cent of these are over 65. The Act, one of the first products of the Scottish Parliament, makes sweeping

68 19 EHRR 139 at para 55-58.
69 (1988) 55 DR 224.
70 Adoption (Scotland) Act 1978, s 16(1)(b) and 65.
71 Children (Scotland) Act 1995, s 45(8) and 93.

reforms as to the law of guardianship of persons *incapax* by way of mental or physical disability, and provides in detail for the smoother administration of their property. The elderly who foresee coming incapacity can now make continuing powers of attorney as to the management of their assets which will continue in force notwithstanding any future loss of capacity by the granter of the power; such powers must be registered with the Office of the Public Guardian who supervises their operation. A 'welfare power of attorney' can also be granted to enable a selected person to make personal welfare and health decisions for the granter if that granter subsequently becomes *incapax* (it has no operation before that time). Finally, the Act also makes provision for consent to medical treatment of the adult *incapax*, and for the management of the finances of persons resident in care homes. These latter two parts of the Act have not yet been brought into force. Empirical research assessing the impact of the AWI(S)A was undertaken from November 1999 to March 2001 and has taken the radical step on interviewing a sample of persons themselves suffering from dementia.

The elderly feature more prominently in non-traditional family law areas of Scots and UK law.

In the field of social security, the legal responsibilities of local authorities towards the elderly were part of the 'Cradle to the Grave' policies of the post-1945 welfare state.[72] Local Authorities had (and have) a duty imposed upon them to provide accommodation to those in need who are ordinarily resident within their area, in Part III of the National Assurance Act 1948. The National Health Care and Community Care Act 1990 imposed no new duties other than the drawing up of 'community care plans' for old people. The Social Work (Scotland) Act 1968 as amended now imposes the duty on local authorities to carry out an assessment of the needs of anyone who appears to be in need of community care services, which by section 94 of the Act includes persons 'who are in need of care and attention arising out of infirmity . . . or age'. Once an assessment has been conducted, the local authority comes under a duty to meet these needs, although this may, arguably, be subject to their budgetary constraints. The disabled elderly also have special provision made for their care. Most recently, the Community Care and Health (Scotland) Act 2002 implements some of the requirements of the Royal Commission on Long Term Care of the Elderly by providing for free nursing care, free personal care and the regulation of charging for non-residential social care. It does not, however, settle the most controversial legal question in this area, which is how far an older person who becomes unable to live on their own should be forced to offset the costs of

[72] Note that the Roman law based obligation of children to aliment their parents (as opposed to parents alimenting children) was only removed by statute in Scotland in 1985. However it was little observed long before that time.

state residential care by the sale of their former residence. Most older people would rather that their home went to their children or family on their death or move into care, than to the state, and so an elaborate case law has evolved in which various avoidance tactics (eg, the conveyance of the house to children before the older person moves into residential care)[73] are tried and countered by the state or the courts. The law as it stands remains unsettled, although it may be clarified by a coming appeal to the House of Lords.

Prior to 1989, social security legislation specified a retirement age as well as a pensionable age and older persons could not claim the basic state pension unless they were retired. This is not the case now and the basic state pension (itself taxable) can be claimed over pensionable age by non-retired persons. The basic state pension is contributory but a married woman who does not qualify can claim a reduced pension on the basis of a pensionable age husband who has entitlement. Pensionable age in the UK is currently 60 for women and 65 for men. This is in the process of being changed and by 2010, pensionable age will be 65 for both sexes (ie, women born after 6 April 1955 will be affected).

In summary, there is no overall legal strategy in Scotland as to the regulation of the rights and interests of the elderly that straddles private and public law. While solutions have been found in recent years for some nagging private law problems (such as the legislation relating to continuing powers of attorneys, and the tidying up of the law of medical consent in relation to *incapaces*), in public law the most intractable problems relate at a basic level to the question of how much public resource is to be provided to meet the needs of an increasingly 'greying' society: a political not a legal issue.

V. CONCLUSIONS

The family is in a process of transition in Scotland. As in other Western European countries, the demographic pattern is of a fairly steady but high rate of divorce, a decline in legitimate birth rate, an increase in the birth rate outside marriage, a decline in marriage, an increase in cohabitation (and in the breakdown of cohabitation, leading to the relatively novel phenomenon outside wartime of a substantial number of adult women under 60 who have never married), and increasing life expectancy for the elderly (with women living around 6 years longer than men). As a result, to pick out just a few striking statistics, in 1999 the number of marriages taking place in

[73] See further E Sutherland, *Child and Family Law* (Edinburgh: T and T Clark, 1999), ch 15.

Scotland was one of the lowest since 1895; and in the latest Scottish Households Survey, only about 15 per cent of households are conventional 'nuclear family' households with an adult couple (married or unmarried) and one or more children living under the same roof; while a third of all households are single-person households (16 per cent of these pensioners living alone). All this has contributed to a society where notions of family, partnership, parent, and kinship have become fluid. Into this mix we can add also the impact of technology, which has lead to fundamental re-conceptions about who is defined as a parent, and whether such definition should be by genetics, gestation, financial support, or social role played.

The legal pattern is equally mixed and uncertain. As has been seen above, most of Scots family law, in as much as it is based around adult relationships, is still founded on marriage as the paradigm status. There is as yet no status of registered partnership, either for same sex or heterosexual couples. Those who choose to cohabit, or those who are unable to marry their partner of choice such as gay and transsexual persons, still suffer from severe legal impediment which can be alleviated, but not altogether removed, by the making of contracts and other deeds such as wills. In any case, the making of cohabitation contracts in Scotland is still unusual, and there is no case law or statute that guarantees such agreements enforceability. Scotland suffers as well from the lack of the remedies used in England and Anglo-American legal systems to provide claims for the unmarried former partner arising out of constructive trust and equity. It is hoped that the forthcoming Family Law Bill for Scotland will at the very least provide heterosexual partners with means to make a legal claim for support from the other partner on the breakdown of the relationship; although it is unlikely to go as far as this writer would like in providing an equivalent system for the division of the assets of the partnership such as is available on divorce for married partners in the Family (Scotland) Act 1985.

As noted above, probably in response to the collapse of marriage as the dominant stable family axis, Scottish family law has in recent years become increasingly centred on emphasising the permanence and responsibilities of the parent-child relationship. Much of this emphasis has been crudely financial: as in the UK as a whole, there is a vested state interest in persuading fathers they have a moral and legal right to pay for their children's upkeep regardless of the dissolution of their relationship with the mother, especially given the low employment rates and high benefit dependency of single mothers. There has been little or no movement in the law towards embracing, as an alternative support structure perhaps, a wider notion of 'family', which might take in, for example, grandparents, unmarried siblings or step-parents. The only reform that is anticipated in this direction is the possibility that step-parents will be able to agree with the natural mother (or father) to share parental responsibilities and rights, in the same way as unmarried parents currently can using section 4 of the 1995Act—perhaps reducing the felt need or tendency to make a formal court application for parental rights, or more commonly, adoption (the latter course being seen as particularly undesirable since it severs all legal connection between the child and one natural parent). The most vociferous demands for reform in recent years have been for equal rights for unmarried fathers, something which will probably be dealt with in statute fairly soon (and will arguably reinforce a false 'nuclear family' paradigm even further).

'Religion, tradition and custom' play little part in modern Scottish family law, and there is little impression of a demand for a more 'multicultural' family law, even though urban Scotland, at least, is certainly a multicultural society. In child law, the welfare principle appears to be a flexible enough standard to allow the courts to take into account issues such as race, colour and religion where they arise as significant, without the need to lay down rigid rules of law which might lead to unfair results in particular cases. In the recent leading case of *Osborne v Matthan*,[74] where custody was disputed between a black natural mother and a white foster mother who had looked after the child for most of her life, the Inner House held that in principle it was in the welfare of the child to be brought up within its own racial and cultural identity, but particular facts might alter the decision granted. On the facts in that case, the white foster mother retained custody of the child.

Finally, is the Scottish family a private or a public institution in law? As has been seen above, traditional private law basically only regulates the relationship between husband and wife and parent and child. The guaranteeing of rights (such as support and accommodation) to other family members, such as the elderly, is mainly now a job for public law, and the state is the guarantor of those rights not the family. Even in those key private law areas of husband and wife, and parent and child, the state now has extensive oversight, either out of concern for the welfare of the child as paramount, or to preserve (at least in theory) minimum standards for formation and dissolution of marriage, marriage being a status and as such of public concern. In this sense the family is clearly a hybrid private-public law institution.

A key area in Scots law, which should be highlighted, where 'public law' interacts with the private sphere of the family is in the prevention of juvenile delinquency and child abuse. Given what we have learnt about physical and sexual abuse and neglect, coupled with the origins of youth crime, it is apparent that the family now offers no guarantees of safety to children, and may not be the best place for some children to grow up. In response, Scotland has developed a unique institution known as the children's hearings

74 1998 SLT 1264.

system, to which children are referred both if they are seen as 'in need' *or* if they are themselves delinquent or showing signs of criminality such as truancy. Neither a criminal court nor a social work venue, the hearing is clearly a public body (and indeed almost wholly replaces the need for persons under 16 to appear in criminal courts); but its concern, from its inception in 1961, has been to provide education, resources and supervision to help and/or rehabilitate the child, within the home if possible, rather than to 'punish', or to remove the child into state care. The hearing is also staffed by lay volunteer members of the community ('panellists') and thus provides a link between the public concept of community and the private notion of family. It is interesting that the hearing is perhaps the best example then, of how modern Scottish family law is currently seen to be moving from being entirely a private law institution to one which has far more of a hybrid private/public character; but the hearing is also widely regarded as a system in crisis exactly because of this character. In this sense it perhaps stands as a metaphor for the current transitional status of the family and family law in Scotland.

Chapter 4

Liability for Defective Products and Services

*Stathis Banakas**

I. TORT: THE GENERAL RULE OF NEGLIGENCE LIABILITY

English law applies a residual negligence rule to liability for defective products and services, following the landmark decision of the House of Lords in *Donoghue v Stevenson.*

A. Products

Liability is restricted, under this general rule, to external injury caused by the product, personal injury or damage to property. It does not extend to damage to the product itself, its loss of value or external pure economic loss. A possible exception is damage to a separable component of a complex product caused by a defective part produced separately. An important consideration in such a case is the time of the passing of title in the product. Such a damage to a separable component must be done after the claimant has acquired such title. Difficulties of demarcation between 'physical' and 'purely economic' loss arise when property or chattels are constructed or manufactured *ab initio* defective, or damaged before the claimant acquired a proprietary interest in them. In cases of bad construction or manufacture several kinds of losses are conceivable. In the first place, the defective property *per se* represents a loss for its owner, in that its market value is less than that bargained for. Secondly, the owner of the property may incur repair or replacement costs, either in order to be able to use it or, even, in order to avert further damage that the defect might cause. Thirdly, the defect may cause further *internal* damage to the property, eg defective foundations may cause damage to the brickwork of a building, or a defective wire may set a car on fire. Fourthly, the defective property may cause *external physical* damage, eg defective car brakes may cause an injury to a passenger in a crash. Fifthly, the defective property may cause *external financial damage.* Defective property is often acquired *with* the defect, and this makes it difficult for the defective construction or manufacture to be presented as an

* University of East Anglia.

'invasion' of an 'existing' proprietary right of the purchaser. In a considerable number of cases, where loss is suffered from a defective product or defectively constructed property, the law of Contract will provide adequate satisfaction to the aggrieved party and the need of a tort claim will not even arise. But there are also cases where, for some reason, the law of Contract can offer no remedy, and the loss is left to lie with the aggrieved party, contrary to what appears to be desirable in the circumstances. It lies in the nature of contractual liability that the contractual action for damages accrues at the time of the breach of the contractual duty and not when the damage caused by it becomes manifested. The period of limitation of the contractual action begins to run against the claimant from the moment of the breach and may well have been completed before any damage appears. On some occasions, as in the case of a defective construction, the appearance of the damage is the first indication of a breach that the claimant can possibly have, and may happen *after* the contractual action has run out.[1] The aggrieved party is, in such a case, left without a contractual remedy and, often, in the absence of the possibility of a tortious claim, with no claim at all.[2]

B. Services

Negligence liability for defective services has developed into a major part of this traditional Tort, mainly with regard to the supply of financial services, advice or information.

The original approach of English law was that, in the absence of a contract, liability for negligent financial advice or information would attach only if a fiduciary relationship existed between the plaintiff and the defendant. This approach was followed by the majority of the Court of Appeal in *Candler v Crane, Christmas & Co.*[3] It was held there that a false statement made carelessly, as opposed to fraudulently, by one person to another, though acted upon by that other to his financial detriment, was not actionable in the absence of any contractual or fiduciary relationship between the parties. It was further held that this rule had in no way been affected by the

[1] *SparhamSouter v Town Developments* [1976] QB 858.

[2] But see s 26 of the Limitation Act 1980: when the action is based on the fraud of the defendant or when the cause of action was concealed by him by fraud, the period of limitation does not begin to run until the plaintiff has discovered the fraud or should, with reasonable diligence, have discovered it. It is noted that 'no degree of moral turpitude is necessary to establish fraud' in this connection, and that the section 'will apply whenever the defendant has committed the wrong, knowingly or recklessly, in circumstances such as to prevent the plaintiff from coming to know of his cause of action': Clerk and Lindsell, *Torts* (London: Sweet & Maxwell, 1998), para 621.

[3] [1951] 2 KB 164, where it was decided that, though the accounts of the company in which the plaintiff had invested had been carelessly prepared and gave a wholly misleading picture of the state of the company, the plaintiff could not recover damages.

emergence of the general principle of Duty of Care in *Donoghue v Stevenson*. Denning LJ, however, dissenting in *Candler*, held that accountants, in preparing and rendering accounts and reports, owed a duty of care not only to their clients but to any third person to whom they knew that their clients were going to show the accounts and reports when, to the knowledge of the accountants, that person would consider the reports and accounts with a view to the investment of money or taking some other action to his profit or detriment. But Denning LJ also made it clear that this duty extended only 'to those transactions for which the accountants knew their accounts were required'.[4] Denning was later shown to have been right, in the seminal decision of the House of Lords in *Hedley Byrne & Co Ltd. v Heller & Partners Ltd.*[5] *Hedley Byrne* while opening the way for recognition of liability in tort for incorrect financial advice or information, also made it clear that the principles applicable in cases of physical harm are not sufficient to cover cases of pure economic loss by negligent advice or information. As Lord Oliver also said in the later case of *Murphy*:

> In the straightforward case of the direct infliction of physical injury by the act of the plaintiff there is, indeed, no need to look beyond the foreseeability by the defendant of the result in order to establish that he is in a 'proximate' relationship with the plaintiff. . . . The infliction of physical injury to the person or property of another universally requires to be justified. The causing of economic loss does not. If it is to be categorised as wrongful it is necessary to find some factor beyond the mere occurrence of the loss and the fact that its occurrence could be foreseen.[6]

Developments since *Hedley Byrne*, in search of principles to govern liability outside contract for incorrect advice or information resulting in pure economic loss, are conveniently reviewed by Nourse LJ in the recent Court of Appeal case of *Bank of Credit and Commerce international (Overseas) Ltd (In liquidation) and Others v Price Waterhouse and* Another.[7] This concerned a consolidated action involving three Plaintiffs : Overseas BCCI Holdings (Luxembourg), SA ('Holdings') and Bank of Credit & Commerce international SA ('SA'). Overseas and SA were wholly owned subsidiaries of Holdings. All three companies went in liquidation following the disastrous collapse of the BCCI group in 1991. The collapse was due to the enormous losses that resulted from the improper and imprudent manner in which the banking activities of the BCCI group had been conducted in the preceding years. These losses had not been revealed in the accounts of the companies. The liquidators of the three companies brought proceedings against their former auditors, both in contract and in tort, alleging breaches of their duties of care. The principal claims against the Defendants related to the audits of the three companies carried out for the

[4] Ibid, at 182. [5] [1964] AC 465. [6] [1991] AC at 398.
[7] 142 SJ LB 86, *The Times* 4 Mar 1998 (CA: Nourse, Brooke LJJ, and Sir Brian Neill).

years 1985 and 1986. The main allegation against the Defendants was that the audits were carried out negligently, and, as a result, the improper and imprudent operation of the banking activities of the companies remained undetected and the companies continued to trade until losses mounted and eventually the BCCI group collapsed.

According to Nourse LJ, the judicial search for a principle or test of liability since *Hedley Byrne*:

> has followed three separate but parallel paths . . .
>
> The *first path*[8] has led to the adoption of what has been called '*the threefold test*'[9]. This test was succinctly stated by Lord Griffiths in *Smith v Eric S. Bush*[10] '. . . . in what circumstances should a duty of care be owed by the adviser to those who act upon his advice? I would answer—only if it is foreseeable that if the advice is negligent the recipient is likely to suffer damage, and there is a sufficiently proximate relationship between the parties and that it is just and reasonable to impose the liability.' . . . Less than a year later, however, some of the difficulties of the threefold test were pointed out in speeches in the House of Lords in *Caparo industries Plc v Dickman* . . . Lord Bridge referred to the concepts of proximity and fairness and continued . . . 'But it is implicit in the passages referred to that the concepts of proximity and fairness embodied in these additional ingredients are not susceptible of any such precise definition as would be necessary to give them utility as practical tests, but amount in effect to little more than convenient labels to attach to the features of different specific situations which, on a detailed examination of all the circumstances, the law recognises pragmatically as giving rise to a duty of care of a given scope.' . . . Lord Oliver expressed similar doubts about the utility of the test . . . he said: '. . . it is difficult to resist a conclusion that what have been treated as three separate requirements are, at least in most cases, in fact merely facets of the same thing, for in some cases the degree of foreseeability is such that it is from that alone that the requisite proximity can be deduced, whilst in others the absence of that essential relationship can most rationally be attributed simply to the court's view that it would not be fair and reasonable to hold the defendant responsible. 'Proximity' is, no doubt, a convenient expression so long as it is realised that it is no more than a label which embraces not a definable concept but merely a description of circumstances from which, pragmatically, the courts conclude that a duty of care exists.' . . . Notwithstanding these reservations, however, the threefold test has retained its value because it focuses attention on three essential questions: (a) Was it reasonably foreseeable that the plaintiff would suffer the kind of damage which occurred ?(b) Was there sufficient proximity between the parties? (c) Was it just and reasonable that the defendant should owe a duty of care of the scope asserted by the plaintiff? . . . Moreover, it is to be noted that the test was used in *Spring v Guardian Assurance Plc* [1995] 2 AC 296, [1994] 3 All ER 129 (see, for example, Lord Woolf at 342B) and in *Marc Rich & Co. AG v Bishop Rock Marine Co Ltd*[11] (see, for example, Lord Steyn at 235–6 of the former report). I have not overlooked the fact, however',

[8] Emphasis added.
[9] Emphasis added.
[10] [1990] 1 AC 831.
[11] [1996] 1 AC 211.

continued the judge, 'that in *Marc Rich* Lord Steyn approved the following passage in the judgement of Saville LJ in the court below: ' . . . the three so-called requirements for a duty of care are not to be treated as wholly separate and distinct requirements but rather as convenient and helpful approaches to the pragmatic question whether a duty should be imposed in any given case. in the end whether the law does impose a duty in any particular circumstances depends upon those circumstances . . . '

. . . The *second path*[12] which has been followed in decided cases uses an '*assumption of responsibility*'[13] test. in *Smith v Eric S. Bush* . . . Lord Griffiths . . . stated that he did not think that 'voluntary assumption of responsibility is a helpful or realistic test of liability.' But in *Henderson Merrett Syndicate Ltd.*[14] Lord Goff, in looking for the principle which underlay the decision in Hedley Byrne . . . , referred to passages in the speeches of Lord Morris and Lord Devlin in that case including a passage in the speech of Lord Devlin . . . where he considered the sort of relationship which gave rise to a responsibility towards those who act upon information or advice and so created a duty of care towards the person so acting. Lord Devlin said: 'I do not understand any of your Lordships to hold that it is a responsibility imposed by law upon certain types of persons or in certain sorts of situations. It is a responsibility that is voluntarily accepted or undertaken, either generally where a general relationship, such as that of solicitor and client or banker and customer, is created, or specifically in relation to a particular transaction.' . . .

Having referred to passages in these speeches Lord Goff continued in *Henderson* . . . 'From these statements, and from their application in *Hedley Byrne*, we can derive some understanding of the breadth of the principle underlying the case. We can see that it rests upon a relationship between the parties, which may be general or specific to the particular transaction, and which may or may not be contractual in nature. All of their Lordships spoke in terms of one party having assumed or undertaken a responsibility towards the other.' . . . It is also to be noted that in *White v Jones*[15], in a speech which was delivered about six months after the speech in Henderson, Lord Goff stated unequivocally . . . that the Hedley Byrne principle was 'founded upon an assumption of responsibility.'

. . . The *third path* [16] which has been followed in the authorities has been to adopt *an incremental approach*[17]. This approach was suggested by Brennan J in his judgement in the High Court of Australia in *Sutherland Shire Council v Heyman*[18]. He rejected the idea that one could introduce some kind of restrictive qualification to limit the prima facie duty produced by a criterion of foreseeability of injury, and continued . . . : 'It is preferable, in my view, that the law should develop normal categories of negligence incrementally and by analogy with established categories, rather than by a massive extension of a prima facie duty of care restrained only by indefinable considerations which ought to negative, or to reduce or limit the scope of the duty or the class of person to whom it is owed.' . . . The wisdom of this approach was recognised by Lord Bridge in *Caparo* . . . and a few months later the

12 Emphasis added.
13 Emphasis added.
14 [1995] 2 AC 145.
15 [1995] 2 AC 207.
16 Emphasis added.
17 Emphasis added.
18 (1984–5) 157 CLR 424.

incremental approach received further support from the House of Lords in *Murphy v Brentwood District Council*[19]: see, for example, the speech of Lord Keith at 461F . . . The incremental approach also has been the subject of criticism But in the absence of some guiding principle of universal application this approach ensures that developments in the law will take place in measured steps'.

The Court of Appeal went on to hold in the *BCCI case* that in special and 'unusual' circumstances, which established the existence of a special relationship based on an assumption of responsibility, the duty of care owed by professional accountants employed to audit the accounts of a bank could extend to another bank, although that bank also had its own independent auditors.

Why does English law have to go down such tortuous paths of Tort liability to resolve the question of protection against incorrect financial information? One important reason is that contractual liability is strictly limited in English law by the doctrines of Consideration and Privity to cases where a contractual price has been agreed as payment for advice or information. When professional people act or advise not in the context of a specific contract but, either in a pre-contractual context with no contract reached at in the end, or in the context of complex, symbiotic long-term arrangements, although important financial and commercial interests are at stake to the full knowledge of all parties involved, and which, moreover, are often fully exploited financially by the adviser, there is no case for Contractual liability. Moreover English law does not know of any precontractual liability for negotiations that have not materialised in a contract.

C. Plaintiff's 'Intended Reliance'

In *Galoo Ltd (In liq) & Others v Bright Grahame Murray (a firm) and another*[20] the Court of Appeal set out to identify the difference between the facts there and those in its previous decision in *Morgan Crucible Co Plc v Hill Samuel Bank* Ltd,[21] that allowed the recovery of the economic loss, as satisfying the test of 'close proximity' established in *Caparo*. The question was, once again, when is an adviser, eg in this case, an auditor, in close proximity with a person suffering loss by relying on his negligently false advice or information? The answer given by the Court of Appeal in *Galoo* was, when the auditor '*intends*' that the third party, a particular identified person, will rely on it.[22] Thus the bidder relying on the auditor's accounts of the target company in *Galoo* had his claim dismissed, because, although he was personally known to the auditor, it was not 'intended' by the latter that he should rely on his accounts. The leading judgement of Glidewell LJ

19 [1991] 1 AC 398.

20 [1995] 1 All ER 16 (CA).

21 [1991] Ch 295.

22 See [1995] 1 All ER 16, 37 per Glidewell LJ; 43–4 per Evans LJ.

relied on Lord Denning's 'classic statement' in *Chandler v Crane Christmas & Co.*[23] The auditor's 'intention' was meant as referring to his knowledge, and willingness, of the reliance of the plaintiff, not any willingness to inflict on him financial injury through such false information. A professional making a false statement in the course of doing his every day job, on the subject matter of his expertise, will find it hard to shift a presumption of negligence in the error. The idea of a 'voluntary assumption of responsibility' (Nourse LJ's 'second path') was used to explain the importance of 'intended reliance'.in *Galoo* it was turned into a new concept of a 'voluntary inter-personal' relationship. This falls short of being a contract only because of lack of consideration proceeding from the plaintiff to the defendant in return for the advice or information.[24] In *Coulthard and others* v *Neville Russell (a firm)*,[25] the Court of Appeal, in another case concerning the civil liability of accountants acting as auditors, considered the issue whether in their function as auditors accountants owed a duty of care to the directors of the audited company to warn on unlawful financial conduct. The facts were as follows: A company acquired the shares of another company of which the plaintiffs were directors. The defendant firm of accountants were appointed auditors of the second company. The first company had borrowed money to purchase the shares of the second and originally it was planned to repay the loan out of dividends declared by the second company. Subsequently, in order to maintain the appearance of capital adequacy in the accounts of the second company, it was suggested that the second company would make a number of loans to the first company to enable it to pay off its loan made in order to acquire it. in fact, these loans by the second company to the first constituted a breach of section 151 of the Companies Act 1985. The second company's Directors were, as a consequence, disqualified under the relevant legislation. They were now suing the auditors of the company alleging that they owed them a duty of care to warn them that the loans were unlawful. They claimed damages for the loss caused to them by the disqualification proceedings that had been brought against them. The auditors had applied to the judge in the High Court to strike out the plaintiffs' claims as disclosing no cause of action. The judge refused, and they appealed. The Court of Appeal held that the liability of professional advisers for failure to give correct advice or accurate information was in a state of development. It was not possible to say that the present claim was bound to fail and therefore the appeal of the auditors should be dismissed. This was an area 'in which the law is developing pragmatically and incrementally. It is pre-eminently an area in which the legal result is sensitive to the facts'.

[23] [1951] 2 KB 164, at 179–84, see above.

[24] [1995] 1 All ER 16, 44 per Evans LJ.

[25] [1998] 1 BCLC 143.

D. Dependence as an Alternative to Reliance

There are a number of important cases where intended reliance is absent, but the law needs to consider a remedy for economic loss. These are cases in which the plaintiff's financial well-being depends, through no choice of his own, on the defendant's correct advice not to the plaintiff, but to *someone else*.

The leading case in England is the House of Lords decision in *Spring v Guardian Assurance plc & others*.[26] The plaintiff applied for work in the financial services industry and sought a personal reference letter from his former employers, a leading insurance firm. The employment rules of the financial services industry required that such a reference be sought and given. It was given, but it was unfavourable, and was found by the trial judge to constitute a negligent mis-statement in the House of Lords it had to be considered whether a duty of care was owed to the plaintiff. Lord Goff reached an affirmative conclusion on the basis of *Hedley Byrne*. He said: 'Where the plaintiff entrusts the defendant with the conduct of his affairs, in general or in particular, the defendant may be held to have assumed responsibility to the plaintiff, and the plaintiff to have relied on the defendant to exercise due skill and care, in respect of such conduct.' But both Lord Goff and Lord Woolf approved in *Spring* the decision of the New Zealand Court of Appeal in *South Pacific Manufacturing Company Limited* v *New Zealand Security Consultants and Investigations Ltd*,[27] where it was held that an investigator reporting on the causes of a fire to an insurance company owed no duty of care to the insured whose claim was rejected because of the allegedly inaccurate report. Lord Goff found that there had been no assumption of responsibility by the investigator to the insured in that case, and Lord Woolf said that the report of the investigator was made pursuant to their contractual duty to the insurer.

Another example of similar type, is *Baker v Kaye*[28]. Mr Baker was a television sales executive. On 28 January 1991, he took up employment with Guild Television Ltd. Three weeks later, however, he was offered a lucrative employment by NBC Europe, a subsidiary of the American giant General Electric, as director of international sales. The offer, which was contained in a letter from GE's human resources manager, was to take effect from 1 March, subject to a satisfactory medical report from the company doctor, Dr Kaye. When the doctor advised GE that a blood test on the plaintiff revealed the possibility of excess social consumption of alcohol, the offer of employment was withdrawn. The plaintiff sued the doctor, alleging negligence in his performance and analysis of the test and his conclusions

[26] [1995] 2 AC 296.
[27] [1992] 2 NZLR 282.
[28] [1997] IRLR 219 (QB).

in his medical report to the company. The High Court held that a medical practitioner retained by a company to carry out pre-employment medical assessments of its prospective employees owes a duty of care to those whom he assesses in carrying out his assessment and in reporting his conclusion; the defendant was, therefore, under a duty to the plaintiff to take reasonable care in carrying out the medical assessment in connection with the job offer, and in making a judgement as to the plaintiff's suitability for employment by reference to the employers' requirements. It was held to be a duty of care that fulfilled all the requirements identified by the House of Lords in *Caparo Industries plc v Dickman*: namely, foreseeability of economic loss, the necessary degree of proximity between the parties and the proviso that it should be just and reasonable in all the circumstances for a duty to be imposed. Not only was it clear that economic loss was a foreseeable consequence of a breach of the duty, but there was also sufficient proximity between the parties to give rise to a duty of care, as the defendant knew that the plaintiff's employment by the company depended solely on the assessment and that to make a non-recommendation could have serious financial consequences. Finally, it was just, fair and reasonable for such a duty to be imposed; there was no conflict between the proper discharge of the defendant's contractual duty to the prospective employers and any duty to the plaintiff, and the plaintiff was dependent upon the medical assessment made by the defendant. The latter was, however, found not liable, as it was not shown that he had breached his duty of care in his assessment of the plaintiff's fitness for the job. But in *Kapfunde v Abbey National Plc and another*,[29] the Court of Appeal, in considering the same question, that is the question whether in assessing the appellant's suitability for employment by Abbey National Plc, a medical practitioner, employed by Abbey National for that purpose, owed her a duty of care, reached a negative conclusion. The Court held that a duty of care will generally be owed to the person to whom a statement is made and who relies on it. In the case of a bank reference or medical report, this is normally the person who asks for it or commissions it. A reference by an employer, however, is likely to be regarded as provided to the former employee, who is the subject of the reference, for his use 'as a passport to future employment', rather than as a service to any particular prospective new employer. The Court disapproved of the Judge's conclusion as to the existence of a duty of care in *Baker v Kaye (supra)*. The doctor's advice is given to the employer or insurer and not to the applicant for a job, who is a patient only in the sense that he is the subject of the examination and advice. The doctor is, therefore, taken to assume responsibility for his advice only to the employer or insurer who commissioned it, and not to the patient.

[29] [1998] IRLR 583 (CA).

E. Incorrect Advice Causing Financial Loss to a Beneficiary of a Client

In the leading case of *White and another v Jones and others*,[30] a solicitor was found liable to the intended beneficiaries of his client, the testator, who died before the solicitor came round to drawing up a will under instructions to confer a benefit on them. The House of Lords (Lord Keith and Lord Mustill dissenting) held that where a solicitor accepted instructions to draw up a will and as the result of his negligence an intended beneficiary under the will was deprived of a legacy the solicitor was liable for the loss of the legacy. Lord Goff and Lord Nolan based their decision on extending the assumption of responsibility by the solicitor towards his client in law to an intended beneficiary. But they made it clear that this assumption of responsibility existed only if the loss of the beneficiary was foreseeable to the solicitor, and if the circumstances of the situation were that there was no confidential or fiduciary relationship between the parties, and neither the testator nor his estate had a remedy against the solicitor. Tort liability was appropriate in such circumstances only because otherwise an injustice would occur, as a result of a lacuna in the law and there would be no remedy for the loss caused by the solicitor's negligence to the beneficiary. Lord Browne-Wilkinson and Lord Nolan chose to adopt the 'incremental approach' (see above), and held that the principle of assumption of responsibility should be extended to a solicitor who accepted instructions to draw up a will, holding him to be in a special relationship with those intended to benefit under it.

This case could have launched a significant expansion of the ambit of professional liability for economic losses to a non-client, but it has not done so. Instead, it has served as an authority for the courts to focus such liability on cases where there is, as Lord Goff put it, a 'lacuna in the law'. A good example of this is cases concerning third-party professional liability to beneficiaries of a trust. *White v Jones* extended in law the expert adviser's assumption of responsibility to his client's beneficiaries. This has given rise to the question of whether an expert advising trustees owes a duty of care to the beneficiaries. In the case of *Royal Brunei Airlines v Tan*,[31] Lord Nicholls, giving the judgment of the Privy Council, said:[32]

> it is difficult to identify a compelling reason why, in addition to the duty of skill and care vis-à-vis the Trustees which the third parties have accepted, or which the law has imposed upon them, third parties should also owe a duty of care directly to the beneficiaries.

[30] [1995] 2 AC 207. [31] [1995] 2 AC 378 (PC). [32] At 391.

In the very recent case of *Hogg Robinson Trustees Ltd. and others v J Alsford Pensions Trustees Ltd. and others*,[33] there is further evidence of the Courts being unwilling to generally recognise third-party liability for economic loss to beneficiaries, in the absence of a lacuna in the law, similar to that which gave ground to the House of Lords to accept the claim of the testator's beneficiaries in *White v Jones*. A fiduciary relationship (and, therefore, also a special relationship) will, normally, exist only between third parties and trustees, and, of course, trustees and beneficiaries. In *Hemmens v Wilson Browne*,[34] a settlor instructed a solicitor to draft a document giving the plaintiff an immediately enforceable right to call at a future date for a sum of £110,000. After the settlor had executed a document drafted by the solicitor, the latter told the plaintiff that the effect of the document was 'akin to a trust' but advised her to consult her own solicitors if she had any doubt in the matter. It ought to have been known to the solicitor that the document failed to give the plaintiff any enforceable right. When the plaintiff called on the settlor to perform his promise he was no longer willing to do so and declined to pay her the promised sum. The plaintiff claimed damages for negligence against the solicitor. The court held that a solicitor might be held to owe a duty of care to the intended beneficiary of an inter vivos transaction who had suffered damage which it was beyond the power of the settlor to put right, but such a duty of care could not be said to exist in all cases of inter vivos transactions. Although it was foreseeable that by failing to exercise due care the defendant might cause the plaintiff loss and although there was a sufficient degree of proximity between them, it was not 'fair, just or reasonable' to give her a remedy against him since the settlor remained capable of fulfilling his original intention and retained a remedy in contract against the solicitor if he chose to exercise it (no lacuna in the law as in *White v Jones*). If the solicitor's client is alive, the client can sue the solicitor for his negligence to confer his benefit on the beneficiary, and this takes care of the need to give the beneficiary an independent action in tort.[35]

F. Professional Liability to a Client: Concurrence of Contract and Tort

In *Henderson v Merrett Syndicates Ltd*, Lord Goff said:[36]

an assumption of responsibility coupled with the concomitant reliance may give rise

[33] High Court, Chancery Division, Lindsay J, signed judgement handed down on 19 Mar 1997.

[34] [1995] Ch 223.

[35] But in *McCullagh v Lane Fox & Partners Ltd* [1996] 18 EG 104 , the Court of Appeal held that an estate agent acting for a vendor owes a duty of care to the purchaser of property, although not on the facts of that case.

[36] [1995] 2 AC 145 at 194.

to a tortious duty of care irrespective of whether there is a contractual relationship between the parties, and in consequence, unless his contract precludes him from doing so, the plaintiff, who has available to him concurrent remedies in contract and tort, may choose that remedy which appears to him to be most advantageous.

The defendants in that case were the providers of services as managers of underwriting syndicates. Lord Goff also said:

It is however my understanding that by the law in this country contracts for services do contain an implied promise to exercise reasonable care (and skill)in the performance of the relevant services . . . [37]

And:

Attempts have been made to explain how doctors and dentists may be concurrently liable in tort while other professional men may not be so liable, on the basis that the former cause physical damage whereas the latter cause pure economic loss . . . But this explanation is not acceptable, if only because some professional men, such as architects, may also be responsible for physical damage. As a matter of principle, it is difficult to see why concurrent remedies in tort and contract, if available against the medical profession, should also not be available against members of other professions, whatever form the relevant damage may take.

And in *Holt and another v Payne Skillington and another*[38] the Court of Appeal confirmed that where there are concurrent claims in contract and tort for professional negligence, it is possible that the scope of the duty in tort may be wider than that in contract.

The existence of a contract between plaintiff and defendant is undisputable proof of an assumption of a duty of care by the latter to the former; and the recognition of the concurrence of contractual and tortious remedies by English law is hardly surprising, in the light of the narrow scope of contractual liability. The interesting question is whether the terms of the contract can be allowed to circumscribe the scope of the duty in tort. This would be unacceptable, if the latter is to be seen as arising *ex lege* (as it normally is). But not so, if its existence depends on a (voluntary) assumption of responsibility. Assumption of responsibility is, however, as we shall now see, a troubled concept. It is objective, and does not depend on the will or knowledge of the defendant. To that extent, the tort duty that comes from it can be, and is, independent from the will of the parties as expressed in the contract that embodies the assumption of responsibility (subject to lawful limitation or exclusion of liability).

[37] Ibid at 193. [38] (1996) 49 Con LR 99.

II. CONTRACT

In Contract, the seller or direct supplier of a defective product is liable to the buyer for products and services that are not of merchantable quality and fit for their purpose. There is no theory of warranty linking the buyer with anyone other than the seller or direct supplier, ie the producer or distributor. But if a product has been bought for use by a third party it may be possible, on the true construction of the contract of sale, for the third party to claim directly from the seller, under the recent Contracts (Rights of Third Parties) Act 1999.

A. Quality & Fitness for Purpose

Under the Sale of Goods Act 1979, section 14, the Supply of Goods (Implied Terms) Act 1973, section 10, the Supply of Goods & Services Act 1982, sections 4 and 9 and the Sale & Supply of Goods Act 1994, section 1, all products or services must be, when sold, of 'reasonable' merchantable quality and fit for their purpose. Similar guarantees, but in the case of sales of consumer goods only, are now been introduced on a pan-European level with Directive 1999/44/EC on 'certain aspects of the sale of consumer goods and associated guarantees'.

B. Consumer Sales

Special protection is offered in case of products sold in consumer sales. Consumer protection became a top European Priority with the new Article 129(a) of the EC treaty inserted as title 'XI, Consumer protection' by the Treaty on European Union of 1992 (Maastricht Treaty):the EU will take 'action to protect the health, safety and economic interests of consumers and to provide adequate information to consumers'. Over 19 major UK statutes and over 42 EC Directives have been produced to address these issues. Directly relevant to this paper among them are the Unfair Contract Terms Act 1977 and the Unfair Terms in Consumer Contracts Regulations 1999 (enacted to implement European legislation).

The Unfair Contract Terms Act 1977 introduced controls of exclusion clauses in consumer contracts, excluding or restricting the seller's liability for non-performance. The Act is built around the idea that an exclusion clause must be 'reasonable' in order to be valid. Reasonableness, is of course, a concept difficult to pin down to a clear definition. In Schedule II, the Act provides evidence of what is considered to be an unreasonable term, in describing factual circumstances against which the reasonableness of contractual clauses should be judged. These associate reasonableness with the bargaining position of the parties, the cost of choice not to enter the contract offered with the exclusion clause, or the existence of alternative sources of satisfaction of the Consumer's needs. Under the 1977 Act, all 'unreasonable' Contract terms in Consumer contracts will be struck down by the courts, whether they are exclusion or limitation of liability terms or other. The, mainly economic, tests of 'unreasonableness' mentioned above show that this Act only introduced a limited protection for consumers.

The Unfair Terms in Consumer Contracts Regulations 1999 provide, in Article 8(1), that an unfair term in a contract concluded with a consumer by a seller or supplier shall not be binding on the consumer; Article 8(2) provides that the contract shall continue to bind the parties if it is capable of continuing into existence without the unfair term. Article 5(1) provides that a contractual term shall be regarded as unfair if it has not been individually negotiated and if, contrary to the requirement of good faith, it causes a significant imbalance in the parties' rights and obligations arising under the contract, to the detriment of the consumer. Under Article 5(2), a term shall always be regarded as not having been individually negotiated where it has been drafted in advance and the consumer has therefore not been able to influence its substance. Article 5(3) further provides that, notwithstanding that a specific term or certain aspects of it in a contract has been individually negotiated, the Regulations shall apply to the rest of a contract if an overall assessment of it indicates that it is a pre-formulated standard contract. Under Article 5(4) it shall be for any seller or supplier who claims that a term was individually negotiated to show that it was. Schedule 2 to these Regulations contains an indicative and non-exhaustive list of terms that may be regarded as 'unfair'. This list includes terms which have the object or effect of excluding or limiting the legal liability of a seller or supplier in the event of the death of a consumer or personal injury to the latter resulting from an act or omission the seller or supplier; giving the seller or supplier the possibility of transferring his rights and obligations under the contract, where this may serve to reduce the guarantees for the consumer without the latter's agreement; excluding or hindering the consumer's right to take legal action or exercise any other legal remedy, particularly by requiring the consumer to take disputes exclusively to arbitration not covered by legal provisions, or unduly restricting the evidence available to him or imposing on him a burden of proof which, according to the applicable law, should lie with another party to the contract.

There is very little that is new in these Regulations, ie that has not been covered already in the Unfair Contract Terms Act of 1977. Except, of course that the concept of 'unfairness' is based on the broad new requirement of 'Good Faith' itself that been forced by the Directive on English law (the Directive's Preamble had made it clear that domestic courts would have to use this concept in defining unfairness, even if national legislators failed to introduce it themselves into domestic law). A leading modern Contract law textbook (S Wheeler and J Shaw, *Contract Law. Cases Materials and Commentary* (Oxford: Oxford University Press, 1994), was first to note that the use of the good faith principle by the Directive shows the strong influence of the German AGB-Gesetz. Wheeler and Shaw suggest that in applying the new rules English judges may need to be influenced by the experience of both civil law and other common law jurisdictions, notably, the American experience with the Good faith rule of the UCC. But, rather pointedly, they go on to remark that it is unlikely a good faith or fairness standard will be any more favourable to the consumer that the older reasonableness standard. It is noteworthy that the Regulations are transposing the absolute minimum of the original Directive, omitting the important provision of Article 7(2) about representative or collective action, already implemented in other European jurisdictions. A leading commercial lawyer, Professor Reynolds, has suggested that this minimalist approach, combined with preserving the Unfair Contract Terms Act of 1977, will create a situation of 'nightmarish complexity' inimical to the philosophy of consumer law which requires simple and 'user-friendly' rules. The U.K. might be accused of an infringement of Article 5 EC for inhibiting the EC's objectives by creating an inconsistent legal regime which creates a 'state of uncertainty as to the possibility available to [Community citizens] of relying on Community law' (relevant is the case of *Commission v France (French Seamen)* Case 167/73). Failure to implement Article 7(2) of the Directive might well lead to Commission action against the UK at the European Court, under Article 5 and Article 189(3) EC. The Regulations provide, as a substitute to representative or collective action, for action by the Director General of Fair Trading, a Governmental watchdog, on behalf of aggrieved consumers (Article 8). One important drawback of the new English implementing Regulations for the consumer is that the burden of proof of bad faith rests with him; the Regulations have paid no heed to contrary suggestions in the Preamble of the Directive. Contrariwise, it is the seller or supplier who must show the 'reasonableness' of his terms under the Unfair Contract terms Act 1977. This adds to the attraction of sticking to what we already have, and will not further the EC's objectives in Consumer protection for a uniform 'good faith' principle across Europe.

III. CONCURRENCE OF CONTRACT AND TORT

English law accepts the cumulation of claims in Contract and Tort. More precisely, the court will award the remedy most appropriate in the circumstances, whether contractual or tortious, if there is a contractual link between the parties. Personal injury claims, as well as most property damage claims, will sound in Negligence (tort), despite the existence of a contractual relationship. Losses of value and other economic losses can only be recovered in Contract.

The possibility of the existence of a contractual relationship between the parties in defective products litigation creates a fundamental point of order between contract and tort. A breach of contract is not always a tort. In view of the broad nature of the tort of Negligence, the scope of which is *a* priori restricted only in relation to the nature of the *damage* at issue, among the various kinds of tortious conduct, Negligence is the tort more likely to coexist with a breach of contract. But as far as defective products are concerned, it must be now taken as firmly established that the existence of a breach of contract does not preclude the plaintiff from suing also in tort. As Megaw LJ said in the case of *Batty*, the decision of the Court of Appeal in *Esso*[39] had put into great doubt the validity of Diplock LJ's finding in an older case,[40] which had stirred the controversy. *Esso,* Megaw LJ said, had the effect of disposing of any objections to the concurrence of contractual and tortious actions in cases of negligence. And the learned judge went on to attack forcefully the suggestion of counsel that because all cases which had so far accepted the tortious action were dealing with claims against professionals exercising a 'common calling', which required a special 'professional skill' (and *Esso* was no different in this respect), the concurrence of an action in tort should only be allowed in relation to claims against such professionals. Megaw LJ found this distinction artificial and rejected it as an 'undesirable development' in the law.[41] It appears that the decision of Oliver J in the *Midland Bank Trust*[42] case has also rejected a limitation of the *Esso* ratio to 'common callings'. This decision has formulated the principle of *Esso* in the broadest possible terms. It virtually contemplates the possibility of a cumulation of contractual and tortious remedies irrespective of the nature of the contractual relationship: no contractual duty of any kind can preclude the concurrent invocation of a claim in tort (provided that there is, of course, such a claim. Such cumulation of a contractual and a tortious action creates certain problems, the most important of which is exemption clauses and the related issue of their impact, if any, on the *tortious* claim. Liability for non-premeditated harm, contractual or tortious, may, in principle, be excluded, by means of an exemption clause or condition. English law is likely to interpret a contractual exemption clause strictly *contra preferentem,* which may mean that the exclusion of *tort ous* liability must either be specifically mentioned, or expressed in terms which cannot but be construed as referring to such liability, too. After the enactment in England of the Unfair Contract Terms Act

39 [1976] QB 801 (CA).

40 *Bagot v Stevens Scanlan & Co., Ltd.* [1966] 1 QB 197 (CA).

41 *Batty v Metropolitan Property Realisations* [1978] 2 WLR 500, 508 f (CA).

42 [1978] 3 WLR 167 (CA).

1977 it is no longer possible to exclude liability for Negligence resulting in death or personal injury. And in cases of 'loss or damage' arising from defective goods in *consumer* use (and resulting from the Negligence of a manufacturer or distributor) section 5 of the same Act provides that 'liability . . . cannot be excluded or restricted by reference to any contract term or notice contained in or operating by reference to a guarantee of the goods'. This provision renders void any contractual surrender by the consumer, in exchange of a guarantee (eg 'repair plus parts'), of his rights in *tort* in respect to such loss. The wording however, of the section, leaves it open whether it refers only to 'physical' losses, or, also, to other losses of less clear 'physical' complexion. 'Loss or damage' can be taken as indicating that the legislator had also in mind the possibility of a consumer claim in *tort* for losses not 'purely' physical.

An interesting question is whether the presence of a contractual relationship gives always rise to a Duty of Care in Tort. Several interesting cases have touched upon this issue. *Junior Books v Veitchi*[43] was a case involving loss of production of a factory, shut down for repairs to a defective (but non-dangerous) floor, laid by sub-contractors of the plaintiff's contractors. *Simaan General Contracting Co v Pilkington Glass Ltd*,[44] was a case in which the sub-contractors failed to install glass to the proper specifications in the curtain walling and the client of their contractors refused to pay the full price to the latter. In *Junior Books* the House of Lords found that the plaintiff was entitled to rely 'reasonably' on the sub-contractors' competence, because there existed a very close proximity between plaintiff and sub-contractors: the former was for the latter the one and only clearly foreseeable and individually identifiable potential victim of their negligence. Lack of privity prevented contractual remedies against the defendants; but liability in tort was inescapable in such an almost 'contractual' entanglement of the parties. In a more restrictive later line of cases, especially in the areas of economic loss from defective buildings and products, *Junior Books is* treated as a *sui-gener*is case confined to its facts. But it is still good support for the proposition that a very close relationship between plaintiff and defendant can be found in such almost contractual entanglements (ie contracts between defendant and third party in plaintiff's favour that are badly performed to the plaintiff's detriment). Such a close relationship may be the basis of a 'reasonable reliance' placed by the plaintiff on the defendant *for the latter to do the job as agreed between him and the third party.* Whether, however, reliance is reasonable, and can support a claim in tort, is a question that must be decided on the basis of the facts of each case: thus in *Simaan General Contracting*, it was found not to be reasonable for the plaintiff to rely on the defendant's compliance with the terms of his contract

43 [1983] 1 AC 520. 44 [1988] QB 758 (CA).

with a third party. *Simaan's* broader significance for English Law lies in the evidence supplied by that case of the reluctance of the law to allow contractual bargains to determine the basis and extent of liability *in tort*, of one of the parties to the contract, towards a third party, in whose favour, or for the benefit of which, the contract was made. But even after *Simaan, Junior Books* will continue to provide authority for the proposition that such contractual bargains can affect in a decisive way the fate of an economic loss claim, to the extent that they give rise to a direct and very high exposure to risk of such loss of a plaintiff that, because of the contract between the defendant and a third party, becomes directly (or, even, *individually*) foreseeable to the defendant. Clearly the latter would be *assuming* a duty of care not to cause economic loss to the plaintiff in such cases; this was implied in the *Junior Books* speeches.

Any contractual clauses in consumer sales will be operational in tort only for injuries other than personal injury or death, and only if the exclusion of tortious liability is incorporated into a clause in a contract of transfer of ownership or possession, and also satisfies the requirement of 'reasonableness'.[45] This only enhances the real impact that a tortious action, if accepted, might have.

IV. STRICT LIABILITY RULE FOR DANGEROUS PRODUCTS: EUROPEAN PRODUCT LIABILITY DIRECTIVE

Following EU Directive 85/374/EEC on Product liability, the United Kingdom enacted the Consumer Protection Act 1987, which introduced a rule of strict liability for dangerous products that are defective and cause personal injury or property damage. More precisely, the Act, following the Directive, relieves the claimant of the burden of proving the negligence of the manufacturer, requiring only that he or she proves the defect, the injury or damage and the causal link between the two. The manufacturer can escape liability by proving that the defect was not due to negligence in the making of the product. This Act has recently been amended by the Consumer Protection Act 1987 (Product Liability) Modification Order 2000, which came into force at the beginning of December of 2001. This order extends the definition of a 'product' to cover all moveable products, including electricity and agricultural products and game. Agricultural products include produce of the soil, of stock farming and of fisheries. There is a 'long stop' special limitation period under the Act of 10 years after the product was put into circulation by the defendant.

[45] And in accordance with the requirement of good faith: see, below, The Unfair Terms in Consumer Contracts Regulations 1999, implementing European legislation.

Under section 11 of the Consumer Protection Act 1987, the Secretary of State is given power to make regulations to ban certain products. And in *R v Secretary of State for Health ex parte US Tobacco International Inc*,[46] the High Court decided that this power extends to applied to both defective goods and those intrinsically dangerous in that in their use there was a risk of personal injury or death.

Very little litigation has been generated by the Act,[47] but an important recent decision has made it clear, contrary to the belief of many experts both the Directive and the Act are interpreted as having introduced genuine strict liability. In *A and Others v National Blood* Authority,[48] the claimants had been infected with Hepatitis C (the virus) through blood transfusions which had used blood products obtained from infected donors. They brought actions for damages against the defendants, the authorities responsible for the production of blood and blood products. During the period when most of the claimants were infected, the risk of such infection through blood transfusions, though known to the medical profession, was impossible to avoid, either because the virus itself had not yet been discovered or because there was no way of testing for its presence in blood. The claims were brought not in negligence, but under the Consumer Protection Act 1987. Article 6(1) of the Directive provided that a product was defective when it did not provide the safety which a person was entitled to expect, taking all circumstances into account, including the presentation of the product, the use to which it could reasonably be expected that the product would be put and the time when the product was put into circulation. Article 7(e) provided the producer with a defence if he could establish that the state of scientific and technical knowledge at the time when he put the product into circulation was not such as to enable 'the existence of the defect' to be discovered. Very significantly the defendants accepted on the trial that a producer's liability under Article 6 did not depend on fault. But they argued that, in assessing whether the infected blood was defective, the unavoidability of the risk was a decisive factor, and that all that the public was entitled to expect was that all reasonably available precautions had been carried out, not that the blood would be 100 per cent safe. The defendants argued that the infected blood should be seen as an inherently risky standard product (ie one which performed as the producer intended) rather than a non-standard product (ie a product which was deficient or inferior in terms of safety from the standard product, and whose harmful characteristic, not present in the standard product, had caused the material injury or damage). They also relied on the fact that they were obliged to produce

[46] [1992] 1 QB 353.

[47] Until 1997, there was an estimated ten reported judgments based on the Directive in the whole of the EU!

[48] [2001] All ER (D) 298.

blood, and that they had no alternative but to supply it to hospitals and patients, as a service to society. Alternatively, the defendants sought to rely on the Article 7(e) defence, contending that an unavoidable risk qualified for protection under it if the producer was unable to discover, by means of accessible information, the defect in a particular product. The judge Mr Justice Burton rejected these arguments. He held that avoidability was not one of the circumstances to be taken into account under Article 6, even in respect of a harmful characteristic in a standard product. In that article, 'all circumstances' meant all relevant circumstances. Avoidability was not a relevant circumstance since it fell outside the purpose of the Directive, which was intended to eliminate proof of fault or negligence.

A. Definition of 'Defect'

Article 3 of the Consumer Protection Act 1987, implementing the European Directive, states that:

> There is a defect in a product . . . if the safety of the product is not such as persons generally are entitled to expect.

Section 3(2) further provides that

> in determining . . . what persons generally are entitled to expect in relation to a product all the circumstances shall be taken into account, including—(a) the manner in which, and purposes for which, the product has been marketed, its get-up, the use of any mark in relation to the product and any instructions for, or warnings with respect to, doing or refraining from doing anything with or in relation to the product; (b) what might reasonably be expected to be done with or in relation to the product; and (c) the time when the product was supplied by its producer to another; and nothing in this section shall require a defect to be inferred from the fact alone that the safety of a product which is supplied after that time is greater than the safety of the product in question.

In *Worsley v Tambrands Ltd* (unreported), the High Court rejected a claim under the Act for damages for toxic shock syndrome ('TSS') suffered by the plaintiff, due to her use of a tampon during a menstrual period, put into circulation by the defendants, on the grounds that the warning and information accompanying the relevant tampons, were adequate to warn the claimant of the potential risk associated with tampon use.

This is not very clear wording. The first clear definition of what is a defect in English (and European) law, is provided again by the recent case mentioned above, where the judge held that the measure was the legitimate expectation of the public and not a risk-utility calculus. More specifically, the judge held that products could be distinguished into standard and non-standard products, the latter meaning products that inherently carried risks. But he held that the primary issue was whether the public at large accepted the non-standard nature of the product, ie whether they accepted that a proportion of the products was defective. This question was, however, one of legitimate expectation, meaning that the court might conclude that the expectation of the public was too high or too low. Questions such as warnings and presentations were important, but the avoidability of the harmful characteristic, the impractability, cost or difficulty of precautionary measures, and the benefit to society or the utility of the product (except in the context of whether, with full information and proper knowledge, the public had and should have accepted the risk) were not relevant. In the instant case, the infected blood products were non-standard products since they were different from the norm that the producer intended for use by the public. They were defective within Article 6 because the public at large was entitled to expect that the blood transfused to them would be free from infection.

B. The Development Risk Defence

Among the defences available to the producer under the European legislation, the most significant, and controversial, is the so-called 'development risk' defence.

Article 7 of the 1985 Directive provides that the producer shall not be liable if he proves:

(e) that the state of scientific and technical knowledge at the time when he put the product into circulation was not such as to enable the existence of the defect to be discovered . . .

Article 4(1) of the Consumer Protection Act 1987 states that a person liable under the Act (and the Directive) will have a defence, if he shows

(e) that the state of scientific and technical knowledge at the relevant time [ie when the product was put into circulation] was not such that a producer of products of the same description as the product in question might be expected to have discovered the defect if it had existed in his products while they were under his control . . .

The European Court of Justice was called upon to decide whether the UK had properly implemented the European Directive in this connection, in proceedings instituted by the European Commission . The Court has recently given its judgment on the issue (Case C-300/95). It concluded that there was nothing to suggest that the UK courts, in interpreting s 4(1)(e), would not be able to achieve the result that the Directive intended.

The Court also held, after acknowledging that the state of scientific and technical knowledge included 'the most advanced level of such knowledge', that

[In] order for the relevant scientific and technical knowledge to be successfully pleaded as against the producer, that knowledge must have been accessible at the time when the product in question was put into circulation.

This implies that it is necessary to establish that the relevant knowledge sted and was accessible, and that the mere fact that someone, somewhere, had more advanced knowledge will not be enough to exclude the defence. The European Court left open the question of how accessibility is to be interpreted. This makes it possible that the defence might be available when the necessary knowledge was not 'reasonably' accessible. But it is , of course, for the producer to establish the facts that provide him with the defence, including the fact that any available knowledge was not 'reasonably accessible' at the time of the circulation of the product.

As illustrated, however, in a recent decision of the Court of Appeal[49] the question of whether the producer might have been expected to have discovered the defect at the time of putting the product in circulation, will often have nothing to do with the state of scientific or technical knowledge at that time. The court held in that case that there was no difficulty in discovering the defect by a simple practical test, and no advance in scientific or technical knowledge was required to enable that test to be carried out. The only reason that it was not carried out was that manufacturers had not thought of doing so. It was decided that the defence under section 4(1)(e) of the Act is simply not engaged in such a case.

V. VICARIOUS LIABILITY

In English law an employer is strictly liable for wrongs committed by an employee in the course of his employment. This liability is extensive, because 'course of employment' is a very large concept that includes all acts or omissions in the place of work, or while coming to or leaving work. Businesses will always be liable for such acts or omissions for which the employee is personally responsible.

VI. CONCLUSION

The concept of product liability was introduced into European legal systems by the Directive of 1985, which, although relatively simple in its provisions, did not prove easy to implement everywhere in Europe. In the UK implementation came relatively quickly, but was followed by scarcity of

[49] *Abouzaid v Mothercare (UK) Ltd* [2000] All ER (D) 2436 (CA) (Pill, Chadwick LJJ and Wright J).

litigation. However, the case of *A and Others v National Blood Authority*,[50] discussed above, has now shown that the Directive can be applied so as to impose a true strict liability on the producer for personal injury and property damage, and one should not exclude the possibility that the courts will also take a hard look at the defence of development risks in the future.

On the contrary, as far as defective services are concerned, the European project has faltered, after the aborted Draft Directive, and English law remains unchanged in its negligence rule. But it is important to underline in this connection that the development of the law relating to liability for negligent advice or information on the grounds of an assumption of responsibility has led to an expansion of professional liability. And although proof of lack of care is still required, it will not be difficult in practice for a claimant to discharge this burden when a professional error has been clearly committed.

[50] [2001] ALL ER (D) 298.

Chapter 5

Present and Future of Real and Personal Security: Scotland

*David L Carey Miller**

I. INTRODUCTION

Scots law pays close attention to a distinction between real and personal rights which, in the context of security, translates into the separate and distinct categories of real and personal security. Confined to a context of creditor and debtor a personal right by definition cannot amount to a right of security; hence the classic statement of Lord President Inglis that a 'mere assignation of corporeal moveables *retenta possessione* is nothing whatever but a personal obligation and creates no preference of any kind'.[1]

As is the case in property law generally,[2] in the field of security, at least in terms of fundamentals, Scotland has greater affinity with the civilian tradition than with the distinctive common law developed in England.[3] But this is not to say that the development of Scots law has remained uninfluenced by English law; in a recent study of security over moveables the author concludes that '[p]ledge, hypothec, and lien have been influenced both by civil law and by English law.'[4]

To be in any sense meaningful, personal security must involve a third person to whom the creditor may look in the event of the debtor failing to meet his or her obligation. In Scots law this form of security is known as

* Professor of Property Law, School of Law, University of Aberdeen. While I alone am responsible for this report I am pleased to acknowledge the contribution of research assistant Christopher Bartlett LL B (Aberd); I am also grateful to my colleague Angelo Forte, Professor of Commercial Law, for helpful responses to points raised in the course of my putting the report into final form.

[1] *Clark v West Calder Oil Co* (1882) 9 R 1017, 1024.

[2] See, generally, Kenneth Reid, 'Property Law: Sources and Doctrine', in Kenneth Reid and Reinhard Zimmermann (eds), *A History of Private Law in Scotland*, vol I (Oxford: Oxford University Press, 2000), 185.

[3] See William M Gordon, 'Roman Influence on the Scots Law of Real Security', in R Evans-Jones (ed), *The Civil Law Tradition in Scotland* (Edinburgh: Stair Society, 1995), 157; for a comment on the difference between the Scots and English perceptions of the concept of 'real right' see George Gretton, 'Trusts' in Reid and Zimmermann (n 2), 480, 507–8.

[4] Andrew JM Steven, 'Rights in Security over Moveables' in Reid and Zimmermann (n 2), 333, 361.

'caution'; the obliged third party being a 'cautioner' subject to a 'cautionary obligation'. Caution gives only a personal right and hence no better claim than that of any other creditor in the circumstances of the cautioner's insolvency.[5] A real right of security and a cautionary right belong, respectively, to the separate and distinct categories of property and obligations.

This paper will focus on certain recent developments relating to real and personal security in Scots law. The treatment will be selective. Comprehensive coverage of the subject matter of real and personal security can be found in the standard sources of Scots law.[6]

The reform of security law in Scotland has tended to be driven by commercial pressure. In 1999 the Justice Minister, Jim Wallace, in announcing the preparation of a Scottish Executive paper on moveable securities, commented:

> there is a perception that businesses in Scotland are being inhibited in raising capital because, under Scots law, they cannot create a security . . . without giving up possession of that property[7]

While it is true that, in principle, in Scots law security cannot be granted over a moveable without possession it is doubtful whether business activity is being inhibited by the position.[8] This said, the hesitant adoption of the *Romalpa* reservation of title doctrine by Scots law[9] does suggest a certain difficulty in reconciling the tension between, on the one hand, principles long recognised as fundamental and, on the other, the perceived needs of a modern commercial society.

It is probably true that the common law pledge[10]—which, of course, functions in terms of the principle that the creditor must have possession—is of marginal commercial significance.[11] It is also true that the non-possessory

[5] But, of course, cautioners are normally selected by creditors on the basis of the relative financial soundness of their position as compared to that of the debtor.

[6] See *The Laws of Scotland: Stair Memorial Encyclopaedia,* 'Rights in Security', vol 20 (Edinburgh: W Green, 1992), paras 1–272 and 'Cautionary Obligations and Representations as to Credit' vol 3 (1994), paras 801–1008. See also, generally, WA Wilson, *The Scottish Law of Debt,* 2nd edn (Edinburgh: W Green, 1991).

[7] Parliamentary Written Answer S1W–1719 per Jim Wallace. See also: *Eighth Report of the Law Reform Committee for Scotland* (1960, Cmnd 1017); *A Review of Security Interests in Property* (1989, DTI); *Security Over Moveable Property in Scotland: A Consultation Paper* (DTI, 1995).

[8] On this issue see Gretton , 'The Reform of Moveable Security Law' (1999) *SLT* 301.

[9] See, generally, DL Carey Miller, *Corporeal Moveables in Scots Law* (Edinburgh: W Green, 1991), 12.01–12.06.

[10] For a definitive account of the history and development of pledge and the other forms of security over moveables see Steven (n 4), 333.

[11] The various forms of common law lien—providing for the right of a creditor to retain the property of the debtor until the debt has been repaid—are, however, significant in particular contexts. See, generally, Wilson, n 6.

credit devices of hire-purchase[12] and retention of title,[13] which while not technically amounting to security, are important in modern law in meeting security needs. The floating charge, which has come to be controversial in Scotland,[14] is also significant. With regards to security over heritable (ie immovable or real) property the need for continued possession has never been an issue, since registration of the interest in security serves as the functional equivalent of according possession to the creditor, in a context in which the real right is characterised by a written title rather than by actual possession.

This paper will examine four topical matters which could be seen as representative of a tendency to follow developments in English law, or, at least, a tension in that regard: first, the impact of the decision of the House of Lords in *Sharp v Thompson*;[15] secondly, the issue of the classification of book debts for the purposes of security; thirdly, developments in standard security law and, finally, recent case law concerning a problem relating to the liability of a spouse for the business debts of his or her partner.

II. *SHARP V THOMPSON*: BENEFICIAL INTEREST AND OTHER DIFFICULTIES

Sharp v Thompson,[16] concerned with the frequently encountered issue of competing claims to property in the context of insolvency, raised fundamental questions concerning Scots property law,[17] with definite implications for security. The jurisprudence of the Court of Session[18] is straightforward and clear[19]—as, arguably, the common law is; unfortunately, however, the House of Lords' jurisprudence[20] is far from a model of clarity, nor, indeed, has it been enthusiastically met.[21] This case deals with fundamental issues of property law but it is relevant to security in being concerned with the competing claims which may arise when insolvency occurs in the circumstances of an incomplete transaction concerned with the transmission of title to land.

12 Regulated by the (UK) Consumer Credit Act 1974.

13 See Carey Miller, n 9.

14 See, eg, Robert Rennie, 'To *Sharp v Thomson*—an Heir' 2000 *SLT* (News) 247, where the learned writer refers to the argument that 'floating charges themselves do damage to our property and registration laws since they require no recording in the Register of Sasines or registration in the Land Registry even where they affect land'.

15 1997 SC(HL) 66

16 Ibid.

17 See, eg, Gretton, 'The Integrity of Property Law and of the Property Registers' 2001 *SLT* (News) 135.

18 1995 SC 455.

19 See my comments in 'Transfer of Ownership' in Reid and Zimmermann (n 2), 301–4.

20 1997 SC (HL) 66 (also reported in: 1997 SLT 636; 1997 SCLR 328).

21 The extensive critical literature is cited in full in the Scottish Law Commission's, *Discussion Paper on Sharp v Thompson* (SLC Paper No 114), July 2001, 4, n 21. For a

In 1989 the purchasers (P) concluded missives to (ie contracted to buy) a flat owned by a construction company (C). In due course possession was given in return for payment of the price, however, contrary to normal practice, no deed of disposition was delivered by the seller on payment by the purchaser. Without registration of the disposition, the purchasers could not become owners. Accordingly, for a period of fourteen months, following full payment by P, C retained ownership while P, on the accepted view,[22] had no more than possession on the basis of a personal right.

Prior to the construction of the property, C had borrowed money from a bank, the loan being secured by a floating charge. A floating charge is a security device which floats over the assets of a corporate debtor pending 'crystalisation', ie actuation by a certain event, typically liquidation. Because no real right of security attaches pending the actuating event, the debtor is free to deal with the property. The floating charge, developed as an 'equitable security' in English law,[23] was introduced into Scots law by the Companies (Floating Charges) (Scotland) Act 1961.[24]

On 10 August 1990 the bank appointed receivers, and within the terms of section 53(7) of the Insolvency Act 1986, the floating charge crystallised. On the previous day the disposition had been delivered to the purchasers' solicitors, but it was only recorded in the Register of Sasines on 21 August—well after crystalisation. The issue before the court was whether the floating charge had attached to the property concerned. This depended on whether, on the date of crystalisation, the flat formed part of the 'property then subject to the charge', ie the property of C, within the meaning of section 53(7).

The House of Lords, in reversing the decision of the Court of Session, held that the purchasers, having paid the price and received a disposition, were to be protected against the sellers' insolvency, even though ownership had not passed to them. The concept of 'beneficial interest', in terms of

comparative law perspective see especially: Reid, 'Equity triumphant: *Sharp v Thompson*' (1996)1 *ELR*, 464; Gretton, 'Scots law in shock: real rights and equitable interests' (1998) 6 *Eur Rev of Private Law*, 403; Ralf Michaels, 'Sharp Distinctions and Floating Transactions—a German view of *Sharp v Thomson*' (1998) 6 *Eur Rev of Private Law* 407; EG Dacoronia '*Sharp v Thomson* and the Principle of Publicity according to Greek Law' (1998) *Eur Rev of Private Law* 413; Anya Fenge 'Englisches Kreditsicherungsrecht versus schottisches Sachenrecht' 2000 *Zeitschrift für vergleichende Rechtswissenschaft* 410 and 'Floating Charge im schottischen Sachenrecht' 2000 *Zeitschrift für europäisches Privatrecht* 342.

[22] See *The Laws of Scotland: Stair Memorial Encyclopaedia* 'Property', vol 18 (1993), paras 606, 640.

[23] See *Government Stock Investment Co v Manila Railway Co.* [1897] AC 81; *Illingworth v Houldsworth* [1904] AC 355. See, generally, Lionel Smith, 'Security' in Peter Birks (ed), *English Private Law*, vol I (Oxford: Oxford University Press, 2000), 5.85–90.

[24] The issue of compatibility with Scottish conveyancing practice was raised by the late Professor W A Wilson in 'Floating Charges' 1962 SLT (News) 53, 55. Difficulties arising in the interaction between a floating charge and a standard security have been identified in recent research: see Scott C Styles, 'Floating Charges and Subsequent Securities' (2001) 6 *SLPQ* 73.

orthodox thinking only known to Scots law in the self-contained area of trusts,[25] was applied to achieve this end. The Lords' starting point was the proposition that one who has delivered a conveyance and accepted payment can no longer be said to hold a beneficial interest in the property. On this analysis, a beneficial interest passed to the transferee although the transferor remained technically owner until such time as the conveyance was registered. The obstacle of the seller's remaining capable of passing a good title to a bona fide third party acquirer, was dealt with by a proposition which, applying questionable logic, assumes a controlling role for the notion of beneficial interest. This approach can be seen in the dictum 'ability to commit such a fraud does not amount to a beneficial right of property'.[26] The obvious difficulty with this proposition is its circularity in answering the question by assuming the very premise which needs to be established—ie whether Scots law recognises a general concept of 'beneficial interest' having something of the quality of a real right.

Section 53(7) of the Insolvency Act 1986 provides that on appointment of a receiver the floating charge attaches to the property of the debtor company. In construing the section, it was stated that regard should be had of the substance and reality of the debtor's interest, and that common sense should be applied:

> There is in my view no principle which requires that the word "property" occurring in relation to crystallisation of a floating charge must be given the restricted meaning sought by the respondents. There is on the other hand everything to be said for giving it a practical, commonsense meaning which is likely to produce fair and equitable results between the parties affected by the crystallisation.[27]

In effect the House of Lords took the radical step of creating a new category of property in the concept of beneficial interest; moreover, although it sought to restrict the innovation to the limited circumstances of the crystallisation of a floating charge it is doubtful whether this was competent—and, hence, effective—given that what was truly in issue was a fundamental property question.[28] The decision has been criticised on a number of grounds with the call for reform becoming more urgent[29] since *Burnett's Trs v Grainger*[30] extended the principle from receivership to sequestration, and thus by implication to other insolvency regimes as well.

[25] See now Reid, 'Patrimony not Equity in the Trust in Scotland', in JM Milo and SM Smits, *Trusts in Mixed Legal Systems* (Nijmegen: Ars Aequi Libri, 2001), 19, 21–2.

[26] 1997 SC (HL) 66 at 77C per Lord Jauncey.

[27] Per Lord Jauncy at 76 F.

[28] See my comments as cited above, n 19.

[29] See R Rennie, 'To *Sharp v Thompson*—An Heir' 2000 *SLT* (News) 247; Gretton, 'Equitable Ownership in Scots Law?' (2001) *5 ELR* 73; Styles, 'Sharp Pains for Scots Property Law: the case of Burnett's Trustees v Grainger' 2000 *SLT* (News) 305.

[30] 2000 SLT (St Ct) 116; appeal to Inner House of Court of Session heard 12, 13 Feb 2002.

In a discussion paper published in July 2001 the Scottish Law Commission (SLC) has invited comment on certain provisional proposals directed to the perceived problems associated with the decision in *Sharp v Thompson*. These proposals are directed to two separate ends, first, to secure the restoration of the fundamental position of Scots law regarding the principles of derivative acquisition, and, secondly, to adjust the relevant laws to provide enhanced protection to an acquiring party from the circumstances of insolvency. The first proposal is outwith present scope but the second aim, being relevant to security, may be elaborated upon in brief terms.

A distinction must be made depending upon whether the disposition was delivered after or before sequestration. The case of post-sequestration delivery involves the possible problem of an unknown existing state of insolvency. This difficulty may arise by reason of the unavoidable delay—between the relevant court order of sequestration and its publication through registration—happening to coincide with delivery of the disposition (a deed of conveyance) and payment of the price. The SLC provisionally proposes an extended period of grace for permitted dealings by a sequestrated party. The period would extend from the date of sequestration to seven days after registration of the insolvency (effectively notice to the world at large to henceforth deal with the trustee) provided that the acquirer was in good faith and gave value on receiving the disposition.

As the SLC explains the case of pre-sequestration delivery in theory raises the possibility of a 'race to the register' between the acquiring party and the trustee but, in practice, the trustee would not normally compete because value has been received by payment of the price to credit of the insolvent estate.[31] Even if the trustee did feel justified in seeking to secure the property for the insolvent estate the formalities involved give the acquiring party a head-start.

Pending registration, the risk of prejudice, through supervening insolvency, to an acquirer who has made payment and received the disposition is largely a theoretical one. The SLC nonetheless proposes a twenty-one day freeze from the date of registration of the first order of sequestration on the rationale that '[t]he trustee should be barred from completing title for a period which is sufficiently long to allow an acquirer, acting with expedition and in accordance with normal conveyancing practice, to register his deed.'[32] An apparent difficulty with this solution is that it appears to concede the legitimacy of a bad faith act by the trustee.[33]

[31] The SLC Discussion Paper (3.21) argues that good faith is not required in a 'race to the register' context because 'the winner is not disqualified merely because he knew that a competitor was also running'. But in the situation in which the seller's estate has already benefited to the extent of the price it would, arguably, amount to bad faith for the insolvent seller's trustee to seek also to obtain the property.

[32] SLC Discussion Paper, para 4.9.

[33] See n 31.

The SLC has made counterpart provisional 'period of grace' proposals applicable to the circumstances of the liquidation or voluntary administration of insolvent companies, floating charges and receiverships as well as for the various forms of execution against property. In these areas also, the aim is to avoid the potential difficulty of the period of vulnerability—between payment and the obtaining of a real right by the acquirer—which appears to be endemic to the Scottish system of conveyancing.[34]

On one view, the proposed solutions would substitute a limited and regulated statutory form of 'beneficial interest' for the blanket one which, arguably, arises from the House of Lords decision in *Sharp v Thompson*.[35] As a reform restricted to the circumstances of conveyancing the better view is that the proposal, if implemented, would be no more than a limited exception to the normal consequences of the transmission of property and, as such, would not affect the distinction between real and personal rights.

III. FIXED AND FLOATING CHARGES IN BOOK DEBTS

In terms of provisions in a chapter in the Companies Act 1985 concerned with the registration of charges in Scotland, a charge to confer security over company property is void unless registered within 21 days of creation.[36] From the point of view of this requirement, a charge may be a security over various forms of incorporeal moveable property including the book debts[37] of a company.[38] But the clause 'so far as any security on the company's property or any part of it is conferred by the charge'[39] shows that the section does not seek to address the fundamental question of the competence of such a charge. It has already been noted that Scots law in 1961 adopted an English development which allows a company to secure any debt or obligation (including a cautionary obligation) by a floating charge 'over all or any part of the property ... which may from time to time be comprised in its property and undertaking.'[40]

[34] Because the system, through its historical development, leaves a dangerous gap between payment of the price by the transferee, on the obtaining of possession, and the acquiring of a title on the act of recording in the Register of Sasines or registration in the Land Registry.

[35] 1997 SC(HL) 66.

[36] Companies Act 1985 s 410(2).

[37] Wilson, *Scottish Law of Debt* (n 6), 106 identifies a book debt as 'a debt arising in the course of a business which would or could in the ordinary course of business by entered in well-kept books relating to that business whether it is in fact entered in the books of the business or not' (see *Independent Automatic Sales Ltd. v Knowles* [1962] 1 WLR 974, 983).

[38] Companies Act 1985 s 410(4) (c)(i).

[39] Companies Act 1985 s 410(2).

[40] Companies Act 1985 s 462(1). Regarding important issues of the ranking of floating charges see Styles, n 24.

An issue long controversial in English law,[41] is whether a charge over present and future book debts takes effect as a fixed security or as a floating charge. Where a company asset is subject to a fixed charge, the company is prohibited from disposing of it or creating a charge over it but an asset subject to a floating charge can be dealt with in the normal course of business. The difference is also important because in principle, on insolvency, a fixed charge ranks higher than a floating charge; classification as a fixed or floating charge may determine the issue of priority over the proceeds of book debts.[42]

In *New Bullas Trading Ltd*[43] the Court of Appeal upheld a scheme to create a fixed charge over present and future debts while leaving the debtor company free to apply the paid proceeds to the ordinary course of its business, in the normal way.[44] Earlier in *In Re Brightlife Ltd,*[45] Hoffmann J, as he then was, took the view that entitlement to deal with proceeds was only consistent with a floating charge—with consequent implications for the relative standing of the security. The decision in *Bullas* has been brought into question by a recent decision of the New Zealand Court of Appeal, *Re Brumark Investments Ltd v Agnew.*[46]

In *Brumark,* a company created in favour of its bank a fixed charge over present and future book debts with the proceeds subject to a floating charge, unless the bank ordered payment into a frozen account when proceeds would be subject to a fixed charge. The question before the court was whether a company could create a fixed charge over book debts which could not be further charged or disposed of but, once collected, would be subject to the floating charge. At first instance,[47] Fisher J followed *New Bullas* and upheld its tandem fixed/floating system.[48] This decision was reversed in the New Zealand Court of Appeal [49] which reaffirmed the orthodox view that a charge on book debts was necessarily floating if the debtor company retained control over the debts and their proceeds.[50]

[41] See Roy Goode, 'Charges over book debts: a missed opportunity' (1994) 110 *LQR* 592.

[42] In terms of s 175(2)(b) of the Insolvency Act 1986 preferential debts (s 386 and Schedule 6; income tax, VAT, various forms of duty, pension contributions, remuneration of employees, etc) 'have priority over the claims of holders of debentures secured by, or holders of, any floating charge created by the company, and shall be paid accordingly out of any property comprised in or subject to that charge'.

[43] [1994] BCC 36

[44] Professor Roy Goode finds a fallacy of reasoning in this decision in the proposition that 'the characterisation of the security over book debts can be divorced from the contractual provisions relating to the application of the proceeds'; see n 41, at 601.

[45] [1987] Ch 200.

[46] [2000] 1 BCLC 353.

[47] (1999) 19 NZTC 15, 159; noted (1999) 115 *LQR* 365.

[48] DW McLauchlan, 'New Bullas in New Zealand: Round Two' (2000) 116 *LQR* 211 notes that the decision recognises 'that there is no reason in principle or policy why a debenture should not provide for a fixed charge on uncollected book debts and a floating charge on their proceeds'.

[49] [2000] 1 BCLC 353.

[50] See McLauchlan, n 48, at 212–13.

The issue of whether a fixed charge over uncollected debts can co-exist with a floating charge over proceeds has not been specifically addressed in Scots law. In principle one might urge that Scots law would do well not to follow *Brumark* but should rather adhere to the earlier but more progressive *Bullas* approach. However, the existing position of Scots law rather means that such a point of view is hypothetical. To bring into being a charge which functions as a fixed security over incorporeal moveable property requires compliance with cumbersome form. A right in security over incorporeal movable property—like an out-and-out transmission of property—requires a formal act of assignation[51] and where the subject of the security is a debt its assignation must be intimated to the party by whom payment is due.[52] This second act is necessary to perfect the right of security in the sense of making it a real security right which, of course, it must be to constitute a preference on liquidation. As already noted, a charge created in this way must be registered within 21 days; failing this the charge becomes void and any debt sought to be secured becomes due.[53]

IV. STANDARD SECURITY: GENERAL DEVELOPMENTS

Distinctive provision governing real security over interests in land—heritable security—is part of Scotland's land law which, most significantly, does not know any general concept of equitable ownership.[54] Professor Kenneth Reid has made this point recently in a comment on the 'mixed system' legal family to which Scots law belongs:

> [i]t is characteristic of mixed legal systems that the mixture is unevenly distributed. Some areas of law are mainly civilian in character, while others draw heavily from the common law. The law of property is always civilian. Mixed systems do not have a separate system of equity, and do not acknowledge the distinction between legal and beneficial ownership.[55]

The main modern form of heritable security, the 'standard security', was introduced as the primary vehicle into a complex context representing a long continuous history of development which was much modified by 19th century legislation.[56]

[51] The Transmission of Moveable Property (Scotland) Act 1862 provides for optional forms.

[52] *Tay Valley Joinery Ltd v CF Financial Services* Ltd 1987 SLT 207, 211. See also *The Laws of Scotland: Stair Memorial Encyclopaedia* 'Rights in Security', vol 20 (1992), paras 46–7; Gretton and Reid, *Conveyancing*, 2nd edn (Edinburgh: W Green, 1999), 22.03–22.04.

[53] Companies Act 1985 s 410(3).

[54] TB Smith, *British Justice: The Scottish Contribution*, Hamlyn Lectures (London: Stevens, 1961), 190: 'no dichotomy between "legal" and "equitable" property.'

[55] 'Patrimony not Equity in the Trust in Scotland', n 25, 19.

[56] For a comprehensive account see WM Gordon, *Scottish Land Law*, 2nd edn (Edinburgh: W Green, 1999), ch 20.

In terms of the Conveyancing and Feudal Reform (Scotland) Act 1970 the method of creating a heritable security over an interest in land for securing a debt is through the use of the standard security.[57] The term 'interest in land' is defined in the Act to mean 'any estate or interest in land, other than an entailed estate or any interest therein, which is capable of being owned or held as a separate interest and to which a title may be recorded in the Register of Sasines'.[58] However, in terms of the Abolition of Feudal Tenure etc (Scotland) Act 2000 (not in force at time of writing[59]) the term 'interest in land' in the 1970 Act is deleted and replaced by 'land or real right in land'.[60] The Land Registration (Scotland) Act 1979[61] requires a heritable security to be registered, and the definition adopted is almost identical to that found in the 1970 Act, but 'interest in land' includes 'estate, interest, servitude or other heritable right in or over land, including a heritable security but excluding a lease which is not a long lease'.[62]

A standard security can be created to function in two distinct forms: one combining the personal obligation to repay with the grant of the real right of security; the other as a pure security form applicable where the personal obligation secured is constituted in a separate instrument.[63] The former is normally used to secure a loan to be applied to the purchase of heritable property (colloquially a 'mortgage bond') whereas the latter is generally used in a commercial context.[64]

The possibility of enlightened borrowing of compatible rules or doctrines is something which comparative law seeks to facilitate. In the context of English and Scots law, however, it is understandable likely that there may be Scottish concern that an English law position is being followed because of the dominant position of English law in the British context rather than for good comparative law reasons.[65] Concern of this sort may be misplaced, unless, of course, the matter is viewed from the a-comparative perspective of retaining native purity regardless.

[57] Section 9(3). The standard text on standard securities is DJ Cusine, *Standard Securities*, (Edinburgh: Law Society of Scotland, 1991).

[58] 1970 Act s 9(8)(b)

[59] See s 77 re commencement.

[60] Schedule 12, para 30(2)(a)(ii).

[61] Section 2(3)

[62] Section 28(1); also subject to pending amended by the Abolition of Feudal Tenure etc (Scotland) Act 2000, Schedule 12, para 39(11)(c) to read: '(a) means any right in or over land, including any heritable security or servitude but excluding any lease which is not a long lease; and (b) where the context admits, includes the land.'

[63] Respectively, Forms A & B of Schedule 2 of the Conveyancing and Feudal Reform (Scotland) Act 1970.

[64] Both forms reflect the accessory character of security; see below.

[65] The longstanding Scottish debate concerning the Sale of Goods Act 1979 is a case in point; see my comments in 'Scots and South African Property: Problem Transplants' in Elizabeth Cooke (ed), *Modern Studies in Property Law*, vol I, 2001, 293.

The Mortgage[66] Rights (Scotland) Act 2001 could be said to reflect 'policy borrowing' from English law. The Act follows the general policy of 1970s English legislation[67] in protecting a residential property standard security debtor from the strict application of a creditor's enforcement rights. The Scottish legislation, however, functions in a distinct way. The debtor must invoke the Act by application to court, this being consistent with the fact that, in principle, a standard security can be enforced without recourse to judicial process. The court is given a discretion under the Act to suspend the exercise of a creditor's enforcement rights, being enjoined to take account of four factors in arriving at its decision. The factors are: the nature of and reasons for default; the debtor's ability to fulfil the relevant obligations within a reasonable period; any action by the creditor to assist in the process of fulfilment; the ability of the debtor and other residents at the premises concerned to find reasonable alternative accommodation.[68]

The accessory nature of security was noted in a matter in which the granting of a standard security was mooted as a means of dealing with a claimed imbalance in the context of the division of matrimonial assets on divorce. The factual details are not important for present purposes but the following dictum of Sheriff Principal Nicholson is worth commenting upon:

> if no order is pronounced against the pursuer for payment by her of a capital sum to the defender, there is, as I see it, no way in which the relationship of debtor and creditor can be constituted with the consequence that there can be no debt which can properly be secured by the grant of a standard security.[69]

This may seem a trite observation in the context of the relevant legislation[70] and forms[71] but seemingly obvious points can have significant implications. As Professors Gretton and Reid have pointed out[72] the importance of the above dictum is shown in another recent case in which a standard security was held to be a nullity because its terms founded the security on an obligation which

[66] The use—by the new Scottish legislature—of the English law term 'mortgage' caused Sheriff NPM Morrison to proclaim in dismay '[p]erhaps we should just abandon Scots law now'; see (2001) 42 *Greens Civil Law Bulletin* 2. Although as a technical term of art Scots law does not know the term 'mortgage bond' it is in general colloquially use and the Scottish Parliament may well have considered it a more 'user friendly' term.

[67] The Administration of Justice Act 1970 s 36, as amended by the Administration of Justice Act 1773, s 8.

[68] For a critical comment on this Act see Reid and Gretton, *Conveyancing 2001*, (Edinburgh: W Green, 2002) (in press).

[69] *Trotter v Trotter* 2001 SLT (Sh Ct) 42, 47. For more detailed comment on this case see Reid and Gretton, loc. cit.

[70] See Conveyancing and Feudal Reform (Scotland) Act 1970, eg, ss 9(3), 9(8)(c), 20(1) (in respect s 20(1)—noted in *UCB Bank PLC v Hire Foulis Ltd (in liquidation)* 1999 SCLR 35—the wording 'arising from the contract to which the security relates' is significant).

[71] See Schedule 2, Forms A and B to the Conveyancing and Feudal Reform (Scotland) Act 1970 where reference is made to the underlying 'personal obligation'.

[72] See n 68.

had in fact been superseded.[73] It is implicit in the maxim *accessorium principale sequitur* that the disappearance of the principal must necessarily cause the extinction of the accessory.

V. STANDARD SECURITY PROBLEMS: GUARANTEES OF A SPOUSE'S BUSINESS DEBTS

The existence of a properly constituted cautionary obligation of guarantee means, of course, that the estate of the third party cautioner is potentially liable to the creditor in the event of the principal debtor's failure to meet the liability concerned. Where one spouse or personal relationship partner stands cautioner for another there is obvious potential for loss to the cautioner, including, of course, the possible loss of the heritable property which is the debtors' home.

Issues relevant to standard security have arisen in developments in Scots law—following precedents of English law—concerning the position of one party in a personal relationship affected by the securing of a commercial loan to the other party. In the circumstance of marriage, or a *de facto* sexual relationship, one party may be burdened with the debts of the other.[74] Scots common law does not protect female cautioners (sureties) under the principle of the Roman *Senatus Consultum Velleianum* and the *Authentica si qua mulier*.[75] A woman of full capacity is bound by her obligations, including those of a cautionary nature without any requirement of renunciation of benefits.

The English decision in *Barclays Bank v O'Brien*[76] appears to have influenced developments in Scots law.[77] In this case it was held that knowledge that the principal debtor is in an intimate relationship with the proposed guarantor should put the creditor on notice as to the possibility of the guarantor's consent having been obtained unfairly. Arising from this, any right the guarantor may have to contest the guarantee should be available against the creditor as well as against the principal debtor. As a response to *O'Brien* the standard practice of banks is to insist that the guarantor has separate legal representation from that of the principal debtor.

The essential thinking of *O'Brien* was extended to Scotland by the

[73] *Albatown Ltd v Credential Group Ltd* 2001 GWD 27-1102.

[74] See Gretton 'Sexually Transmitted Debt' 1997 *SLT* (News) 195; Professor Gretton acknowledges the provenance of his title as Miranda Hope's, 'Equity's Treatment of Sexually Transmitted Debt [1997] *Feminist Legal Studies* 35.

[75] See HF Jolowicz *Roman Foundations of Modern Law* (Oxford: Clarendon Press, 1957), 171–2; see also comments by Professor Gretton, loc cit.

[76] [1994] 1 AC 180.

[77] See Euan McKendrick 'The Undue Influence of English Law', in HL MacQueen (ed) , *Scots Law in the 21st Century* (Edinburgh: W Green, 1996), 214.

House of Lords in *Smith v Bank of Scotland*.[78] Lord Clyde (a Scottish Law Lord) addressed the policy issue specifically:

> I have not been persuaded that there are sufficiently cogent grounds for refusing the extension to Scotland of the development which has been achieved in England by the decision in *Barclays Bank Plc v O'Brien*. On the contrary, I take the view that it is desirable to recognise a corresponding extension of the law in Scotland.[79]

One may contrast this dictum to the approach of Lord President Hope in the First Division of the Court of Session[80] who stated that reform should be a matter left to the Scottish Law Commission. In *Smith* a wife sought to reduce (ie set aside) a standard security—given jointly with her husband over their matrimonial home—in favour of the defender bank which had financed a business loan to a firm in which her husband was a partner.

The House of Lords has extended the policy basis of *O'Brien* to Scotland but, as Professor Gretton has shown, the ratios are not the same.[81] This has been reaffirmed by later cases such as *Royal Bank of Scotland v Clark*.[82] However, the essential point remains that in terms of basic policy position Scots law has adopted the English position—not, of course, in itself a necessarily negative fact.

In a similar vein, in *Royal Bank of Scotland Plc v Wilson*[83] two brothers, acting in partnership, and their wives granted standard securities to the bank. The debts secured included any business debts of any party. After such debts were incurred, the bank sought to enforce the security. Both wives resisted enforcement on the basis the bank should have told them what was happening, and in failing to do so, its conduct amounted to bad faith. It was held, however, that since both wives had received legal advice when executing the securities, and with no undue influence or misrepresentation being averred,[84] the defence was irrelevant.

In *Ahmed v Clydesdale Bank Plc*[85] a husband and wife had purchased a flat financed by a loan from a bank and secured by a standard security over the property, the deed concerned providing for present and future liability. Some years later, when the husband wished to obtain a further advance for business purposes the bank asked the wife to sign a guarantee but she refused to do so. The advance was nonetheless granted. In an action to reduce the standard security over her half share of the property the wife

[78] 1997 SC (HL) 111. For a valuable comment on this decision and the issue in general see ADM Forte 'Good Faith and Utmost Good Faith: Insurance and Cautionary Obligations in Scots Law', in A Forte (ed) *Good Faith in Contract and Property Law* (Oxford: Hart, 1999, 77.

[79] At 120–1.

[80] 1996 SLT 392.

[81] See above n 74, 196.

[82] 2000 SLT (Sh Ct) 101

[83] 2000 GWD 17-689

[84] See *Braithwaite v Bank of Scotland* 1999 SLT 25; on this case see Forte (n 78), 95–6.

[85] 2000 GWD 27-1037

argued that the bank had acted in bad faith in the knowledge that she was not prepared to accept liability for the further advance. Her action of reduction failed, a relevant consideration being that she had received legal advice when the original security was granted.

On one view, it was predictable that reduction would be refused because it was not contended that the validity of the standard security was affected by the circumstances under which it was granted. What seems anomalous, however, is that in the case of a pure cautionary obligation at least the implied consent of the cautioner would be required to make good his or her liability for a future advance.[86]

Finally, it may be noted that *Broadway v Clydesdale Bank plc*[87] could be taken to suggest that the floodgates of litigation may be opening up. On the basis of this decision in addition to litigation between the cautionary wife and lender, an action against the solicitor who supervised the transaction also becomes a real possibility.

VI. CONCLUSION

While the perceived need to escape from the requirement of possession by the creditor has long been a spur for reform of the law relating to security over movables, the development of commercial law, facilitating the purchase of consumer goods on credit, has tended to leave traditional security devices in the lurch. That review of the general law of security over movables is not perceived as a matter of high priority is demonstrated by the succession of official proposals for reform which have come to nothing.[88]

The pressure for a uniform law of security between England and Scotland, as a matter of commercial utility,[89] has, to a significant extent, been met by the growth of a UK commercial law. Plausible reasons of commercial expediency have driven this development.[90] In the new

86 See *The Laws of Scotland: Stair Memorial Encyclopaedia*, 'Cautionary Obligations and Representations as to Credit' vol 3 (1994), paras 909–14.

87 2000 GWD 19-763

88 See David O'Donnell & DL Carey Miller 'Security over Moveables: a Longstanding Reform Agenda in Scots Law' 1997 *ZEuP* 807.

89 The report of Professor AL Diamond 'A Review of Security Interests in Property' (1989) considered both English and Scots law and recommended legislation to introduce an Art 9 US Uniform Commercial Code approach to security interests created by agreement; although Professor Diamond recommended separate legislation and separate registries the substance of his proposal was directed towards uniformity a la Art 9 (see O'Donnell and Carey Miller, n 85, 811–14).

90 This issue goes back to Victorian Britain to which the Scottish commercial contribution was, of course, significant; see AF Rodger, 'The Codification of Commercial Law in Victorian Britain' (1992) 108 *LQR* 570, 581–2.

devolved dispensation the reserving of matters pertaining to consumer protection—notably the sale and supply of goods and hire-purchase[91]—is a limit on the development of the otherwise devolved private law. The overall picture is not a tidy one and, as certain of the developments considered in this paper show, there is a continuing tension between, on the one hand, a reform agenda driven by commercial utility, and, on the other, pressure to adhere to fundamental principles of private law. In this regard, the priority should be a legal regime which best serves the relevant interests of Scotland, achieved by reform which is functionally compatible with Scots law. While the pressures referred to have produced a certain Anglicisation of Scots security law one could hardly say that the development, in modern law, has been in ignorance or intolerance of the law of Scotland.

None of this is to say that Scots law lacks any significant internal force; the reaction of the system to *Sharp v Thompson*, discussed in this paper, puts the lie to this. It is worth noting that a proposal to extend the availability of the floating charge form of security to natural persons[92] may well have died a death as a result of this case. Developments in the important area of standard security also show the dynamic character of Scots law although, even here, English law influence can be detected.

As aspects of the law commented on in this paper show, while policy emanating from the larger and faster-developing English system may be influential, the technical development of the law proceeds in a manner which fits the native jurisprudence of Scotland. In a certain sense this represents a microcosm of the wider picture of European integration and harmonisation in the field of commercial law.

91 See the Scotland Act 1998, Schedule 5, C7.

92 A 1994 Department of Trade and Industry consultation paper, 'Security over Moveable Property in Scotland' incorporating a draft bill 'Floating Charges and Moveable Securities (Scotland)' has not come to anything.

Chapter 6

Present and Future of Real and Personal Security: England

*Gerald McCormack**

I. INTRODUCTION

This paper endeavours to address the current state of play and also to assess the likely prospects for reform of the law pertaining to real and personal security in England. 'Real security' is interpreted as meaning security over property, particularly personal property. Security over land is a particular and specialised topic where the relevant principles are well established and the law is relatively stable. By contrast, the area of personal property securities is more dynamic though English law has generally been resistant to the growing influence of Article 9 of the American Uniform Commercial Code.[1] 'Personal security' is understood as referring to the two main institutions of suretyship and independent or 'demand' guarantees.

A. 'Real Security'

English law is essentially pragmatic when it comes to the recognition of security interests in property. The overall approach however is facilitative and enabling. There are almost no limits on the category of assets that may be used as security and the procedures for the creation of security interests are quite flexible and informal. The law is pragmatic rather than functional for transactions that serve the same economic ends are often visited with different legal consequences. The latter state of affairs has attracted criticism but so far the legislature has resisted efforts to recast English law along the lines of Article 9 of the US Uniform Commercial Code. Article 9 attempts to apply similar rules to all transactions that in economic terms are

* Professor of Law, University of Manchester.

[1] It could be argued that the provisions of the Insolvency Act 1986 display the influence of Art 9. The Act introduces a new procedure—administration—designed partly for the rescue of ailing companies and during the currency of an administration there is a moratorium on the enforcement of security claims against a company. This moratorium extends to claims to repossess goods in the company's possession pursuant to reservation of title agreements. In this respect the legislation adopts a broader conception of 'security' than is common in English law.

intended to serve as security. There is a comprehensive definition of 'security interest' as meaning an interest in personal property that secures payment or performance of an obligation and also the interest of a buyer of accounts. Moreover, Article 9 embodies a near-comprehensive registration obligation, ie public notice of security interests must be given. Under English law, by contrast, certain transactions that in economic terms might be regarded as creating a security interest are not subject to any public registration or filing requirements that might alert other potential creditors or, indeed the world at large, to the existence of the security interest. This paper will look at the key features of the English law pertaining to security interests and draw some comparisons with the functional approach of Article 9.

B. What is Security?

English law is characterised by an absence of statutory definition of security interests. One must fall back on judicial interpretations that, necessarily, are conditioned and qualified by the circumstances of a particular case. A notable example is provided in the judgment of Browne-Wilkinson VC in *Re Paramount Airways* Ltd[2] where the following definition of security was accepted: 'security is created where a person (the creditor) obtains rights exercisable against some property in which the debtor has an interest in order to enforce the discharge of the debtor's obligation to the creditor.'

Clearly this is not a comprehensive definition for it does not recognise the fact that security may be granted to secure the obligations of somebody other than the grantee. Professor Sir Roy Goode, acknowledging the 'third party' issue, has defined a security interest as a right given to one party in the asset(s) of another party to secure payment or performance by that other party or by a third party.[3] On his analysis a security interest:[4]

1) arises from a transaction intended as security;
2) is a right in rem;
3) is created by a grant or declaration, not by reservation;
4) if fixed, or specific, implies a restriction on the debtor's dominion over the asset;
5) cannot be taken by the creditor over his own obligation to the debtor.

[2] [1990] BCC 130 at 149. See also the comments of Lord Scott in *Smith v Bridgend County Borough Council* [2001] UKHL 58 at para 53 that 'a contractual right enabling a creditor to sell his debtor's goods and apply the proceeds in or towards satisfaction of the debt is a right of a security character'.

[3] See RM Goode, *Legal Problems of Credit and Security*, 2nd edn (London: Sweet & Maxwell, 1988), at 1. See generally for a definitional exposition of security Fidelis Oditah, *Legal Aspects of Receivables Financing* (London: Sweet & Maxwell, 1991), ch 1.

[4] Ibid, at 1–2.

These characteristics ascribed to a security interest cannot be accepted in their entirety—in particular no (5) which suggests that it is a conceptual impossibility for a bank to be granted a charge over its own indebtedness to a customer.[5] There is a strong contrary view that a debt is simply an item of property and, like any other item of property, it may be charged to anybody that the creditor wishes.[6] This pragmatic approach appealed to Lord Hoffmann in *Re BCCI (No 8)*[7] who spoke for a unanimous House of Lords in categorically rejecting the doctrine that it was conceptually impossible for a security interest to be taken by a creditor over his own obligations to the debtor. In Lord Hoffmann's view, the law should be slow to declare a practice of the commercial community to be commercially impossible given the fact that the law was fashioned to suit the practicalities of life. He added that legal concepts, such as 'proprietary interest' and 'charge', were no more than labels given to clusters of related and self-consistent rules of law. Such concepts did not have a life of their own from which the rules were inexorably derived. In fact, English law has long taken a non-doctrinaire view towards the recognition and enforcement of security interests in property. Lord Hoffmann highlighted the example of the charge that, as he pointed out, is a security interest created without any transfer of title or possession to the beneficiary. An equitable charge could be created by an informal transaction for value and over any kind of property. The workhorse of the secured credit industry in England has traditionally been the charge, particularly the floating charge but there are many different types of security right recognized under English law. These will now be examined.

II. DIFFERENT TYPES OF SECURITY RIGHTS

There are three basic distinctions; first, between legal and equitable security interests, secondly, between possessory and non-possessory security interests and thirdly, between consensual and non-consensual security interests. These various distinctions cut across one another. The main types of security interest are mortgages, charges, pledges, and liens, both common law liens and equitable liens.

The distinction between legal and equitable security interests is perhaps most confusing to a non-common lawyer but it is easy to exaggerate the importance of the distinction in practice. The distinction stems from the historical separation between law and equity and the fact that certain kinds

[5] As was held by Millett J in *Re Charge Card Services Ltd* [1987] 1 Ch 150.

[6] See, eg, William Blair 'Cash deposits as a form of security' in *Butterworths Banking and Financial Law Review 1987*, at 163, 173–4; P Wood (1987) 8 *Co Law* 262.

[7] [1998] AC 214.

of security right were only recognised in courts of equity, as distinct from courts of common law, prior to the unification of the court structure in the 1870s. For example, a mortgage of future property was void at common law and consequently, any security interest in future personalty must necessarily be equitable in nature.[8] The distinction retains some importance in the context of priorities. Legal interests are said to bind the whole world whereas equitable interests are said to bind all, save for a bona fide purchaser of a legal interest in the same property for value without notice of the prior equitable interest. The priority issue is however affected by the question of registration because, generally speaking, a charge created by a corporate debtor is invalid in the event of the debtor going into liquidation.[9] Moreover, if an equitable security interest on property requires registration then the fact of registration should infect the holders of subsequent legal security interests in the same property with notice.

The distinction between possessory and non-possessory security interests is highly significant in practical terms. Mortgages, charges, and equitable liens are non-possessory security interests; in other words, the lender does not have possession of the items used as security whereas the pledge and the common law lien are possessory in nature, ie the lender is entrusted with possession of the items used as security. Finally, mortgages, charges and pledges are consensual security interests, ie in other words they are created by agreement between the parties. Liens, on the other hand, are non-consensual, ie they arise by operation of law, irrespective of the agreement of the parties, in certain defined circumstances. A brief description of each of these types of security right is appropriate.

A. Mortgages and Charges

In many contexts the phrases 'mortgage' and 'charge' are used interchangeably whereas in other settings 'charge' is defined so as to encompass a 'mortgage'. There is however a distinction between the two concepts. As Slade J explained in *Re Bond Worth Ltd*[10] the technical difference between a 'mortgage' and a 'charge' lies in the fact that a mortgage involves a

[8] See, eg, *Lunn vThornton* (1845) I CB 379; *Tailby v Official Receiver* (1888) 13 App Cas 523.

[9] Section 395 Companies Act 1985. See also the comments of Lord Hoffmann in *Smith v Bridgend County Borough Council* [2001] UKHL 58 at para 19: 'Section 395 . . . was intended for the protection of the creditors of an insolvent company. It was intended to give persons dealing with a company the opportunity to discover, by consulting the register, whether its assets were burdened by floating and certain fixed charges which would reduce the amount available for unsecured creditors in a liquidation. Whether this was a realistic form of protection and whether the choice of registrable charges was entirely logical is not presently relevant.'

[10] [1980] Ch 228.

conveyance of property subject to a right of redemption, whereas a charge conveys nothing and merely gives the chargee certain rights over the property as security for the loan.[11] In other words, a mortgage involves the transfer of rights of ownership whereas the phrase 'charge' is a general umbrella expression to cover a right of recourse to property for security purposes.[12] The chargee has certain rights over the property of the chargor to ensure the payment of money due or the performance of some other obligation. The chargee is entitled to resort to the property only for the purpose of satisfying some liability due to him, and, whatever the form of the transaction, the chargor has an equity of redemption to have the property restored to him once the liability has been discharged.

In *Re BCCI (No 8)* Lord Hoffmann described an equitable charge as

> a species of charge, which is a proprietary interest granted by way of security. Proprietary interests confer rights in rem which, subject to questions of registration and the equitable doctrine of purchaser for value without notice, will be binding upon third parties and unaffected by the insolvency of the owner of the property charged. A proprietary interest provided by way of security entitles the holder to resort to the property only for the purpose of satisfying some liability due to him (whether from the person providing the security or a third party) and, whatever the form of the transaction, the owner of the property retains an equity of redemption to have the property restored to him when the liability has been discharged.

B. Pledges

A pledge has been described as the actual or constructive delivery of possession of an asset to a creditor by way of security.[13] In the case of a pledge the pledgee (lender) is given possession of the items pledged whereas ownership of the items remains with the pledgor (borrower). As possessor, the pledgee is said to enjoy a 'special property' in the goods but the general property however, or what might be termed 'ownership' still belongs to the pledgor.[14] To constitute a pledge, delivery of possession need not be contemporaneous with the making of a loan but it should be stressed that

[11] Ibid, at 250.

[12] See also the comments of Buckley LJ in *Swiss Bank Corporation v Lloyds Bank Ltd* [1982] AC 584: 'An equitable charge which is not an equitable mortgage is said to be created when property is expressly or constructively made liable or specifically appropriated, to the discharge of a debt or some other obligation, and confers on the chargee a right of realisation by judicial process, that is to say, by the appointment of a receiver or an order for sale . . . '

[13] See generally Goode, op cit, at 10 and see also EL Sykes *The Law of Securities*, 4th edn (Sydney: Land Book Co, 1986), 649–62 and NE Palmer, *Bailment*, 2nd edn (London: Sweet & Maxell, 992) Ch 24.

[14] The pledgee has an inherent right to sell unredeemed chattels after the loan period has expired. In *Matthew v TM Sutton Ltd* [1994] 4 All ER 793 it was held that a pledgee who sells unredeemed chattels for more than the sum owed by the pledgor holds the surplus as a fiduciary on trust for the pledgor.

the actual or constructive delivery of possession is indispensable. The requirement of delivery means that the class of assets capable of forming the subject matter of a pledge is confined to goods and to documentary intangibles which are 'documents embodying title to goods, money or securities such that the right to these assets is vested in the holder of the document for the time being and can be transferred by delivery with any necessary indorsement.'[15] Consequently pledges may be created in respect of bills of lading and other documents of title to goods but not over common commercial contracts. The fact that a bill of lading may be pledged signifies the usefulness of pledges for the financing of international trade. The requirement however that a creditor takes a pledge over a document which is actually a document of title suggests the limitations of the pledge as a security vehicle. Bills of lading are documents of title and so too are bearer share certificates but not warehouse receipts nor certificates relating to registered shares.[16] On the other hand, the usefulness of the pledge mechanism has been extended by judicial validation of three techniques. The first is that of 'constructive delivery of possession'. The second is that of attornment—if goods are in the possession of a third party rather than the debtor, the third party can 'attorn' to the creditor i.e. undertake to hold the goods for the benefit of the creditor as is demonstrated by the following example:[17]

> If, for instance, the debtor is an art dealer who has deposited works of art with an auction house, the auction house can, by attorning in favour of the creditor (ie by confirming, at the request of the debtor, that it holds the works of art on behalf of the creditor), transfer constructive possession in the works of art to the creditor.

The concepts of 'constructive delivery of possession' and attornment were explained by the Privy Council in *Official Assignee of Madras v Mercantile Bank of India Ltd*:[18]

> At common law a pledge could not be created except by a delivery of possession of the thing pledge, either actual or constructive. It involved a bailment. If the pledgor had the actual goods in his physical possession, he could effect the pledge by physical delivery; in other cases he could give possession by some symbolic act, such as handing over the key of the store in which they were. If, however, the goods were in the custody of a third person, who held for the bailor so that in law his possession was that of the bailor, the pledge could could be effected by a change of the possession of the third party, that is by an order to him from the pledgor to hold for the pledgee, the change being perfected by the third party attorning to the pledgee,

[15] Goode, op cit, at 11.

[16] *Harrold v Plenty* [1901] 2 Ch 314.

[17] Richard Calnan 'Taking Security in England', in Michael Bridge and Robert Stevens (eds), *Cross-Border Security and Insolvency* (Oxford: Oxford University Press 2001), 17 at 19.

[18] [1935] AC 53 at 58–9.

that is acknowledging that he thereupon held for him; there was thus a change of possession and a constructive delivery; the goods in the hands of the third party became by this process in the possession constructively of the pledgee.

The third technique is that of the 'trust receipt'. The fact that goods are released back by the 'pledgee' to the 'pledgor' will not prejudice the claim to a pledge in certain circumstances where the release takes place under the auspices of a trust receipt. The 'trust receipt' is a document that permits a pledgee to release goods to his pledgor as agent for sale and trustee of the proceeds but simultaneously maintaining his pledge interest.[19]

Reference has occasionally been made to another form of possessory security right based on contract; namely the contractual lien.[20] It is clear that contractual liens and pledges are akin. Certainly they share many of the same characteristics; in particular they both depend on delivery of possession to the creditor. Millett LJ however distinguished between them in *Re Cosslett (Contractors) Ltd*[21] saying that in the case of a pledge the owner delivers possession to the creditor as security, whereas in the case of a lien the creditor retains possession of goods previously delivered to him for some other purpose.

C. Liens—Common Law Liens

A common law lien is a right to retain possession of an asset until discharge of an outstanding debt and is to be distinguished from an equitable lien that is essentially a form of non-possessory security interest arising by operation of law. The distinction between the two concepts has been expounded in the following terms:[22]

> An equitable lien differs from a common law lien in that a common law lien is founded on possession and, except as modified by statute, merely confers a right to detain until payment, whereas an equitable lien, which exists quite irrespective of possession, confers on the holder the right to a judicial sale.

In *Tappenden v Artus*[23] Diplock LJ compared the common law remedy of a possessory lien with other 'primitive remedies' such as abatement of nuisance, self-defence or ejection of trespassers to land. The remedy was a self-help one. Diplock LJ said the possessory lien was a remedy in rem exercisable on the goods and its exercise required no intervention by the courts, for it was exercisable only by a person who had actual possession of the

[19] See generally *North Western Bank Ltd v Poynter, Son and Macdonalds* [1895] AC 56; *Re David Allester* [1922] 2 Ch 211.

[20] *George Barker Ltd v Eynon* [1974] 1 WLR 462.

[21] [1998] Ch 495.

[22] *Halsbury's Laws of England*, 4th edn (London: Butterworths, 1973), vol 28, para 551.

[23] [1964] 2 QB 185.

goods subject to the lien. A common law lien afforded a defence to an action for recovery of the goods by a person who, but for the lien, would be entitled to immediate possession.

Common law liens are non-consensual in nature and are confined to historically determined situations.[24] Statute however has sometimes recognised or created lien-type rights. Section 88 Civil Aviation Act 1982 which was considered in *Bristol Airport plc v Powdrill*[25] serves as a case in point. The section conferred on airport authorities the right to detain aircraft to force payment of unpaid airport charges. The Court of Appeal took the view that the statutory right of detention was a 'lien or security' over property within the meaning of section 248 of the Insolvency Act 1986. In general a common law lien equals a passive power of detention. The lienee may however, have a power of sale in the case of a statutorily-conferred lien as is the situation with section 88 Civil Aviation Act 1982. Moreover, statute sometimes invests a lienee with a power of sale in other circumstances.[26]

D. *Liens—Equitable Liens*

Equitable liens are more expansive in nature than common law liens in that they are not dependent on possession.[27] It has even been suggested that 'the equitable lien is a dangerous and elusive enemy of the law of [pari passu distribution of a debtor's assets in an insolvency]' and that as 'applied to some bankruptcy cases, it seems as well named as the Holy Roman Empire, for it is neither equitable nor a lien'.[28] An equitable lien is a form of equitable charge arising by operation of law. In other words, it[29] is a right against property which arises automatically by implication of equity to

[24] See Bridge *Personal Property Law*, 2nd edn (London: Blackstone, 1996), at 142–3. Professor Bridge points to general confluence between the conferment of a lien and the exercise of a common calling. See also AP Bell, *Modern Law of Personal Property in England and Ireland* (London: Butterworths, 1989), at 138–9.

[25] [1990] Ch 744.

[26] See, eg, Torts (Interference with Goods) Act 1977, ss 12 and 13. Moreover, under the Civil Procedure Rules 1998, r 25.1(1)(C)(v) the court has power on the application of any party to a cause or matter to order the sale of any property which is the subject of a claim or as to which any question may arise on a claim and which is of a perishable nature or which for any other good reason it is desirable to sell quickly.

[27] Adopting the words of Lord Mersey in *Kreglinger v New Patagonia Meat and Cold Storage Co Ltd* [1914] AC 25 at 46. See generally on equitable liens the decision of the High Court of Australia in *Hewett v Court* (1983) 149 CLR 639 which case is extensively discussed by Hardingham 'Equitable Liens for the Recovery of Purchase Money' (1985) 15 *Melbourne University Law Review* 65.

[28] M McLaughlin (1927) 60 *Harvard Law Review* 341 at 389, referred to by Phillips in ch 39 of NE Palmer and E McKendrick (eds), *Interests in Goods*, 2nd edn (London: LLP, 1998), at pp. 992-993.

[29] (1983) 149 CLR 639. The case is extensively discussed by Hardingham 'Equitable Liens for the Recovery of Purchase Money' (1985) 15 *Melbourne University Law Review* 65.

secure the discharge of an actual or potential indebtedness.[30] An equitable lien may be enforced by obtaining an order of sale from the court.[31] The best known equitable liens are the vendor's lien for unpaid purchase money and the purchaser's lien; both arising in the case of contracts for the sale of land.[32] The former is founded on the principle that 'a person, having got the estate of another, shall not, as between them, keep it, and not pay the consideration'.[33] The purchaser's lien rests on the converse principle that he who has agreed to convey property in return for a purchase price will not be allowed to keep the price if he fails to convey the property as agreed.[34]

III. ENGLISH LAW AND THE ESSENTIALS OF A MODERN LAW OF SECURITY INTERESTS

It is widely believed, at least among the international lending community that a modern law of security interests must be founded on five key elements.[35] First, the security right must adhere to the essential qualities of a property right (right in rem). Secondly, the law should provide for the granting of security in the widest possible range of circumstances. Thirdly, the existence of a security right over property must be effectively publicised. Fourthly, there should be a rapid and cost-effective means of recovering the debt from the secured asset and, fifthly, the cost of creating, maintaining and exercising the right should be kept at a reasonable level.[36]

Adopting a broad-brush approach, English law essentially implements these principles.[37] First, security rights in English law are rights in rem. In other words, they are enforceable against third parties and not just *inter partes*, ie between debtor and creditor. Secondly, English law does provide for the granting of security in the widest possible range of circumstances.

[30] Ibid, at 220. Reference was made *inter alia* in this connection to *Re Bernstein* [1925] Ch 12 at 17–18 and *Re Bond Worth Ltd* [1980] Ch 228 at 251.

[31] *Bowles v Rogers* (1800) 31 ER 957; *Re Stucley* [1906] 1 Ch 67.

[32] Under s 41-3 Sale of Goods Act 1979 an unpaid seller of goods has a possessory lien and also a right to stop goods in transit but the courts have refused to recognise equitable liens in sale of goods transactions that operate independently of the legislation—*Re Wait* [1927] 1 Ch 606.

[33] *Mackreth v Symmons* (1808) 15 Ves 329, at 340; 33 ER 778, at 782.

[34] See *Rose v Watson* (1864) 10 HLC 672 at 684.

[35] See Fairgrieve 'Reforming Secured Transactions Laws in Central and Eastern Europe' [1998] *EBLR* 254.

[36] See also the Preface to the Model Law on Secured Transactions (London: European Bank for Reconstruction and Development (EBRD), 1994).

[37] See for a comparison between the Model Law and English Law G McCormack and F Dahan [1999] *Company, Financial and Insolvency Law Review* 65 and more generally J Norton and M Andenas (eds), *Emerging Financial Markets and Secured Transactions* (London: Kluwer, 1998).

Through the floating charge it is possible to create security over the entirety of a company's business operations by simply charging the company's undertaking. It is also possible to create a fixed charge over almost any asset provided that the company debtor is restricted in the manner that it can deal with the assets that form the subject matter of the security. For instance, the courts have acknowledged the possibility of creating a fixed charge over future receivables provided that the chargee pays the proceeds of the receivables into a special bank account under the control of the chargor.[38]

Thirdly, in the main, English law publicises the existence of security interests over property through the registration of company charges regime. There is general legislative and judicial hostility to the recognition and enforcement of secret security interests and this hostility is based on the avoidance of detriment to other creditors. Such creditors may advance credit to a company on the basis that its assets are unencumbered and are prejudiced if it later emerges that the company has in fact given security for some or all of its existing debts. Part XII of the Companies Act 1985 sets out specifically the categories of charge that necessitate registration for effectiveness in the event of a corporate debtor's liquidation. Not all charges require registration but the most common categories of charge are within the scope of the registration requirement including floating charges and fixed charges over land, goods, and debts.[39] The register is open to public inspection and, in this way, third parties are alerted to the scope of a company's secured borrowings.

There is no requirement of registration in the case of pledges and common law liens but the fact that the creditor has possession of the items used as security may be taken as the functional equivalent of notice. There are no notification or registration requirements in the case of security interests arising by operation of law, ie equitable liens. This is a gap in the system and is, perhaps, the main reason why the judges have set their face against any extension of the category of equitable liens. There is however, an even larger gap in the system in that English law adopts a narrows conception of security interests. In economic terms, there are many strategies for taking what would be regarded as the functional equivalent of security but which do not, in a legal sense, involve the creation of a security interest. In other words, there are various ways, outside the creation of a charge, in which a creditor may improve its position in the event of the debtor's insolvency.[40]

[38] *Siebe Gorman v Barclays Bank* [1979] 2 Lloyd's Rep. 142; *Re Brightlife Ltd* [1987] Ch 200; *Agnew v Commissioner of Inland Revenue* [2001] AC

[39] eg, charges over goods, land, book debts, and floating charges.

[40] See generally on the company charge registration system WJ Gough, *Company Charges*, 2nd edn (London: Butterworths, 1996); McCormack , *Registration of Company Charges* (London: Sweet & Maxwell, 1994).

Fourthly, English law provides for a rapid and cost-effective means of recovering secured debts from the secured asset. From the point of view of a charge holder there is an especially efficacious method of enforcing security rights in England through the appointment of a receiver.[41] A chargeholder may appoint a receiver out-of-court pursuant to a facility contained in the instrument of charge. Although nominally the agent of the borrowing company to which he was appointed, the basic function of the receiver is to realise the secured assets for the benefit of the secured creditor. Fifthly and finally, under English law the cost of creating, maintaining, and exercising security interests appear to be at reasonable levels in that there are no notarisation fees or other levies payable on instruments of charge. Registering a charge and searching the register are subject to payment of a small fee but there are no other transaction costs apart of course from lawyer's remuneration.

Insofar as English law is judged against the benchmark of these principles then it scores quite well. The main pluses are the freedom to create security interests in almost all classes of assets and the general absence of procedural barriers in respect of the creation of security interests. The minuses, on the other hand centre, around the relatively formalistic preoccupations of the law and the lack of a comprehensive registration obligation. These pluses and minuses will now be considered.

A. Scope of Security Rights

It is with respect to the scope of assets that may be used as security that English law has earned its reputation for being favourably disposed towards the secured creditor.[42] In the nineteenth century legal practitioners and the courts responded to the growing needs of commerce by the development of an all-encompassing form of security—the floating charge. As a result of the Industrial Revolution, the bulk of a company's assets could now be in the form of raw materials, manufactured goods or goods in the process of manufacture, stock-in-trade and debts owed to the company by trade customers. The existing fixed forms of security over land and buildings could not capture these assets. Moreover the advent of the limited liability company meant that bank lending on a totally unsecured basis was an even more hazardous proposition.[43] Judicial reaction to this state of affairs was twofold. First, the validity of mortgages on after-acquired property—both

[41] It has been suggested however in the White Paper 'Insolvency—A Second Chance' (Cm. 5234, 2001) that the power of a floating charge holder to appoint an administrative receiver over a company's assets should be removed.

[42] See generally on the history and development of the floating charge RR Pennington, 'The Genesis of the Floating Charge' (1960) 23 *MLR* 630.

[43] Limited Liability Act 1855.

goods and receivables—was recognised.[44] Secondly, the floating charge was given the judicial imprimatur and this made it possible to create a security interest over the entire existing and future assets of an undertaking.[45] A floating charge is essentially a charge on a class of assets, both present and future, which permits the company creating the charge to dispose of a 'clean' title to the assets which form the subject matter of the charge until some event occurs which causes the chargeholder to intervene. Such an event is called a 'crystallising' event. Put another way, the corporate debtor has management autonomy with respect to the category of assets covered by the floating charge.[46]

In the seminal case *Illingsworth v Houldsworth*[47] Lord Macnaghten distinguished between the fixed charge and the floating charge in the following terms:[48]

> A specific charge, I think, is one that without more fastens on ascertained and definite property or property capable of being ascertained and defined; a floating charge, on the other hand, is ambulatory and shifting in its nature, hovering over and so to speak floating with the property which it is intended to affect until some event occurs or some act is done which causes it to settle and fasten on the subject of the charge within its reach and grasp.

The essence of the floating charge is that it does not inhibit a company from disposing of assets within the category covered by the charge in the ordinary course of its business without reference to, or the consent of the person entitled to the benefit of the charge. The acquirer of the asset gets a good title that is completely unimpaired by the charge. A specific charge, on the other hand, prevents a company from disposing of an unencumbered title to the assets, the subject-matter of the charge. While the kind of assets over which the security is taken provides a reasonably safe guide for characterising the nature of the security, it is not failsafe. The real distinction turns on the management autonomy which a floating charge confers on the chargor. The chargor has management autonomy insofar as the category of assets charged is concerned until that autonomy is brought to an end by a

[44] *Holroyd v Marshall* (1862) 10 HLC 191.

[45] *Re Panama, New Zealand and Australian Royal Mail Co.* (1870) 5 Ch App 318.

[46] The chargor's management autonomy was recognised by Millett LJ in *Re Cosslett(Contractors) Ltd* [1998] Ch 495 at 510: 'The essence of a floating charge is that it is a charge, not on any particular asset, but on a fluctuating body of assets which remain under the management and control of the chargor, and which the chargor has the right to withdraw from the security despite the existence of the charge. The essence of a fixed charge is that the charge is on a particular asset or class of assets which the chargor cannot deal with free from the charge without the consent of the chargee. The question is not whether the chargor has complete freedom to carry on his business as he chooses, but whether the chargee is in control of the charged assets.' This passage was approved of by Lord Hoffmann in *Smith v Bridgend County Borough Council* [2001] UKHL 58 at para 60.

[47] [1904] AC 355.

[48] Ibid. at 358.

process known as crystallisation whereupon the floating charge becomes fixed. The floating charge has been likened to a charge over a fund of assets. When crystallisation occurs the charge settles on the assets then within the fund.

The centrality of the floating charge in English lending practice was acknowledged by the Privy Council in *Agnew v Commissioner of Inland Revenue*. Lord Millett said:

> The floating charge is capable of affording the creditor, by a single instrument, an effective and comprehensive security upon the entire undertaking of the debtor company and its assets from time to time, while at the same time leaving the company free to deal with its assets and pay its trade creditors in the ordinary course of business without reference to the holder. Such a form of security is particularly attractive to banks, and it rapidly acquired an importance in English commercial life which . . . should not be underestimated.

On the other hand, the floating charge does not enjoy as high a ranking in the debtor's insolvency as the fixed charge. Legislation since 1897 has given priority to preferential creditors over claims by floating charge holders whereas the fixed charge will rank ahead of preferential creditors. The categories of preferential debts are set out in a schedule to the Insolvency Act and basically cover certain tax and employee claims. These may be quite numerous in the event of a corporate debtor's insolvency and secured lenders have adoped two techniques in an attempt to outflank claims by preferential creditors. The first is to widen the grounds for crystallisation. As traditionally understood a floating charge crystallised or, to use non-technical terminology, converted into a fixed charge, where the floating charge holder appointed a receiver over the debtor's assets or upon the commencement of the debtor's winding up. In *Re Woodroffes (Musical Instruments) Ltd*[49] it was decided that the cessation of a company's business brought about the crystallisation of a floating charge. This occurred because cessation removed the *raison d'être* of the floating charge which was to permit the company to carry on business in the ordinary way. The big breakthrough however came in *Re Brightlife Ltd*[50] where it was held that notice given by the chargee to the charger could convert a floating charge into a fixed charge. The judge, Hoffmann J, said that it was not open to the courts to restrict the contractual freedom of parties to a floating charge. He pointed to the limited and pragmatic interventions by the legislature in the area and suggested that these rendered it wholly inappropriate for the courts to impose additional restrictive rules on grounds of public policy.[51]

[49] [1986] Ch 366 affirmed (1984) 54 ALR 397.

[50] [1987] Ch 200.

[51] [1971] NZLR 909. See also *Deputy Commissioner of Taxation v Horsburgh* [1983] 2 VR 591 and *Re Obie Ltd (No 2)* [1984] 2 ACLC 69 and McLaughlan [1972] *NZLJ* 300.

The decision opens the door for clauses that stipulate for crystallisation on the occurrence of events such as the borrowing of the company exceeding a certain level or its assets falling below a stated sum. Such clauses are referred to as 'automatic crystallization' clauses and aim to give the floating charge holder as prominent a place as possible in the queue of creditors. The clauses however carry the practical disadvantage that crystallization may outside at a time that is outside the knowledge of the charge holder and the legal implications of the debtor continuing to trade in these circumstances is by no means certain. The Insolvency Act 1986, has however, considerably reduced the attractions of automatic crystallisation clauses by defining a floating charge as a charge which, as created, was a floating charge.[52] The consequence is that even if a floating charge has crystallised automatically prior to receivership or liquidation, it still ranks after the preferential creditors. A crystallised floating charge will still however, take priority over a prior ranking floating charge, a subsequently created equitable fixed charge and execution creditors. As far as execution creditors are concerned, there is one caveat to this statement. It seems that a person dealing with a company prior to crystallisation and aware of the existence of the floating charge is entitled to assume the continuance of the company's managerial autonomy until cessation of that autonomy by crystallisation has been brought to his attention.[53]

The second technique used by secured lenders in an attempt to outflank claims by preferential creditors has been to draft security documents in such a way that the fixed charge takes up territory that had traditionally been occupied exclusively by the floating charge.[54] In particular, 'receivables'—debts owing to the borrower—have traditionally been the subject of a floating charge in they are a class of circulating assets and normally the company creating the security expects to be to able to continue to collect the receivables and use the proceeds thereof in the ordinary course of its business. Nevertheless, in a seminal case, *Siebe Gorman & Co. Ltd v Barclays Bank*, a company gave a debenture to a bank which purported to include a first fixed charge on existing and future book debts. The court upheld the characterisation for three reasons. Firstly, the charge was described as a first fixed charge though this point alone was not conclusive for the test is one of substance rather than form. Secondly, the debenture contained a negative

52 See Insolvency Act 1986, s 251.

53 *Legal Problems of Credit and Security* 2nd edn (London: Sweet & Maxwell, 1988), at 70–1. In the Australian case *Horsburgh v Deputy Commissioner of Taxation* (1984) 54 ALR 397 McGarvie J at 413 doubted whether 'modern equity would be forced to run in such established grooves that if employees received pay and customers bought goods from a company, while reasonably unaware that the property of the company, had become subject to a fixed equitable charge, they would be losers.

54 See generally Goode 'Charges over Book Debts: a Missed Opportunity' (1994) 110 *LQR* 592.

pledge clause, ie the company was prohibited from charging or assigning the debts in favour of anybody else other than the bank. The judge however, was more persuaded by a third feature of the debenture which obliged the debtor, even before the bank had taken any steps to enforce its security, to pay into the debtor's account with the bank all moneys which it might receive in respect of the debts. While there were no express prohibitions on withdrawals from this account, Slade J held that the debenture, on its true construction, gave the bank rights to prevent the company from spending, in the ordinary course of business, all or any of the proceeds of book debts paid into the account. Were this not so, he would have been inclined to regard the charge, for all the wording of the debenture, as doing no more than 'hovering over' and, so to speak, floating with the book debts. *Siebe Gorman* is a very favourable decision from the point of view of the security interest holder. The judge was prepared to infer the existence of provisions, not expressly stated in the debenture, which ultimately proved decisive in the resolution of the fixed/floating charge debate. In other cases the courts have not been prepared to make similar inferences.[55]

At the heart of the fixed/floating charge characterisation exercise lies an unresolved tension. The lender wants to have a fixed charge but the borrower wants to be able to use the proceeds of charged debts in the ordinary course of its business. Doctrine however, in the shape of *Siebe Gorman* seems to insist that some restrictions on this freedom are necessary before a fixed charge label can be attached to the security interest. Recently, the decision of the Privy Council in *Agnew v Commissioner of Inland Revenue* have reiterated the point that 'labelling' and 'non-assignment' clauses in the debenture are insufficient to constitute a charge over book debts a fixed charge. Lord Millett said categorically:[56]

> A restriction on disposition which nevertheless allows collection and free use of the proceeds is inconsistent with the fixed nature of the charge; it allows the debt and its proceeds to be withdrawn from the security by the act of the company in collecting it.

The court appeared to approve *Siebe Gorman*, subject to the caveat that the implied restrictions on withdrawals of the proceeds of debts, once collected, were real and substantial in practice. In other words, a charge on book debts could be a fixed charge if the proceeds of the debts collected by the chargor were required to be paid into a blocked account with the charge holder. It was said:[57]

[55] See *Re Brightlife Ltd* [1987] Ch 200. See also *Hart v Barnes* (1982) 7 ACLR 310; *Re Keenan Bros Ltd* [1986] BCLC. 242; *Supercool Refrigeration and Air Conditioning v Hoverd Industries Ltd* [1994] 3 NZLR 300; *Re Cosslett (Contractors) Ltd* [1998] Ch 495.

[56] [2001] 3 WLR 454 at 467.

[57] [2001] 3 WLR 454 at 470.

Such an arrangement is inconsistent with the charge being a floating charge, since the debts are not available to the company as a source of its cash flow. But their Lordships would wish to make it clear that it is not enough to provide in the debenture that the account is a blocked account if it is not operated as one in fact.

In Agnew it was also held that it was not possible to create a fixed charge over uncollected book debts and, to couple this in the same debenture, with a floating charge on the proceeds of realisation of the selfsame debts.[58] Such a hybrid form of security was upheld by the Court of Appeal in *Re New Bullas Trading Ltd* where, rationalising the conclusion of the court, Nourse LJ stated:[59]

There being usually no need to deal with it before collection, [a company's book debt] is at that stage a natural subject of the fixed charge. But once collected, the proceeds being needed for the conduct of the business, it becomes a natural subject of the floating charge. While the company is a going concern, it is no less an advantage to the lender that the debt should be collected and the proceeds used in the business. But on insolvency, a crystallised floating charge on proceeds which, in the event supposed, are all the more likely to have been dissipated, may be worthless; whereas a fixed charge enabling the lender to intercept payment to the company may be of real value.

Re New Bullas Trading Ltd has been criticised on conceptual grounds. In particular, it has been argued that the distinction drawn in the case between the book debts before collection, and after realisation, is unrealistic and artificial because a debt is worth nothing unless and until it is turned into money. In *Agnew* the Privy Council rejected *New Bullas* as wrongly decided.[60] Lord Millett said:[61]

While a debt and its proceeds are two separate assets . . . the latter are merely the traceable proceeds of the former and represent its entire value. A debt is a receivable; it is merely a right to receive payment from the debtor. Such a right cannot be enjoyed in specie; its value can be exploited only by exercising the right or by assigning it for value to a third party. An assignment or charge of a receivable which does not carry with it the right to the receipt has no value. It is worthless as a security. Any attempt in the present context to separate the ownership of the debts from the ownership of their proceeds (even if conceptually possible) makes no commercial sense.

[58] The judgment smacks of commercial commonsense. The court was not bound by subjective indications of intention. Reference was made in this connection to the comments of Lord Templeman in *Street v Mountford.* Rather the task of the court was to discover what mutual rights and obligations the parties, objectively speaking, intended to create. Once this task had been completed, then the court would engage in the characterisation exercise. This was a legal exercise that was unconstrained by the label which the parties had chosen to apply to their agreement. See also the comments of Lord Scott in *Smith v Bridgend County Borough Council* [2001] UKHL 58 at para 53 that 'once contractual rights have, by the process of construction, been ascertained, the question whether they constitute security rights is a question of law that is not dependent on their intentions.'

[59] [1994] I BCLC 485 at 487.

[60] [1994] 1 BCLC. 485.

[61] [2001] 3 WLR 454 at 469.

Essentially, the borrower in both *New Bullas* and *Agnew* was left in control of the process by which the charged assets were extinguished and replaced by different assets which were not the subject of a fixed charge and which were at the free disposal of the borrower. This, according to the court in *Agnew*, was inconsistent with the nature of a fixed charge.

The fixed/floating charge distinction has attracted a lot of attention in recent years because of the different priorities accorded the two types of charge. The priority issue has engendered a degree of criticism but this does not detract from the overall contribution that the floating charge has made to the financing of business in England. In particular, the floating charge can provide global security over existing and future assets of the borrower to cover existing and future indebtedness and, while its priority ranking is relatively weak, these attractions are not to be ignored. Viewing the law through the lens of the secured creditor, the development of the floating charge is a 'definite' plus as far as the English position is concerned. In this respect, English law compares very favourably with pre-Article 9 US law which did not recognize any equivalent of the floating charge on the basis that it was incompatible with the nature of a security interest that the debtor should have dominion over the assets used as security.[62] This state of affairs was transformed by Article 9.[63] Article 9 however also goes beyond current English law by adopting a wider conception of security interests, for example, by embracing reservation of title or factoring agreements, that in English eyes would be viewed as 'quasi-security' rather than security strictly so-called. The Company Law Review steering group recently in its final report *Modern Company Law for a Competitive Economy* drew attention to the English legal treatment of 'quasi-security interests' ie functionally equivalent legal devices and the possibility of enacting a comprehensive register of security interests along North American lines.[64] The formalistic distinctions of English law will now be examined in some detail.

[62] *Benedict v Ratner* (1925) 268 US 354; *Zartman v First National Bank* (1907) 189 NY 267. There is also something of a feeling expressed in the pre-Article 9 American cases that all the debtor's property should not be swept away by security interest holders and that the debtor should have a 'cushion' of free assets that is available for payment of debts owing to unsecured creditors.

[63] Art 9 was most recently revised in 1998 with the revision coming into force on 1st July, 2001; for access to the revised version of Art 9 see the National Conference of Commissioners on Uniform State Laws website, <http://www.nccusl.org/>

[64] *Modern Company Law For a Competitive Economy: Final Report, Volume 1* (July 2001), at 247: 'Although charges created by companies over their assets other than land must far outnumber similar charges created by other debtors, it would not be sensible to consider a notice-filing system for company charges without at the same time considering a similar system for all charges over property other than land and for functionally-equivalent legal devices (often termed "quasi-security" devices).'

B. Formalism of the English Law of Security Interests

In *Chow Yoong Hong* v *Choong Fah Rubber Manufactory*[65] Lord Devlin observed that there are many ways of raising cash besides borrowing. To adjust the statement slightly, there are many ways in which a person who has 'advanced' money might enhance its prospects of recovery in the event of the debtor's insolvency besides being party to the creation of a charge. These methods include the following: (1) sale and leaseback/hire purchase; (2) title retention/conditional sale; (3) agency sales financing; (4) factoring/assignment of receivables; (5) *Quistclose* trusts. These are all 'quasi-security' devices and will now be considered.

1. Quasi-Security—Sale and Leaseback/Hire Purchase

A uncommon financing technique involves the sale of goods or land followed by a lease back. In all probability, the vendor will never have parted with possession and, in practice, it may be difficult to distinguish a genuine sale and lease-back from the creation of a creation over the property in question. In a leading case, *Re George Inglefield Ltd*,[66] Romer LJ attempted to explain the essential differences. He said:[67]

> In a transaction of sale the vendor is not entitled to get back the subject-matter of the sale by returning to the purchaser the money that has passed between them. In the case of a mortgage or charge the mortgagor is entitled, until he has been foreclosed, to get back the subject-matter of the mortgage or charge by returning to the mortgagee the money that has passed between them. The second essential difference is that if the mortgagee realises the subject-matter of the mortgage for a sum more than sufficient to repay him, with interest and the costs, the money that has passed between him and the mortgagor he has to account to the mortgagor for the surplus. If the purchaser sells the subject-matter of the purchase, and realises a profit, of course he has not got to account to the vendor for the profit. Thirdly, if the mortgagee realises the mortgage property for a sum that is insufficient to repay him the money that he has paid to the mortgagor, together with interest and costs, then the mortgagee is entitled to recover from the mortgagor the balance of the money . . . If the purchaser were to resell the purchased property at a price which was insufficient to recoup him the money that he has paid to the vendor, of course he would not be entitled to recover the balance from the vendor.

These distinctions, while easy to state on paper, may become blurred in practice. For example, sale agreements may include options to repurchase

[65] [1962] AC 209 at 216
[66] [1933] Ch 1.
[67] [1933] Ch at 26–7. It was made clear in *Durhan Bros v Robertson* however, [1898] 1 QB 765 that once the security nature of a transaction is established, equity will imply a right of redemption; see at 772 per Chitty LJ Having regard to this fact Fidelis Oditah [1992] JBL 541 at 546 argues that the speech of Romer LJ gives very little, if any, useful guidance.

and also profit sharing clauses under which the original vendor shares in profits from resales as well as provisions whereby the vendor agrees to indemnify the buyer in respect of any losses incurred on a resale.

The modern form of hire purchase agreement in relation to goods builds on the clear theoretical distinction between a sale and a lease or hire of goods. Hire purchase entails a hiring coupled with an option to purchase.[68] In legal terms however, there is a lot to be said for the view that this description is, in reality, a legal fiction that bears little or no relation to reality.[69] In legal terms there is a contract for the hiring of goods coupled with an option on the part of the hirer to purchase the goods.[70] While the agreement subsists, the property in the goods remains in the owner and the hirer has no power to dispose of them. Moreover, although the hirer has an option to purchase the goods it is not under a binding obligation to do so.[71]

Normally a hire purchase transaction involves three parties, namely, a dealer, finance house and hirer. Goods are sold by the dealer to the finance house who then lets them on hire-purchase terms to a hirer who had no prior interest in the goods. The tripartite nature of the transaction makes it difficult to argue that in reality it constitutes a loan. But the essential principle remains the same, irrespective of the fact that there are only two parties as when the owner of goods sells them to a finance house and takes a lease-back under a hire purchase agreement.

2. *Quasi-Security—Retention of Title Clauses*

Title retention clauses may take many forms but basically the clause refers to a situation where the seller of goods retains title to those goods until they have been paid for.[72] This is the simplest and perhaps the most common form of title retention clause but more complicated variants are possible. Under a 'current account' clause the seller retains title until all debts owing by the buyer to the seller have been paid and not just indebtedness arising under the particular contract of sale. A 'proceeds' or 'tracing' retention of title clause permits the buyer to resell the goods in the ordinary course of business before the original debt has been discharged but transfers the seller's claim to the proceeds generated by the resale. 'Products' clauses are

[68] See for a definition of a hire purchase agreement *Benjamin's Sale of Goods*, 3rd edn (London: Sweet & Maxwell, 1987), 45, para. 53.

[69] See generally, Crowther Committee Report Cmnd. 4569, 175–6.

[70] For a modern analysis see *Forthright Finance Ltd v Carlyle Finance Ltd* [1997] 4 All ER 90.

[71] On hire-purchase see generally Goode, *Consumer Credit Law* (looseleaf) (London: Butterworths, 1989); Guest, *The Law of Hire-Purchase* (London: Sweet & Maxwell, 1966); Goode, *Hire-Purchase Law and Practice*, 2nd edn (London: Butterworths, 1970).

[72] For a comprehensive analysis see McCormack *Reservation of Title*, 2nd edn (London: Sweet & Maxwell, 1995).

used in quite complex factual scenarios where the goods supplied have formed all or part of the raw materials in a process of manufacture. With such a clause the supplier of the raw materials is claiming all or part of the finished article.

English law holds that security interests created by grant, but not by way of reservation, in the main require registration.[73] Part 12 Companies Act 1985 requires that certain charges created by companies must be registered to be valid in the event of the company going into liquidation. How does this charge analysis apply to retention of title clauses? Basically, 'simple' retention of title clauses and current account clauses have been given the judicial imprimatur but the more complex variants—namely, 'proceeds' and 'products' clauses have met with judicial disfavour.[74] The analysis goes like this—with a simple clause and a current clause the seller is merely retaining ownership of the goods until satisfaction of some condition. Until this condition is fulfilled the buyer does not acquire any bit of ownership that he can hand back to the seller by way of a security interest.[75] On the other hand, where goods have been sold, the seller's claim does not translate readily into the resale proceeds. Originally the courts were prepared to recognise the seller's claim on the basis that in reselling the seller was acting in a dual capacity ie as an agent *vis-à-vis* the original seller but as a principal as far as the resale buyers were concerned so that the latter were not brought into direct contractual relations with original seller.[76] More recently however, the courts have moved away from this analysis holding that seller's entitlement to resale proceeds is a limited interest by way of charge since it comes to an end upon the discharge of the original purchase price.[77] Likewise 'product claims' have attracted the disapproval of the courts. The dominant view is that where there is a mixture of heterogeneous goods in the manufacturing process a new product—nova species—is created which belongs, initially at least, to the manufacturer, so to speak.[78]

3. *Quasi-Security—Assignment of Receivables*

In England receivables financing may take one of two forms—either the

[73] As we have Browne-Wilkinson VC (as he then was) adopted the following definition of security in *Re Paramount Airways Ltd* [1990] BCC 130 at 149: 'security is created where a person (the creditor) obtains rights exercisable against some property in which the debtor has an interest in order to enforce the discharge of the debtor's obligations to the creditor.'

[74] See generally McCormack *Reservation of Title*, 2nd edn (London: Sweet & Maxwell, 1995).

[75] See *Clough Mill Ltd v Martin* [1985] 1 WLR 111; *Armour v Thyssen Edelstahlwerke AG* [1991] 2 AC 339.

[76] *Aluminium Industrie Vaassen BV v Romalpa Aluminium Ltd* [1976] 1 WLR 676.

[77] See, eg, *Pfeiffer Weinkellerei-Weineinkauf GmbH Co. v Arbuthnot Factors Ltd* [1988] 1 WLR 150; *Compaq Computer Ltd v Abercorn Group Ltd* [1991] BCC 484.

[78] *Borden v Scottish Timber Products Ltd* [1981] Ch 25; *Re Peachdart Ltd* [1984] Ch 131.

creation of charges, whether fixed or floating, on receivables (debts) or else the outright assignment of receivables which is referred to as factoring.[79] Factoring, or the absolute assignment of receivables, serves as the functional economic equivalent of taking a charge over the receivables. Factoring of debts is a well-recognised and established economic activity with many of the major financial institutions having factoring subsidiaries. A factoring transaction does not have to be registered but where a company creates a charge over its debts, registration is a necessity.[80] There are also other reasons, apart from registration, why it is also important to distinguish between the assignment of a debt and the creation of a 'mere' charge over it. In the case of an assignment of a debt, the assignee takes subject to all rights of set-off and other defences that were available against the assignor, but only those existing when the debtor receives notice of the assignment. The chargee of a debt is not, however, the owner of it and certain consequences ensue. First, rights of set-off and defences remain exercisable by the debtor against the grantor of the security interest, whether these arise before or after the debtor receives notice of the charge. Secondly, the debtor is not obliged to pay the chargee on receiving notice of the charge. It is even the case that, unless the charge is combined with an authority from the chargor to pay the chargee, the debtor is not entitled to make payment to the chargee but remains obliged to paying the chargor.

Of course the factoring of debts equates to a loan of money on the security of debts to the extent that ready cash is released to the assignor. The latter receives money upfront rather than having to wait for the debts to mature, or to be collected. Factoring however, can serve functions other the immediate release of funds. For instance, if it is done on a notification basis then the factor is relieved of the responsibility of collecting the debts. The factor may also take over the burden of accounts administration. Factoring may also take on some of the features of credit insurance if the factor assumes the responsibility for the debtor failing to pay as distinct from the assignor being under an obligation to accept a reassignment of bad debts.

Receivables financing is often carried out in a manner that blurs the distinction between the outright sale of receivables and their transfer by way of security.[81] In English law, it is possible to mortgage a debt by an assignment of the debt to the mortgagee coupled with a provision for reassignment of the debt once the obligation to which the mortgage relates has

[79] See generally Freddy Salinger, *Factoring Law and Practice*, 3rd edn (London: Sweet & Maxwell, 1999); Oditah, op cit.

[80] The distinction between factoring and the creation of a charge over debts was explored at length by the House of Lords in *Lloyds & Scottish Finance v Cyril Lord Carpet Sales Ltd* [1992] BCLC. 609.

[81] See Bridge, Macdonald, Simmonds, and Walsh 'Formalism, Functionalism and Understanding the Law of Secured Transactions' (199) 44 *McGill LJ* 567 at n 46.

been discharged. The formalities for legal assignments of debts are laid down in section 136 Law of Property Act 1925. One of the requirements is that an assignment be 'absolute' and 'not purporting to be by way of charge only.'[82] It is perfectly possible, nevertheless, that an assignment is 'absolute' for purposes of section 136 and still operate by way of security. The test for the application of section 136 is whether for the time being the assignor has unconditionally transferred to the assignee the right to receive payment from the debtor. On the other hand, if the assignor is a corporate body, the transaction will require registration under Part 12, Companies Act 1985 where the assignor retains an equity of redemption ie if the transaction is by way of mortgage. With a mortgage the assignee has ownership of the debt transferred subject to the assignor's right of redemption. A charge of a debt however, gives the chargee not ownership of the debt but rather preferential rights thereto.[83] Professor Goode has suggested that to facilitate a transfer of the legal title to the debt in case the chargee wishes to dispose of it, the default provisions in the charge should (1) confer a power of attorney on the chargee to collect or dispose of the debt and to convert the charge into a mortgage by executing an assignment in the name of the chargor.[84] It has been argued that these powers diminish to vanishing point any remaining distinctions between a mortgage and a charge.[85] Be that as it may, the distinction, in legal terms, clearly remains between an outright transfer of debts and the transfer subject to an equity of redemption. In other words, there is still a fundamental distinction between factoring of debts and the creation of a security interest in the same.

4. *Quasi-Security—Agency Sales Financing*

Agency sales financing is a fairly complicated form of financing technique that was employed in ***Welsh Development Agency v Export Finance Co Ltd***[86] and the technique is perhaps best explained by looking at the facts of the case. These basically involved an exporter of computer software gaining finance for its export trade transactions by selling the software in question

[82] *Burlinson v Hall* (1884) 12 QBD 347. See also *Bovis International Inc. v Circle Ltd Partnership* (1995) 49 Con LR 12 at 29 where Millett LJ said 'an assignment does not cease to be absolute merely because it is given by way of security and is subject to an express or implied obligation to reassign on redemption'.

[83] Denman J stated in *Tancred v Delagoa Bay and East Africa Railway Co.* (1889) 23 QBD 239 at 242 that ' a document given by way of charge' is not one which absolutely transfers the property with a condition for reconveyance, but is a document which only gives a right to payment out of a particular fund or particular property, without transferring that fund or property'.

[84] [1994] JBL 172 at 174.

[85] See Oditah, op cit, at 96.

[86] [1992] BCLC. 148. The case is analysed by Oditah [1992] JBL 541. Contrast *Re Curtain Dream plc* [1990] BCLC 925.

to a financier and then fulfilling the overseas orders as the financier's agent. The financier acted as an undisclosed principal with the foreign buyers dealing at all times with the software supplier. The buyers made payment into a bank account that was in the name of the software supplier but which was under the complete control of the financier. The price that the financier paid the software supplier for the goods was not fixed at the outset but was subject to variation depending on the speed with which the foreign buyers paid for the goods. The financing arrangement also had a termination clause under which, on cessation of the agreement, the supplier would satisfy all claims owing to the financier by the foreign buyers and, when this payment had been made, the financier would transfer all interests it had in the goods to the supplier. It is important to note that the financing technique purported to involve a sale of goods rather than an assignment of debts.

It seems that, in the particular case, this form of financing arrangement was used because of a clause in a prior lending agreement under which the supplier covenanted not to factor, discount or assign its debts. Breach of this undertaking would entitle the lender to appoint a receiver. Unfortunately, the software supplier experienced financial difficulties and it was argued that the financing arrangement was invalid for non-registration on the basis that, in reality, it represented a charge over goods rather than an absolute sale.[87] The Court of Appeal rejected this proposition. The transaction was not a sham because there was no evidence that the parties intended rights and obligations to apply inter se other than those set out in the agreement. Moreover, looking at the internal workings of the transaction, there was nothing therein that was necessarily incompatible with the transaction being one of sale. The termination clause was like a repurchase agreement and options to repurchase were not uncommon in sales transactions. Furthermore, price variation clauses were often found in sales contracts.

5. *Quasi-Security—Quistclose /Conditional Purpose Trusts*

Some trusts may be regarded as serving a security type function and, in particular, the conditional purpose or 'Quistclose' trust.[88] Under a

[87] See also the comments of Lawrence LJ in *Re George Inglefield Ltd* [1933] Ch 1 at 23: 'As the law stands at present, there is nothing to prevent a limited company from selling its assets without giving notice of that sale to the public or to anyone else, remaining in possession of the assets so sold, with the consent of the buyer, and obtaining credit on the faith of that possession. If such a state of things ought to be remedied it is for Parliament to supply the remedy. All that the Court has to do . . . is to ascertain whether there has, in fact, been a sale of the assets and to give effect to the transaction if that be the case.'

[88] See generally on the Quistclose Trust Priestley 'The Romalpa Trust and the Quistclose Trust', in Paul Finn (ed), *Equity in Commercial Relationships* (North Ryde, NSW: Law Book Co, 1987); Goodhart and Jones (1980) 43 *MLR* 489; Bridge (1992) *OJLS* 333 and C Rickett (1991) 107 *LQR* 608.

'Quistclose' trust money is advanced subject to the condition that it is applied for a particular purpose. If this purpose is not fulfilled or is no longer capable of accomplishment the money is said to be held on a secondary trust for the payer rather than being part of the debtor's assets available for payment to the debtor's general creditors. The courts have held that debt and trust can coexist - in other words that that the same transaction can give to the legal relationship of debt and also to a trust. It has been contended that a Quistclose trust constitutes a security interest in that the 'payer is to be protected from the claims of other creditors of the payee' on the latter's insolvency and thus 'clearly evinces an intention to seek and provide security'.[89] On this analysis, the Quistclose trust secures performance of the debtor's obligation to carry out the purpose of the advance.

Having said that however it must be recognised that the Quistclose trust is not a conventional security interest. In the typical advance the secured assets and the moneys advanced are quite clearly separate and the former secures the latter. With a Quistclose trust the payer is asserting a de facto security interest in the advance itself and it is not the failure to repay that is secured but rather the execution of the primary trust purpose. If the primary trust purpose is carried out the payer is converted from a secured into an unsecured creditor.[90] Under a Quistclose trust the payee (debtor) never acquires beneficial ownership but is rather a trustee—a conduit for the transmission of funds whereas the rationale of the OPSSA is the protection of the debtor's residual ownership. The generally accepted view is that the Quistclose trust does not fall within the scope of the company charge registration system.

IV. PRESSURE FOR REFORM OF THE ENGLISH LAW OF SECURITY INTERESTS

It is possible to say that there are a number of pressure points for reform of the English law of security interests. These can be considered under various heads; (a) the Article 9 agenda; (b) the corporate rescue agenda; (c) dissatisfaction with the existing priority regime; (d) impact of 'dematerialisation'/new technologies. These heads will now be addressed.

A. *The Article 9 Agenda*

There have been many calls for fundamental reform of English law pertaining

89 See Bridge (1992) *OJLS* 333 at 345–6 and 360–1.
90 See Bridge, *et al* , op cit, 567, at n 156.

to security interests along North American lines.[91] Perhaps the most radical blueprint for reform was that contained in the 1989 Report by Professor Aubrey Diamond commissioned by the Department of Trade and Industry. Diamond concluded his review of the law by stating that a security interest could be taken in almost anything provided that an appropriate method was used but it was not always easy to decide which method was appropriate.[92] In his view, the English law suffered from three main defects; namely, compartmentalisation, complexity, and difficulty in determining priorities.[93] The compartmentalisation problem was overriding and stemmed from the fact that the law lacked a functional basis. The law was divided into rigid compartments making it fragmented and incoherent. Essentially similar transactions were treated by the law in very different ways which had the effect of complicating the legal issues quite unnecessarily. Complexity and uncertainty was also compounded by the old division between common law and equity that loomed large in the security law field. Common law and equity had been administered in parallel but separate court systems before the 1870s and, while both sets of principles were now administered in the same courts, the different historical antecedents of similar security law rights contributed to complexities in exposition and characterisation. For example a purchaser of goods who bought, not knowing of any security interest in them, might be in a radically different position depending on whether the security interest was legal or equitable. Simply stated, there were difficulties in determining priorities and priority problems were exacerbated by the fact that there were so many different ways of achieving similar economic ends. The Diamond prescription for England was comprehensive reform along the lines of Article 9 of the US Uniform Commercial Code and the Canadian Personal Property Security legislation. More recently, the Company Law Review Steering Group in its Final Report recommended that the Law Commission should be requested to examine the whole issue of security interests over property other than land. In fact, the Steering Group proposals in relation to company charges are very much in line with Article 9, for example, notice filing and the time of registration being used as a point of reference for determining priorities.[94]

In the early 1990s however, the Government decided not to accept the Diamond recommendations and it remains to be seen whether the passage

[91] See also Crowther Committee Report on Consumer Credit (1971) Cmnd 4596; Cork Committee Report on Insolvency Law and Practice (1982) Cmnd 8558.

[92] Op cit at 31.

[93] See generally 31–3 of the Diamond Report 'A Review of Security Interests in Property' (HMSO, 1989).

[94] *Modern Company Law For a Competitive Economy: Final Report Volume 1* (July 2001) at 247.

of years will lead to a change of heart. The Government's reluctance to embrace Diamond was based on three interlinked reasons.[95] First, in its view, there was no major constituency pressing for reform. Secondly, it was suggested that reform would be disruptive and, in view of proposed registration requirements, potentially costly to government and to business and thirdly, there was the possibility of EU harmonisation measures in this sphere. Somewhat surprisingly, this distant prospect, which has not yet come to pass except in a minor way, was felt to preclude domestic legislative initiatives.[96]

While the governments' case for not implementing Diamond may not be entirely convincing, it is certainly arguable that Diamond overstated the defects of the present system. Certainly banks and other users of the system are reasonably happy with its operation and remain to be convinced that reform would bring appreciable benefits without accompanying disadvantages. This point is made when one looks at the desirable features of a modern system of personal property security law as enunciated by bodies like EBRD. In large measure, English law complies with these desirable features. Moreover, while English law has recognised title retention clauses without the need for registration such clauses do not intrude too greatly on a bank's security. In the main, the superpriority status enjoyed by trade creditors using title retention clauses only extends to the original good supplied and does not embrace proceeds or products. In any reform of the law that might benefit lenders in certain respects there is the corresponding danger that these hard-won advantages might be lost. As one commentator has concluded[97] 'the English bank has obtained all the freedom it needs to make its position ironclad. It is therefore hardly surprising that the banks are not pressing for a reform along the lines of Article 9.' Nevertheless, the final report of the Company Law Review Steering Group has put the question of Article 9 type reforms in England back on the agenda.[98]

B. The Corporate Rescue Agenda

The second major pressure point for reform of the English law of security interests stems from a desire on the part of Government to promote the rescue or rehabilitation of ailing businesses. The focus of insolvency law reform has increasingly been on the promotion of a rescue culture and this

95 Vol 189 H.C debates, col 482, 24 Apr 1991.

96 The recently enacted EU Late Payment in Commercial Transactions directive 2000/35/EC however contains provision for the recognition of a 'simple' retention of title clause throughout the Community. The text of the directive can be viewed through the Europa website <http:// www.europa.eu.int/> or in the official journal—OJ L 2000/35, 8.8.2000.

97 'How far is Art 9 Exportable? The English Experience' (1996) 27 *Can Bu. LJ* 196, at 221.

98 See also Goode 'Insularity or Leadership? The Role of the United Kingdom in the Harmonisation of Commercial Law' (2001) 50 *ICLQ* 751, at 759–60.

has been part of a growing international trend to encourage a more collective approach to corporate rescue mechanisms. Moreover, there is a concern that the procedure of administrative receivership is insufficiently concerned with the goal of maximizing economic value and, additionally, is excessively oriented towards protecting the secured creditor's position to the neglect of other parties.[99] Under existing law, a secured creditor with a floating charge over the whole or substantially the whole of a company's assets, may appoint an administrative receiver without having to seek court approval. The vast majority of receivership appointments are made on this basis. Although designated an agent of the corporate debtor, the primary task of an administrative receiver is to realise the charged assets for the benefit of the creditor by whom he was appointed. The receiver owes only limited duties to the company and to other debtors. In particular, the receiver is not obliged to delay a sale of the charged assets merely because delay is likely to result in a substantially higher value being obtained at a later stage.

In the Insolvency Act 1986 a new procedure—'administration'—was introduced to facilitate the objective of encouraging the continuation and disposal of a debtor's business as a going concern, wherever possible. Where a company is actually or potentially insolvent, the court may appoint an administrator if this is likely to result in the achievement of one or more of the statutory objectives. Once the order of appointment is made, the administrator takes charge of the company's affairs and formulates a plan with a view to achieving the objectives for which he was appointed. In carrying out his functions, an administrator owes his duties to all interested parties and not exclusively to secured creditors. The Insolvency Act 1986 however permits a floating, but not a fixed chargeholder, to block the appointment of an administrator to an ailing company. This power of veto enshrined in the Insolvency legislation has led to the practice whereby lenders who are already secured up to the hilt by fixed charges over a company's most valuable assets will, nevertheless, take a floating charge over the same assets.[100] The instrument containing the floating charge will be shorn of the usual covenants—hence the expression 'lightweight' floating charge. The sole purpose of including the additional floating charge security in these circumstances is for the secured lender to acquire the power of veto over the appointment of an administrator. The legislative provision strengthens the position of the floating charge in English lending practice.

The floating charge is under partial threat at the moment however, as a result of the proposals contained in the DTI/Insolvency Service White Paper

[99] See generally the DTI Report 'A Review of Company Rescue and Business Reconstruction Mechanisms' (Nov 2000).

[100] Such floating charges were given the judicial imprimatur in *Re Croftbell Ltd* [1990] BCLC. 844; on which see Oditah 'Lightweight Floating Charges' [1991] *JBL* 49.

'Insolvency—A Second Chance'.[101] The White Paper recommends that floating chargeholders should lose the unilateral right to appoint an administrative receiver over a company's assets and also the power to block the appointment of an administrator. The White Paper however, also proposes a balancing measure. At the moment, preferential creditors are paid ahead of floating, but not fixed, charge holders in a liquidation or receivership. Preferential debts cover certain tax (Crown) claims and employee claims. The White Paper suggests that Crown preference, but not employee preference would be abolished, with a certain proportion of floating charge realisations being set aside for unsecured creditors so as to ensure that the fruits of the abolition of Crown preference were enjoyed by all creditors.[102] These proposals, if implemented, would seriously detract from the status of the floating charge.

C. Dissatisfaction with the Current Priorities Regime

Another pressure point for reform comes from practitioner dissatisfaction with the existing priority rules. There is no single reference point for determining priorities between competing security interests in the same property. Unlike the position in the US under Article 9 of the UCC, registration is not per se a priority determinant. Under English law interests that involve the use of absolute title by way of security, such as interests under trusts and 'simple' retention of title clauses,[103] enjoy super-priority status. Moreover, they are not subject to any requirement of registration.[104] As far as charges, strictly co-called are concerned, while failure to register a registrable charge will result in the invalidation of the charge in the event of the corporate debtor going into liquidation, once registration has been duly effected then priority among competing charges turns on the date of creation. In other words, fixed charges rank amongst themselves according to the order of creation but, on the other hand, a floating charge is postponed, priority-wise, to a fixed charge irrespective of the order in which the two charges were created.[105]

If however, a floating charge instrument contains a 'negative pledge' or

[101] Cm 5234, July 2001.

[102] See the statement at para 2.20 of the White Paper: 'Where there is no floating chargeholder, the benefit of abolition will be available for the unsecured creditors. Where there is a floating charge-holder (in relation to a floating charge created after the coming into force of the legislation), we would ensure that the benefit of the abolition of preferential status goes to unsecured creditors. We will achieve this through a mechanism that ringfences a proportion of the funds generated by the floating charge.'

[103] Put shortly, the property never comes into the beneficial ownership of the insolvent.

[104] The registration obligation contained in Part 12 Companies Act 1985 only applies to charges created by a company.

[105] See McCormack 'Priority of Charges and Registration' [1994] JBL 587.

'restrictive ' clause, ie a clause forbidding the creation of any subsequent security having priority to the floating charge and a subsequent fixed charge holder has actual notice, not just constructive notice, of the restrictive clause, then the floating charge holder will be paid out of the assets in question in priority to the floating charge holder.[106] It appears that the practice of submitting details of a negative pledge clause among the particulars of a charge delivered for registration does not automatically fix the subsequent fix chargee with notice of the negative pledge clause though it is something from which notice may be inferred.[107] Registration of negative pledge clause is not required by statute. In practice though, a bank which is thinking about making a secured loan to a corporate borrower will consult the register of charges and, in this way, previous secured borrowings by the company will come to light.[108] The priority rules are further complicated by apparent judicial acceptance of the proposition that where a second floating charge covers only part of the assets covered by a prior floating charge, then the second floating charge will have priority provided that the first instrument of charge authorises the creation of subsequent charges having this effect.[109]

Where there is more than one assignment of the same debt, then prior-

[106] n *G & T Earle Ltd v Hemsworth Rural District Council* (1928) 44 TLR 605 Wright J said: ' . . .the debentures having been duly registered . . . the plaintiffs, like all the world, are deemed to have constructive notice of the fact that there are debentures. But it has never been held that the mere fact that persons in the position of the plaintiffs have constructive notice of the existence of debentures also affects them with constructive notice of the actual terms of the debentures or that the debentures are subject to the restrictive condition to which these debentures were subject. No doubt it is quite common for debentures to be subject to this limiting condition as to further charges, but that fact is not enough in itself to operate as constructive notice of the actual terms of any particular set of debentures.' See *also Re Standard Machine Co Ltd* (1906) 95 LT 829 *and Wilson v Kelland* [1910] 2 Ch 306.

[107] But of Farrar (1976) 40 *Conv* (NS) 397 who argues for the existence of inferred actual knowledge rather than constructive knowledge. He suggests that the failure on the part of a subsequent chargee to inspect the register might give rise to an inference of actual knowledge particularly since restrictive clauses are so common. The argument seems inconsistent however with *Re Valletort Sanitary Steam Laundry Co* [1903] 2 Ch 654 and *Welch v Bowmaker (Ireland) Ltd* [1980] IR 251. Farrar has previously suggested (1974) 38 Conv (NS) 315 that restrictive clauses may be inconsistent with the nature of a floating charge but reaches the conclusion that 'it would now seem too late for the point to be raised' (at 318).

[108] If a fixed chargee has priority over a floating chargee in a particular case because the fixed chargee has actual notice of a restrictive clause in the floating charge debenture, this gives rise to circularity problem. What about the preferential creditors who, in terms of priorities, are in between the fixed and floating charges? There has been some judicial disagreement on this issue. One view holds that by coming after the floating charge, the fixed charge should therefore come after the preferential creditors—*Re Portbase Clothing Ltd* [1993] Ch 388. Another possible solution is the subrogation solution, ie that by virtue of the altered priorities between them, the floating chargeholder stands in the shoes of the fixed chargeholder to the extent of the amount secured by the fixed charge and therefore the floating chargeholder will be paid ahead of preferential creditors by the degree to which liabilities are secured by a fixed charge—*Re Woodroffes (Musical Instruments) Ltd* [1986] Ch 366.

[109] *Re Automatic Bottle Makers* [1926] Ch 412; *Re Benjamin Cope & Co.* [1914] 1 Ch 800. See also *Griffith v Yorkshire Bank Ltd* [1994] 1 WLR 1427; *Re H. & K. Medway Ltd* [1997] 1 WLR 1422.

ity among competing assignments is determined by the order in which notice of the assignments is given to the debtor save where a subsequent assignee has actual or constructive notice of an earlier assignment at the time that the subsequent assignment is made. In the latter situation priority is governed by a simple 'first-in-time-has-priority' rule. The complexities in the law governing priorities has led to calls for clarifying legislation or at least private law solutions negotiated amongst secured parties. As one commentator has said:

> The priority rules are a potential minefield for secured creditors. The rules vary depending on the nature of the assets concerned, floating charges are governed by a different set of rules altogether, and there is yet another set of rules for money lent after the creditor has received notice of a subsequent charge . . . For all these reasons, it is common practice for secured creditors to enter into a priority agreement with any other secured creditor of which they become aware.

There seems little doubt that new rules which make priority turn, in the first instance at least, on the date of registration (or perfection where it is possible to perfect by a method other than registration) would bring a necessary degree of simplicity and clarity to the law.

D. The Impact of 'Dematerialisation' and New Technologies

It is submitted that in England the advent of new technologies, growing computerisation and the use of electronic commerce, has not had a major impact on the substantive law of security interests.[110] At the moment, charges over a company's portfolio of shares are not registrable. This is perhaps the most significant gap in the existing system of registration of company charges. It has been rationalised, not entirely convincingly, on the basis that a company's portfolio of shares may be changing all the time and consequently, a requirement of registration might impede transactions where speed is of the essence and cause lenders to become reluctant to accept shares as security. A number of security possibilities present themselves. The first is the pledge but this can only be used in relation to bearer shares which are most uncommon in England.[111] The second is the floating charge which may be, and is, employed with facility and ease. On the other hand, the floating charge holder is in a weaker priority position than other secured creditors with fixed security interests. For this reason, lenders may wish to take either a legal mortgage or an equitable charge over shares. A

[110] See generally for a brief discussion of the process involved in the taking of security over shares Richard Calnan 'Taking Security in England', 17, at 40–1 and for a discussion of the impact of 'dematerialisation' see Joanna Benjamin *Interests in Securities* (Oxford: Oxford University Press, 2000) and Jacqueline Lipton *Security over Intangible Property* (Sydney: LBC Information Services, 2000), at 69–84.

[111] *Harrold v Plenty* [1901] 2 Ch 314.

legal mortgage is possible only in relation to existing shares whereas an equitable charge may extend over after-acquired shares. With a legal mortgage the lender becomes the legal owner of the shares and is registered as such in the books of the relevant company and there is a covenant to reconvey the shares to the borrower once the loan is repaid. Lenders however may be reluctant to go on the register of members and this leaves the equitable charge as the alternative security option. The equitable charge though can be trumped by subsequent registered holders of the shares who acquire the shares bona fide, for value, and without notice of the earlier equitable interest. Because of the absence of any registration requirement pertaining to shares the status of a bona fide purchaser may be relatively easy to establish. For this reason equitable chargees may wish to obtain possession of the relevant share certificates but, of course, this is not possible where the shares exist in dematerialised form.[112]

V. PERSONAL SECURITY

The expression 'personal security' refers to two major institutions ie suretyship and independent or demand guarantees.[113] Contracts of suretyship have been recognised for centuries but the judicial recognition of 'demand guarantees' or 'performance bonds' is a relatively recent phenomenon although it was remarked in *Gold Coast Ltd v Caja de Ahorros* that they have now been a feature of commercial life for many years. Back in 1978 in the *Edward Owen* case Lord Denning said that the 'performance bond is a new creature as far as we are concerned'. This is an area where confusion in terminology abounds and the expression 'guarantee' or 'contract of guarantee' is often, and traditionally, used to refer exclusively to contracts of suretyship whereas independent or demand guarantees are often called performance bonds. Moreover,

> the term 'performance bond' or 'performance guarantee' is sometimes used to denote a genuine contract of guarantee or indemnity. To make matters even more confusing, a guarantee or indemnity may be given in circumstances in which one might expect to find a true performance bond. The nature of the particular contract, whether it happens to be a guarantee or an indemnity, or a performance bond, and whether the normal incidents of a contract of that class have been modified, is ultimately a question of construction in each case, and is often very difficult to resolve . . .[114]

[112] The practical steps a lender might take to protect itself in this situation are discussed in Lipton *Security over Intangible Property* (London: Sweet & Maxwell, 2000), at 69–84.

[113] See generally on this area G Andrews and R Millett *Law of Guarantees* 3rd edn (London: Sweet & Maxwell, 2000); K McGuinness *Law of Guarantee*, 2nd edn (Scarborough, Ont.: Carswell, 1996).

[114] *American Home Assurance Co. v Hong Lam Marine Pte Ltd* [1999] 3 SLR 682, a deci-

A. Surety Guarantees

There is no modern statutory definition of suretyship but the expression is described in section 4, Statute of Frauds 1677 as 'any special promise to answer for the debt, default, or miscarriage of another person'. The description has been turned into modern legal terminology as a promise to accept liability for the failure of another party to perform legal obligations, existing and future, and arising from any source.[115] A suretyship contract is a secondary or accessory contract. In other words, the liability of a surety is conditional on the liability of a principal debtor and is co-terminous with that liability. If certain circumstances arise which happen to reduce the liability of the principal debtor or even to extinguish it altogether, then the liability of the surety is proportionately reduced or eliminated. A surety guarantor is relieved from liability, either absolutely or to the extent by which its position has been prejudiced, where there has been some alteration of the creditor/principal debtor relationship that is potentially to the detriment of the surety. If, for example, a creditor binds itself contractually to give a principal debtor more time to pay the debt, without reserving its rights against the surety, the surety may be detrimentally affected.[116] A surety is entitled to be indemnified by the principal debtor in respect of any sums that it is required to pay to the creditor and by giving a principal debtor more time to pay, a creditor may conceivably increase the likelihood that a surety's indemnity *vis-à-vis* the principal debtor could become worthless. The creditor has changed the risk position of the surety, without its consent, and for this reason, the surety is relieved of responsibility. The liability of the surety is tied strictly to the underlying base contract and legally binding modifications of that base contract which are not obviously to the surety's advantage will discharge the surety.

B. Demand Guarantees

The courts in England have treated the demand guarantee as an autonomous performance undertaking analogous to the commercial letter of credit.[117] Demand guarantees are sometimes used to secure the performance of the seller under a sales contract and are commonly used to secure

sion of the Singapore Court of Appeal that is referred to by Jack, Malek, and Quest, *Documentary Credits*, 3rd edn (2000), at 357.

115 *Hampton v Minns* [2002] 1 WLR 1 at 24.

116 See generally on discharge of a surety from liability *Moschi v Lep Air Services* [1973] AC 331; *Natwest Bank v Riley* [1986] BCLC. 268; *Ankar Proprietary Ltd v Natwest Finance* (1987) 162 C.L.R. 549; *Standard Chartered Bank v Walker* [1982] 1 WLR 1410; *China and South Sea Bank v Tan* [1990] 1 AC 536.

117 See generally Jack, *et al*, op cit, ch 12.

the performance of a contractor's obligations to the employer in the case of a construction contract. In the latter situation, a bank will provide the guarantee at the request of a contractor and the guarantee is issued for the benefit of the employer. The contractor stands in a similar position to the applicant for a commercial credit and the position of the bank equates with that of the issuing bank in the letter of credit context. Moreover, the position of the employer is analogous to that of the beneficiary under a letter of credit. The guarantee undertaking given by the bank to the employer is separate and distinct from the original base contract and the bank is not concerned with disputes between employer and contractor. One can stretch the letter of credit analogy too far however.[118] The bank under a letter of credit is the first port of call for payment insofar as the seller of goods is concerned. If the underlying base contract is performed according to its terms then the seller will receive payment from the bank who in turn will be reimbursed by the buyer. On the other hand, a demand guarantee should only be called in practice if something has gone wrong in terms of the underlying base contract. Nevertheless, the courts have stressed the letter of credit analogy in cases such as *Edward Owen v Barclays Bank International*[119] where Lord Denning said:

> A performance bond . . . has many similarities to a letter of credit . . . It has long been established that when a letter of credit is issued and confirmed by a bank, the bank must pay it if the documents are in order and the terms of the credit are satisfied. Any dispute between buyer and seller must be settled between themselves . . . All this leads to the conclusion that the performance guarantee stands on a similar footing to a letter of credit. A bank that gives a performance guarantee must honour the guarantee according to its terms. It is not concerned in the least with the relations between the supplier and the customer; nor with the question whether the supplier is in default or not. The bank must pay according to its guarantee, on demand, if so stipulated without proof or conditions. The only exception is where there is a clear case of fraud of which the bank has notice.

Under English law demand guarantees and standby letters of credit are treated alike. The difference between the two is more a matter of business practice than strict legal rights.[120] A standby credit is payable against documents which evidence or at least

[118] See the comments of Eveleigh LJ in *Potton Homes Ltd v Coleman Contractors Ltd* (1984) 28 *BLR*, 19 at 29.

[119] [1978] 1 QB 159, 171. See also *Esal (Commodities) Ltd v Oriental Credit Ltd* [1985] 2 Lloyds Rep 546.

[120] The similarity between the two undertakings was explored in *Kvaerner John Brown Ltd v Midland Bank plc* [1998] BCLC 446 at 449 where Creswell J said: 'Standby credits issued by banks at the request of a seller or contractor in favour of a buyer or employer are sometimes used in lies of first demand bonds in respect of major long-term sales or construction contracts ... Similar principles for present purposes apply both in relation to standby credits and first demand bonds. In the case of a first demand bond or a standby credit, banks assume irrevocable obligations. It is only in exceptional cases that the courts will interfere with the machinery of irrevocable obligations assumed by banks. Such obligations are regarded as

suggest that the applicant is in breach of an obligation owed to the beneficiary. The underlying obligation may be the performance of a supply or construction contract or the repayment of a loan. In the international oil trade standbys are used as a fall-back payment mechanism. Because of the difficulty of obtaining a set of documents which conform to letter of credit stipulations, standbys are used which can be satisfied by the submission of less rigorous documentation if, following an agreed period after the oil has been delivered, the supplier has not been able to obtain payment by other means. The demand guarantee follows the substance of the standby credit in that the bank gives its irrevocable undertaking to pay against specified documents but, in its purest form, the bank simply undertakes to pay against the beneficiary's first written demand for payment without any further documentation. Unlike the case of standbys, the conventional letter of credit structure of advice and confirmation of the credit by a foreign bank is not appropriate. Instead, the beneficiary will normally require that a local bank actually issue the demand guarantee and the applicant's bank will authorise or mandate the issue. The applicant's bank issues its own undertaking to the local bank to reimburse that bank for any payment it makes under the prime instrument.

C. *The Demand Guarantee/Surety Guarantee Distinction*

Demand guarantees should be distinguished from guarantees by way of surety. The essence of a surety-type guarantee is that, unless otherwise agreed between the parties, the guarantor's liability is co-extensive with that of the party for whose obligation the guarantee is given. Consequently, the guarantor is liable only when that party is liable and only to the extent of that party's liability. By way of contrast, a demand guarantor or issuer of a standby credit is liable when the conditions stipulated in the undertaking are fulfilled, without regard to the underlying contractual position. The issuer of a demand guarantee or standby credit may, therefore, be liable to pay the beneficiary even where the applicant is not actually in default and may be liable to pay sums in excess of those for which the applicant would be personally liable.[121]

This difference in legal result has spawned considerable litigation exploring the parameters of the distinction between demand guarantees and surety guarantees. For example, in the construction industry, advance payment guarantees are often issued to employers who make stage payments to contractors and similarly, refund guarantees are a common

collateral to the underlying rights and obligations between the businessmen at either end of the banking chain.'

[121] See Jack, *et* al, op cit, at 357: 'under [a demand] guarantee, payment must be made against documents, under a [surety] guarantee, proof of primary liability is required which means that there will have to be an extensive investigation of the facts and possibly a lengthy trial before payment will be ordered.' See also on this area *Howe-Richardson v Polimex-Cekop* [1978] 1 Lloyd's Rep. 161; *Esal (Commodities) Ltd v Oriental Credit Ltd* [1985] 2 Lloyd's Rep. 546.

feature of the shipbuilding industry. It appears however, that there is no standard practice in relation to such guarantees; they can either be in the form of demand guarantees or surety guarantees. In *Gold Coast Ltd v Caja de Ahorros del Mediterraneo*[122] Tuckey LJ explained that, in deciding upon the nature of the undertaking in a particular case, the court had to construe the instrument in its factual and contractual context having regard to its commercial purpose. In the *Caja de Ahorros*, the Court of Appeal referred approvingly to the following illumination of the distinction offered in a leading practitioner textbook:[123]

> Where an instrument i) relates to an underlying transaction between parties in different jurisdictions, ii) is issued by a bank, iii) contains an undertaking to pay on demand (with or without the words first and/or written) and iv) does not contain clauses excluding or limiting the defences available to a guarantor, it will almost always be construed as a demand guarantee.

Often the courts will face a difficult task of construction in correctly classifying the nature of the legal relationships assumed by the parties. For example, as in *Trafalgar House Construction Ltd v General Surety and Guarantee Co* Ltd,[124] the contract may contain somewhat contradictory language, describing itself as a performance bond but also using language redolent of suretyship. In *Trafalgar House* the House of Lords decided that the instrument in question was a surety guarantee for a number of reasons. It used suretyship expressions and moreover, bonds in similar form had existed for more than 150 years and had been treated by the parties thereto and by the courts as guarantees.[125]

Because of the fact that a demand guarantee is independent of the underlying base contract, a demand guarantor cannot avail of traditional defences available to a surety guarantor. The independence principle means that there is no room for traditional surety defences to operate. In actual fact, the wording of the contract between creditor and surety guarantor will often exclude or restrict the operation of surety defences. This has led some commentators and courts to the view that there is not so much a stark dichotomy between surety guarantees on the one hand and demand guarantees on the other but rather a spectrum of guarantees. In *Moschi v Lep Air Services Ltd*,[126] for example, Lord Reid said that there was not a general rule applicable to all guarantees. Parties were free to make any agreement they liked and the court had to determine the meaning of the particular agreement Lord Diplock said in the same case that where a

122 2001 WL 1476275.
123 *Paget's Law of* Banking, 11th edn (London: Butterworths, 1996).
124 [1996]1 AC 199.
125 [1996] 1 AC 199 at 205 per Lord Jauncey.
126 [1973] AC 331 at 344.

contractual promise could correctly be classified as a guarantee it was open to the parties expressly to exclude or vary any of their mutual rights or obligations which would otherwise result from its being classifiable as a guarantee.[127] Every case, he added, depended upon the true construction of the actual words in which the promise was expressed.

The spectrum of guarantees would range from traditional surety guarantees with all the implied trappings and trimmings on one end to completely autonomous demand guarantees on the other. The mere fact, however, that a document uses words excluding traditional surety defences, will not transform what is otherwise a demand guarantee into a surety guarantee. Such a clause was one of the features that persuaded the House of Lords in *Trafalgar House* that the relevant instrument was a true guarantee but it did not prove decisive in tipping the balance in favour of a suretyship construction in the *Caja de Ahorros* case.

D. Letters of Comfort

Insofar as surety guarantees are at the bottom end of the spectrum to the extent that liability is concerned, then so-called 'letters of comfort' are off the spectrum. In more cases than not under English law a 'letter of comfort' will provide only moral comfort to a lender to a creditor. The leading case is *Kleinwort Benson v Malaysia Mining Corp*[128] where the Court of Appeal held that a letter of comfort to a lender stating that it was the policy of the parent company to ensure that its subsidiary was 'at all times in a position to meet its liabilities' in respect of a loan made by the lender to the subsidiary did not have contractual effect as a promise regarding the parent company's future intentions towards its subsidiary. On the facts, the letter of comfort was expressed to be only a statement of present fact and not a promise as to future conduct. Bearing in mind the context in which the letters were written they were not intended to be anything other than a representation of fact giving rise to a moral responsibility. It should be noted, and was noted by the Court of Appeal, that during the course of the negotiations the parent company was asked by the lender to provide a legal guarantee of the subsidiary's debts. It had refused and, in consequence of so doing, the subsidiary was charged a higher rate of interest on the loan to reflect the increased risk that the lender was assuming.

The *Kleinwort Benson* decision has been criticised as excessively technical[129] but nevertheless, the case does not foreclose the possibility that

[127] [1973] AC 331 at 349.

[128] [1989] 1 WLR 379.

[129] See the Australian case *Banque Brussels Lambert SA v Australian National Industries* (1989) 21 NSWLR 502. Some commentators have distinguished between 'hard' and 'soft' letters of comfort. Basically a letter of comfort is considered 'soft' if all it includes is the issuer's statement of his awareness of his transaction and a description of his connection with the affil-

'letters of comfort' will be held to have legal consequences where the facts are stronger and different. This point was reiterated by Chadwick J in *Re Atlantic Computers plc*[130] who said that the question for the court in each case is whether, as a matter of construction, in the light of whatever surrounding circumstances may be relevant and admissible, the parties intended to make a contractual promise for the future or to give only a warranty as to present intention.

VI. CONCLUSION

At the moment the law of personal security in England is relatively stable. For example, the autonomy and independence of the demand guarantee from the underlying contract is well-established. The fundamental principles of surety guarantees are also well entrenched though there is a case for rationalisation and reformulation of the law applicable to surety defences. By contrast, the law of 'real' security has attracted more criticism and controversy with unflattering comparisons often being made between the provisions of English law and Article 9 of the US UCC. The latter has been depicted as the 'most modernised, rational and comprehensive system of security interests in the present world'[131] and, viewed in this light, English law is seen to contain a number of undesirable features. While this may well be the case, there are a number of countervailing considerations. First, resort may be had to the old Holmesian dictum that the life of the law has been logic rather than experience. Secondly, while Article 9 may be rational and comprehensive it is certainly not simple and straightforward in its drafting. While Article 9 may have a greater conceptual unity than the law applicable to security interests in England it is highly questionable whether it is any less complex. This is particularly so given the recent revision of Article 9 which has significantly added to its length and complexity. Nor is clarity in communication—an important goal of legislative policy—necessarily better achieved in the United States than in England—neither Article 9 nor any legislative restatement of the English position would win any prizes for literary elegance or the quality of the prose. Legal advisers

iate. A mere indication that the issuer does not have the intention of decreasing his stake in the affiliate in the foreseeable future does not necessarily change the nature of the facility. It becomes a 'hard' letter of comfort only if the issuer assumes a commitment of one type or another, such as his undertaking to see to it that the affiliate remains in a position to perform its financial duties or a promise to retain the existing shareholding. The letter of comfort in the *Kleinwort Benson* case, on this analysis would be of the 'hard' variety and thus legally binding.

130 [1995] BCLC 696.

131 Comment quoted by Diamond (1989) 42 CLP 231, at 241. The comment comes from the report *Study on Security Interests* that Professor Drobnig prepared for UNCITRAL; see vol 8 UNCITRAL Yearbook (1977), 171 at s 2.6.2.3

however, feel comfortable with the existing precepts of English law and the advantages of familiarity are not easily forsaken. Moreover, and more importantly, the credit industry as a whole, and banks in particular, see no obvious merits in moving over to a new system and this reluctance seems well founded, at least from their point of view. Writing a new legislative blueprint risks reopening old controversies, long since resolved in favour of banks, on the scope of secured creditors' rights. When the alternatives remain to be determined, the attractions of the 'tried and trusted' are obvious. Theoretical perfection can and may be sacrificed at the alter of practical utility and while New Zealand has recently gone down the Article 9 route,[132] this is not necessarily any reason for England to follow suit; at least without careful consideration of the consequences. Of course all the issues should be explored when, as recommended by the Company Law Review Steering Group, the Law Commission addresses the whole area of personal property securities. Pending such fundamental review the most likely avenue for reform of the English law of 'real' security is through the vehicle of measures designed to facilitate corporate rescue and the rehabilitation of ailing companies.

[132] Personal Property Securities Act 1999. Up-to-date information on the implementation schedule for this legislation can be found on the following website—<http://www.ppsr.govnz/>.

PART THREE: CIVIL PROCEDURE

Chapter 7

Mediation in Scotland: an Eluded Opportunity?

*Margaret Ross**

I. BACKGROUND

This paper examines the state of mediation in Scotland at present and offers some ideas for its place in the future. Although for many purposes Scotland is a part of the United Kingdom, it has a separate legal system, devolved government and distinct social and administrative factors that influence the use of processes for resolution of disputes.

The legal system of Scotland has its roots in Roman law, however it is now more properly categorised as a mixed legal system, influenced to an increasing extent by case law, including decisions of the House of Lords in civil cases originating in Scotland, and by statute law of a regulatory nature applying across the United Kingdom. Scotland has a history of private ordering of dispute determination, particularly in arbitration which, originating in the thirteenth century, is substantially older than the process of adjudication in courts.[1] Scotland is a relatively small jurisdiction in terms of population, [2] number of courts and judges,[3] and size and diversity of legal professions.[4]

Even in this small country cultural differences survive between east and west, inland and coastal, highland and lowland, and although the racial mix is dominated by white Caucasians, there are pockets of racial and ethnic diversity. Business and education swell the non-Scottish-born popu-

* University of Aberdeen.

[1] RLC Hunter, *The Law of Arbitration in Scotland* (Edinburgh: W Green, 1987), ch 1.

[2] Approximately 5 million.

[3] There is one supreme court (a college of justice comprising 32 Judges) for civil proceedings in Edinburgh acting through its 22 Outer House judges as a court of first instance in civil cases with jurisdiction over the whole of Scotland, and through its 10 Inner House judges as a civil appeal court. A network of 49 local courts dealing with civil and criminal business is staffed by approximately 120 judges ('sheriffs'). Serious criminal cases are tried by the supreme court judges acting as a High Court in Edinburgh and on circuit.

[4] The profession is divided into two branches solicitors (with rights of audience in sheriff courts) and advocates (with rights of audience in all courts). Experienced solicitors may undertake additional training in order to secure rights of audience in the supreme court as solicitor advocates.

lation; there is a history spanning more than 500 years of higher education establishments, originally outnumbering the total of those in the rest of the United Kingdom, and in recent years expansion of traditional industrial expertise into electronics and offshore oil production has brought varied experience of dispute resolution to the Scottish domain. Devolved legislative competence to a Scottish Parliament in Edinburgh[5] has brought about unprecedented interchange of ideas between the policy-makers and legislators and those engaged in the delivery and analysis of legal and social mechanisms. Justice and health have been the major areas of activity of that new Parliament in its first two years.

The system of sheriff courts in Scotland,[6] with jurisdiction over virtually all types of civil case and all but the most serious criminal cases ensures that courts are geographically accessible to all but those living in the remotest parts. However, cost, and, to a lesser extent, administrative backlog, create difficulties of access to courts which, although on a smaller scale than those examined by Lord Woolf in relation to England and Wales[7] are nevertheless pervasive disincentives to litigation. Lawyers in Scotland have a heritage of providing wide-ranging advice, both legal and practical, and of negotiating settlement in the majority of cases,[8] either before or after litigation has commenced. Although risk management within the profession, coupled with the advance of 'blame culture' has fostered partisanship, the polarising effect and inherent gamble of litigation is widely recognised, and efforts to settle cases prior to evidential hearing in court, are well established in the practice of litigation. Recent research has revealed gaps in provision of advice in relation to some problems of a legal nature, and considerable need for advice from those who are not lawyers, but who are trained to the appropriate level to provide information and advice which is low cost, easily accessible and understandable.[9]

Against a background of private ordering, compactness, and desire for practical advice it might be assumed that mediation would have found fertile ground in Scotland. The reality is that the opportunity to embrace mediation as a realistic and realisable process of dispute resolution has not yet been grasped with widespread enthusiasm and confidence.[10] The situation has

[5] Scotland Act 1998. The Scottish parliament was established by election in May 1999.

[6] Ibid, n 4.

[7] Interim Report to the Lord Chancellor on the Civil Justice System in England and Wales, June 1995; Final Report: *Access to Justice*, July 1996.

[8] S Moody and R Mackay, *Alternative Dispute Resolution in Scotland* (Edinburgh: W Green, 1995), para 1.2.7.

[9] *Review of Legal Information and Advice Provision in Scotland* (Edinburgh: Scottish Executive, 2001); Genn and Paterson, *Paths to Justice Scotland* (Oxford: Hart Publishing, Oxford, 2001).

[10] In 1995 Moody and Mackay noted that ADR was a 'latecomer to Scotland' but that it 'would not go away', Moody and Mackay, op cit, para 10.5.1–10.5.2.

been described variously: '(t)he concept of ADR has not been uniformly embraced within the various areas of civil dispute';[11] 'the legal system currently provides somewhat uneven access to mediation, and the scope for mediation appears to be under-exploited';[12] and, in December 2001, 'mediation has not taken hold in Scotland, outwith the family and community fields'.[13]

II. THE DEVELOPMENT OF MEDIATION IN SCOTLAND

A. Labelling and Images

Mediation as it is does exist in Scotland can include any process by which a neutral third party is used to assist parties who are in dispute, not to impose a determination upon the dispute, but to empower the parties to identify, discuss and, if possible, agree upon a way forward through[14] the dispute. This description, which bears some similarities to the definition of mediation adopted in Australia in 1999,[15] is intentionally broad. It avoids some of the features of traditional definitions which may have acted as disincentives to the assumption of mediation as a *standard* tool for resolution of disputes, rather than an infrequently used *alternative*. Mediation in Scotland is most often discussed under the collective banner of alternative dispute resolution, which first emerged in Scotland in the 1980s, but it found initial recognition in the context of reordering of family relationships, for which a conciliation service,[16] provided by trained volunteers, was developed in 1984. The piecemeal contexts in which the terms conciliation, mediation and alternative dispute resolution arose in Scotland provided little scope for focused development. Furthermore, the uncertainty of terminology has at once exemplified and intensified the lack of clarity and security in the processes.

[11] R Mays and B Clark, *Alternative Dispute Resolution in Scotland* (Edinburgh: Scottish Office Central Research Unit, 1996).

[12] J Lewis, *The Role of Mediation in Family Disputes in Scotland*, Legal Studies Research Findings No 23, (Edinburgh: Scottish Office Central Research Unit, 1999).

[13] Scottish Consumer Council, *Consensus without going to court: Encouraging Mediation in non-family civil disputes in Scotland* (Edinburgh, 2001).

[14] This avoids the expectation that the process will resolve the whole dispute. This will normally be the aim and the aim may be achieved, but even a mediation that has failed in resolving the whole dispute, is likely to change the shape of the dispute and to open up possibilities for negotiated settlement of the remainder, or more closely focused litigation.

[15] 'A process in which the parties to a dispute, with the assistance of a neutral third party (the mediator), identifies the disputed issues, develop options, consider alternatives and endeavour to reach agreement. The mediator has no advisory or determinative role in regard to the content of the dispute or the outcome of its resolution, but may advise on or determine the process of mediation whereby resolution is attempted.'

[16] Later renamed Family Mediation Scotland.

B. Conciliation

'Conciliation' was used by the first family mediation services in Scotland[17] to describe a negotiation facilitated by a neutral third party, enabling a communicative approach to decision-making about children arising from relationship breakdown. This was in contrast to the polarised and distant process of determination of issues by the court with which many family practitioners were dissatisfied.[18] It was confused by some potential users with the concept of *reconciliation*, and to some the term suggested undue concession to the wishes of the other party. Nevertheless the take-up of conciliation services was significant.[19] The process was provided by trained volunteers, under the auspices of a charitable company with an organising committee of those eager to offer an alternative to the traditional referral to the court in the absence of direct or assisted negotiation.[20] The presence of family lawyers and judges on those organising committees reflected perceived need for another process and promoted referrals. The process involved facilitated negotiation between the parents, but concentrated on the interests of the child by reducing conflict between parents, paving the way for children to be involved with both parents and for parents sharing the responsibility of the child's upbringing despite the breakdown of their relationship.[21] In that context some evaluation by the conciliator of the positions of the parties was possible, and the conciliator might suggest settlement terms.[22] The child was not invited to attend, but with increasing recognition of the right of the child to be heard[23] increased participation by children has been accommodated. The process was renamed family mediation in 1987.

The term conciliation had become more widely known in Scotland through employment relations legislation. Since 1976 the state-funded Advisory Conciliation and Arbitration Service (ACAS) has offered a free conciliation process (effectively facilitative, mainly non-evaluative, shuttle mediation) in all applications[24] before the employment tribunal (the body

[17] The first service was in established in Edinburgh for the Lothian area in 1984. The process had been described and advocated to the Scottish legal profession by J Wright, 'Matrimonial Conciliation' (1981) 26 *Journal of the Law Society of Scotland* 432.

[18] Lewis, op cit.

[19] S Matheson and H Gentleman, *The Scottish Family Conciliation (Mediation) Service (Lothian)*, (Scottish Office Central Research Unit, 1986).

[20] Moody and Mackay, op cit, ch 3.

[21] Ibid, para 3.2.1.

[22] Ibid, para 3.6.6.

[23] UN Convention on the Rights of the Child, Article 3; Moody and Mackay, op cit, para 3.8.6; E Sutherland and A Clelland, *Children's Rights in Scotland*, 2nd edn (Edinburgh: W Green, 2001).

[24] Applications are commonly made without lawyer involvement, not least because no legal aid is available for the tribunal procedure.

with exclusive jurisdiction over employment disputes at first instance).[25] The process is widely and easily understood, and has been well received.[26] Its success may be due in part to the relative inexperience of many parties (and lawyers) in appearing before the tribunal; the automatic offer of the service, free of charge, at a critical stage in the relatively short pre-hearing procedure of tribunal applications; and the desire of both parties for negotiating autonomy within the highly regulated area of employment relations.

C. Mediation

Although mediation in family cases is now in regular used albeit on to a variable degree across Scotland,[27] the use of mediation in other contexts remains limited.[28] In 2001 the Journal of the Law Society of Scotland (the professional journal issued to all practising solicitors), featured articles about mediation aimed at raising awareness in the profession.[29] The articles are descriptive of simple practical mediation processes, and although written by those who are knowledgeable and experienced it is paradigmatic of the low level of baseline acceptance of mediation that the topic required this type of coverage after more than 15 years of available mediation processes, including mediation by trained solicitor mediators. Evaluation of mediation activity has been undertaken,[30] but the low volume of cases makes it difficult to evaluate, articulate and replicate positive features and available data has not been put to particular effect to address negative perceptions.

It is at least possible that the label 'mediation' creates in the mind of a party an unacceptable vision of 'meeting in the middle',[31]of giving substantive ground in a distributive manner to the other party, and/or of giving way procedurally by releasing information that might have been withheld in the

[25] Rather confusingly the same body in its exercise of dispute prevention and resolution in the collective employers: employees arena is charged with 'conciliation' to describe facilitated negotiation, but 'mediation' to describe a more evaluative process verging, at its most interventive, upon arbitration, Moody and Mackay, op cit, paras 7.2.1 and 7.4.1.

[26] Ibid, paras 7.6.1–7.6.4.

[27] J Lewis, op cit.

[28] Scottish Consumer Council, *Consensus without going to court: Encouraging Mediation in non-family civil disputes in Scotland* (Edinburgh,2001).

[29] J Sturrock and D Semple, 'Mediating a cultural revolution' (2001) 46 *Journal of the Law Society of Scotland* 21; A Hall Dick and E Malcolm 'Let Mediation take the strain' (2001) 46 *Journal of the Law Society of Scotland* 24; R McKenzie 'The Falkirk experience' (2001) 46 *Journal of the Law Society of Scotland* 32, S Clark 'Learning from across the Altantic' (2001) 46 *Journal of the Law Society of Scotland* 33.

[30] See further below. It is perhaps cynical to note that evaluation has been funded and effected only in areas of mediation activity where funding by the state is an issue.

[31] A term used in a report evaluating family mediation in Scotland, F Myers and F Wasoff, *Meeting in the Middle: A Study of Solicitors' and Mediators' Divorce Practice* (Legal Studies Research Findings No 25, Scottish Executive Central Research Unit, 2000).

adversarial process.[32] This is an unfortunate vision because it is not reflective of the expansion of options that mediation can create; of the non-distributional nature of the process; of the fact that it is open to any party to walk away from the process without reaching agreement.

Mediation also emerged in 1987 in Scotland in the minor criminal case context[33]—by way of diversionary reparation and mediation processes practiced in a few areas (funding issues dictated initially that these would be inner cities) under schemes provided by SACRO[34] In this context, the image of meeting in the middle is displaced by the concept of the offender accepting the need to make reparation, and coming to an agreed plan for reparation after mediated (invariably shuttle) discussions with the victim. The process of mediation in this context is, it is submitted, more obviously evaluative than facilitative, although it operates differently for the parties according to the situation. In the main it will be the offender who has to be educated by the mediator regarding public and social unacceptability and direct impact of offending behaviour upon the victim (evaluation), but the corresponding understanding by the victim of the private and social factors that drive the offender to offend enrich the process and social understanding.

D. Alternative Dispute Resolution

The term alternative dispute resolution (ADR) was introduced to Scotland from the USA, Australia and England. In some quarters it met the resistance that one would associate with the somewhat pejorative use of 'alternative': different, difficult to understand, threatening, uncertain. Indeed those committed to the benefits of ADR have sought to improve its press by re-labelling it as 'additional', 'appropriate' or 'assisted'[35] and more recently 'effective'[36] dispute resolution. The term is in some respects equated only with consensual methods of dispute resolution, particularly conciliation and mediation. However it can be a very broad umbrella term for all adjudicative and evaluative processes other than litigation[37] including arbitration.[38] The selling point for ADR in Scotland to date has been substitution

32 Although this is not necessary

33 Moody and Mackay, op cit, para 2.3.1 et seq.

34 The acronym originally referred to the Scottish Association for the Care and Resettlement of Offenders, but now describes the renamed organisation Safer Communities and Reducing Offending.

35 Moody and Mackay, op cit.

36 The Centre for Dispute Resolution (CEDR) an ADR agency and training body is now styled the Centre for *Effective* Dispute Resolution.

37 ADR in Scotland; Scots Commercial Law

38 Adjudicative and evaluative processes outwith mediation and conciliation not within the focus of this paper.

for the adversarial process of litigation[39] which may be an understandable point of contrast, but in reality it is used in a variety of ways in and around the court process. Indeed, concentrating upon ADR as a means of removal of a dispute from the security of the understood court system probably has acted against its acceptance and development in the general arena of civil disputes. Not least, lawyers who traditionally service the court system are effectively gatekeepers of referral to their business-threatening mediation in many commercial and family disputes. The public, somewhat superficial, appreciation of court processes with the perception that this will achieve 'justice' and vindication of rights is a powerful image to displace.

That various methods of resolving, or at least reshaping, disputes are used in advance of or alongside litigation is not in question. However, these are largely ad hoc and not perceived, nor presented, under the label of Alternative Dispute Resolution. Nevertheless they provide hope that the shift of equilibrium towards party-owned and party-centred dispute resolution is achievable in Scotland. Mediation is the most powerful of shareable tools for dispute handling. In some contexts piloting, followed by practice in mediation has established a toehold at least.

III. THE CURRENT PRACTICE OF MEDIATION AND CONCILIATION IN SCOTLAND

Although the mediation practice in Scotland is limited in volume, nevertheless it is available to those who wish to use it (and in some situations only those who can afford it) in the following range of situations.

Family disputes through the charitably funded Family Mediation Scotland service (some areas of Scotland can only offer mediation of child issues),[40] and on all issues through lawyers trained as mediators (collectively operating as CALM)[41] funded privately or by legal aid in certain circumstances (subject to assessment of means);[42]

Commercial disputes, privately funded, or, by legal aid if litigation has been commenced and permission is obtained from the legal aid board.

[39] A leaflet to increase public awareness entitled *Resolving Disputes Without Going to Court* was published by Scottish Courts Administration in August 1996.

[40] All issues mediation is available from this body only where the local provider is confident in the training and ability of their mediators to deal with this.

[41] Comprehensive Accredited Lawyer Mediators.

[42] The Scottish Legal Aid Board has embraced the role of mediation in family disputes, having successfully piloted funding for pre-litigation mediation, and extended the scheme on an indefinite basis in to mediation pre and post litigation.

Consumer disputes, where industry or advice agency schemes are in place, or where in the context of small claim actions in the sheriff court, the sheriff assumes the evaluative, mediatory mantle, which is permitted by the court rules.[43]

Community disputes, where community mediation facilities are available, mainly funded by central government,[44] which may involve qualifying factors for access to the facility such as location, social band or other conditions of sponsorship.

Victim–offender schemes (as diversions away from prosecution rather than post-prosecution restorative measures),[45] where a scheme is in operation. The application of the scheme to a particular case depends upon agreement from the prosecutor and the victim. Cases can be mediated only after referral from the police to the prosecutor and before the prosecutor commences proceedings. Schemes involving juvenile offenders (who are subject to the jurisdiction of Children's Hearings rather than the court) are being piloted in some areas.

Employment and workplace disputes, through the statutorily established Advisory Conciliation and Arbitration Service (ACAS) if there is a collective dispute or a case already before the employment tribunal, and privately arranged if there is a workplace issue between individuals.

Professional service complaints procedures increasingly include mediation schemes, ie complaints are routinely referred to mediation, although this does not preclude further action if the mediation is unsuccessful or a mediator's evaluation of the situation is not accepted.[46]

Educational disputes, privately arranged and funded and at times promoted by procedures for dealing with complaints or grievances, including peer mediation carried out by mediation-trained senior students.

[43] Small Claims Rules 1988, (SI 1988/1976) Rule 13.

[44] J Dignan and A Sorsby, *Resolving Neighbour Disputes through Mediation in Scotland* Development Department Research Programme Research Findings No 64 (Edinburgh: The Scottish Office Central Research Unit, 1999).

[45] Although compensation orders may be made as part of the sentencing process there is no process at present for mediation as part of a sentence. This in part mirrors the lack of victim input in the sentencing process, but since there are moves in Scotland towards additional victim involvement in sentencing, further exploration of mediation in this context may occur.

[46] Examples are Scottish Motor Trades Association; Law Society of Scotland complaints scheme, Royal Institution of Chartered Surveyors complaints scheme. See also R Christie 'Complaints against solicitors: Conciliation or confrontation' (1994) 39 *Journal of the Law Society of Scotland* 43.

Relationship mediation, available privately basis from those with training in mediation and, usually, background training or experience in human sciences or human resources.

IV. EVALUATION OF EXISTING MEDIATION PRACTICE IN SCOTLAND

A. Mapping the Use of Mediation

Some work has been done in the latter half of the 1990s to map the extent of use of alternative dispute resolution across the board in Scotland,[47] and more recently to suggest means of encouraging mediation. Research projects evaluating processes of mediation in Scotland have to some extent been hampered by the low volume of mediation work,[48] and perhaps reveal more about the obstacles to the use of mediation in Scotland than to its overwhelming success. Nevertheless, set against the small size of Scotland, the outcomes are significant, and advance the debate about increased use of mediation.

Family mediation, as the most widely established of mediation processes has been the most widely examined. Matheson and Gentleman in 1986[49] and Jones in 1990[50] examined the Family Conciliation/Mediation services then available, and noted their effectiveness in achieving settlement. There were improved settlement rates the sooner after separation the process was started, and even after litigation had commenced and parties had become entrenched in positions good settlement rates were achieved if the litigation was still at an early stage. Parties felt that they had been 'helped' by mediation, reflecting the fact that even if settlement in whole had not been achieved,[51] there had been an improvement of some sort in relationships or the perception of the dispute. A study by Lewis[52] in 1999 revealed that even by that late stage lawyers had little knowledge or experience of mediation, and if clients opted into the process or were referred to it by the court, their lawyers were unable to reassure them as to the process or its past effectiveness. Awareness and acceptability for ethnic families was even poorer.[53]

[47] R Mays and B Clark, *Alternative Dispute Resolution in Scotland,* Edinburgh: Scottish Office Central Research Unit, 1996). The state of ADR in Scotland is examined from the perspectives of the various subject areas in which it was then available in Moody and Mackay, op cit. The most up-to date review is Scottish Consumer Council, *Consensus without going to court:Encouraging Mediation in non-family civil disputes in Scotland* (Edinburgh, 2001).

[48] Mays and Clark, op cit.

[49] Matheson and Gentleman, op cit,

[50] R Jones, *Family Conciliation in Scotland* (Edinburgh: Scottish Office, 1990).

[51] Settlement rates of at least one issue were recorded at over 70 per cent.

[52] Lewis, op cit.

[53] V Pankaj, *Family Mediation Services for Minority Ethnic Families in* Scotland,Legal Studies Research Findings No 36 (Edinburgh: Scottish Executive Central Research Unit, 2001).

Despite low levels of lawyer awareness, family mediation nevertheless amongst those who do have some awareness, carries the somewhat disabling preconception of being 'better' at dealing with child issues than judicial alternatives, an assumption promoted by some members of the judiciary and lawyers who routinely refer cases involving children to mediation.[54]

Myers and Wasoff[55] reported in 2000 following a qualitative study involving interviews with mediators (both lawyer and non-lawyer) and non-mediator family lawyers. The study did not involve attendance at the process of mediation itself.[56] The findings indicate that non-mediator family lawyers adopt a conciliatory approach in dealing with family disputes, and by a process of evaluation of parties' conduct and positions against the known attitudes of the courts, coupled with realistic advice, disputes are often resolved between parties and their agents without resorting to the process of mediation itself. This conclusion is perceived by critics to belittle the fundamental differences between the role of the mediator and that of the pragmatic family lawyer.[57] The study involves a small sample, but given the relatively small cohort of family lawyers and mediators operating in Scotland, the sample is not insignificant. Process difficulties in obtaining access to mediation sessions (or recent accounts of them) appear to have been over-played when the study was designed. The study also examines a very narrow point in relation to family mediation, and is more illuminating in its conclusions about family lawyers. Lewis's study in 1999 draws out more disturbing information about patchy knowledge and access. More research could be done to examine the reasons for variation in access and confidence levels amongst professionals and disputants.

Victim: offender mediation as it then operated in Scotland was examined by Warner who, reporting in 1992,[58] who notes that mediation is potentially very valuable to participants, but more particularly to the offender in terms of avoiding the humiliation of the court process. An evaluation of the economics of the process did not reveal savings in cost.[59] The absence of a systematic and reliable funding process for the former as compared to that existing for the latter prevented the process from being available other than to a minority of victims and offenders.[60] A sense of unease which some

[54] Lewis, op cit.

[55] Myers and Wasoff, op cit.

[56] It is understood that this was because of difficulty in arranging access to the process.

[57] J Scoular and C Irvine, 'A review of 'Meeting in the Middle'' 2001 14 *Scots Law Times (News)* 125.

[58] S Warner, *Making Amends: Justice for Victims and Offenders* (Aldershot: Averbury, 1992).

[59] M Knapp and A Netten, 'Reparation, mediation and prosecution: Comparative costs', in Warner, op cit, at ch 8.

[60] Warner, op cit, 136, 149, 155.

accustomed to the criminal justice system might have felt with a process of private reparation—even for minor crimes—was not replicated by participants (including prosecutors, victims and accused).[61] This process of mediation involves departure from norms of public understanding of dealing with criminal conduct, with complicity on the part of the prosecutor. It is less open to assumption that the alternative process must be better, having to overcome as it does the instinctive expectation of public disapproval of the conduct whatever the wish of the victim. However, as in some other jurisdictions, the process of reparation and mediation in criminal cases remains a marginal one, limited by funding, types of criminal conduct and prosecutor attitudes. As yet in Scotland possibilities of promoting mediation before the stage of referral to the prosecution do not exist, except in relation to juvenile crime. In statutory offences where there is a time limit upon commencement of prosecution this may prevent the referral, which, if unsuccessful, would preclude prosecution due to lack to time bar.

Community mediation has been examined in the context of neighbour disputes in which it commonly is used[62] and in wider community issues.[63] Community mediation has been an area of growth in the last decade and mediation is firmly placed in a range of tools for dealing with anti-social conduct and community environmental issues. A large degree of agency (ie police, housing authorities) support for it is necessary, but this has been forthcoming. The fact that community tensions require multi-agency action and cooperation sets an environment within which mediation can blossom. However funding constraints, and instances of poor interaction between relevant agencies are the main obstacles to uptake and success.

B. Evaluation Processes

Evaluating ADR has been the domain of researchers funded by the state, as the references will confirm. There are limited funding opportunities for research other than the Central Research Unit of the Scottish Government, and their interest in evaluation is enhanced by the fact that government and local authority funding has been behind much of the processes that have been researched. There has been less evaluative activity in relation to privately-funded mediation, but satisfied customers of this have been open in support of the process,[64] and provide repeat business.

[61] Ibid, 138.

[62] Dignan and Sorsbury, op cit.

[63] R McKay and A Brown, *Community Mediation in Scotland: A study of its Implementation* (Edinburgh: Scottish Office Central Research Unit, 1998).

[64] Such as in promotional literature for CEDR whose trained mediators operate in Scotland as well as in England and Wales.

Some academic and critical analysis has been undertaken in Scotland in relation to mediation as a process,[65] its contextual development and the issues that it must address, [66] particularly in the family mediation context.[67] Increasingly, evaluation and analysis notes the gaps between theory and reality. Much more *evaluation* by mediators than theoretical models would suggest is found to occur in practice or to be desired by those who attempt mediation.[68] The theoretical emphasis of mediation on future conduct and relationships rather than on past (poor) conduct and relationships is not necessarily what is desirable in family or community mediation—reflection on past conduct may be vital to improvement for the future.[69]

Some interesting material about evaluation and mediation also emerges from studies of traditional legal processes and remedies. Thus in a study of Options Hearings in sheriff court civil actions[70] (in which the sheriff is expected to ensure expeditious progress of the case after both parties have set out their legal and factual cases in written pleadings) considerable difference in judicial approach to intervention is identified,[71] and in a study of the use of civil remedies in relation to neighbour disputes it emerges that much court procedure in this area is avoided by housing management techniques, many of which are conciliatory in nature, and by referral to community mediation services, if available in the area.[72] The Scottish Consumer Council has noted that the lack of a civil justice review in Scotland such as that carried out by Lord Woolf in England and Wales has meant that there is no systematic review of the state of consensual dispute resolution in Scotland,[73] nor the awareness-raising and procedural promotion that such

[65] See for example Scoular, 'Process Notes: Mediation in Family Disputes', in Scoular (ed), *Family Dynamics* (Edinburgh: Butterworths, 2001); W Semple 'Mediation as a form of ADR' (1994) *Journal of the Law Society of Scotland* 406.

[66] R Mays and B Clark, 'The Legal Profession and ADR' 1996 *Juridical Review* 389; ead, 'Funding ADR in Scotland' 1997 *Scots Law Times (News)* 29.

[67] Semple 'Mediation as a form of ADR', 406, and rejoinders by F Raitt, 'Mediation as a form of ADR' (1995) 40 *Journal of the Law Society of Scotland* 182 and A Oswald 'Mediation in Family Disputes' (1996) 41 *Journal of the Law Society of Scotland*, 115. Raitt 'Informal Justice and the Ethics of Mediating in Family Disputes' 1997 2 *Juridical Review*, 76.

[68] R Mackay and A Brown *Community Mediation in Scotland,* Legal Studies Research Findings No 24 (Edinburgh Scottish Officer Central Research Unit, 1999), Lewis, op cit.

[69] Mackay and Brown, op cit.

[70] E Samuel and R Bell, *Defended Ordinary Actions in the Sheriff Court: Implementing Ordinary Cause Rules (1993),* Legal Studies Research Findings No 8 (Edinburgh: Scottish Office Central Research Unit, 1995.

[71] Similar to the divergence of judicial approaches identified in the examination of family mediation referrals by Lewis, op cit.

[72] R Atkinson, T Mullen, and S Scott, *The Use of Civil Legal Remedies for Neighbour Nuisance in Scotland* (Edinburgh: Scottish Executive Central Research Unit, 2000), chs 3 and 6.

[73] A review of the business of the Outer House of the Court of Session makes no mention of processes to expedite resolution, *Review of the Business of the Outer House of the Court of Session*, Lord Cullen (1995).

an exercise can achieve. So, in the absence of a review of civil justice has there been any institutationalisation of mediation in Scotland?

V. INSTITUTIONALISING MEDIATION

The epitome of institutionalisation of mediation would be its use on the order of the court. There are no compulsory mediation schemes within court procedures in Scotland. There are rules of court that permit (but do not require) the sheriff or judge to refer a matter to mediation. These are relatively well known in the context of family proceedings,[74] but now are also in rules for expediting commercial actions.[75] In this commercial context they are dependent to a lesser extent upon the judge's decision to invoke some mediation process, and to a greater extent upon the parties' decision to use the speedier and more flexible court process for commercial actions.[76] If the parties invoke the expeditious procedure, the court must do all it can to expedite an outcome, including investigating the use of alternative dispute resolution. In the family action context research indicates powerfully that practice varies greatly from court to court[77] and although mediation is used greatly in some areas[78] it is used infrequently in others.[79] Much seems to depend upon the individual knowledge of the judge or sheriff dealing with the case, to the extent that if a case is heard by one resident judge rather than another in the same court, the chances of referral to mediation will be different. Perhaps the extension of powers of sheriffs to expedite the determination of the case in general[80] and issues involving children in particular[81] prompt the more adventurous of sheriffs to attempt to secure settlement by evaluative dialogue involving parties and their agents in court, but the more traditional judicial approach of refereeing up to the point of adjudicating is still very much in evidence.[82] It is to the good that there is now wider scope for judges to guide parties, which may encourage them to negotiate or self-refer to mediation. However without the power to require parties to attempt a process of facilitated negotiation the predominant image within the court system appears is hasty negotiation at the door of the final court hearing.

[74] Act of Sederunt (Ordinary Cause Rules) 1993 ('OCR') rule 33.22 (Sheriff court); Rules of the Court of Session 1994 ('RCS') rule 49.23.

[75] RCS rule 47.12.

[76] Both procedures are optional, and cannot be used unless both parties agree. RCS ch 47; OCR rule 40.12A (introduced with effect from 1 Mar 2001).

[77] Lewis, op cit.

[78] See also McKenzie 'The Falkirk Experience' (2001) 46 *Journal of the Law Society of Scotland*, 32.

[79] Lewis, op cit.

[80] OCR rule 9.12.

[81] OCR rule 33.22A (by compulsory child welfare hearing early in the proceedings which the parties must attend).

[82] Samuel and Bell, op cit.

In order for mediation to be required routinely or even encouraged by the court it is essential for knowledge levels to be improved. Calls for training of lawyers, and particularly the judiciary, have been made for a number of years,[83] but levels of awareness are still considerably below those in other jurisdictions.[84] The matter of judicial appointments and training has only recently been taken to a new level of independence and professionalism in Scotland[85] and it is to be hoped that the situation will improve as a result of increased training, and of enhanced awareness levels in a new generation of legal personnel who may have been exposed to mediation. Some attempt has been made to alert lawyers to the opportunities as compared to perceived threats that mediation may create.[86]

Education about mediation has not been part of the core curriculum of university legal education in Scotland, but in recent years some universities have introduced material on an optional basis,[87] and the core curriculum now adopted for providers of the professional qualifying degree and postgraduate 'bridge' diploma creates an expectation (albeit somewhat minimalist) of education and skills training in consensual dispute resolution as well as in legal instutions.

After a report by the Scottish Law Commission dealing with concerns about confidentiality and privilege in family mediation,[88] statutory protection from discovery of the process of family mediation is found in the Civil Evidence (Family Mediation)(Scotland) Act 1995. The Act only applies to mediation conducted by an approved service. In fact the two pre-existing organisational providers of family mediation in Scotland were approved without undergoing an evaluation process, Family Mediation Scotland and The Law Society of Scotland. In the commercial context there is no express protection from disclosure of what occurs in the mediation, nor is there similar requirement for institutional approval of available processes. The difference is no doubt in keeping with the perception of freedom of choice

[83] Most recently by the Scottish Consumer Council, *Consensus without going to court: Encouraging Mediation in non-family civil disputes in Scotland* (Edinburgh, 2001), paras 3.3, 6.9.

[84] R Mays and B Clark, 'The Legal Profession and ADR', 1996 *Juridical Review*, 389.

[85] A judicial appointments board was established by the Bail, Judicial Appointments etc (Scotland) Act 2000.

[86] J Sturrock and D Semple, 'Mediating a cultural revolution'; Hall Dick and Malcolm 'Let Mediation take the strain', McKenzie 'The Falkirk experience', Clark 'Learning from across the Atlantic' M Stone, *Representing Clients in Mediation* (Edinburgh: Butterworths, 1998).

[87] The author's course in Alternative Methods of Dispute Resolution at Aberdeen University is currently the only self-contained course on this topic available in Scotland, although others cover mediation and other processes within substantive courses such as Jurisprudence, Family Law, Commercial Law, see Scottish Consumer Council, *Consensus without going to court:Encouraging Mediation in non-family civil disputes in Scotland* (Edinburgh, 2001), para 6.7.

[88] Scottish Law Commission, *Report on Evidence: Protection of Family Mediation* (Scot Law Com No 136) (1992).

and commercial acuity of the parties in commercial disputes, and some protection from disclosure is afforded by the privileges attaching to negotiation.[89] However evaluation reveals poor levels of understanding of matters of confidentiality and privilege outwith the traditional legal context.[90]

There has been no hint in Scotland of a general expectation of mediated settlement in court proceedings such as that promoted by the Woolf Report and the Civil Procedure Rules 1999 in England and Wales. That is not to say that there is no movement towards mediated settlements. It is known that parties have many justiciable events in their lives, most of which are not referred to the courts, but require some advice or assistance for their determination, even if the determination is simply to a decision not to take the matter further. The extent of pre-institutional need for dispute advice and assistance has been assessed as part of the review of legal information and advice provision in Scotland.[91] A proposed Community Legal Service for Scotland,[92] would be expected to act as a gateway for referral to appropriate services to enable the individual to access appropriate advice and assistance. The extension of the Institutional continuum to incorporate a community legal service should act as a platform for inclusion of mediation processes, whether within the court process or as a preliminary, satellite, or postscript.[93] However, adjectival law is not the only vehicle for change. Mediation can be built into substantive law, following the example of conciliation in employment law and ideally a combination of both can generate the institutional momentum for change.

A statement to the effect that disputes involving government departments in the United Kingdom might be referred to mediation instead of litigation is a welcome statement of confidence in the consensual process. Mediation has been a successful means of resolution of disputes of public law and the public–private interface, particularly in environmental disputes,[94] although the confidentiality that is often seen as a strength of

89 Concessions made for the purposes of negotiation only are protected from being disclosed or founded upon in subsequent court proceedings, but unequivocal admissions, albeit made in a negotiation context, are not so protected, *Daks Simpson Group v Kuiper* 1994 *Scots Law Times* 689.

90 Mackay and Brown, op cit.

91 *Review of Legal Information and Advice Provision in Scotland* (Edinburgh: Scottish Executive 2001); Genn and Paterson, op cit.

92 Mirroring to some extent that brought into existence in England and Wales in 2000 with statutory basis in the Access to Justice Act 1999.

93 eg, it would be possible to follow the model proposed in New Zealand for adoption cases, requiring the court to approve a parenting plan as a condition of the adoption order in court, but disputes about the implementation of that plan after the court order had been made, would not be justiciable, but referable to mediation, *Adoption and its Alternatives: A Different Approach and a New Framework* (Report No 65, Sept 2000).

94 eg, negotiated arrangements for access or development under the Wildlife and Countryside Act 1981 Part II.

consensual dispute resolution may be seen as a disadvantage in matters of public interest. Concerns about the lack of public access to the outcomes of mediated settlements should not be underestimated, and there would be difficulty in achieving justiciable and legitimated outcomes if there were so few events put to open adjudication that no precedents were available. However, these are issues to consider when there is effective choice of mediation within the institutional continuum, not when the level of awareness in Scotland is too low for effective decision-making.

VI. PROFESSIONALISING MEDIATION

Despite the low level of use of mediation in Scotland there is a reasonable-sized pool of those who have undergone mediation training.[95] Family mediation is provided by lawyers who are accredited as family mediators by the Law Society of Scotland after undergoing an approved training programme. They self-organise as CALM (Comprehensive Accredited Lawyer Mediators) which has devised a code of conduct for mediators and the mediation process. Breach of that code of conduct by the mediator would jeopardise continued provision of services under that banner. Non-lawyer family mediators train under the aegis of Family Mediation Scotland which in turn is affiliated to the UK-wide National College of Mediators. Training in family mediation is normally geared to family cases only and is not transferable to other contexts. Even in the relatively buoyant arena of family mediation most accrediting bodies have had to reduce the requirements of mediation practice for routine re-accreditation since no mediators could satisfy the minimum experience originally specified.

Commercial mediators (ie those who may undertake paid mediation of any civil dispute, but not normally family disputes) may be trained and accredited by a number of commercial organisations most operating UK wide,[96] but one purely Scottish training bodies now exists (drawing upon mediation experience from Scotland and abroad).[97] Professional bodies such as the Law Society of Scotland, Faculty of Advocates, Royal Institution of Chartered Surveyors, will require that training has been undertaken with a training provider recognised or accredited by them before the mediator may provide services linked to their professional status. Failures in the process of conducting mediation in so far as they may also

[95] Approximately 65 Lawyer mediators for non-family disputes and 50 in family disputes (out of a legal profession of over 8000), and 100 non-lawyer family/other mediators. See also Scottish Consumer Council, *Consensus without going to court: encouraging Mediation in non-family civil disputes in Scotland* (Edinburgh, 2001), Lewis, op cit.

[96] eg, CEDR, ADR Group, IDR. Mediation UK, Mediation Bureau.

[97] Core Mediation Ltd.

breach the professional ethics or rules of conduct will be actionable or open to disciplinary procedures of that profession. Some training organisations are also accrediting bodies[98] with codes of conduct breach of which involves loss of accreditation. Mediators employed by the state or non-governmental public bodies are few, the main exception being those in the employment relations arena who are employed and trained by ACAS.

Community mediation and victim–offender mediation has tended to be within the domain of community and social working organisations who provide or secure training through the public or voluntary sector. Training is for the purposes of the project in hand, and is not normally transferable into domains such as family or commercial mediation (although some consumer, landlord/tenant, education issues may fall within the broad term of community mediation).[99] Quality of training and expertise within these particular areas may be very high, with more opportunity for shadowing, co-mediation and sharing of experience than occurs in the private mediation field.

VII. WHAT WILL THE FUTURE HOLD FOR MEDIATION IN SCOTLAND

It is alarming to note that so many reviews of mediation and alternative dispute resolution in Scotland have noted both its evident potential, and its notable lack of activity. That little appears to have been learnt from what has been happening and evaluated to date suggests that leaving the acceptance of mediation to the passage of time and experience is too modest and passive an approach. The passivity of response to date is not fully understood but perceived hurdles are lack of awareness by members of the public and professionals, resultant lack of confidence and resort to known processes, resistance by those whose livelihood depends upon the traditional processes (lawyers in particular), and lack of funding to permit countrywide, on demand, access to processes.[100] The key to these being overcome is increased knowledge and experience of, and resultant confidence in, mediation processes. Even legal professionals who may see mediation as limiting the need for traditional legal advice would be able to see that referral to mediation does not remove the need for legal advice, but may lead to a win-win outcome for the client from which the lawyer stands to gain in terms of goodwill.

[98] eg, CEDR.

[99] Such as that undertaken in the Edinburgh Mediation Project. This is annexed to the sheriff court in Edinburgh and, under the management of the Scottish Consumer Council and Citizens Advice Scotland, offers mediation services in small value civil actions.

[100] Scottish Consumer Council, *Consensus without going to court: Encouraging Mediation in non-family civil disputes in Scotland* (Edinburgh, 2001), ch 5.

In an ideal world interest in mediation would be such that it would always be the process of choice before disputants resort to any process in which a third party is empowered to make a decision in their place. Whilst it has always been the author's hope that such a position would be achieved in Scotland, mature reflection upon the evidence to date and the progress or lack of it over the past decade, suggest that mediation in Scotland requires to be driven from the institutional end of the dispute resolution spectrum. The conceptual difficulty with court-imposed referral to mediation[101] has not acted as a barrier to court-annexed mediation in other jurisdictions, where there is evidence not only that court-annexed mediation can be put in place but that it can change the culture of litigious pursuit. The culture change required is one that is difficult to articulate because viewed from the standpoint that mediation is at least worth trying, arguments to the contrary sound reactionary and narrow. Arguments for mediated processes and outcomes on the other hand are both obvious and persuasive, but even the more open-minded in Scotland appear to want to wait to see how it works for others before attempting or advising mediation, and so the dilemma of low usage continues.

The benefit of evaluative material is in a sense outweighed by its overwhelming discovery of low usage. The data concerning agreement rates is buried amongst anxieties and points for further evaluation. However, very importantly, the evaluations consistently reveal the strength of, failing which the need for, the mediator to carry out some evaluation in order for the process to achieve movement and enriched awareness. This may reveal that Scots instinctively prefer to be guided by objective evaluation towards resolution of disputes, but it may be a mere symptom of low awareness of the empowerment that a consensual process can achieve. One hopes that evaluative mediation is not the only model that can find acceptance in Scotland, but, if that model is what is needed in order to engage this nation with the process, it is little price to pay in the short term for a process that can so clearly deliver in its goal for long term improvement of relations.

[101] Prevailing even in ibid, para 2.3, using amongst other grounds the human right to a hearing. This ignores the fact that compulsory referral to mediation would not preclude parties from failing in reaching or implementing an agreement, in which case it remains justiciable.

Chapter 8

ADR in England and Wales

*Loukas A Mistelis**

I. INTRODUCTION

The judiciary is traditionally regarded as one of the three state powers. Hence it is the duty of the state to organise a justice system, build the necessary legal and tangible infrastructure, recruit judges and make the services available to the public at a small cost. The state subsidises the system by employing and often training judges and accordingly guaranteeing their competence and independence. Depending on cultural attitudes, judges and courts are deemed either an emanation of state and expression of state power (civil law model) or mere service, albeit public service providers (common law model).

In the wave of liberalisation and privatisation of public services that swept the western world as well as the so-called emerging markets in the late twentieth century alternatives to state judicial systems have been introduced. The United Kingdom[1] has been one of the driving forces of such reforms in Europe; the motto of reform was 'access to justice'.[2] In particular,

- Parallel to the state judicial system a private independent but binding justice system exists and is activated at the initiation of disputants. Arbitration arguably predates state courts and is nowadays widely used for private commercial disputes, often with an international element. Its

* Clive M Schmitthoff Senior Lecturer in International Commercial Law, School of International Arbitration, Centre for Commercial Law Studies, Queen Mary, University of London, L.Mistelis@qmul.ac.uk

[1] Northern Ireland and Great Britain comprise the United Kingdom, the principal geographic area to which parliamentary expressions apply. But, as in the case of Great Britain, the United Kingdom is a larger area than one associates with English law.

[2] See ch 1 of *Access to Justice: Interim Report to the Lord Chancellor on the civil justice system in England and Wales*, published by the Stationery Office in June 1995. *Final Report: Access to Justice*, July 1996. Both reports were prepared by a Working Party headed by Lord Woolf. See also M Cappalletti and BG Garth, *Access to Justice, Volume 1: A World Survey* (**PLACE**: Sijthoff & Noordhoff, 1978). See also recently Hazel Genn, *Paths to Justice: What People Do and Think About Going to Law* (Oxford: Hart Publishing, 1999) Hazel Genn and Alan Paterson, *Paths to Justice Scotland: What People in Scotland think and do about Going to Law* (Oxford: Hart Publishing, 2001).

statutory introduction in the late seventeenth century[3] was justified as an alternative to a rigid and formalistic litigation system.[4] In arbitration disputants retain the arbitrators, and pay all relevant expenses. Over the years arbitration has been institutionalised and often judicialised.

- More recently, in the late twentieth century, systems of alternative dispute resolution (ADR)[5] were introduced and were often entrenched in the legal system overnight. Some ADR systems are significantly older but there are no sufficient records and rarely a regulatory regime. Modern ADR is a voluntary system, according to which the parties enter a structured negotiation or refer their disputes to a third party for evaluation and/or facilitation of resolution. Especially in the light of the facts that the justice system was flooded by disputes of variable importance and complexity, and that the parties are almost invariably intimidated by the atmosphere in the court room and the litigation process itself, ADR has now become a acceptable and often preferred alternative to judicial settlement or settlement of disputes by arbitration.

This paper uses the general term 'ADR' rather than the specific terms of 'mediation' and 'conciliation'; the purpose is to draw conclusions relevant for all ADR types. Where necessary definitions will be given and delimitation will be made. Moreover, the term ADR is used in its European context which does not include arbitration.[6] Hence, for the purposes of this paper ADR covers a variety of processes which provide an alternative to litigation

[3] The earliest law dedicated to arbitration in England was in 1698. It enabled the courts, with the parties' consent to refer the disputes to arbitrators but did not limit the court's right to intervene or control the arbitration process. See further MJ Mustill and SC Boyd, *Commercial Arbitration*, 2nd edn (London and Edinburgh: Butterworths,1989), at 434–48.

[4] See, eg, VV Veeder, 'Evidential Rules in International Commercial Arbitration: From the Tower of London to the New 1999 IBA Rules', 65 *Arbitration 291* (1999), at 293.

[5] See generally H Brown and AL Marriott, *ADR Principles and Practice*, 2nd edn (London: Sweet & Maxwell, 1999); R Bernstein, J Tackaberry, AL Marriott, and D Wood, *Handbook of Arbitration Practice*, 3rd edn (London: Sweet & Maxwell/Chartered Institute of Arbitrators, 1998), at 585–601; T Stipanowich and P Kneckell, *Commercial Arbitration at Its Best* (London: CPRI and ABA, 2001); M Hoellering, *Comments on the Growing Inter-Action of Arbitration and Mediation in International Dispute Resolution: Towards an International Arbitration Culture*, ICCA Congress Series No 8 (The Hague: Kluwer, 1998), at 121–4; K Mackie, D Miles, and W Marsh, *Commercial Disputes Resolution: An ADR Practice Guide*, 2nd edn (London: Butterworths, 2000); M Freeman, *Alternative Dispute Resolution* (Aldershot: Dartmouth, 1995); J Nolan-Haley, *Alternative Dispute Resolution in a Nutshell*, 2nd edn (St Paul: West, 2001); E Carroll and K Mackie, *International Mediation: The Art of Business Diplomacy* (The Hague: Kluwer 2000).

[6] See, eg, JDM Lew, L Mistelis, and S Kröll, *Comparative International Commercial Arbitration* (forthcoming, Kluwer 2002); E Gaillard and J Savage, *Fouchard Gaillard Goldman on International Commercial Arbitration* (The Hague: Kluwer, 1999); A Redfern and M Hunter, *Law and Practice of International Commercial Arbitration*, 3rd edn (London: Sweet & Maxwell, 1999). See also Y Dezalay and B Garth, *Dealing in Virtue: International Commercial Arbitration and the Construction of a Transnational Legal Order* (Chicago and London: University of Chicago Press, 1996).

(through the courts) and binding arbitration. Classic (binding) arbitration requires the agreement of the parties for proceedings to commence but does not require their agreement for the resolution of the dispute. In ADR such an agreement is a prerequisite for settlement.

The leading English textbook defines ADR as follows:

> a range of procedures that serve as alternatives to litigation through the courts for resolution of disputes, generally involving the intercession and assistance of neutral and impartial third. In some definitions, and more commonly, it excludes not only litigation, but all forms of adjudication.[7]

We will follow this definition with a qualification. The term adjudication has become of term of art in the UK as it has a specific meaning in the context of construction disputes. Accordingly the word adjudication should be replaced by 'binding arbitration', although as far as English law is concerned, the attribute binding is not an essential part of the definition: arbitration under English law is final and binding.

This paper deals with ADR in England[8] and provides a bird's-eye view of the current infrastructure. Some limited comparative remarks will also be made. While the wider term ADR is used the focus is on mediation and conciliation.

In particular, we first look briefly at the evolution and development of ADR in England in the context of civil justice reforms (section II), and the established regulatory and institutional support before examining the various types of ADR and the types of disputes referred to ADR in England as well as the institutionalisation and professionalisation of ADR (section III). Finally we will attempt a prediction about the future of ADR in the UK (section IV).

II. EVOLUTION AND DEVELOPMENT OF ADR IN THE UK

The history of ADR in the United Kingdom is a companion of the history of the debate about civil justice reform. In this section the references of the stages of evolution of ADR in the UK (II.A) are followed by the qualitative assessment of the shift of focus of disputes referred to ADR (II.B) and

[7] Brown and Marriott, op cit, at para. 2-001 [footnotes omitted]

[8] English law applies in England and Wales. Great Britain, the political geographic term for England, Wales, and Scotland, has no common legal system. Many English statutes are applicable in Scotland, but the Scottish private law is based primarily on the civil law and principally on Roman law, the result of an alliance with the continent in the fourteenth and fifteenth centuries intended to inhibit recurrent English expansion. After union with England in the Treaty of 1707, the development of Scottish law was influenced largely by the English common law. Since the accession of the United Kingdom in the European Community, some aspects of private law are harmonised at European level for both England and Scotland.

finally an attempt is made to integrate ADR in the web of dispute resolution mechanisms available in England and Wales (II.C).

A. History of ADR in the UK—Civil Justice Reform

The introduction of the discussion paper of the Lord Chancellor's Department on Alternative Dispute Resolution in November 1999 states that

> This Government has embarked on the most radical programme for the modernisation of the civil justice system for 120 years. Encouraging and improving the ways which enable those with legal problems to avoid disputes, or to resolve them outside the court system, have an important part to play in that programme.[9]

Indeed significant reforms have taken place in the 1990s. First, in 1996 we had the introduction of the new English Arbitration Act[10] and on 26 April 1999 the Civil Procedure Rules Civil Procedure Rules (CPR)[11] came into effect and replaced the Rules of the Supreme Court (RSC) and County Court Rules (CCR). The CPR implement the changes recommended by Lord Woolf's 'Access to Justice'[12] and also provide wide support for ADR.

We will look at these reforms grouped by the decade in which they were introduced.

1. 1960s

The discussion in the 1960s is predominately North American and concentrates on a widespread criticism of state institutions and the role of state. The debate seems to evolve also around the concepts of 'judgment' and 'settlement'.[13] The discussion had a theoretical-jurispudential[14] and/or a historical-comparative[15] flavour.

[9] Published in Nov 1999. Available also at <http://www.lcd.gov.uk/consult/civjust/adr/indexfr.htm>.

[10] Arbitration Act 1996 (c 23) which came into force on 31 Jan 1997.

[11] Civil Procedures Rules (SI 1998 no 3132) which came into force on 26 Apr 1999; the rules are also accessible at <http://www.lcd.gov.uk/civil/procrules_fin/menus/rules.htm> (last visited on 26 Jan 2002).

[12] Lord Woolf, *Access to Justice: Interim Report to the Lord Chancellor on the Civil Justice System in England and Wales* (June 1995) and *Final Report: Access to Justice*, July 1996. See also <http://www.lcd.gov.uk/civil/finafr.htm> (last visited on 26 Jan 2002).

[13] See M Palmer and S Roberts, *Dispute Processes: ADR and the Primary Forms of Decision Making* (London: Butterworths,1998), at 25–6.

[14] Ibid.

[15] See, eg, JP Dawson, *A History of Lay Judges* (Cambridge, Mass: Harvard University Press,1960); id, *The Oracles of Law* (Ann Arbor: University of Michigan Law School, 1968).

2. 1970s

The (further American) debate in the 1970s focused on the pitfalls of litigation and adjudication and the merits of settlement.[16] It also addressed the role of lawyers and has been critical of the adversarial nature of proceedings before courts and other dispute processes where lawyers were involved.

3. 1980s[17]

The discussion acquired more structure and depth in the 1980s. The concept of informal justice was introduced, and 'informalism' was explored and criticised.[18] A related matter was the option of resolving disputes without lawyers or without reference to law.[19] Moreover 'settlement' came under fire and become the topic of extensive and seminal academic discussion.[20] Finally, it appears that the 1980s appear to be the decade during which the term ADR creeps into general use.[21]

A further impact of the wider debate is that academic lawyers now refer to dispute processes rather than litigation or adjudication and that the word dispute has acquired a wider meaning.[22]

In the UK a practice direction was issued relating to conciliation in family proceedings: ie Practice Direction (Family Division: Conciliation Procedure) 2 November 1982.[23] According to the statement a pilot conciliation was put in operation from January 1983.[24] Towards the end of the 1980s we also have the first UK ADR institutions.

[16] See, eg, WE Burger, 'Agenda for 2000 AD—Need for Systematic Anticipation', 70 Federal Rules Decisions, 92–4 (1976); see also Palmer and Roberts, op cit, at 27–9.

[17] Ibid, at 29–44.

[18] See RL Abel (ed), *The Politics of Informal Justice, Volume 1: The American Experience; Volume 2: Comparative Studies* (New York: Academic Press, 1982); B de Sousa Santos, 'Law and Community: The Changing Nature of State Power in Late Capitalism', in Abel, op cit, vol 1, at 261–3; MR Damaska, *The Faces of Justice and State Authority* (New Haven and London: Yale University Press, 1986)

[19] See JS Auerbach, *Justice Without Law? Resolving Disputes Without Lawyers* (Oxford: Oxford University Press, 1983); D Bok, 'A Flawed System of Law and Practice Training', 33 *Journal of Legal Education*, 570–85 (1983); LL Riskin and J Westbrook, *Dispute Resolution and Lawyers* (St Paul, Minn: West 1987); JS Murray, AS Rau, and EF Sherman, *Processes of Dispute Resolution: The Role of Lawyers*, 1st edn (Westbury, New York: Foundation Press, 1989), 2nd edn 1996).

[20] See OM Fiss, 'Against Settlement', 93 *Yale Law Journal*, 1073–90 (1984); AW McThenia and TL Schaffer, 'For Reconciliation' 94 *Yale Law Journal*, 1660–8 (1985); Fiss, 'Out of Eden' 94 *Yale Law Journal*, 1669–73 (1985).

[21] See Palmer, M and Roberts S, op cit, at 45.

[22] See Brown and Marriott. op cit, at paras 1-001–1-042; P Stein, *Legal Institutions: The Development of Dispute Settlement* (London: Butterworths, 1984).

[23] [1982] 1 WLR 1420 (no 2) [1984] 1 WLR 1326; they were both cancelled by a subsequent direction in 1991.

[24] See further A Bottomley, 'Resolving Family Disputes: A critical review', in M Freeman (ed), *State, Law and the Family: Critical Perspectives* (London and New York: Tavistock, 1984); S Roberts, 'Mediation in Family Disputes', 46 *Modern Law Review*, 337–57 (1983).

4. 1990s

Discussion about ADR in the UK was fully developed only in the 1990s with focus on 'litigation-mania'[25] and the crisis in civil justice.[26] In the early 1990s two reports were published with recommendations about ADR, one commissioned by the General Council of the Bar,[27] the other by the Law Society.[28] At the same time a new practice direction was issued to replace the pilot conciliation scheme used in family proceedings and to reflect changes in the Children Act: Practice Direction (Family Division: Conciliation Procedure) 18 October 1991.[29] All these changes have received some criticism.[30]

It is intriguing that in England the driving force for all reforms were lawyers involved in commercial litigation, a few academics, and the courts. As far as the government is concerned, both the Lord Chancellor's Department[31] and the Department of Trade and Industry[32] also played a significant role in the enhancement of ADR.

In fact the commercial court that was founded in 1895 with a specialist mandate has been in the forefront of procedural innovation and prides itself on the speed with which matters can be resolved. A high percentage of cases before the Commercial Court are settled before trial, although very often at a late stage after substantial costs have been incurred and following a considerable number of court hearings. In 1993, while recognising that there are certain types of dispute which will always have to be resolved at trial, such as those on which the parties require an authoritative ruling, the court decided to experiment, very tentatively, with the possibility of encouraging parties to use one of the developing methods of ADR, such as mediation and conciliation, as a possible additional means of resolving at an earlier stage of the proceedings, either particular issues arising in a case or the dispute itself.[33]

[25] B Markesinis, 'Litigation-Mania in England, Germany and the USA: Are We So Very Different?' (1990) 49(2) *Cambridge Law Journal*, 233–76.

[26] AAS Zuckerman, *Civil Justice in Crisis. Comparative Perspectives of Civil Procedure* (Oxford: Oxford University Press, 1999).

[27] Beldham LJ, General Council of the Bar, Committee on ADR, Report, Oct 1991.

[28] H Brown, The Law Society, Courts and Legal Services Committee, ADR Report, 71/1991.

[29] [1992] 1 All ER 431, [1992] 1 WLR 147, [1992] 1 FLR 228; Brown and Marriott, op cit, para A3-007, at 636.

[30] See, eg, P Robertshaw and J Segal, 'The Milking of ADR?' (1993) 12 *Civil Justice Quarterly*, 23–8.

[31] See <http://www.lcd.gov.uk> and <http://www.courtservice.gov.uk/notices/chanc/ ultra_new_chan_guide/Pt17.htm >.

[32] See <http://www.dti.gov.uk> and <http://www.dti.gov.uk/er/individual/et.htm>.

[33] A Pugh-Thomas, 'The Commercial Court of England and Wales and Alternative Dispute Resolution', *International Company and Commercial Law Review* (ICCLR) 1999, 10(1), 26–30, at 26.

This encouragement took the form of a practice statement: Practice Statement (Commercial Cases: Alternative Dispute Resolution) 10 December 1993.[34] Cresswell J, who was then in charge of the commercial list, indicated in the statement that, although judges in the Commercial Court would not themselves act as mediators or be involved in any ADR process, they would

> in appropriate cases invite parties to consider whether their case, or certain issues in their case, could be resolved by means of ADR. By way of example only, ADR might be tried where the costs of litigation are likely to be wholly disproportionate to the amount at stake. The Clerk to the Commercial Court thereafter kept a list of individuals and bodies offering mediation, conciliation and other ADR services.[35]

The practice statement provided that parties or their legal advisers, before the hearing of a summons for directions, answer various questions set out in a questionnaire, the questions being designed to ensure that parties did consider the possibility of attempting to resolve the particular dispute or particular issues by mediation, conciliation or otherwise. That initiative was in part prompted by the court's awareness of the use of ADR techniques in other jurisdictions and the increasing interest of major national and international commercial enterprises in ADR and their expressed support for its development.[36]

The Commercial Court clearly moved cautiously. Next a Practice Direction (HC Civil Litigation: Case Management) by Lord Taylor of Gosforth was published on 24 January 1995.[37] This Direction aims at reducing cost and delay in litigation by, *inter alia*, requesting parties and their counsel to consider ADR. Four months later ADR was added in Section 14 of the Chancery Guide (April 1995) and parties were again reminded of ADR and the list of mediators kept by the Court.[38] Finally on 26 July 1995 Sir Thomas Bingham, MR issued a Practice Statement addressing the issue in relation to the Court of Appeal again encouraging the use of mediation.[39]

Waller J issued another Practice Statement (Commercial Cases: Alternative Dispute Resolution) (no 2) on 7 June 1996,[40] assessing and improving the statement by Cresswell J. In this new statement the use of

[34] [1994] 1 WLR 14; [1994] 1 All ER 34; Brown and Marriott, op cit, paras A3-008, at 637.

[35] [1994] 1 WLR 14.

[36] A Pugh-Thomas, ICCLR 1999, 10(1), 26–30, at 26.

[37] [1995] 1 All ER 385; [1995] 1 WLR 508; Brown and Marriott, op cit, para A3-009, at 638.

[38] Ibid, para A3-003, at 631.

[39] Ibid, para A3-010, at 640. This Statement was accompanied by a Direction which entered into force on 4 Dec 1995, [1995] 3 All ER 847, [1995] 1 WLR 1188.

[40] [1996] 1 All ER 383; [1996] 1 WLR 1024; Brown and Marriott, op cit, para A3-011, at 643. See also the more recent [1998] 1 Lloyd's Rep 126, 30 Sept 1997.

early neutral evaluation is encouraged as a means of reducing costs and delay. In particular, the direction provided, *inter alia*, that, if it appeared to a judge

> that the action before him or any of the issues arising in it are particularly appropriate for an attempt at settlement by ADR techniques but that the parties have not previously attempted settlement by such means he may invite the parties to take positive steps to set in motion ADR procedures.

The judge was empowered, where appropriate, to 'adjourn the proceedings then before him for a specified period of time to encourage and enable the parties to take such steps'.

The Court of Appeal few months later published ADR Guidelines (Paragraph 11) for the Court of Appeal—ADR Scheme.[41] According to these guidelines a pro bono scheme was introduced from 1997 and legal aid was offered to cover the costs of ADR for an assisted party. Next, a Practice Direction (Family Division: Family Proceedings: Financial Dispute Resolution) was issued on 16 June 1997 by Sir Stephen Brown addressing, in particular, financial dispute resolution as a meeting held for the purposes of conciliation.[42]

Finally, Appendices 2 and 3 of the Second Report of the Commercial Court Committee Working Party on ADR (ADR Orders in the Commercial Court) was issued on 14 July 1998 under the Chairmanship of Colman J.[43] This Working Party started reviewing the interaction between the legal and judicial process and ADR as early as May 1995 by looking at materials and practice on court-annexed ADR schemes in Canada, the United States, Australia and New Zealand. It concluded there was no objection in principle to the court adopting a substantially more driven approach to pre-trial settlement using, where appropriate, more persuasive means than merely requiring lists of questions to be answered in writing, as envisaged by the December 1993 practice direction. They were, in particular, influenced by the fact

- that it is in the interests of good court management and of the whole body of litigants that courts should not be clogged with heavy litigation where the parties have not even tried to achieve settlement by other means;
- that the efficient use of judicial manpower required that judges should be enabled if not to drive litigants from the judgment seat, at least to deter

[41] Brown and Marriott, op cit, para A3-002, at 630–1. See also the more recent [1999] 2 All ER 490; [1999] 1 WLR 1027, 19 Apr 1999.

[42] [1997] 3 All ER 768, [1997] 1 WLR 1069, [1997] 2 FLR 304, [1997] 3 FCR 476; Brown and Marriott, op cit, para A3-013, at p 647; See also *Rose v Rose*, Court of Appea1, 20 Feb 2002, reported in the *The Times* 12 Mar 2002.

[43] Brown and Marriott, op cit, paras A3-004-5, at 631–4.

them from rushing there headlong before they had made reasonable efforts to try other means of resolving their disputes; and

- that the conservation and more efficient use of judicial resources was a strong justification for the courts actively to promote the resolution of civil disputes by means less costly to the state and less demanding on judicial time.[44]

The working party rejected the possibility of allowing the court to order a stay of proceedings until ADR had been tried as they feared that any such order would give justifiable grounds for complaint that litigants were being unduly deprived of their rights to have their disputes resolved in court; and they were of course conscious that, in a great many of the disputes referred to the Commercial Court in London, both parties were foreign,[45] had been attracted to London by the high standing of the court, but could well choose to litigate in other sophisticated jurisdictions if they disliked the court's procedures, to the prejudice of London's position as a major financial and commercial centre. Finally, the court put in place a system for monitoring how successful the practice direction was in encouraging the resolution of disputes by ADR: as a further example of persuasion, the practice direction made it plain that the commercial judges would expect the parties to have thought carefully about ADR before 'the hearing of the first *inter partes* summons at which directions for the interlocutory process of the action are given' and allowed the parties to inform the court of the progress of any ADR attempt to invite the court to allow further time.[46]

Before completing their work, the working party looked again at whether the Commercial Court's Listing Office should carry on the practice of maintaining lists of institutions offering ADR-accredited members and lists of retired members of the judiciary who might wish to be appointed as mediators and, in the case of the latter, they should indicate that some of those included might not have received ADR training: except for retired judges, other individuals would not be personally identified but litigants would be left to obtain the names of suitable mediators from one or other of the listed institutions.

44 A Pugh-Thomas, ICCLR 1999, 10(1), 26–30, at 27.

45 According to various statistics published in the press in England and the website of the Law Society 80 per cent of the cases before the Commercial Court have at least one foreign party and in almost 50 per cent of the cases both litigants are foreign: <http://www.lawsoc.org.uk/dcs/fourth_tier.asp?section_id=3456&Caller_id=AboutUs#6133> (last visited 18 Feb 2002).

46 Pugh-Thomas, above, at 27.

B. ADR and Civil Justice Reform

While the working party under the Chairmanship of Colman J was deliberating, commercial court judges had found that making an order suspending the periods of time within certain interlocutory steps in the proceedings were required to be taken while the parties explored resolving their dispute by some form of ADR, was disadvantageous as it often led to the parties taking far too long to agree whether or not to attempt mediation and, if so, to identify the mediator. Instead of leading to a resolution of the litigation, such an order just added a layer in the dispute resolution process and merely caused delay. Court records showed that at least sixty-seven ADR orders had been made between June 1996 and July 1998 and it was thought that there might have been further orders which had not been notified to the Listing Office.[47] Professor Hazel Genn published an evaluation report of the Bloomsbury Central London County Court pilot mediation scheme. One of her conclusions was that, other than in the large City law firms, 'few parties or solicitors had any experience of mediation and were not knowledgeable about the process', and indeed there was some evidence of suspicion, if not active hostility, towards the process.[48]

A survey by the National Consumer Council found in 1995 that three out of four people in serious legal disputes were dissatisfied with the civil justice system. In fact, out of 1,019 respondents, 77 per cent claimed that the system was too slow, 74 per cent said it was too complicated, and 73 per cent said it was unwelcoming and dated.[49] This was also the conclusion of the 1988 Civil Justice Review and it was against this background that the Lord Chancellor set up the Committee in 1994 under Lord Woolf to produce a report on *Access to Justice*. In less than a year, Lord Woolf published an interim report,[50] and his final report was published in July

[47] The Listing Office had also, during that period, received ten letters recording that ADR had either not been proceeded with or having been attempted had failed, but in fact, and this is a common experience in commercial disputes generally when they are referred to ADR, at least one of the cases was known to have settled subsequently. Unfortunately, what the court record did not show was whether the other cases settled because the parties resorted to one of the well-known ADR procedures or by reason of traditional direct bilateral negotiations, but the working party felt that did not matter as, if the parties responded to an ADR order by achieving a settlement by traditional negotiation within the time designated by the order, that achieved one of the objectives of the procedure, namely settlement by a cheaper and less complicated mechanism than a full High Court trial. Pugh-Thomas, A, ICCLR 1999, 10(1), 26–30, at 28.

[48] Hazel Genn, The Central London County Court/Pilot Mediation Scheme—Evaluation Report, accessible at <http://www.lcd.gov.uk/research/1998/598esfr.htm > (last visited 26 Jan 2002). During the period of her study, mediation was offered in 4,500 cases, but only 160 mediations took place. She found that 62 per cent of mediated cases reached a settlement at the mediation appointment and that mediation achieved earlier settlement.

[49] *Seeking Civil Justice: A Survey of People's Needs and Experiences* (1995), NCC.

[50] *Access to Justice—Interim Report to the Lord Chancellor on the Civil Justice System in England and Wales* (HMSO, June 1995).

1996.[51] The Government made recommendations and in February 1997 the Civil Procedure Act 1997 received Royal Assent.

Lord Woolf identified the problems of formal and inflexible proceedings, endemic delays, in short described a rather depressing picture of English civil justice system which is incomprehensible to litigants, costs significant sums of money and makes no or little use of modern technology. The report concluded that the time [1995] had not yet arrived for a system of court-annexed ADR or for any other form of mandatory procedure leading to ADR but added, at paragraph 32:

> It is to be hoped that most lawyers will regard it as their responsibility to be able fully to acquaint their clients with the options but, nonetheless, the courts must encourage their use. There is some evidence that ADR is less effective when the parties have not chosen for themselves to participate in it, and that is another reason for not making it compulsory. There are also indications, however, that parties are often reluctant to make the first move towards a negotiated settlement or to suggest ADR, in case this is interpreted by their opponents as a sign of weakness. Legal advisers who are not themselves experienced in ADR often adopt a similar attitude, and so the court itself, as a neutral third party, has an important role in pointing out what options are available.[52]

Following the two Woolf Reports[53] and the Civil Procedure Act 1997, most recommendation were effected from 26 April 1999 through the Civil Procedure Rules 1998.[54] The civil justice reform had four main objectives:

- Simplification of procedure (including expediency and cost reduction through an underlying principle of proportionality);
- Judicial case management (requiring judges to actively manage the resolution process by watering down the adversarial system;
- Pre-action protocols (aiming at encouraging contact between parties and better exchange of information; hoping that a settlement may be facilitated); and
- Alternatives to court procedure

The first three issues will not be addressed in this paper[55] and the focus

[51] *Final Report—Access to Justice* (HMSO, July 1996).

[52] Lord Woolf, *Access to Justice—Interim Report to the Lord Chancellor on the Civil Justice System in England and Wales* (HMSO, June 1995), at 143.

[53] See <http://www.lcd.gov.uk/civil/finalfr.htm> (last visited 26 Jan 2002).

[54] See <http://www.lcd.gov.uk/civil/procrules_fin/menus/rules.htm> (last visited 26 Jan 2002).

[55] But see Adrian AS Zuckerman, 'Justice in Crisis: Comparative Dimensions of Civil Procedure', and Michalik, Paul, 'Justice in Crisis: England and Wales', both in Zuckerman, *Civil Justice in Crisis. Comparative Perspectives of Civil Procedure* (Oxford: Oxford University Press, 1999) at 3–52 and 117–65 respectively; JA Jolowicz, 'The Woolf Reforms', in Jolowicz, *On Civil Procedure* (Cambridge: Cambridge University Press, 2001), 386–97; Zuckerman, 'Lord Woolf's Access to Justice: Plus ça change . . .' (1996) 59 *Modern Law*

is one the enhancement of out of court settlement mechanisms. There are three different ways,[56] in which the Woolf Reports and the Civil Procedure Rules attempt to promote ADR:

- The payment system has been changed so as to enable claimants and defendants alike to make offers relating to the allocation of costs;[57]
- The settlement at the earliest possible stage is encouraged by pre-action protocols[58] and an active case management;[59]
- Official encouragement is given to the avoidance of litigation through recourse to alternative dispute resolution.[60]

Lord Woolf's report contained an entire chapter to ADR entitle 'Alternative approaches to dispensing justice'[61] and most views found an expression in the Civil Procedure Rules.[62] The Civil Procedure Rules are undoubtedly the most fundamental change in civil litigation for more than a century. It seems that the objective of simplification of procedure in court supported by encouragement of settlement out of court has been successful. During May to August 1999, there was a 25 per cent reduction in the number of proceedings issued in the county courts compared to the same period the previous year. By the end of January 2000 there was a further fall of another 23 per cent.[63]

Review 773; M Zander, 'The Woolf Report: Forwards or Backwards for the New Lord Chancellor?' (1997) 16 *Civil Justice Quarterly* 208; Woolf 'Lawyers, Medics and the Courts' (1997) 16 *Civil Justice Quarterly* 302; Zander, 'The Government's Plans on Civil Justice' (1998) 61 *Modern Law Review* 382; S Flanders, 'Case Management: Failure in America? Success in England and Wales? (1998) 17 *Civil Justice Quarterly* 308.

[56] Jolowicz, 'The Woolf Reforms', 386–97, at 392.

[57] CPR, rule 36 available at <http://www.lcd.gov.uk/civil/procrules_fin/contents/parts/part36.htm> (last visited 26 Jan 2002); Lord Woolf Final Report, ch 14; previously RSC order 22.

[58] CPR Rule 1.4.2 available at <http://www.lcd.gov.uk/civil/procrules_fin/contents/parts/part01.htm#rule1_4> (last visited 26 Jan 2002); See also <http://www.lcd.gov.uk/civil/procrules_fin/menus/protocol.htm> where protocols are listed: eg, Protocol for the Construction and Engineering Disputes, Pre-Action Protocol for Defamation; Pre-Action Protocol for Personal Injury Claims; Pre-Action Protocol for the Resolution of Clinical Disputes; Pre-Action Protocol for Professional Negligence; Lord Woolf Final Report, at 107.

[59] See Flanders, 'Case Management: Failure in America? Success in England and Wales? (1998) 17 *Civil Justice Quarterly* 308. See also *Cowl and Others v Plymouth City Council*, Judgment 14 Dec 2001, reported in *The Times* 8 Jan 2002, (CA) *per* Lord Woolf, LCJ

[60] See, eg, CPR rule 3.1 available at <http://www.lcd.gov.uk/civil/procrules_fin/contents/parts/part03.htm#rule3_1> and CPR rule 26.4. available at <http://www.lcd.gov.uk/civil/procrules_fin/contents/parts/part26.htm#rule26_4> (both last visited 26 Jan 2002).

[61] Lord Woolf Interim Report, ch 18; Lord Woolf Final Report, at 107.

[62] See, eg, CPR rules 26.4 and 1.4(2)(e), at <http://www.lcd.gov.uk/civil/procrules_fin/menus/rules.htm> (last visited 26 Jan 2002).

[63] G Slapper and D Kelly, *The English Legal System*, 5th edn (London and Sydney: Cavendish Publishing, 2001), at 286. According to <http://www.cedr.co.uk www.cedr.co.uk>, the drop in the number of claims issued in the Queen's Bench Division since the introduction of the CPR has been 37 per cent. See *Resolutions*, Issue no 28 (Summer 2001), at 3.

Several surveys were conducted by law firms to assess the impact of reforms. In a survey by Eversheds published in 2000 nearly two-thirds of the respondents did not think the reforms would make them less likely to start proceedings, but 43 per cent said they were settling cases earlier and almost half said their lawyers were handling disputes differently. Mediation or ADR in general is becoming more popular: 41 per cent have used it, compared with 30 per cent in 1998.[64]

C. Two Recent Cases

The encouragement of the parties to recourse to ADR has been manifested by the Court of Appeal in several recent decisions. Most notably, in *Cowl v Plymouth City Council*,[65] Lord Woolf, the architect of the Civil Procedure Rules, himself delivered a clear and unconditional reminder to those involved in public law cases to remember that trial litigation should be the last resort. Refusing judicial review to residents over the closing of the local authority home where they lived, he stated at the outset of his judgement:

> The importance of this appeal is that it illustrates that, even in disputes between public authorities and the members of the public for whom they are responsible, insufficient attention is paid to the paramount importance of avoiding litigation whenever this is possible. Particularly in the case of these disputes both sides must by now be acutely conscious of the contribution alternative dispute resolution can make to resolving disputes in a manner which both meets the needs of the parties and saves time, expense and stress.

Lord Woolf further suggested that the court might on its own motion fix a hearing at which the parties could be required to explain what they had done to resolve a dispute without resort to the courts. The issue of which disputes are apt for mediation was then the focus in Lord Woolf's judgment. He replies to those critical of ADR with a summary on why to mediate, fit for a textbook:

> We do not single out either side's lawyers for particular criticism. What followed was due to the unfortunate culture in litigation of this nature of over-judicialising the processes which are involved. It is indeed unfortunate that, the process having started, instead of the parties focussing on the future they insisted on arguing about what had happened in the past. The parties should have been able to come to a sensible conclusion as to how to dispose of the issues which divided them. If they could not do this without help, then an independent mediator should have been recruited to assist. That would have been a far cheaper course to adopt. Today sufficient should be known about ADR to make the failure to adopt it, in particular when public money is involved, indefensible.

[64] See above and (2000) *The Times*, 2 May.

[65] See *Cowl and Others v Plymouth City Council*, Judgment 14 Dec 2001, reported in *The Times* 8 January 2002 (CA) *per* Lord Woolf, LCJ, [2001] EWCA Civ 1792.

The terms negotiated and agreed during the appeal and annexed to the judgement read like a well-crafted settlement agreement from a mediation.

In *Asian Sky Television plc v Bayer-Rosin*,[66] the claimants sued their former solicitors for negligence and breach of contract over a complex conveyancing transaction in 1992. The quantification of damages involved complex valuation issues. Proceedings were issued in 1995, but progress with the action was very slow. Shortly after the CPR came into effect in April 1999, the claimant's solicitors suggested mediation in a 'without prejudice' telephone call. The defendants' solicitors said they would consider it, though privately doubting its attractiveness with a gap between the parties being £100,000 to £6 million. A month later £200,000 was paid into Court by Part 36 offer, and two months later the defendants themselves suggested that mediation might be tried.

The action stagnated until April 2000, at which point the defendants sought to strike it out under CPR Part 3.4. The Master had not been told of the telephone suggestion for mediation by the claimant in April 1999 and struck the case out, criticising the claimant's apparent failure to accept mediation proposed by the defendant in September 1999. Allowing the appeal and permitting the claim to continue on stringent terms, Clarke LJ accepted that the mediation offer made by the claimant in April 1999 was genuine and that had the Master known of it, he would have viewed the claimant's culpability differently.

III. FROM DOMESTIC MEDIATION DEALI SOCIALLY SENSITIVE MATTERS TO NG WITH BUSINESS MEDIATION

While ADR and, in particular, conciliation and mediation have been successfully introduced in domestic, consumer, and family matters for several decades, in the last stages of the introduction of ADR the focus shifted on business disputes. It now appears that the construction industry is the single largest user of ADR services. In fact, there are strong arguments for using ADR mechanisms in a wide spectrum of disputes.

Factors affecting 'ADR-ability' of disputes include the nature and value of the dispute, the legal or not nature of dispute (eg, is the question one of determination of rights and obligations of the parties or one of assessment of quality or quantification of damages), the attitude and financial resources of the parties, the desired outcome, and the balance of representation. In any event both parties must be willing to submit their dispute to a form of alternative dispute resolution, or willing to try a form of assisted settlement. If both parties are not willing, there can be prob-

66 [2001] EWCA Civ 1792.

lems in enforcing an apparently contractual agreement to try mediation or conciliation.

Part III of the Family Law Act 1996 allows for the provision of publicly funded mediation in family proceedings. Over 250 mediation services have concluded contracts with the Legal Aid Board and further contracts were granted to ensure nationwide coverage by autumn 2000. Section 29 of the Act, which requires those seeking legal aid for representation in family proceedings to attend a meeting with a mediator to consider whether mediation might be suitable in their case, was implemented in over 60 per cent of the country as of 1999 and it was intended to be in force across England and Wales in 2000.

A. Factors For and Against ADR[67]

Any form of ADR will be worth considering where the cost of court proceedings is likely to equal or exceed the amount of money at issue. This is undoubtedly one of the main incentives for ADR. The others relates to situations where the parties are connected with long-standing business relationship and they wish to maintain them.

Because ADR is completely voluntary, the best time to consider using it is before a dispute has arisen, or when it has arisen but the disputants communicate with each other.

Mediation is seldom effective without previous negotiations having been held. Good negotiations can be hampered by excessive posturing by counsel and the use of litigation techniques. Mediations proceed more effectively when the parties are skilled negotiators as a matter of training or experience.

Where parties wish to preserve an existing relationship, mediation or conciliation may be helpful. For example, not all neighbour disputes are necessarily suited to mediation, particularly where there are serious issues of harassment or mental health problems.[68] Arbitration may be suitable in cases where there is no relationship to preserve, and a rapid decision is needed.[69]

When available, trade association arbitration schemes, utility regulators,

[67] See Brown and Marriott, op cit, ch 2 and *passim*; E Carroll and K Mackie, *International Mediation: The Art of Business Diplomacy* (The Hague: Kluwer, 2000), at 11–40; Lord Chancellor's Department, *Alternative Dispute Resolution, A Discussion Paper* (Nov 1999), at 10–16.

[68] Dignan, Sorsby, and Hibbert, 'Neighbour Disputes: Comparing the Cost-effectiveness of Mediation and Alternative Approaches' (Centre for Criminological and Legal Research at the University of Sheffield, Oct 1996).

[69] In a recent survey of the American Arbitration Association Global Centre for Dispute Resolution only 8 per cent of the respondents rated the maintenance of future relations as a significant feature of arbitration.

and ombudsmen can provide a cheaper alternative for an individual seeking redress against a company or large organisation, but they may be limited in the redress they can provide. Early neutral evaluation might be applicable in cases where there is a dispute over a point of law, or where one party appears to have an unrealistic view of their chances of success at trial. Where there is a technical dispute with a great deal of factual evidence, mediation or determination by an expert in that area might be best. Moreover, parties involved in a commercial dispute may prefer to use a form of ADR to keep sensitive commercial information private. Mediation has achieved settlement in many apparently intractable multi-party cases.

In her research into the scheme at Central London County Court, Professor Genn indicated that mediation might not be appropriate in cases where there is a significant imbalance of power.[70] One should add to that the imbalance of skill and experience in negotiations.

Litigation is the only option where one party needs to set a legal precedent or obtain an injunction, or where one party is refusing to acknowledge the problem or engage in negotiations. Several remedies will not normally be available in ADR proceedings.

The first and most obvious obstacle to an effective mediation is any lack of a *bona fide* desire to settle. Probably the other greatest obstacle to a successful mediation is lack of authority to settle on the part of one or both of the parties. If the individuals at the mediation session misunderstand the role of the mediator, and if the mediator is not skilled enough to make them comfortable with the process and everyone's role in it, the mediation will be in trouble.

B. *Current Court-Annexed ADR in England and Wales*[71]

While private ADR has been around for considerable time, at least for business and construction disputes, court-annexed or court encouraged ADR is rather recent. There is limited (in terms of time) but considerable experience in England and Wales.

Currently there are the following systems, briefly described above:

- Commercial Court and the Technology and Construction Court[72]

[70] Genn, The Central London County Court/Pilot Mediation Scheme—Evaluation Report, accessible at <http://www.lcd.gov.uk/research/1998/598esfr.htm> (last visited 26 Jan 2002).

[71] See Brown and Marriott, op cit, paras 3-043–3-080.

[72] CPR Rule 1.4. available at <http://www.lcd.gov.uk/civil/procrules_fin/ contents/parts/part01.htm#rule1_4> (last visited 26 Jan 2002); See also <http://www.lcd. gov.uk/civil /procrules_fin/menus/protocol.htm> where protocols are listed: eg, Protocol for the Construction and Engineering Disputes, Pre-Action Protocol for Defamation; Pre-Action Protocol for Personal Injury Claims; Pre-Action Protocol for the Resolution of Clinical Disputes; Pre-Action Protocol for Professional Negligence.

- Family law disputes[73]
- Court of Appeal[74]
- Central London County Court[75]
- Patents County Court[76]
- Employment Tribunals[77]

The increasing numbers of court-annexed or court encouraged ADR have led to less cases litigated in English courts. Undoubtedly, the introduction of ADR was not the only reason, as it has been described above. The very introduction of the Civil Procedure Rules not only encourages parties to settle their disputes by recourse to ADR, it also discourages parties from litigating small claims, by introducing a principle of proportionality, according to which litigation costs should be ideally lower than the amount in dispute.

Mediation has often been received well by the parties but there are occasions where parties rejected mediation. It is intriguing to reproduce here a table produced by Professor Genn indicating the reasons for rejecting mediation (see page 214).

A search in Lexis and WESTLAW conducted on 31 January 2002 for reported and unreported cases in all UK courts gives 766 returns for conciliation, 274 returns for mediation, and 95 returns for ADR. These numbers are from definitive as provided that ADR is successful only very few ADR cases will end in court. The majority of the returns are from years 1997–2001; one more indication of the quantitative as well as qualitative importance ADR has acquired in recent years (see page 215).

This table cannot be any evidence about court-annexed or court encouraged ADR. However, it is an accurate picture of conciliation cases which end to litigation. Not surprisingly, the majority of cases (23 per cent) relate

[73] Rules 2.71 to 2.77 of the Family Proceedings Rules 1991, Pilot Scheme organised by the Solicitors Family Law Association in 1998 that has become the national norm as of June 2000. See also [1997] 3 All ER 768 [1997] 1 WLR 1069 [1997] 2 FLR 304 [1997] 3 FCR 476.

[74] See Brown and Marriott, op cit, para A3-002, at 630–1. See also the more recent [1999] 2 All ER 490; [1999] 1 WLR 1027, 19 April 1999; *Thompson v Commissioner of Police of the Metropolis (and Hsu v Commissioner of Police of the Metropolis)* [1997] 2 All ER 762; *Cowl and Others v Plymouth City Council*, Judgment 14 Dec 2001, reported in *The Times* 8 Jan 2002, (CA) *per* Lord Woolf; *Asian Sky Television plc v Bayer-Rosin*, [2001] EWCA Civ 1792.

[75] Genn, op cit at <http://www.lcd.gov.uk/research/1998/598esfr.htm>.

[76] See, eg, *Unilever v Procter and Gambler* [1999] 2 All ER 691 *per* Laddie J. A recent case in the Court of Appeal dealt with trademark issues: *World Wide Fund for Nature (formerly World Wildlife Fund) v World Wrestling Federation Entertainment Inc*, 27 Feb 2002, reported in The Times 14 Mar 2002.

[77] See DTI News Release no P/2001/30 dated 20 July 2001, which announced the review of employment disputes resolution and DTI document entitled *Routes to Resolution: Improving Dispute Resolution in Britain*, available at <http://www.dti.gov.uk/er/individual/et.htm> (last visited on 26 Jan 2002).

Reasons given to the Court by claimants and defendants for rejecting mediation[78]

Reasons for rejecting mediation given on mediation reply form sent to court	Claimants (207 responses) %	Defendants (197 responses) %
Mediation 'inappropriate' (no explanation)	17	10
No common ground/case won't settle	14	12
Complex evidence/expert evidence	17	18
Dispute over fact/law / both	11	4
Case will settle in any case	11	9
Need a court ruling / want to go to trial	9	8
No merit in claim / defence	6	8
Offer of mediation too earlyinlitigation	3	15
Not appropriate for personal injury cases	6	7
Too expensive to mediate	4	1
Want case transferred to arbitration	0	4
Just don't want to do it	1	5

to employment disputes. It is, however, surprising that 7.89 per cent of the cases go up to the House of Lords and that 31.3 per cent go up to the Court of Appeal. It is also worth noting that there significantly less cases in Scotland (see table on pp 216–217).

This table cannot be any evidence about court-annexed or court encouraged ADR either. However, it is an clear picture of mediation cases which end to litigation. It is remarkable that the single largest court for mediation cases is the Civil Division of the Court of Appeal as more than 50 per cent of the cases end there. The Queen's Bench Division and the Chancery Division are the second largest users with almost 19 per cent and 5.5 per cent respectively. Family mediation cases rarely result in litigation and one can conclude that they are overall more successful out-of-court settlements. Both the need for privacy and threat of costs force parties to settle family disputes out of court. Finally, there are significantly more mediation than conciliation cases in Scotland.

Finally ADR cases in UK courts and a classification of their subject matters (see table on p 217):

[78] Research Papers 1997, no 5/98 the Central London County Court Pilot Mediation Scheme—Evaluation Report by Professor Hazel Genn. Reproduced also in Brown and Marriott, *ADR Principles and Practice*, para 3-067.

Conciliation Cases per Court

Court	Number of cases	Percentage
European Court of Justice	4	
European Court of Human Rights	1	
House of Lords	60	7.89
Court of Appeal (no further indication)	65	8.4
Court of Appeal (Criminal Division)	1	
Court of Appeal (Civil Division)	176	22.9
Court of Appeal total	242	31.3
High Court of Justice (no indication of division)	4	
Queen's Bench Division	82	10.69
QBD Technology and Construction Court	2	
QBD Commercial Court	16	
QBD Administrative Court	1	
QBD Crown Office List	13	
QBD total	114	14.88
Chancery Division	35	
Chancery Division (Companies Court)	1	
Chancery Division total	36	4.69
Family Division	45	5.8
National Industrial Relations Court	45	5.8
Industrial Tribunal	62	8.0
Employment Appeals Tribunal	130	16.9
Employment and Industrial Tribunals total	237	23.7
Court of Session (Scotland)	1	
Court of Session: Inner House	1	
Court of Session: Outer House	9	
Court of Session total	11	1.43
Admiralty Division	6	
Sheriff Court	1	
Birmingham County Court	1	
Restrictive Practices Court	3	
Vat and Duties Tribunals	1	
Various courts and tribunals total	12	1.56
Total of cases (all courts)	766	

Mediation Cases per Court

Court	Number of cases	Percentage
European Court of Human Rights	3	
House of Lords	11	
Privy Council	4	
House of Lords and Privy Council	15	5.47
Court of Appeal in Chancery	1	
Court of Appeal (Criminal Division)	1	
Court of Appeal (Civil Division)	139	50.71
Court of Appeal total	141	51.46
The High Court of Justice in Northern Ireland	1	
King's Bench Division	1	
Queen's Bench Division	18	
QBD Technology and Construction Court	5	
QBD Commercial Court	15	
QBD Administrative Court	7	
QBD Crown Office List	6	
QBD total	52	18.98
Chancery Division	22	
Chancery Division (Companies Court)	1	
Chancery Division total	23	8.39
Family Division	15	5.47
Employment Appeals Tribunal	4	
Court of Session (Scotland)		
Court of Session: Inner House	2	
Court of Session: Inner House (Extra Division)	1	
Court of Session: Outer House	7	
Court of Session total	10	3.64
Courts of Probate and Divorce	1	
Admiralty Division	3	
Sheriff Court	2	
Chancery Court of York, [Judicial committee]	1	
Vat and Duties Tribunals	3	
Various courts and tribunals total	10	3.64
Total of cases (all courts)	274	

ADR Cases per Court

Court	Number of cases	Percentage
Court of Appeal (no further indication)	2	
Court of Appeal (Civil Division)	68	
Court of Appeal total	70	73.68
Queen's Bench Division	6	
QBD Technology and Construction Court	1	
QBD Commercial Court		3
QBD Administrative Court	2	
QBD (Official Referees' Business)	3	
QBD total	15	15.79
Chancery Division total	3	3.16
Family Division	2	2.10
Employment Appeals Tribunal	2	2.10
Court of Session: Outer House	1	
Court of Session total	1	
The High Court of Justice in Northern Ireland	1	
Vat and Duties Tribunals	1	
Various courts and tribunals total	2	2.10
Total of cases (all courts)	95	

The smaller number of 'ADR cases' that are finally referred to litigation allows us a further classification according to subject matter. This revealed the following results:

- 54 cases or 65.1 per cent were ADR cases relating to socially sensitive areas in the public interest. In particular,
    - 12 were consumer disputes;
    - 12 were family law cases;
    - 1 was a community dispute; and
    - 29 were public (administrative) law disputes.
- 29 cases or 34.9 per cent were ADR cases relating to financial disputes. In particular,
    - 15 were commercial law disputes;
    - 3 were financial disputes;
    - 2 were insurance disputes;
    - 8 were construction disputes; and
    - 1 dispute was relating to maritime law.
- 10 cases or 10.63 per cent were ADR cases with a foreign element relating to the parties or the subject matter of the dispute.

It is compelling that the Court of Appeal has dealt with seventy ADR cases in the last few years and that the largest number of cases are of commercial nature. The number of twenty-nine public law cases is also impressive.

In any event the 1,135 cases which are reported in Lexis and WESTLAW UK are cases which for some reason were not finally resolved by conciliation, mediation or another ADR form. They are indicative of the growing number of cases that are now referred to ADR.

IV. ADR IN THE WEB OF DISPUTE RESOLUTION MECHANISMS

ADR is now an established dispute resolution method in the web of various mechanisms for the settlement of disputes. The main focus of ADR remains on domestic disputes although it is often used for international disputes as well. In principle, every state should have ADR mechanisms for domestic disputes as the regulatory competence will be restricted to such cases, or cases which are otherwise within the jurisdiction of the national regulator. It is difficult, if not impossible, to have accurate statistics about the use of ADR, as the mediation agreement is a private agreement of the parties and can normally be enforced voluntarily. Only when one of the parties to such an agreement wishes not to be bound by the agreement, state courts may be used.

A. Some Statistical Data

The Department of Trade and Industry commissioned a report, published in 2000[79] about the non-judicial resolution of international commercial disputes. ADR was considered but only data from CEDR was collected. Other institutions or private mediators were not asked to provide any data. This is also true for arbitration cases, although an estimate is given for *ad hoc* arbitrations.

The table on page 219 indicates that the number of commercial ADR cases has doubled since 1998 and that ADR accounts for roughly one-tenth of international commercial disputes resolved in London. If one excluded maritime (and marine insurance) disputes, then ADR cases account almost for one-third of the commercial dispute resolution with an international element.

It appears that the encouragement of ADR has been the most successful PPP (public private partnership) project of recent UK governments; a tradi-

[79] Source: BI—*Dispute Resolution in London* (2000), eds Judith Gill, Lord Hacking, Arthur Marriott, and Peter Rees.

Non-judicial Resolution of international commercial disputes in London[80]

Institution	1998	1999	2000
Ad hoc arbitrations (estimate)	500	500	500
CEDR (ADR commercial)	257	450	467
LCIA	70	56	81
ICC	50	70	80
LMAA	3191[81]	N/A	N/A
Trade Associations	500	500	N/A

tionally public service is now offered and performed by private providers, often with some support of public funds, to the extent that legal aid is now also made available to users of ADR services. The success of this form of PPP in dispute resolution can also be confirmed by statistics published by CEDR[82] according to which in 2000/01 27 per cent of all cases administered by CEDR were cases referred to it by courts. In particular, it was 8 per cent in 1998/99, 19 per cent in 1999/00, and 27 per cent in 2000/01.[83]

B. ADR and Arbitration

The relation between ADR and arbitration is not clearly defined and there is often no obligation for an arbitration tribunal to stay proceedings in favour of ADR. It is possible to use ADR before or during arbitration and there are several hybrids: arb/med, med/arb, etc.[84]

The use of ADR before arbitration is an added layer of dispute resolution and such multi-step dispute resolution clauses are becoming more frequent although there are not always welcome. A prominent example can be seen in the famous Channel Tunnel case:[85]

Settlement of Disputes

(1) If any dispute or differences shall arise between the Employer and the Contractor during the progress of the Works . . . , then . . . such dispute or difference shall at the instance of either the Employer or the Contractor in the first place be referred in writing to and be settled by a Panel of three persons (acting as independent

[80] Ibid, at 5.

[81] Number in 1997.

[82] <http://www.cedr.co.uk www.cedr.co.uk>.

[83] Summer 2001 (issue no 28) Resolutions, at 3, also available at <http://www.cedr.co.uk www.cedr.co.uk>.

[84] See below under 3.2.

[85] Excerpts from Clause 67 of the Channel Tunnel contract, *Channel Tunnel Group v Balfour Beatty Ltd* [1993] 1 All ER 664 at 672 a–e.

experts but not as arbitrators) who shall unless otherwise agreed by both the Employer and the Contractor within a period of 90 days after being requested in writing by either party to do so, and after such investigation as the Panel think fit, state their decision in writing and give notice of the same to the Employer and the Contractor. . . .

(2) The Contractor shall in any every case continue to proceed with the Works with all due diligence and the Contractor and the Employer shall both give effect forthwith to every such decision of the Panel . . . unless and until the same shall be revised by arbitration as hereinafter provided. . . .

The *Channel Tunnel* clause required an attempt to resolve disputes by reference to a Panel and if either party was not satisfied could have the decision of the Panel reviewed and revised by arbitration. Such a clause can only operate if well defined and reasonable time-limits for the completion of each stage of dispute resolution are set; otherwise the parties may be involved in too lengthy and uncertain a process.

A careful drafting makes such a multi-step dispute resolution agreement effective and enforceable. This is however difficult to assess if the ADR stage is expressed to be in the form of 'good faith negotiations'. This question was considered in *Halifax Financial Services Ltd v Intuitive Systems Ltd*.[86] In this case, a contract for software design included a provision to the effect that in the event of any dispute arising, the parties 'would meet in good faith and attempt to resolve the dispute without recourse to legal proceedings'. The clause further provided for structured negotiations with the assistance of a neutral or a mediator. McKinnon J considered that this clause was 'not nearly an immediately effective agreement to arbitrate, albeit not quite'[87] as in *Channel Tunnel*.[88] The decision in *Halifax Financial Services* has been correctly criticised as unduly traditional (and dated) and not in accordance with the accepted approach of the courts both in England and in other jurisdictions of giving effect to dispute resolution mechanisms agreed by the parties.[89]

C. ADR and Litigation

The relation between ADR and litigation has been now settled as a result of the court-annexed ADR described above and all practice directions

[86] [1999] 1 All ER 303. See also the note Okanunle Olatawura,, 'Managing Multi-Layered Dispute Resolution Under the Arbitration Act 1996—Smashing Bricks of Intention' 4(3) *International Arbitration Law Review* 70–3 (2001).

[87] See above.

[88] [1993] 1 All ER 664 at 678 *per* Lord Mustill.

[89] See Brown and Marriott, *ADR Principles and Practice*, 2nd edn (London: Sweet & Maxwell, 1999), para 6-064.

issued to express the newly adopted guidelines for courts.[90] If there was any doubt left, this was lifted by the Court of Appeal in *Cowl v Plymouth City Council*.[91] Parties *must* consider non-judicial settlement of their dispute via ADR before resorting to courts. The question is whether ADR can be made a compulsory dispute resolution step and whether such compulsion would be in conformity with the Human Rights Act and the European Convention of Human Rights. In other words should a court stay proceedings and refer parties to ADR? Is that a possible violation of section 6 of the Human Rights Act 1998 which guarantees the rights to a fair and public trial? None of the two cases[92] referring to mediation in the European Court of Human Rights addressed this issue.

Current English law works on three premises:

- The existence of an agreement to refer disputes to ADR is a prerequisite for the commencement and validity of ADR proceedings.[93] Such agreement may be expressed or implied and may have been entered into before or after the dispute has arisen. Under EC (and UK) law in consumer disputes ADR is possible if the parties agree to refer their dispute to ADR for resolution only after the dispute has arisen.[94]
- ADR, unlike arbitration and litigation arguably does not operate on the principle of fairness but on the principle that the parties jointly try to achieve a mutual acceptable resolution of their dispute. The neutral or the mediator should, however, appear to and be neutral and impartial.
- Should either party find the resolution of the dispute by ADR unsatisfactory, a recourse to courts is always possible.

On the basis of the three principles above, ADR is undisputedly in conformity with the Human Rights Act, as ultimately the courts can review ADR settlements.

90 See above under 2.1.4 and 2.1.5.

91 See *Cowl and Others v Plymouth City Council*, Judgment 14 December 2001, reported in *The Times* 8 January 2002 (CA) *per* Lord Woolf, LCJ.

92 *Hokkanen v Finland* (Case No 50/1993/445/524), European Court of Human Rights, [1996] 1 FLR 289, 23 Sept 1994; *Elsholz v Germany* (app no 25735/94 European Court of Human Rights (Grand Chamber), [2000] 3 FCR 385, 13 July 2000.

93 See *Jewo Ferrous BV v Lewis Moore (A Firm)*, 19 May 2000, CA, 2000 WL 774981 (CA); *Stafford Engineering Services Ltd's Licence of Right (Copyright) Application*, [2000] RPC 797, 1999 WL 33210358 (PO).

94 See EC Unfair Contract Terms Directive 93/13/EEC OJ L95, 21 Apr 1993, 29–34. Please note that Statutory Instrument 1999 No 2083 The Unfair Terms in Consumer Contracts Regulations 1999 makes no reference to ADR but it in Schedule 2 (q) declares arbitration not covered by legal provisions unfair, if there is no opportunity to review the decision in the courts.

V. REGULATORY AND INSTITUTIONAL SUPPORT

The development of ADR in England and Wales has been the result not only of civil justice reforms and changes in the dispute resolution culture but was also of the increased institutionalisation (III.A), evolution of many ADR mechanisms (III.B), and professionalisation of ADR providers (III.C).

A. Institutionalisation

In the United Kingdom, mediation as we currently know it could be said to have its roots in the formation of the Advisory, Conciliation and Arbitration Service (ACAS)[95] which was set up in 1974. This body was set up specifically to deal with industrial disputes and it continues to do so to this day.

However, England had no commercial mediation service available until 1989 when IDR Europe Limited, which now trades as ADR Group,[96] was set up. This was followed in 1990 by the establishment of the Centre for Dispute Resolution (CEDR).[97] Meanwhile, community mediation was beginning to be explored as a viable means of resolving neighbour disputes with a number of programmes being set up throughout the country in the early 1990s, including the Newham Conflict and Change Project,[98] Bristol Mediation,[99] and Mediation UK.[100] At the same time, the use of mediation in the Family Division of the UK Court system was being actively promoted.

The main ADR providers in the United Kingdom include:[101]

- *Adjudication.co.uk* is a adjudicator nominating body which also provides adjudication services and information.[102] Adjudication is a

[95] See <http://www.acas.org.uk/>.

[96] See <http://www.adrgroup.co.uk/>.

[97] See <http://www.cedr.co.uk/>.

[98] Newham Conflict and Change Project, Christopher House, 2a Streatfield Avenue, London E4 2LA, England.

[99] See <http://transatlantic.telewest.co.uk/5.html>.

[100] See <http://www.mediationuk.org.uk/>.

[101] See lists at <http://www.venables.co.uk/arbitrat.htm> and <http://www.eej-net.org.uk/Ukprocess/RegADR/regadr.html>. The latter site lists bodies that participate in EEJ-Net and provide quality services. They include registered bodies dealing with banking, building societies, carpet cleaning, consumer credit, estates, financial services, funerals, furniture, floor coverings, and allied trades, housing, insurance, investment, legal services, mail order, and pensions. Most schemes are relying on Ombudsmen. See also <http://www.pensions-ombudsman.org.uk> for information about the pensions ombudsman scheme; <http://www.abta.com> for the Association of British Travel Agents scheme and <http://www.eej-net.org.uk/UKprocess/RegADR/Legal/legal.htm> for the legal services Ombudsman for England and Wales and <http://www.slso.org.uk> for the Scottish Legal Services Ombudsman.

[102] <http://www.adjudication.co.uk>.

statutory procedure relating to UK legislation concerning Adjudication in the construction and telecommunications industries.[103]

- *Adjudication Society* is a not-for-profit society promoting resolution of construction disputes by means of adjudication.[104] The scope is similar to that of the 'sister site' adjudication.co.uk.
- *ADR Chambers (UK) Ltd* is an Alternative Dispute Resolution Group consisting of retired Law Lords, Lords Justices, High Court Judges, Circuit Court Judges and other retired judges, as well as retired and practising barristers and solicitors who are trained and dedicated to helping parties resolve disputes in an expeditious and cost-effective manner. The members of the group are independent contractors under the umbrella of ADR Chambers and provide support services to the members and clients. The group has its own mediation rules and also offers training services.[105]
- *Alternative Dispute Resolution (ADR) Group* was founded in 1989 and is a specialist mediation provider. ADR Group arranges mediations in disputes relating to banking, insurance, contract, probate, financial services, contract disputes, as well as medical negligence and personal injury. It offers training in mediation in general as well as specific family mediation training. It also offers case selection for mediation and confidential advice to disputants.[106]
- *Arbitration a Commercial Initiative (formerly Arbitration for Commerce and Industry)* provides extensive administered commercial dispute resolution services including arbitration, mediation, early neutral evaluation and mini trial.[107]
- *The Association of Northern Mediators*, based in Leeds, promotes the use of mediation throughout the region. It provides at no cost, lists of mediators divided up into local and subject groupings.[108] They have recently produced a report about mediation in the north of England.[109] The survey contrasted mediation activity in the first and second halves of

103 See, eg, Housing Grants, Construction and Regeneration Act 1996; Scheme for Construction Contracts (England and Wales) Regulations 1998; Construction Contracts (England and Wales) Exclusion Order 1998; Housing Grants, Construction and Regeneration Act (England and Wales) (Commencement no 4) Order 1998; Scheme for Construction Contracts (Scotland) Regulations 1998; The Construction Contracts (Scotland) Exclusion Order 1998; Housing Grants, Construction and Regeneration Act 1996 (Scotland) (Commencement no 5) Order 1998.

104 <http://www.adjudication.org>, in association with the Disputes Review Board Foundation, USA and the Major Projects Association, UK.

105 <http://www.adrchambers.co.uk>.

106 <http://www.adrgroup.co.uk>.

107 <http://www.aci-arb.com>.

108 <http://www.northernmediators.co.uk>.

109 See A Glaister, *Mediation Trends in the North of England*, available at <http://mediate.com/articles/glaister.cfm>.

2000. The total number of mediations monitored were 214, 90 in the first half and 124 in the second half. There was a 30 per cent growth in the numbers of mediations between the first and second halves of last year. The survey also reveals how appointments of mediators were made[110] and the significant role institutionalisation of arbitration has played in the development of ADR. The 30 per cent increase is almost exclusively due to the institutions:

First Half 2000	Second Half 2000
Agreed: 24	Agreed 26
Appointment by ADR Group, Academy	Appointment by ADR Group,
Academy of Experts and CEDR: 62	of Experts and CEDR: 85
	Appointtment by other ADR institutions: 5
Court schemes: 2	Court schemes: 8
Total: 90 mediations	Total: 124 mediations

- *Centre for Effective Dispute Resolution (CEDR)* is the most high profile ADR institution in the UK and one of the leading international bodies in the field of ADR, dispute management and conflict prevention in the world. It was launched in 1990 with the backing of the confederation of the British Industry (CBI). It is the flagship for raising the understanding, profile and use of ADR, both in the UK and internationally·[111] It has its own rules and an extensive training programme. CEDR Solve arranged 467 commercial mediations in 2000/01. 27 per cent of mediations referred to CEDR Solve were court-referred, compared with 19 per cent the previous year and 8 per cent the year before that.

The construction industry remains CEDR Solve's largest user group at 14 per cent.

Further, 108 cases were referred to CEDR Solve through industry schemes, an increase by 18 per cent. CEDR Solve offers dispute resolution schemes for organisations which include the Employment Service, National Council of Voluntary Organisations, Age Concern and the Independent Housing Ombudsman.

CEDR was also recently involved in a survey entitled Attitudes to

110 See Glaister, above.

111 < http://www.cedr.co.uk>.

Types of dispute mediated by CEDR Solve in 2000/01 (percentage)[112]

Professional negligence:	17
Construction:	14
Financial:	7
IT:	6
Clinical negligence/Personal injury	5
Employment:	4
Shipping:	4
Engineering:	4
Partnership:	3
Insurance:	3
Intellectual property:	3
Property:	2

Mediation.[113] Some of the most important conclusions are discussed below.

- *The Centre for Business Arbitration* provides reasonably priced dispute resolution services within the reach of the medium and small business. It provides both arbitration and mediation. Panelists are lawyers drawn from the specialist Bar and cover among other areas real property, trust disputes, company share and partnership disputes and financial services.[114]
- *Chartered Institute of Arbitrators* is a professional body with over 9,000 members (practitioners in law, construction, shipping, finance, insurance commodities, agriculture, accountancy and medicine) in eighty-four countries. The headquarters are in London. Its object is to promote and facilitate the determination of disputes by arbitration and alternative means of dispute resolution other than resolution by the court.[115] For these purposes the Chartered Institute has its own rules and offers accreditation and training courses.
- *Chartered Institute of Arbitrators, Scottish Branch* aims to promote the use of arbitration in Scotland as a means of dispute resolution, both domestically and internationally. The site offers free access to the Scottish Arbitration Code which has been developed in conjunction with the Scottish Council for International Arbitration and the Scottish Building Contract Committee.[116]

[112] See *Resolutions*—Issue no 28, Summer 2001, at 3.
[113] In association with the Legal Director and Pinsent Curtis Biddle. The results were published in June 2001. Available at
[114] <http://www.arbitration.lincolns-inn.com>.
[115] <http://www.arbitrators.org>.
[116] <http://www.scottish-arbitrators.org>.

- *Construction Contracts Mediators' Group (CCMG)* provide access to a group of mediators who specialise in construction contract disputes. Each mediator has experience of the difficulties which can arise and need to be overcome in order to enable construction contract disputes to be settled amicably, economically, and on terms acceptable to the parties.[117]
- *Financial Ombudsman Scheme.* It deals with consumer complaints about financial firms which are regulated by the Financial Services Authority, and some unregulated firms after 1 January 2001. It is set up by law to help settle individual disputes between consumers and financial services providers. According the FOS can consider most personal finance disputes. Accordingly the FOS can help with most financial complaints about banking services, credit cards issued by banks and building societies, endowment policies, financial and investment advice, health and loan protection insurance, household and buildings insurance, investment portfolio management, life assurance, mortgages, motor insurance, personal pension plans, private medical insurance, savings plans and accounts, stocks and shares, travel insurance, and unit trusts and income bonds. The service is free to consumers and the FOS decisions are binding on financial firms but not on consumers.[118]
- I*ndependent Mediation for Clinical Disputes (IMCD)* is a specialist mediation, conciliation and arbitration service provider for clinical negligence and personal injury disputes. The service is available either directly to the public or via a legal representative. IMCD also offers training courses to solicitors, claims managers, insurance service providers upon mediation awareness, and case/client preparation.[119]
- *LCIA Mediation* The London Court of International Arbitration is arguably the oldest arbitration institution, having been in existence since 1892. It is a truly international organisation, and this is reflected in its membership and the wealth of international experience in administering cases.[120] It provides a comprehensive international dispute resolution service, and has introduced its own mediation rules.[121]
- *Mediation UK* is an independent firm providing practical, cost efficient solutions for parties who find themselves in dispute. It offers services in matrimonial, corporate, employment, personal injury, and medical negligence cases.[122] Another major of activity is community disputes.

[117] <http://www.ccmg.co.uk>.
[118] <http://www.financial-ombudsman.org.uk>.
[119] <http://www.imcd.co.uk>.
[120] <http://www.lcia-arbitration.com/town/square/xvc24>.
[121] <http://www.lcia-arbitration.com/town/square/xvc24/rulecost/mediation.htm>. See also Adrian Winstanley, 'LCIA: The LCIA Introduces New Mediation Procedure', 2(3) *International Arbitration Law Review* N31–N32 (1999).
[122] <http://www.mediationuk.com>.

- *Royal Institution of Chartered Surveyors (RICS)*[123] is a major body in this field. For example, in 1999, the RICS appointed nearly 8000 arbitrators, experts, adjudicators and mediators to resolve disputes concerning land, property and construction. Over 450 cases were referred under agricultural legislation, and approximately 600 arbitrators and adjudicators were appointed in building/construction disputes.[124] The main ADR services relate to property problems, lease renewals (PACT), and rent reviews. Professional Arbitration on Court Terms (PACT) is a new scheme offered by RICS and the Law Society, for the resolution of lease renewal disputes. PACT is aimed at unopposed lease renewals under the Landlord and Tenant Act 1954 and offers the opportunity for disputes to be resolved without the necessity of going to court.[125]
- *Syndicus* is a group of consultants and practitioners in complaints handling, dispute resolution and training. Syndicus has a special emphasis on ombudsmen issues.[126]
- *South Western ADR*[127] was set up in 1998 to support the Woolf Reforms and is now firmly established in the region (and beyond) as a leading provider for ADR services to the public.
- *UK College of Family Mediators*[128] is the professional standards-setting watchdog and public information providing body for family mediation in England, Scotland, Wales and Northern Ireland. It provides information on how family mediation works and on finding a mediator and it also provides ADR services.

The recent survey of the Association of Northern Mediators has also shown that disputants prefer to rely on services provided by institutions rather than trying to agree on a mediator themselves. The survey below establishes the direct link between the growth of ADR and the ADR institutions, where the ADR institutions have taken front line responsibility in raising public awareness (see table on top of p 228).

The wide range of disputes administered and the healthy competition between the many ADR services providers have contributed to the public awareness and the significant increase of ADR in the UK. It is fact of life that at the beginning of a dispute the parties can agree on very little. ADR institutions not only assist the parties but also create an environment in

123 <http://www.rics.org>.

124 <http://www.rics.org/resources/services/drs>.

125 See JE Adams, 'The Woolf Reforms and Property Litigation' [1999] *Conveyancer and Property Lawyer* 459-461; VM King, 'PACT Gets Into Training', I(5) *Landlord and Tenant Review*, 103–4 (1997); A Salata, and N Cheffings, 'Resolving Property Disputes in the Millennium, 4(4) *Landlord and Tenant Review*, 78–84 (2000)

126 <http://www.syndicus.co.uk,http://www.syndicus.co.uk/const.php?fp=whatwedo>.

127 <http://www.southwesternadr.co.uk>.

128 <http://www.ukcfm.co.uk,http://www.ukcfm.co.uk/training.htm>.

Sources of information about mediation	2000 %	2001 %
Current legal firm	49	56
CEDR	28	41
Industrial / Trade Association	0	11
Other mediation organisation	7	14
Legal directories / publications	6	12
Other	0	36
No answer	0	2

which disputes are administered professionally and in which disputes can be resolved to the satisfaction of the parties.

1. ADR Mechanisms[129]

Essentially there are two forms of dispute resolution: one which imposes a decision and determines issues definitively, such as expert determinations and baseball arbitrations; the other provides the basis to help the parties reach an agreed solution or settlement, such as negotiation, mediation/conciliation, mini-trial, neutral listener, early neutral or expert evaluation. In a recent survey about actions taken in resolving disputes the following results were published:

Actions taken in Resolving Disputes[130]
(Base: Those that have had a serious dispute)

What was your action?	2000 %	2001 %
Holding face to face discussions	79	74
Sending letters to the other party yourself	87	77
Instructing a professional adviser to act on your behalf	83	72
Going to independent mediation	18	19
Going to court/tribunal	46	52
Arbitration	N/A	16
Other	3	5

[129] See Brown and Marriott, *Principles and Practice* (London: Sweet & Maxwell, 1999), at 15–20.

[130] Attitudes to Mediation (June 2001) available at <http://www.cedr.co.uk/library/articles/CEDR_PCB_survey.pdf>, at 8.

The table above gives the immediate action businesspersons would take without considering types of disputes. The classification below attempts at ascertain the relevance and function of the various ADR mechanisms.

2. *Definitive determination*[131]

These are all mechanisms to achieve a final determination of the dispute by the intervention of a third party who imposes a decision. Once the mechanism is agreed upon neither party can unilaterally withdraw from the process. The parties can still settle the dispute themselves but if not, then a binding determination will be made which, in principle, is enforceable through the courts. Most of these mechanisms are known in the UK although they are not as popular as in the US. They are normally used as ADR techniques within a mediation, conciliation or negotiation process. The main mechanisms of definitive determination include:

- *Rent-a-judge or private judging*: This is a court-annexed or private ADR process. It is available where statutes or local court rules permit court referral of cases to neutral third parties, usually retired judges, for formal trials. The procedure followed by the retired judge or neutral is usually akin to that in a common court trial. The decision of the neutral is referred to the competent court, and is considered to be a judgment of the court. Generally the parties' rights to appellate review and enforcement of the decision are the same as if the judgment had been entered into by a court. It is also possible where parties wish to expedite or avoid the delay of the courts. This mechanism is known[132] but not common in the UK.
- *Baseball arbitration*: This is also known as final or last offer or pendulum arbitration. This process involves the parties narrowing the risk themselves by the claims and admissions made and it ties the hand of the arbitrators as to the extent of the awards they can make. Following its submission in a binding arbitration, each party also submits its best offer to the tribunal in a sealed envelope. The tribunal's responsibility is to choose the best offer that comes nearest to its own assessment. The arbitrators do not have to make assessments as to the correct level of damages, but rather which party is nearer to the mark, and that is the amount awarded. The effect of this procedure is to compel the parties to narrow their demands because an over-stated claim will almost certainly result in the award going to the other side. Final offer arbitration is potentially unfair unless all parties have essentially equal access to the

131 See Lew, Mistelis, and Kröll, *Comparative International Commercial Arbitration* (The Hague: Kluwer, 2002), at paras 1-31–1-42.

132 <http://www.adrchambers.co.uk>.

basic facts. This technique is also known as 'baseball' arbitration because it is used in the negotiation of professional athletes' contracts in the US. It is actually an ADR rather than an ADR process in that the third party assists the party in reaching an agreement and does not make own decisions.

- *Expert determination*:[133] This is the referral of a dispute to an independent third party to resolve by using his own expertise. It is particularly useful for resolving valuation disputes, such as intellectual property, technical issues, accounting disputes and earn-outs under company accounts. It can be cheaper and quicker than arbitration as the expert can conduct his own investigations without relying upon, or waiting for, information to be provided by the parties. A decision of an expert cannot be directly enforced in the same way as an arbitration award. There is no appeal from the decision of an expert. Unlike an arbitrator, an expert can be sued for negligence. Expert determination is quite popular in the UK for valuation of, for instance, shares or commodities.
- *Adjudication*:[134] This involves the binding, but not necessarily final, resolution of disputes on an expedited basis. It acts as a form of interim dispute resolution, although its effect may often be to dispose of disputes without further proceedings. In the United Kingdom it is required by statute for all contracts involving the carrying out of construction operations.[135] However, it is also commonly included in contracts for construction or engineering work elsewhere, where it may also be referred to a Dispute Adjudication Board (DAB) or a Dispute Review Board (DRB). The adjudicator is required to reach his decision in a specified, short period of time. Under UK statute this is only 28 days from the reference of the dispute to him, extendable only by agreement of the parties or by up to 14 days with the agreement only of the referring party. Frequently, in large infrastructure projects a time for

[133] See Kendall, *Expert Determination*, 3rd edn (London: Sweet & Maxwell, 2001).

[134] See Stevenson and Chapman, *Construction Adjudication* (Bristol: Jordan, 1999); Seppala, 'The New FIDIC Provision for a Dispute Adjudication Board', 8 *Revue de Droit des Affaires Internationales*, 967–88 (1997); Morris, 'Adjudication as Operated on the Construction of the Dartford River Crossing (The Queen Elizabeth II Bridge)', 60 *Arbitration* 13–16 (1994);

[135] See, eg, Housing Grants, Construction and Regeneration Act 1996; Scheme for Construction Contracts (England and Wales) Regulations 1998; Construction Contracts (England and Wales) Exclusion Order 1998; Housing Grants, Construction and Regeneration Act (England and Wales) (Commencement no 4) Order 1998; Scheme for Construction Contracts (Scotland) Regulations 1998; The Construction Contracts (Scotland) Exclusion Order 1998; Housing Grants, Construction and Regeneration Act 1996 (Scotland) (Commencement no 5) Order 1998. See also Davies, 'Section 9 of the English Arbitration Act 1996 and Section 108 of the Housing Grants, Construction and Regeneration Act 1996: A Conflict Waiting to be Exploited', 13 *Arbitration International*, 411–16 (1997).

adjudication is expressly provided for in the Agreement. Critically, once the adjudicator has made his decision it is binding on the parties and is immediately enforceable. However, it cannot be enforced as an arbitral award but must be sued upon for enforcement.

Whether or not a decision is enforced, unless the contract expressly provides that the adjudicator's decision is also final, the parties may have the dispute re-heard in its entirety by whatever ultimate dispute resolution method they have chosen, whether arbitration or the national courts. The ultimate tribunal is in no way bound by the adjudicator's decision and it re-hears the dispute afresh, rather than reviewing or hearing an appeal from the adjudicator's decision. If the ultimate tribunal comes to a different conclusion to the adjudicator's decision, its judgment or award will replace the decision, with money being repaid if necessary.

B. Mechanisms Requiring Parties' Agreement for Resolution of Dispute[136]

All of the mechanisms below require the parties to conclude the settlement agreement between themselves. These procedures aim to bring the parties closer, to understand the respective position of the other side, and to help the parties see the weaknesses of their own case. This should, in principle, with or without the assistance of a third party, enable the parties to agree the terms for the settlement of their differences. If no agreement is possible, the parties can resort to arbitration or the courts for the determination of their dispute. The main mechanisms requiring parties' agreement for resolution of dispute include:

- *Negotiation*:[137] Straightforward negotiations between the parties or their advisors are always the most obvious but not the easiest way of reaching a consensus and to compromise the controversy. Negotiation is the most flexible, informal, and party-directed method; it is the closest to the parties' circumstances and control, and can be geared to each party's own concerns. Parties choose location, timing, agenda, subject matter and participants. Negotiation should normally be the first approach at resolution of any dispute. However, negotiations may fail because of previous poor relations, intransigent positions of the parties, neither party being prepared to lose 'face' and the fact that a party cannot be pressured against its wishes from adopting an unreasonable position.

[136] See Lew, Mistelis, and Kröll, op cit, at paras 1-43–1-53.

[137] See Brown and Marriott, op cit, ch 6, at 103–26; Palmer and Roberts, op cit, ch 3, at 63–100.

- *Mediation/conciliation:*[138] Mediation is a process whereby a mediator, that is a neutral third party, works with the parties to resolve their dispute by agreement, rather than imposing a solution. It is sometimes known as conciliation but in England the terms are used interchangeably. Historically, and because of the slightly different methods applied in mediation and conciliation in public international law, they were perceived as different processes. Consequently mediation sometimes refers to a method where a mediator has a more proactive role (*evaluative mediation*) and conciliation sometimes refers to a method where a conciliator has a more facilitating mediator role (*facilitative mediation*).

Mediation can be more effective than simple negotiations. This is because the mediator works with the parties to effect a compromise, either by suggesting grounds of agreement or forcing them to recognise weaknesses in their cases. The mediator may, if required, evaluate the merits of the parties' cases in a non-binding manner. However, the mediator cannot make a binding adjudicatory decision. The parties can obtain any remedy they wish; the only limits are on what they can agree. This differs from the position in litigation, arbitration and expert determination, where the court or tribunal is limited to remedies available at law.

In the above-mentioned survey *attitudes to mediation*[139] six tables provide important information about the developments in mediation in the UK.

First, the question was: Have your company's external legal firm ever spoken to you about mediation as a means of ADR? The results were:[140]

Yes:	65 per cent
No:	33 per cent
Don't know:	2 per cent

Two in three firms have been spoken to about mediation by their external legal advisors. This figure has increased from 61 per cent in the previous study.

Secondly, the question was: How strongly do you agree or disagree with the suggestion that mediation should be made compulsory if a business dispute goes to court? The results were:[141]

[138] See Brown and Marriott, op cit, chs 7–15, at 127–351; Palmer and Roberts, op cit, ch 4, at 101–60.

[139] Attitudes to Mediation. A survey by the Legal Director in association with CEDR and Pinsent Curtis Biddle. The results were published in June 2001. Available at <http://www.cedr.co.uk/library/articles/CEDR_PCB_survey.pdf>.

[140] Ibid, at 13.

[141] Ibid, at 26.

Should mediation be made compulsory?		
	2000 %	2001 %
Strongly agree	9	13
Tend to agree	29	19
Neither agree nor disagree	14	7
Tend to disagree	20	24
Strongly disagree	28	37

While parties recognise the merits of mediation they do not wish it to become mandatory.

Thirdly, the question was: Do you use dispute resolution clauses? The results were:[142]

Yes:	73 per cent
No:	23 per cent
Don't know:	4 per cent

Three in four companies claim that their contracts with suppliers/customers currently contain clauses about the process to follow if a dispute occurs. Of these, 55 per cent claim that mediation is included in the process. This suggests that approximately two in every five companies mention mediation in their contracts. Amongst those that do not have a clause in their contracts, 64 per cent say they would consider such a clause.

Fourthly, the question was: What, if any, do you consider the benefits of mediation to be? The results were[143]

Benefits of mediation?	%
Less expensive	61
Quicker response	47
Preserves relationships	40
Better for both sides	10
Avoids court action	14
More effective	7
You get an independent view	8
Keeping things private	21
Other (specify)	25
Don't know	2

[142] Ibid, at 27. [143] Ibid, at 21.

Fifthly, the question was: And what do you consider the drawbacks of mediation to be? The results were:[144]

Drawbacks of mediation?	%
A solution is not guaranteed	34
Want the resolution to be legally binding	21
It is a slower process	15
Extra costs	15
Other sides may not agree to participate	11
Other parties may not behave with honesty	14
There may not be a winner	10
Other	37
Other (specify)	6

Finally, the question was: At what point in a serious dispute would you consider using mediation? The results were:[145]

Most effective source of dispute	Very/quite effective %	Fairly/Very ineffective %
Accountants	36 (30)	58 (64)
Business consultants	18 (13)	80 (79)
Industry associations	33 (39)	64 (60)
Mediation organisations	65 (52)	28 (31)
Solicitors	89 (87)	9 (14)

- *Mediation/arbitration (med-arb)*:[146] This can happen where parties agree that if mediation does not result in a negotiated settlement, the dispute will be resolved by arbitration and the mediator is converted into an arbitrator. In this process, there is initially facilitative mediation (the mediator does not evaluate the strength of the parties' cases) followed by binding arbitration. What is unique in this situation is that the mediator

144 Attitudes to Mediation, at 22.

145 Ibid, at 23.

146 See Hill, 'MED–ARB: New Coke or Swatch?', 13 *Arbitration International* 105–10 (1997); Motiwal, 'Alternative Dispute Resolution in India', 15 *Journal of International Arbitration* 117–28 (1998).

is converted into an arbitrator, in order to make a determinative decision if the mediation fails. The idea of the same individual acting as both a mediator and then an arbitrator gives serious misgivings. In view of the confidential and prejudicial information during the mediation process, it is generally considered that the mediator would be compromised to then convert himself into an arbitrator to make a decision on the merits. In these circumstances many parties would not be fully open and frank with the mediator for fear of being prejudiced at the arbitration stage. The introduction of med-arb has been recently advocated in the UK.[147]

- *Mini-trial/executive appraisal*:[148] In mini-trials, voluntary court-style procedures are adopted which involve the parties presenting a summarised version of their case (including calling evidence and making submissions) before a tribunal. The tribunal may ask questions and comment on evidence and arguments. The tribunal can be a neutral advisor who, following the presentation, advises the parties on how he sees the strengths and weaknesses of their case. Where the tribunal consists of neutrals, it can render a non-binding decision, which is intended as an aid to the parties' further negotiation toward settlement. Alternatively, the tribunal can consist of senior executives of the companies in dispute perhaps with a neutral chairman, who use the mini-trial as a springboard for settlement discussions (*executive appraisal*). Parties to a mini-trial may agree that the neutral advisor will not act as an arbitrator or mediator. A mini-trial aims at facilitating a prompt and cost effective resolution of a complex litigation case concerning mixed questions of fact and law. Its goal is to keep the problem as a 'businessperson's problem,' to narrow the area of controversy, to dispose of collateral issues, and to encourage a fair and equitable settlement.
- *Early neutral evaluation/non-binding appraisal*:[149] Parties present their cases in the early stages of a dispute to a neutral evaluator. The evaluator, following an oral presentation by each party, confidentially assesses the arguments and submissions. The assessment is not binding on the parties. No records of assessment are kept and the evaluation is considered 'off the record'. The aim is to demonstrate to each party the strengths and weaknesses of its case. This is intended to help parties to settle their differences by subsequent negotiation or perhaps with an independent mediator.

[147] P Newman, 'Mediation–Arbitration (MedArb); Can it Work Legally', 60(3) *Arbitration* 173 (1994).

[148] See Brown and Marriott, op cit, at paras 16-038–16-077; Palmer and Roberts, op cit, at 227–8.

[149] See Brown and Marriott, op cit, paras 16-83–16-101; Palmer and Roberts, op cit, at 228–30 and 274–7. See also [1996] 1 All ER 383; [1996] 1 WLR 1024; [1998] 1 Lloyd's Rep 126, 30 Sept 1997.

- *Ombudsman*: This institution is an expression and reflection of the activity of modern state. It represents a procedure for the redress of complaints about the way in which decisions are made. Although originally it was introduced for the examination of complaints of maladministration[150] it now has extended to a number of regulated industries.[151] Ombudsmen normally receive complaints from citizens or consumers recipients of a service provided by regulated industry (including but not limited to former state monopoly). After examination of the complaints attempts are made to settle the case. The decision is not binding on the parties unless they agree so. In other words, the ombudsman is an impartial referee who investigates complaints about many public and some private organisations and suggests settlements.

A great variety of ADR mechanisms is now well established in the UK and a large scope of disputes is now resolved by ADR. There are horses for courses and disputants have a wide choice of options for settling their disputes by whatever mechanism appears to be adequate in the given set of facts and the particular circumstances of the parties.

C. ADR as a Profession

Another factor that contributed to the shift from litigation to non-judicial settlement of disputes can be seen in the change of attitude of lawyers towards disputes and dispute settlement. This change in attitude is not only typical for lawyers but also for other professions dealing with or affected by disputes and their settlements.

At a recent survey the question was: If you felt a serious dispute was developing, how effective do you believe each of the following sources of advice would be in informing you about how to resolve the dispute? The results were:[152]

150 Since 1967 the Parliamentary Commissioner for Administration (PCA), and since 1974, the Ombudsman for local government in England, Wales, Scotland, and Northern Ireland. Later Health Service Commissioners were introduced, and the European Ombudsman was appointed by the European Parliament with Art 195 (ex Art 138(e) of the EC Treaty.

151 eg, for telecommunications, financial services, energy, railway. See, eg, <http://www.pensions-ombudsman.org.uk> for the pensions ombudsman scheme, <http://www.financial-ombudsman.org.uk> for the Financial Services Ombudsman, <http://www.eej-net.org.uk/UKprocess/RegADR/Legal/legal.htm> for the legal services Ombudsman for England and Wales and <http://www.slso.org.uk> for the Scottish Legal Services Ombudsman. The Disability Rights Commission also operates an Ombudsman scheme.

152 Attitudes to Mediation (June 2001) at <http://www.cedr.co.uk/library/articles/CEDR_PCB_survey.pdf>, at 12 (2000 results in brackets).

When to use mediation in a serious dispute?	%
Pre-issue	65
Allocation questionnaire stage	6
Case Management Conference (CMC) stage	16
Exchange of witness statements	6
Exchange of expert reports	5
Listing questionnaire stage	2

The results are compelling. Disputants rely on lawyers for the settlement of their dispute and solicitors are the most trusted advisers in case of disputes. This is surprising as lawyers were accused of causing all problems relating to traditional court procedure. Extreme adversarial process, lengthy litigious proceedings were anathema for those seeking reform. It seems that the recent Woolf reforms have produced results. Many of the leading City law firms have now a distinct ADR group within their litigation or dispute resolution group. However, the credit is not exclusive to the Woolf Reforms. The second most trusted group in the list above are mediation organisations. This is not surprising, because as we have seen above ADR institutions have made a major campaign across the UK to raise public awareness and to educate potential disputants of the merits and drawbacks of ADR. Many lawyers have been trained and re-trained to provide ADR services. In this section we examine essential mediator's skills (III.C.1) and the training available in the UK (III.C.2) before assessing the relevance of accreditation (III.C.3)

1. *Mediator's skills*[153]

Many factors affect the quality of the mediation process. Among them the model of mediation, the Code of Practice upon which it is based and the techniques employed by the mediator. The most important factor is the quality of the mediator. It is difficult to determine what makes a good mediator. Being a good mediator obviously requires a significant personal and professional commitment and skill. It appears that the four fundamental assets are:

- Theoretical understanding
- Practical skills
- Ethical awareness and
- Emotional sensitivity.
- The next three assets are desirable:

[153] This section is based on Brown and Marriott, op cit, chs 15 and 21.

- Sound judgment
- Personal empathy and
- Substantive knowledge.

Creativity, flexibility and balance may also be relevant. However, good listening skills is essential as well as the ability of making the disputants listen. Further good use of language, the ability to summarise and management skills is what forces the parties to settle.

- Effectively the mediator performs the following roles and functions:
- Manager of the process
- Information gatherer
- Facilitator
- Reality tester and evaluator
- Scribe and
- Settlement supervisor.

While a number of skills are character or personal attributes, such as personal empathy and substantive knowledge, the majority of them can be acquired by successful training.

2. *Training Courses*

A variety of ADR training courses are offered by various ADR institutions, ranging from generic information on ADR to hands-on workshop type workshops and university level graduate and postgraduate studies. Here are some of them:

- *Alternative Dispute Resolution (ADR) Group* provides general ADR training courses falling into three categories. (a) Training to become a mediator; (b) Mediator post qualification; and (c) Training in advocacy.[154] It also offers specialist family mediation training.[155]
- *Centre for Effective Dispute Resolution (CEDR)*[156] is arguably the largest provider of training. In addition to CEDR's five-day Mediator Skills Training course, which leads to assessment for CEDR accreditation, CEDR offers continuing professional development events for mediators. CEDR also provides a range of awareness courses and educational seminars on mediation and other aspects of effective dispute resolution. Through its system of intensive, practical training and assessment CEDR Accreditation[157] is recognised as an international benchmark of mediation excellence. On the final two days of CEDR's five-day Mediator Skills

[154] <http://www.adrgroup.co.uk/training/index.html>.
[155] <http://www.adrgroup.co.uk/family/frame_src-fam.html>.
[156] <http://www.cedr.co.uk/index.php?location=/training/default.htm>.
[157] <http://www.cedr.co.uk/index.php?location=/training/accred.htm>.

Training course participants are rigorously assessed by CEDR faculty members, themselves practising mediators, and around 70 per cent achieve accreditation. Accredited mediators are eligible to become registered with CEDR's continuing professional development scheme, which provides a framework for individual development. Registered mediators are recognised in the UK and internationally as offering a service of quality and integrity. Accreditation with CEDR is no guarantee of CEDR Solve mediation appointments, although CEDR accreditation is widely recognised by other mediation providers. Participants who demonstrate exceptional talent during assessment for accreditation may be invited to join CEDR Solve's core group of mediators where they will be given the opportunity to act as an assistant mediator to continue their development through experience before becoming a lead mediator. All CEDR Solve mediators go through a rigorous system of performance monitoring which includes client and peer feedback. No specific qualifications or experience are needed to undertake the Mediator Skills Training course and participants from different professions and backgrounds are encouraged.

- *Chartered Institute of Arbitrators*:[158] The Institute provides specialist training for mediators. The primary course lasts five days and uses role-play exercises, interactive group exercises, video clips, demonstrations and formal lectures. Successful completion of the five-day course will entitle graduates to apply for Associate Membership of the Institute. The five-day course may be followed by a two-day accreditation course, successful completion of which will entitle graduates to apply for Membership of the Institute.
- *Academy of Experts*[159] offers a number of training courses and educational seminars.
- *UK College of Family Mediators*[160] is a specialist body that offers training for family mediators.

3. Accreditation

The introduction of training courses bears the question as to whether and to what extent it is appropriate to accredit and regulate ADR practitioners.[161] In the UK most of the institutions mentioned above as training courses providers also perform an accreditation function. However, their standards may vary.[162]

[158] <http://www.arbitrators.org/events/mediation.htm>.
[159] <http://www.academy-experts.org/trainingmedexp.htm>.
[160] <http://www.ukcfm.co.uk/training.htm>.
[161] Brown and Marriott, op cit, at para 24-001.
[162] CEDR in its *Response to the Lord Chancellor's Department ADR Discussion Paper* at 3 suggests that it is an inappropriate conclusion that 'what is needed is more training, agreed standards, or worst of all external regulation' (Feb 2000).

Accreditation can be advantageous:

- It sets benchmark standards;
- It inspires public confidence; and
- It is consistent with the movement towards the introduction of reliable public standards.

Accreditation is not an absolute indication of competence neither is a guarantee for those who have passed the accreditation exam that they will have a career in ADR. What the accreditation ensures is the observance of certain standards. In a number of cases parties to a dispute may want to have a person with a specific profile appointed who is not necessarily an accredited mediator. Hence, while accreditation is, in principle, welcome should be used as a yardstick rather than a ruler. It will indicate a set of skills but it should not bar other respected practitioners from providing ADR services. This is the case also with arbitration and the system has worked so far successfully.

What is essential is a certain level of self-regulation of ADR practitioners. This will include a Code of Practice and regulation of the profession which the ADR practitioner normally performs. Accordingly, a person who is member of the Law Society should apply the same ethical standards also in ADR proceedings. Also the requirement for continuing professional development may also be useful.

In the UK there are several Codes of Practice. These include:

- Law Society Family Mediation Code[163]
- Law Society Civil and Commercial Mediation Code[164]
- UK College of Family Mediators Code
- CEDR Model Mediation Procedure[165]
- Mediation UK Standards for Mediators and
- City Dispute Panel Expert Determination Guidelines.[166]

The current system which is a combination of accreditation and self-regulation is satisfactory and there have been no problems reported. The indirect self-regulation is welcome; the accreditation should not be used to create new clubs for mediators. In several areas, parties wish to have maximum autonomy and this should be respected in a voluntary process.

163 < http://www.lawsoc.org.uk/dcs/third_tier.asp?section_id=2253&Caller_ID=NS81>.
164 Ibid.
165 <http://www.cedr.co.uk/library/documents/procedure_agreement.pdf>.
166 See Brown and Marriott, op cit, App II, at 563–90.

VI. CONCLUDING REMARKS

ADR has developed considerably in England over the last few years and has acquired a distinct position in the dispute resolution landscape. In all fields of civil and commercial dispute resolution ADR plays an increasingly significant role. A large numbers of ADR institutions has emerged; they all provide comprehensive training and information as well as dispute resolution services. The qualitative and ethical standards are high although more may and will be done in the future towards increased self-regulation.

The courts have also acknowledged the importance of ADR. Several schemes of court-annexed or court encouraged ADR exist and the Civil Procedure Rules support out of court settlement of disputes. The full potential of the Woolf Reforms and the emergence of ADR will unfold in the next few years.

The landscape changes far too fast for us to give an accurate picture; hence, it is rather impressionistic or futuristic. The future, no doubt, will see the increase of online dispute resolution in consumer disputes as well.[167] In any event, modern ADR in England is a successful PPP (public private partnership) as the private sector assumes the role of a public service provider. This is consistent with current economic ideology and the trends for globalisation and settlement of disputes without strict application of law.

167 See <http://www.ecodir.org> and <http://www.arbitrators.org/drs/onlineapps.htm>.

PART FOUR: COMMERCIAL LAW

Chapter 9

Protection of Minority Shareholders

*Janet Dine**

I. INTRODUCTION

A. Sources of Law

UK company law has a Companies Act 1985 which was a consolidation of a number of previous statutes. It has been amended, most notably by the Companies Act 1989 which inserted a considerable number of new sections into the 1985 Act retrospectively. There are also a number of statutory instruments (secondary legislation), most notably SI 1985/805 and SI 1985/1052 which set out model articles of association for different types of company. These articles are deemed to be adopted by companies unless there the articles of individual companies are drafted so as to exclude the model articles. It should also be noted that European Community legislation may be implemented in the UK by statutory instrument. An example is the implementation of the EC twelfth Directive on single member companies. The Companies Act 1985 requires two members, the Companies (Single Member Private Limited Companies) Regulations 1992 SI 1992/1699 permit single member companies.

Despite the quantity of legislation, case law remains of great importance and attempts to understand company law without using sufficient case-law would be doomed to failure. In particular, one minority shareholder protection action 'the derivative action' has no legislative base, it is entirely to be found in case-law. Codes of practice in the UK have focused more on general corporate governance, eg, non-executive director appointments and managerial salaries, so deal with protection of shareholders generally rather than minority shareholder protection. The Stock Exchange Regulations require equal treatment of all shareholders in a takeover and require a mandatory bid to be made to all shareholders after acquisition of more than 20 per cent of shares. This is a major protection for minorities whose shares would be less valuable if they do not have a sufficient number of shares to exercise some voting power, eg by a blocking minority.

* Professor of Law at the University of Essex.

Most of the protections for minorities are specific and mandatory the requirement that a change of articles should be 'bona fide for the benefit of the company' acts as protection for minorities and case law claims that it is representative of the general rules governing the exercise of majority power.[1]

Suggestions for Reform have been made by the Law Commission and by a recent Department of Trade and Industry Review. A Companies Bill is expected during this Parliament but its contents are completely unknown.

B. Concept of Minority

The UK concept of minority relates solely to the exercise of a right to vote, a minority shareholder is one who cannot exercise 51 per cent of the voting power. There are no specially protected categories. Shareholders exercise their right to protection on an individual basis, their entitlement to vote depends on the correct entry existing on the company's register of shareholders.

C. General Legal Context

The duties of the board are defined solely in relation to 'the company' and no distinction is made between majority and minority shareholders. There is a duty to act 'bona fide for the benefit of the company' but the court has always taken the view that it will not substitute its commercial judgment for that of the board and would only interfere if the decision were wholly unreasonable. The board has a very wide discretion. For companies registered prior to 1 July 1985, the relationship between the general meeting of shareholders and the board was usually governed by an article similar or identical to Article 80 of the Table A annexed to the Companies Act 1948. This read:

> The business of the company shall be managed by the directors who may pay all expenses incurred in promoting and registering the company, and may exercise all such powers of the company as are not, by the Act, or by these regulations, required to be exercised by the company in general meeting, subject, nevertheless, to any of these regulations, to the provisions of the Act and to such regulations, being not inconsistent with the aforesaid regulations or provisions as may be prescribed by the company in general meeting; but no regulations made by the company in general meeting shall invalidate any prior act of the directors which would have been valid if that regulation had not been made.

This appeared to reserve to the general meeting a power to make regulations to govern the conduct of directors. The scope of this power was

[1] *Allen v Gold Reefs of W. Africa* [1900] 1 Ch 656.

most uncertain until the judges determined the balance of power issue firmly in favour of the directors to the detriment of the powers of the general meeting. Thus in *Automatic Self Cleansing Filter Syndicate Company Ltd v* Cunningham,[2] the Court of Appeal held that a resolution passed by a simple majority of shareholders (an ordinary resolution) was not effective. The resolution purported to order the directors to go ahead with an agreement to sell the whole of the assets of the company. The directors believed that this was an unwise course. Warrington J said:

> The effect of this resolution, if acted upon, would be to compel the directors to sell the whole of the assets of the company, not on such terms and conditions as they think fit, but upon such terms and conditions as a simple majority of the shareholders think fit. But it does not rest there. Article 96 [this was very similar to Article 80 of Table A to the 1948 Act above] provides that the management of the business and control of the company are to be vested in the directors. Now that article, which is for the protection of a minority of the shareholders, can only be altered by a special resolution, that is to say, by a resolution passed by a three-fourths majority, at a meeting called for the purpose, and confirmed at a subsequent meeting. If that provision could be revoked by a resolution of the shareholders passed by a simple majority, I can see no reason for the provision which is to be found in Article 81 that the directors can only be removed by a special resolution. It seems to me that if a majority of shareholders can, on a matter which is vested in the directors, overrule the discretion of the directors, there might just as well be no provision at all in the articles as to the removal of directors by special resolution. Moreover, pressed to its logical conclusion, the result would be that when a majority of the shareholders disagree with the policy of the directors, though they cannot remove the directors except by special resolution, they might carry on the whole of the business of the company as they pleased, and thus, though not able to remove the directors, overrule every act which the board might otherwise do. It seems to me on the true construction of these articles that the management of the business and control of the company are vested in the directors, and consequently that the control of the company as to any particular matter, or the management of any particular transaction or any particular part of the business of the company, can only be removed from the board by an alteration of the articles, such alteration, of course, requiring a special resolution.

This approach was recently adopted in *Breckland Group Holdings Ltd v London and Suffolk Properties* Ltd,[3] where the court held that since the company's articles of association adopted regulation 80 of Table A of Schedule 1 to the 1948 Companies Act, the conduct of the business of the company was vested in the board of directors, and the shareholders in general meeting could not intervene to adopt unauthorised proceedings.

It seems to have been the case that the general meeting could not interfere in management decisions by way of an ordinary resolution, even under

[2] [1906] 2 Ch 34. [3] [1989] BCLC 100.

the 1948 Companies Act. The 1985 equivalent is Article 70 of the Table A attached to the Companies Act 1985 (by SI 1985 No. 805). This reads:

> Subject to the provisions of the Act, the memorandum and the articles and to any directions given by special resolution, the business of the company shall be managed by the directors who may exercise all the powers of the company. No alteration of the memorandum or articles and no such direction shall invalidate any prior act of the directors which would have been valid if that alteration had not been made or that direction had not been given. The powers given by this regulation shall not be limited by any special power given to the directors by the articles and a meeting of directors at which a quorum is present may exercise all powers exercisable by the directors.

The justification for the insistence that there should be no interference in director-control save by a special resolution was well expressed *in Gramophone and Typewriter Ltd v Stanley*, where Buckley LJ said:[4]

> The directors are not servants to obey directions given by the shareholders as individuals; they are agents appointed by and bound to serve the shareholders as their principals. They are persons who may by the regulations be entrusted with the control of the business, and if so entrusted they can be dispossessed from that control only by the statutory majority which can alter the articles.

When coupled with the knowledge that a very few persons can hold a large number of the shares in a company, that directors can be entrenched by multiple voting provisions, and that shareholders with small stakes in a company rarely take an interest in meetings, it can be seen that 'shareholder democracy' is an extremely hollow concept and the directors will often have complete freedom from control in managing the business.

II. SPECIFIC SITUATIONS

A. Where the Board of Directors Ceases to Function

The above analysis holds good for the situation where the board of directors is a functioning organ of the company. If for some reason the directors are unable or unwilling to exercise their powers of management, those powers revert to and are exercisable by the company in general meeting. In *Alexander Ward & Co Ltd v Samyang Navigation Co Ltd*,[5] the House of Lords held that the company could act through its two shareholders to recover its debts. This was possible despite an article in the company's constitution which read as follows: 'The business of the Company shall be managed by the Directors, who . . . may exercise all such powers of the

[4] [1908] 2 KB 89. [5] [1975] 2 All ER 424.

company as are not by the [Hong Kong] Ordinance or by these Articles required to be exercised by the Company in General Meeting.'

The company had no directors at the relevant time. Lord Hailsham said:

In my opinion, at the relevant time the company was fully competent either to lay attestments or to raise proceedings in the Scottish courts. The company could have done so either by appointing directors, or, as I think, by authorising proceedings in general meeting, which in the absence of an effective board, has a residual authority to use the company's powers. it had not taken, and did not take the steps necessary to give authority to perform the necessary actions. But it was competent to have done so, and in my view it was therefore a competent principal . . . So far as regards the powers of general meeting, in *Gower Modern Company Law*, it is stated:[6]

> It seems that if for some reason the board cannot or will not exercise the powers vested in them, the general meeting has been held effective where there was a deadlock on the board, where an effective quorum could not be obtained, where the directors are disqualified from voting, or, more obviously, where the directors have purported to borrow in excess of the amount authorised by the articles.

Moreover, although the general meeting cannot restrain the directors from conducting actions in the name of the company, it still seems to be the law (as laid down in *Marshall's Valve Gear Co. v Manning, Wardle & Co*,[7] that the general meeting can commence proceedings on behalf of the company if the directors fail to do so. In that case counsel attempted to draw a distinction between the cases supposed in this passage, where the directors were for some reason unable or unwilling to act, and the instant case where there were no directors. I see no difference in the distinction . . .

B. Duties Imposed on Majorities?

There is considerable weight of authority to support the proposition that a shareholder may exercise his right to vote as he pleases and does not have any duty to take into account the interests of others or of the company. In *Pender v Lushington*[8], Jessel MR said:

[A] man may be actuated in giving his vote by interests entirely adverse to the interests of the company as a whole. He may think it more for his particular interest that a certain course may be taken which may be in the opinion of others very adverse to the interests of the company as a whole, but he cannot be restrained from giving his vote in what way he pleases because he is influenced by that motive.

An inroad into this principle appeared to be made by the judgment in the case of *Clemens v Clemens Bros Ltd.*[9] In that case a challenge was made to a resolution to issue further shares to directors. This would have had the

[6] 3rd edn 1969, 136–7.

[7] [1909] 1 Ch 267.

[8] (1877) 6 Ch D 70. See also *North West Transportation v Beatty* (1887) 12 App Cas 589.

[9] [1976] 2 All ER 268

effect of substantially reducing (from 45 per cent to below 25 per cent) the voting power of the plaintiff. Foster J said:

I think that one thing which emerges from the cases to which I have referred is that in such a case as the present Miss Clemens is not entitled to exercise her majority vote in whatever way she pleases. The difficulty is in finding a principle, and obviously expressions such as 'bona fide for the benefit of the company as a whole', 'fraud on a minority' and 'oppressive' do not assist in formulating such a principle.

I have come to the conclusion that it would be unwise to try to produce a principle, since the circumstances of each case are infinitely varied. It would not, I think, assist to say more than that in my judgement Miss Clemens is not entitled as of right to exercise her votes as an ordinary shareholder in any way she pleases . . . I cannot escape the conclusion that the resolutions have been framed so as to put into the hands of Miss Clemens and her fellow directors complete control of the company and to deprive the plaintiff of her existing rights as a shareholder with more than 25 per cent of the votes . . . They are specifically and carefully designed to ensure not only that the plaintiff can never get control of the company but to deprive her of what has been called her negative control. Whether I say that these proposals are oppressive to the plaintiff or that no one could honestly believe that they are for her benefit matters not. A court of equity will in my judgment regard these considerations as sufficient to prevent the consequences arising from Miss Clemens using her legal right to vote in the way she has and it would be right for a court of equity to prevent such consequences taking effect.

This passage is clearly irreconcilable with the traditional view above. The right to vote as a shareholder pleases derives from the idea that the right to vote is a property right that should not be subject to equitable restraints.

C. *Alteration of Articles*

Only in one area of minority shareholder protection has the imposition of a duty on the majority been taken seriously, that is, in the case of alteration of the articles of association. The courts have held that an alteration must be 'bona fide for the benefit of the company'.

Section 9 of the Companies Act 1985 reads as follows:

(1) Subject to the provisions of this Act and to the conditions contained in its memorandum, a company may by special resolution alter its articles.
(2) Alterations so made in the articles are (subject to this Act) as valid as if originally contained in them, and are subject in like manner to alteration by special resolution.

By section 16 of the Act a member will not be bound by alterations made after he has joined the company in so far as they make him liable to pay extra money to the company. There are special provisions which apply when the rights attached to classes of shares are to be varied (see section

125 et seq). This cannot be done simply by special resolution. The general rule is that articles may be altered by a special (75 per cent majority) resolution. This rule can put very considerable power in the hands of the majority. The number of shareholders making up such a majority may be very small, perhaps only one person. Because of this the court has found it necessary to control this power. The rule that has been formulated is that an alteration of articles is valid only if it is in good faith (bona fide) and for the benefit of the company as a whole. At first sight this would seem to be a stringent control, but closer examination of the cases shows a considerable reluctance to intervene in favour of an aggrieved minority, and great confusion as to what is actually meant by 'bona fide for the benefit of the company as a whole'.

In *Allen v Gold Reefs of West Africa Ltd*, Lindley MR said:[10]

> the power conferred by [what is now section 9 of the Act] must, like all other powers, be exercised subject to those general principles of law and equity which are applicable to all powers conferred on majorities and enabling them to bind minorities. It must be exercised, not only in the manner required by law, but also bona fide for the benefit of the company as a whole, and it must not be exceeded. These conditions are always implied, and are seldom, if ever, expressed. But if they are complied with I can discover no ground for judicially putting any other restrictions on the power conferred by the section than those contained in it.

The judge went on to say that shares were taken on the basis that articles were subject to alteration. It would therefore require very clear evidence of an undertaking by the company to treat a particular shareholder differently; an undertaking that a particular article would not be altered. However, where there was an agreement that would be broken by the alteration of the articles of association, the company would be liable for a breach of contract brought about by the change of article:

> A company cannot break its contracts by altering its articles, but, when dealing with contracts referring to revocable articles, and especially with contracts between a member of the company and the company respecting his shares, care must be taken not to assume that the contract involves as one of its terms an article which is not to be altered' (ibid).

1. *Bona Fide for the Benefit of the Company*

Given that a resolution to alter articles will be regarded as valid if it is passed 'bona fide for the benefit of the company', and invalid if this can be shown not to be the case, do the cases throw light on what is meant by that phrase?

[10] [1900] 1 Ch 656.

In *Brown v British Abrasive Wheel*[11], the company was in need of raising further capital. The 98 per cent majority were willing to provide this capital if they could buy up the 2 per cent minority. Having failed to effect this by agreement, the 98 per cent proposed to change the articles of association to give them power to purchase the shares of the minority. The proposed article provided for the compulsory purchase of the minority's shares on certain terms. However, the majority were prepared to insert any provision as to price which the court thought was fair. Despite this the court held that the proposed alteration could not be made. Astbury J held that the alteration was not for the benefit of the company as a whole. One reason for this was that there was no direct link between the provision of the extra capital and the alteration of the articles. Although the whole scheme had been to provide the capital after removing the dissentient shareholders, it would in fact have been possible to remove the shareholders and then refuse to provide the capital. Astbury J's judgment seems to determine that two separate criteria must be met: the judgment must be 'within the ordinary principles of justice' and it must be 'for the benefit of the company as a whole'. So far as the latter requirement was concerned, the company seems to have been identified with the shareholders and the reality of the whole plan seems to have been overlooked, for the judge ignored the plan to provide capital on the grounds that there was no formal link between this and the alteration. He also said that the alteration would benefit the majority and not the company as a whole, thus ignoring the company's separate existence as a commercial entity in need of further funding.

Brown v British Abrasive Wheel was not followed in the later case of *Sidebottom v Kershaw, Leese & Co. Ltd*[12], and the approach taken by the judge in the Brown case was criticised. In *Sidebottom* an alteration was approved although it provided for the compulsory purchase of shares. One difference between this case and Brown is that the ability to purchase the shares was limited to a situation where the shareholder in question was carrying on business in direct competition with the company. The relationship between this article and the benefit of the company was therefore much clearer. In *Sidebottom* two of the Court of Appeal judges made it clear that they believed that in Brown, Astbury J had been wrong to regard good faith and the company's benefit as two separate ideas. The important question was: was the alteration for the benefit of the company as a whole?

Settling the important question and determining its meaning proved to be two different things. *In Dafen Tinplate Co Ltd v Llanelly Steel Co. (1907) Ltd*,[13] the plaintiff company was a member of the defendant company. The defendants realised that the plaintiffs were conducting business in a manner detrimental to their interests. In fact they were buying steel

[11] [1919] 1 Ch 290. [12] [1919] 1 Ch 290. [13] [1920] 2 Ch 124.

from an alternative source of supply. There was an attempt to buy the plaintiff's shares by agreement but this failed. The defendant company then altered its articles by special resolution to include a power to compulsorily purchase the shares of any member requested to transfer them. It was this alteration that was the subject of the action. The court held that the alteration was too wide to be valid. The altered article would confer too much power on the majority. It went much further than was necessary for the protection of the company. The judge seemed to be using the 'bona fide for the benefit of the company' test in an objective sense, that is, he was judging the situation from the court's point of view.

A different view of the meaning of this important question was taken in *Shuttleworth v Cox Bros & Co (Maidenhead) Ltd* [1927] 2 KB 9. In that case the company had a board of directors appointed for life. The alteration to the articles provided that any one of the board of directors should lose office if his fellow directors requested in writing that he should resign. The alteration was directed at a particular director whose conduct had not been satisfactory. Again the words 'bona fide for the benefit of the company' were interpreted as one condition. This time, however, the court approached the question from the point of view of the subjective belief of the shareholders. Scrutton LJ said: 'the shareholders must act honestly having regard to and endeavoring to act for the benefit of the company.' Bankes LJ agreed and added:

> By what criterion is the court to ascertain the opinion of the shareholders on this question? The alteration may be so oppressive as to cast suspicion on the honesty of the persons responsible for it, or so extravagant that no reasonable man could really consider it for the benefit of the company. In such cases the Court is, I think, entitled to treat the conduct of shareholders as it does the verdict of a jury and to say that the alteration of a company's articles shall not stand if it is such that no reasonable man could consider it for the benefit of the company . . . I cannot agree with what seems to have been the view of Peterson J in *Dafen Tinplate Co. v Llanelly Steel Co* . . . that whenever the Court and the shareholders may differ in opinion upon what is for the benefit of the company, the view of the court must prevail.

If this passage is right, the court will only intervene in the most extreme cases—when no reasonable man could believe that the alteration could be good for the company. One of the considerations that caused the courts to withdraw from their more interventionist stand is the fact that shares and the right to vote attached to shares are regarded as property rights. It would be unrealistic, in the words of Dixon CJ in *Re Peter's American Delicacy*[14] '[to] suppose that in voting each shareholder is to assume an inhuman altruism and consider only the intangible notion of the benefit of the vague abstraction . . . "the company as an institution".'

[14] (1939)61 CLR 457 (High Court of Australia).

Two other cases show the reluctance of the court to intervene. In *Greenhalgh v Arderne Cinemas Ltd*,[15] a change in articles which effectively removed the plaintiff's pre-emption rights was approved, despite the reference in the judgment to the factor of discrimination as a factor which would cause a resolution to be disallowed by the courts. It must be clear that any discrimination between majority and minority shareholders would not be sufficient to cause a resolution to fail the bona fide test, since many alterations of articles will cause adjustments between classes of shareholders from which some will emerge better off than others. An example of this is to be found in *Rights and Issue Investment Trust Ltd v Stylo Shoes Ltd*.[16] In that case the effect of the alteration was (amongst other things) to halve the voting rights of a number of ordinary shareholders as against the rights held by management. Despite this the resolution was upheld. The management shares had not been voted and the resolution had been passed by the requisite majority. The court refused to interfere. It seems that if discrimination is to be a ground for interference it will have to be some very clear, perhaps vindictive discrimination that is alleged before the court will be moved to upset the normal voting patterns of the company and declare a resolution invalid.

D. Protection by the Supervisory Board and Auditors

There are no special protections afforded by a supervisory board, and the auditors do not pay special regard to the interests of minority shareholders.

E. Majorities and Quorum

The Act is silent as to the number of members who must be present before the proceedings at the meeting are to be regarded as valid. The articles will determine the relevant number. Article 40 of Table A provides: 'Two persons entitled to vote upon the business to be transacted, each being a member or a proxy for a member or a duly authorised representative of a corporation, shall be a quorum.'

If this article is excluded by the company's articles and not replaced by an article providing for a quorum, section 370(4) will apply. This provides that 'two members personally present are a quorum'. The quorum of meetings may also be contained in shareholder's agreements.[17]

Except in the case of a single member company , no single member can constitute a quorum, even if representing several shareholders.[18] This rule

[15] [1951] Ch 286. [16] [1965] Ch 250.
[17] See *Harman and another v BML Group* [1994] 2 BCLC 674.
[18] See *Re M.J. Shanley Contracting Ltd* (1979) 124 SJ 239.

is displaced when the meeting is called by the court or the Department of Trade and Industry under the powers in sections 371 and 369 Companies Act 1985.

F. Resolutions

The decisions of a meeting are arrived at by voting on resolutions.

(i) Ordinary resolutions

An ordinary resolution will be sufficient for any decision unless the legislation decrees that the particular decision can only be taken by extraordinary or special resolution. An ordinary resolution is one passed by a simple majority of members who vote on it.

(ii) Extraordinary resolutions

Section 378(1) provides:

> A resolution is an extraordinary resolution when it has been passed by a majority of not less than three fourths of such members as (being entitled to do so) vote in person or, where proxies are allowed, by proxy, at a general meeting of which notice specifying the intention to propose the resolution as an extraordinary resolution has been duly given.

Such a resolution is sometimes required in order to vary class rights, to initiate or permit payment of a class of creditors in a voluntary winding up (see s.125 Companies Act 1985; sections 84 and 165 Insolvency Act 1986).

(iii) Special resolutions

Alteration of articles by special resolution is perhaps the most important instance (section 9 CA 1985) section 378(2) provides:

> A resolution is a special resolution when it has been passed by such a majority as is required for the passing of an extraordinary resolution and at a general meeting of which not less than 21 days' notice specifying the intention to propose the resolution as a special resolution, has been duly given.

Thus, a three-quarters majority of the members validly casting votes at the meeting is required for a special resolution, but in addition 21 days' notice must be given.

(iv) Voting

The voting rights of the shareholders will normally be set out in the articles. The usual method of voting is to take a show of hands. In this case, each member will have one vote. However, in some circumstances a member, dissatisfied with the outcome of a show of hands, may call for a 'poll'. The standard article appearing in Table A (Article 54) provides that on a poll 'every member shall have one vote for every share of which he is the holder'.

It can clearly be seen that the outcome of a vote on a poll may radically differ from that on a show of hands. The right to demand a poll is therefore of considerable importance. The circumstances in which a poll may be demanded may appear in the articles. However, the Companies Act provides a 'minimum standard' for the articles. It reads:

(1) A provision contained in a company's articles is void in so far as it would have the effect either—

(a) of excluding the right to demand a poll at a general meeting on any question other than the election of the chairman of the meeting or the adjournment of the meeting; or

(b) of making ineffective a demand for a poll on any such question which is made either—

(i) by not less than 5 members having the right to vote at the meeting; or

(ii) by a member or members representing not less than one-tenth of the total voting rights of all the members having the right to vote at the meeting; or

(iii) by a member or members holding shares in the company conferring a right to vote at the meeting, being shares on which an aggregate sum has been paid up equal to not less than one-tenth of the total sum paid up on all the shares conferring that right.

(2) The instrument appointing a proxy to vote at a meeting of a company shall be deemed also to confer authority to demand or join in demanding a poll; and for the purposes of subsection (i) a demand by a person as proxy for a member is the same as a demand by the member.

G. Disclosure

The major requirement for disclosure is, of course the company accounts which must be prepared in accordance with the EC fourth and seventh Directives. The Stock Exchange requires disclosure of a number of corporate governance issues, including salaries and benefits of directors and the makeup of the board (executive and non-executive directors). The Combined Code which requires amongst other things the maintenance of a 'sound system of internal control' The London Stock Exchange issued guidance on the implementation of this requirement which stresses management of significant risks since 'a company's system of internal control has a key role in the management of risks that re significant to the fulfilment of the company's business objectives'.[19]

[19] Internal Control: Guidance for Directors on the Combined Code, Stock Exchange, 27 Sept 1999.

In order to ensure a proper system of internal control the board must consider (i) the nature of the risks facing the company; (ii) the likelihood of the risk materialising; (iii) the company's ability to reduce the impact of such risks, if they do materialise costs relative to benefits. However, it is doubtful if any of these requirements are of specific assistance to minorities. The DTI reform committee suggested an 'Operating and Financial Review' should be filed by large companies. This would include information about environmental and social performance as well as financial data.

III. SPECIAL RIGHTS

A. Information

There are no special rights given to minorities to require information but a single member can require the holding of an Annual General meeting (AGM) of a private company (which may otherwise elect not to hold one) and, in the event of default, the Secretary of State may direct the holding of such a meeting. (section 366A CA 1985) Also members representing not less than 10 per cent of the total voting rights may require the holding of an Extraordinary General meeting. (section 368(1) CA 1985). Application may be made to the court to order the holding of such a meeting if there is default. Section 376 provides that members may require the company to distribute notice of any resolution intended to be moved at the next AGM. This requires one-twentieth of the total voting rights or not less than 100 members holding shares in the company on which an average of at least £100 has been paid up (s 376(2) CA 1985.

B. Special Audit

The only mechanism for a special audit is a Department of Trade and Industry Inspection. The department is given various powers to investigate the affairs of companies. One way that this can be done is by the appointment of an inspector to look into the affairs of a company. The appointment can be instigated in a variety of ways:

(i) On the order of the court

The Department of Trade must appoint an inspector to investigate the affairs of a company if the court so orders (section 432(1) Companies Act 1985).

(ii) On the application of the company

Section 431(2)(c) provides that inspectors may be appointed on the application of the company. The application must be accompanied by evidence showing a good reason why the company's affairs should be investigated and even then the department have a discretion as to whether or not an inspector will be appointed. Few inspectors have been appointed under this power.

(iii) Fraud, unfair prejudice or withholding of information

The department also has a discretion to appoint inspectors where there is evidence of a company's affairs being conducted in a fraudulent or unfairly prejudicial way, that it proposes to act unlawfully or that 'its members have not been given all the information with respect to its affairs which they might reasonably expect' (section 432(1)(b)).

Although some inspectors have been appointed under this section, there is grave danger that the mere announcement of the appointment of inspectors will bring lasting damage to the reputation of the company that cannot be reversed even if the allegations prove to be unfounded at the end of the day. Because of this difficulty the Companies Act 1967 introduced a wide range of powers which the Department of Trade and Industry could use more discreetly to determine whether allegations of misconduct were soundly based. sections 447–452 CA 1985 now enable the department to require the production of books and papers, to ask for a search warrant if there are grounds for suspecting that articles requested have not been forthcoming and to search premises in respect of which a warrant is issued. Criminal penalties are available for providing false statements and for falsifying, mutilating or destroying documents. It is a defence to show that there was no intention to conceal the state of affairs of the company or to defeat the law. The department's officers are acting in a police capacity when they require the production of books and papers. They are not acting in a way similar to judges. The court will therefore not exercise its power to review decisions taken by those who act in a judicial or quasi-judicial capacity. However the notice requiring the production of books and papers must not be unreasonably or excessively wide.[20]

Part XV of the Companies Act gives the Department of Trade wide powers to investigate the ownership of shares in any company and to impose restrictions on the transfer of those shares while it does so.

C. Conduct of Assemblies

A single member can require the holding of an Annual General meeting (AGM)of a private company (which may otherwise elect not to hold one) and, in the event of default, the Secretary of State may direct the holding of

[20] *R v Secretary of State for Trade, ex parte Perestrello.*

such a meeting. (section 366A CA 1985) Also members representing not less than 10 per cent of the total voting rights may require the holding of an Extraordinary General meeting. (section 368(1) CA 1985). Application may be made to the court to order the holding of such a meeting if there is default. Section 376 provides that members may require the company to distribute notice of any resolution intended to be moved at the next AGM. This requires one-twentieth of the total voting rights or not less than 100 members holding shares in the company on which an average of at least £100 has been paid up (section 376(2) CA 1985. A meeting must be adjourned if a resolution of the meeting so decides.[21]

Apart from the situation regarding alteration of articles, resolutions will only be nullified if they contravene the articles of association.

IV. RIGHT TO CAUSE THE COMPANY TO SUE IT'S DIRECTORS

A. The Rule in Foss v Harbottle

There is such a right but its exercise is fraught with difficulties. If a right has been infringed which is in law a right belonging to a company (for example, the misapplication of company property the only proper plaintiff is the company itself. This rule has come to be known as the rule in *Foss v Harbottle* [22]because this is the case in which the rule was first clearly established. In *Bamford v* Bamford,[23] Lord Justice Russell said:

> it would be for the company to decide whether to institute proceedings to avoid the voidable allotment: and again this decision would be one for the company in general meeting to decide by ordinary resolution. To litigate or not to litigate, apart from very special circumstances, is for decision by such a resolution.

As a general principle this is admirable because it has the advantage of avoiding the problem of many actions being commenced simultaneously by all members that believed themselves to be aggrieved by a particular action of the management. However, real problems occur when the alleged perpetrators of the wrong against the company also control the general meeting. In those circumstances, of course, it is most unlikely that the members of the general meeting will resolve to sue themselves. When this happens, if the wrong done is serious enough a shareholder may be permitted to sue on behalf of the company. Four major difficulties confront such a plaintiff:

1. The standing of the plaintiff and his entitlement to sue must be settled

[21] For the law regarding polls see above 'voting'.
[22] (1843) 2 Hare 461.
[23] [1970] Ch 212.

as a preliminary matter before the substantive complaint has been heard. This involves the plaintiff in establishing that the alleged wrongdoers are 'in control' of the company. Further, the action must be brought bona fide for the benefit of the company for wrongs to the company for which no other remedy is available and not for an ulterior purpose. In *Barrett v Duckett and others*[24] the action was brought to harass an ex son in law and thus was not permitted.

2. The plaintiff must show that the company suffered a wrong of such an order that it would be unfair to permit the general meeting to ratify the wrong. The ambit of this requirement is most uncertain. It seems clear that actions wholly outside the power of the company to perform cannot be ratified by ordinary resolution, only by the special procedure under section 35 Companies Act 1985. It is certain that minor wrongs against the company can be ratified. There remains an enormous area of uncertainty providing a potential pitfall to a plaintiff in this sort of action.

3. The plaintiff must prove the actual commission of the serious wrong against the company by those controlling it. This in itself is a difficult task since the plaintiff is not, by definition, a controller of the company and so he will in all likelihood have limited access to information concerning the internal management of the company.

4. If the plaintiff can surmount these three not inconsiderable hurdles he will have succeeded in his action. During the course of the case he is always at peril as to costs. Even if he succeeds, the principal beneficiary of the action is the company in whose favour judgment will be given. The actual gain to the plaintiff may thus be very small. His only gain may be the right to participate in the fortunes of a better-managed company. It is perhaps not surprising that this type of action is infrequently brought, particularly in view of the remedy introduced in 1980 and now to be found at sections 459–61 of the 1985 Act. When a company is in liquidation the liquidator will be able to bring an action in the company's name and thus breaches of duty may more easily be made the subject of court proceedings. Nevertheless a 'derivative' action (that is, an action permitted because the court decides that an exception should be made to the rule in *Foss v Harbottle* is still an option open to a plaintiff who wishes to complain about the mismanagement of his company while it is still in business. The action is termed 'derivative' because the right that the plaintiff seeks to have enforced is not his own: it 'derives' from the company. The four difficulties faced by such a plaintiff must be examined in more detail.

[24] [1995] 1 BCLC.

B. Locus Standi—Who is in Control of the Company?

In *Birch v Sullivan*[25] the court said that when an individual plaintiff institutes a derivative action to enforce a right belonging to the company, he must specifically allege in his pleadings, and be prepared to prove, that those in control of the company would prevent the company from suing in its own name. If there is any challenge to that allegation the matter must be determined as a preliminary issue.[26] The great difficulty is in determining an effective test which will embrace all circumstances in which the persons complained about are 'in control' of a company. In *Prudential Assurance Co. Ltd v Newman Industries Ltd (No 2)*,[27] the judge who first heard the case believed that the court should examine the realities of the situation. He said:

> if the defendants against whom relief is sought on behalf of the company control the majority of votes, the action will be allowed to proceed whether a resolution that no action should be brought by the company has been passed or not; so also, if the persons against whom relief is sought do not control a majority of the votes but it is shown that a resolution has been passed and passed only by the use of their votes . . . But there are an infinite variety of possible circumstances . . . If shareholders having a majority of votes in general meeting are nominees, the court will look behind the register to the beneficial owners to see whether they are the persons against whom relief is sought: see *Pavlides v Jensen*.[28]There seems no good reason why the court should not have regard to any other circumstances which show that the majority cannot be relied upon to determine in a disinterested way whether it is truly in the interests of the company that proceedings should be brought.

The judgment of the Court of Appeal in that case left matters most unclear. The suggestion was made that if 'control' was an issue the court should grant an adjournment 'to enable a meeting of shareholders to be convened by the board, so that he can reach a conclusion in the light of the conduct of, and proceedings at, that meeting'. This would seem to imply rejection of the idea that all matters which might in fact affect control of the company should be investigated. The approach suggested by the Court of Appeal would to some extent confine the court to taking into account matters which appeared, so to speak, 'on the face of' the meeting. However, the judgment offers no very clear guidance as to what matters should be taken into account. Even if it did, the Court of Appeal's words would be of doubtful value, since the issue of the *Foss v Harbottle* rule had become irrelevant to the outcome of the case by the time it was heard in that court. The judges had refused to hear counsel's arguments on the proper scope of *Foss v*

25 1958] 1 All ER 56.
26 *Prudential Assurance Co. Ltd v Newman Industries Ltd (No. 2)* [1982] Ch 204.
27 [1981] Ch 257.
28 [1956] Ch 565.

Harbottle and were careful to point out that they were not expressing a 'concluded' view on the scope of the rule in *Foss v Harbottle*. The extent to which a court can probe the reality of the situation to determine control thus remains uncertain. What is clear from *Smith v Croft (No 2)*[29] is that a minority shareholder who would otherwise be able to sue on behalf of the company, under an established exception to the rule in *Foss v Harbottle*, may nevertheless be prevented from doing so if a majority of the members, independent of the wrongdoers, is opposed to the litigation. If a majority of the oppressed minority is not prepared to support the action it cannot go ahead.

Two other restrictions are that a defendant may raise not only defences which would be valid against an action by the company, but also defences that would only be valid against the plaintiff personally.[30] It has also been held that a minority shareholder may not bring a derivative action when a company has gone into liquidation. Only the liquidator can represent the company after that moment.[31]

C. Serious Wrongdoing by Those in Control

An essential distinction that is made in company law is between actions by the controllers of the company which cannot be 'ratified' by the majority of the company voting in a general meeting and those that can be ratified. Ratification is a concept borrowed from agency law where it is used to describe the process of retrospective validation of an agent's acts. If an agent acts outside the authority conferred upon him by his principal, the principal can at a later date approve the action of the agent and agree to be legally bound by any transaction entered into by that agent. In company law, if the directors of the company have acted in breach of their duties it is open to the shareholders on some occasions but not on others to vote that such directors will not be sued in respect of those breaches of duty. The major difficulty is in identifying what breaches are ratifiable and can be forgiven and which are not ratifiable and will therefore found an action provided the wrongdoers are in control of the company in the sense discussed above. However, there is another curious feature of ratification which must be noted. Where a breach of duty is ratifiable it may be so ratified by a majority vote notwithstanding that the wrongdoers make up part or the entire vote in favour of ratification. It is argued at the beginning of this chapter that the courts have made a fundamental mistake as to the value of ratification. However, as matters stand the distinction that is crucial to the ratification issue is the type of wrongdoing that has occurred.

29 [1988] Ch 114.
30 *Nurcombe v Nurcombe* [1985] 1 All ER 65.
31 *Fargo Ltd v Godfroy* [1986] 3 All ER 279.

D. *What Actions Make Up a Wrong Which Cannot be Ratified?*

The categories that are identifiable from the cases are:

1. Where the act complained of is ultra vires or illegal (see section 35 CA 1985).
2. Where there is a 'fraud on the minority'.

It is clear in the aftermath of the *Prudential* case that there is to be no exception to the rule in *Foss v Harbottle* simply 'where the interests of justice so require'.

(i) Ultra vires and illegal acts

It was for some time unclear whether an ultra vires or illegal act was a wrong done to individual shareholders as well as a wrong done to the company. If it could be regarded as infringing the personal rights of shareholders, each shareholder would have a personal right to sue on his own behalf and would not need to invoke the derivative action. However, it now seems clear, following *Smith v Croft*, that all cases in which compensation is sought on behalf of the company for past ultra vires or illegal acts are to be regarded as cases brought on behalf of the company. They will therefore have to be in the derivative form. This does not affect the personal right of a shareholder to sue to restrain an action which is about to occur and which will be ultra vires or illegal. The role of ultra vires will be much diminished in the future because of the Companies Act 1985 section 35. An example of illegality and ultra vires is *Smith v Croft* itself. Ultra vires acts may now be ratified by a special resolution of the company (section 35 Companies Act 1985) but another special resolution will be required to relieve directors or others from any liability incurred because of their involvement in the ultra vires transaction.

(ii) Fraud on the minority

It should be noted that 'fraud' in this context has a special meaning unconnected with any considerations of deceit or of criminal law notions of fraud. Some actions may involve crimes, others may not. Over the years commentators have discerned various categories of fraud on the minority from the cases but all agree that the cases are difficult to reconcile with one another and in some cases behaviour can be found which fits more than one of the categories. Perhaps the proper way to regard the cases is to extract the total wrongdoing of the controllers and ask whether this is behaviour that can be condoned by a (possibly partial) majority vote? Categories which have been identified are:

1. Expropriation of the company's property.
2. Mala fide breaches of duty.
3. Negligent acts from which the directors benefit.
4. Use of powers for an improper purpose.

To some extent these categories are merely a way of saying that where there has been a breach of duty by directors the court will examine all the facts to determine whether it is such a serious matter that it cannot be 'forgiven' by ratification. Obviously, taking the company's property is the clearest example of such a situation, so that is an identifiably separate category. With regard to the other instances of breach of duty it is doubtful whether there is value in attempting to do more than look at the sum total of the behaviour of the controllers in order to assess whether a proper case can be made for *Foss v Harbottle* to be disapplied. For that reason breaches of duty not involving expropriation of company property are divided into non-ratifiable acts which are then distinguished from ratifiable acts. Amongst the latter are: bona fide incidental profit making; use of powers for an improper purpose; and negligence which does not benefit the directors.

E. Expropriation of Company Property

In *Menier v Hooper's Telegraph Works*[32] a rival company had a controlling interest in the company concerned. They used this controlling interest to settle an impending action between the two companies in their favour. The judge said that the majority had 'put something into their pockets' at the expense of the minority. This fell squarely within the fraud on the minority exception and would not be permitted. Similarly, in *Cook v Deeks*,[33] the directors diverted to themselves contracts which they should have taken up on behalf of the company. It was held that directors holding a majority of votes would not be permitted to make a present to themselves.

A case falling on the other side of the line, where the behaviour was held to be mere incidental profit-making by the directors so that the breach of duty could have been ratified is *Regal Hastings Ltd v Gulliver*.[34] In that case, Regal Hastings Ltd owned a cinema. The directors decided to acquire two other cinemas with a view to the sale of the whole concern. They formed a subsidiary company. The owner of the cinemas demanded that the subsidiary should have a paid up capital of £5,000 before he would grant a lease. The directors subscribed for £3,000 of the shares and Regal Hastings for £2,000. The concern was then sold and the directors ultimately made a profit on their shares. The court said that the directors were in breach of

[32] (1874) LR 9 Ch D 350. [33] [1916] 1 AC 544. [34] [1942] 1 All ER 378.

their duties. As this had involved making a profit out of the fiduciary relationship in which they stood to the company they were bound to repay the profits they had made.

F. Breaches of Duty

Here, as elsewhere, the only clear distinction between breaches of duty which are ratifiable and those that are not lies in the extent to which the behaviour is regarded as villainous. In *Atwool v* Merryweather,[35] a company was formed to acquire a mine from Merryweather. In fact the mine was worthless and the formation of the company and its subsequent flotation was nothing more than a conspiracy to defraud the public. It was held that the company could get back the money it had paid for the worthless mine despite the fact that the majority had voted against this course of action.

Other examples include *Alexander v Automatic Telephone Co.*[36], where the directors holding the majority of the shares tried to avoid paying the full price for their shares, while requiring all other members to do so; and *Estmanco (Kilner House) Ltd v GLC*[37]. The latter case is interesting, since the judge seemed to take an overall view of the wrongdoing without seeking to put it carefully into categories. The court came to the conclusion that a derivative action would lie where the end result of the breaches of duty was to 'stultify the purpose' for which the company had been formed.

G. Negligent acts which benefit a director

In *Daniels v Daniels*[38] the court held that a minority shareholder who has no other remedy may sue where directors use their powers intentionally or unintentionally, fraudulently or negligently in a manner which benefits themselves at the expense of the company.

This last case shows that benefit to themselves provides a dividing line between ratifiable and non-ratifiable actions because it was held in *Pavlides v Jensen*[39] that an individual plaintiff would not be permitted to sue where the claim was based on negligence alone. No exception to the rule in *Foss v Harbottle* would be made in such a case.

H. Use of Powers for an Improper Purpose

Clear instances of actions that are ratifiable occur where powers given to the directors for one purpose are misused. An example of this is when

[35] (1867) 5 Eq 464.
[36] [1900] 2 Ch 56.
[37] [1982] 1 WLR 2.
[38] [1978] Ch 406.
[39] [1956] Ch 565.

shares are issued to fend off a take-over or otherwise to alter the balance of voting power within a company. The courts have held that the power to issue shares must only be used where the primary purpose of the issue is to raise capital.[40] However, where the directors have misused these powers the courts have consistently allowed ratification by a majority vote at a general meeting provided that the holders of the newly issued shares were not allowed to exercise votes attached to the new shares.[41]

One last category of cases must be mentioned. They are the cases concerned with the alteration of articles. It has been held that an individual may prevent the alteration of articles of association where that alteration was not made bona fide for the benefit of the company. However, the cases do not make it clear on what basis the action is brought. If it is brought on the basis that a personal right has been infringed, then it could be argued that the preservation of the integrity of the articles is the concern of every shareholder and any breach of those articles could be remedied by a personal action. This would allow the multiplicity of suits to prevent which the rule in *Foss v Harbottle* was invented. However, that rule is rarely mentioned in that series of cases so it may be the case that the upholding of the articles can be achieved by a personal action. However, if that is not the case another category must be added to the 'fraud on the minority' cases. That is where alteration of the articles is attempted by a majority in control of the company but that alteration is not bona fide for the benefit of the company.

V. RIGHT TO A MINIMUM DIVIDEND?

There is no such right. Payment of dividends is always a matter of discretion for the board.

VI. PRE-EMPTION RIGHTS

Sections 89–96 of the Companies Act 1985 set out a procedure which must be followed if the company is raising new capital but already has shareholders who own ordinary (equity) shares. Those shareholders have the right to be offered a proportion of the new securities which correspond to the proportion of 'relevant shares' (ordinary shares) already held by them. The shares must be offered on the same or more favourable terms than the eventual offer to the public. The definition of 'relevant shares' excludes

[40] *Bamford v Bamford* [1970] Ch 212.
[41] Ibid; *Hogg v Cramphorn Ltd* [1967] Ch 254.

shares that have a right to participate in a distribution only up to a specified amount (non-participating preference shares).

The shareholders then have twenty-one days in which to accept the offer. This right applies to public and private companies but may be excluded by the memorandum or articles of a private company. Private companies must not contravene the ban on offering shares to the public. Private companies may thus make restricted rights offers only in respect of equity securities (ordinary shares) provided the offer is limited to its own shareholders or its employees.

In a public company pre-emptive rights may be overridden by a general authority given to directors under section 80 Companies Act 1985 or may be removed by a special resolution of the company (see section 95 Companies Act 1985).

VII. EMERGENCY ACTION

The only cases where shareholders may cause the company to sue management are set out above

VIII. OTHER

The right to vote by proxy (and by mail) is normally regarded as in favour of management since the incumbent board may solicit proxies (with the company paying the expenses). The common form of a proxy is to permit management to use the member's share as it deems fit.

IX. GENERAL REMEDIAL RIGHTS

A. General Remarks

The list of remedies above is far from exhaustive, a much more powerful remedy is provided by statute. There is also an extensive and complex system which applies in two situations a) where share rights are to be varied (section 125 CA 1985) or b) where there is a merger or de-merger or company rearrangement. In these cases the shares must be divided into separate class meetings and decisions are made by special resolution. In the case of mergers, de-mergers and rearrangements the final outcome is determined by the court but it will normally only refuse to approve the outcome if procedure has not been followed or the result is manifestly unreasonable (including manifestly unfair to a minority (section 425 CA 1985).

The right to seek dissolution of a company is statutory, the only provision that may be in the company's statutes is provision for a limited term or dissolution on the happening of a particular event. There is nothing to prevent the statutes providing for the appointment of a director by a minority although the possibility of enforcement of such a provision is open to doubt and it must be noted that by section 303 CA 185 a director can always be dismissed by a simple majority of shareholders. Auditors must be appointed annually by a company unless a private company has passed a resolution to dispense with this. In that case any member may deposit written notice with the company proposing to bring the appointment of auditors to an end. Directors must then convene a general meeting and if they do not the member may do so (section 393 CA 1985).

Shareholders of a private company that has passed a resolution approving the giving of financial assistance for the acquisition of shares may apply to the court for cancellation of such a resolution if they hold not less than 10 per cent of the nominal value of the company's issued share capital.

The derivative action is explained above. There is no right to a derivative action for personal damage. In a challenge to a resolution changing the company's articles the challenge must be based on the allegation that the change was not bona fide for the benefit of the company but one way this might be shown is by allegations that it discriminated unfairly against a minority. Resolutions generally may only be challenged if it can be shown that proper procedure was not followed or that they infringed a particular right of a shareholder given generally to that class of shareholders by the articles of association.

As explained above, the court will never substitute its own business judgment for that of the company so can only declare resolutions void. They will not rectify them.

B. Judicial or Public Body Protection

The only mechanisms are those already discussed, the judicial review of resolutions, derivative action and DTI inspections.

There is no doubt that the court's attitude to minority shareholders is driven by the perception that they have entered into a consensual arrangement of their own free will and have therefore taken the risk of an unfavourable outcome. The courts will therefore be extremely careful to enforce all procedural protections provided in law and in the company statutes but it is very rare to find instances of sympathetic treatment by the courts that go beyond those protections. This is more marked where the decision has been taken by substantial majorities.

X. EXIT

In this part, I set out the other really significant remedy available to minority shareholders. Because of the confusion and difficulties surrounding derivative actions a simpler and more comprehensive remedy was introduced for the protection of minorities. S459 and s4 61 provide

s. 459 (1) A member of a company may apply to the court by petition for an order under this Part on the ground that the company's affairs are being or have been conducted in a manner which is unfairly prejudicial to the interests of its members generally or of some part of its members (including at least himself) or that any actual or proposed act or omission of the company (including an act or omission on its behalf) is or would be so prejudicial.

(2) The provisions of this Part apply to a person who is not a member of a company but to whom shares in the company have been transferred or transmitted by operation of law, as those provisions apply to a member of the company; and references to a member or members are to be construed accordingly.

461. (1) If the court is satisfied that a petition under this Part is well founded, it may make such order as it thinks fit for giving relief in respect of the matters complained of.

(2) Without prejudice to the generality of subsection (1), the court's order may—

(a) regulate the conduct of the company's affairs in the future,

(b) require the company to refrain from doing or continuing an act complained of by the petitioner or to do an act which the petitioner has complained it has omitted to do,

(c) authorise civil proceedings to be brought in the name and on behalf of the company by such person or persons and on such terms as the court may direct,

(d) provide for the purchase of the shares of any members of the company by other members or by the company itself and, in the case of a purchase by the company itself , the reduction of the company's capital accordingly

(3) If an order under this Part requires the company not to make any, or any specified, alteration in the memorandum or articles, the company does not then have the power without leave of the court to make any such alteration in breach of that requirement.

(4) Any alteration in the company's memorandum or articles made by virtue of an order under this Part is of the same effect as if duly made by resolution of the company, and the provisions of this Act apply to the memorandum or articles as so altered accordingly.

(5) An office copy of an order under this Part altering, or giving leave to alter, a company's memorandum or articles shall, within 14 days from the making of the order or such longer period as the court may allow, be delivered by the company to the register of companies for registration; and if a company makes default in complying with this subsection, the company and every officer of it who is in default is liable to a fine and, for continued contravention, to a daily default fine.

[(6) The power under [section 411 of the Insolvency Act] to make rules shall, so far as it relates to a winding-up petition, apply for the purposes of a petition under this Part.]

The following passage from the judgment of Slade J later cited with approval by Nourse J in *Re RA Noble (Clothing) Ltd*[42] gives a general overview:

I do not think it necessary or appropriate in this judgment to attempt any comprehensive exposition of the situations that may give rise to the court's jurisdiction under s 75. Broadly, however, I would say this. Without prejudice to the generality of the wording of the section, which may cover many other situations, a member of a company will be able to bring himself within the section if he can show that the value of his shareholding in the company has been seriously diminished or at least seriously jeopardised by reason of a course of conduct on the part of those persons who have had de facto control of the company, which is unfair to the member concerned. The test of unfairness must, I think, be an objective, not a subjective one. In other words it is not necessary for the petitioner to show that persons who have had de facto control of the company have acted as they did in the conscious knowledge that this was unfair to the petitioner or that they were acting in bad faith; the test I think is whether a reasonable bystander observing the consequences of their conduct would regard it as having unfairly prejudiced the petitioner's interests.

The House of Lords had their first occasion to consider the section 459 remedy in *O'Neill v* Phillips.[43] In that case Phillips owned all the share capital of a construction company. This was divided into 100 £1 shares. O'Neill was originally employed as a manual worker, but was later promoted and eventually given 25 shares and made a director. Phillips told O'Neill that he hoped that O'Neill would eventually take over the day-to-day running of the business and would then have 50 per cent of the profits. Phillips then retired and O'Neill ran the company as *de facto* managing director. The profits were then shared on a 50/50 basis. O'Neill guaranteed the company's bank account. There were suggestions that when certain asset targets were met, O'Neill would be given a 50 per cent shareholding. However, due to a recession in the building trade this never happened. Phillips resumed control of the company while O'Neill ran the company's business abroad, principally in Germany. At an acrimonious meeting, Phillips told O'Neill that in future he would no longer receive 50 per cent profits and would henceforward only get a salary and dividends on his 25 per cent shareholding. O'Neill terminated his guarantee of the company's bank account. He petitioned, alleging unfair prejudice because of the termination of the equal profit sharing and repudiation of the understanding that his stake in the company would increase to 50 per cent. The court at first instance dismissed the petition on the twin grounds that no concluded

42 [1983] BCLC 273.

43 [1999] BCC 600.

agreement for profit sharing had been reached and that refusal to allot more shares did not prejudice O'Neill in his capacity as member. The Court of Appeal reversed this decision on the grounds that, although there was no concluded agreement to allot more shares, O'Neill had a legitimate expectation that he would receive them when the relevant targets had been reached, and a legitimate expectation to 50 per cent of the profits. The House of Lords restored the first instance judgment. Lord Hoffman's judgment ranged over the major issues concerning section 459 and will be considered as the definitive text for some time to come. He said:

In section 459 Parliament has chosen fairness as the criterion by which the court must decide whether it has jurisdiction to grant relief. Court must decide whether it has jurisdiction to grant relief. It is clear from the legislative history (which I discussed in *In re Saul D Harrison & Sons Plc* [1995] 1 BCLC 14, 17–20) that it chose this concept to free the court from technical considerations of legal right and to confer a wide power to do what appeared just and equitable. But this does not mean that the court can do whatever the individual judge happens to think fair. The concept of fairness must be applied judicially and the content which it is given by the courts must be based upon rational principles. As Warner J said in In *re JE Cade & Son Ltd*: 'The court . . . has a very wide discretion, but it does not sit under a palm tree.[44]

. . . a member of a company will not ordinarily be entitled to complain of unfairness unless there has been some breach of the terms on which he agreed that the affairs of the company should be conducted. But the second leads to the conclusion that there will be cases in which equitable considerations make it unfair for those conducting the affairs of the company to rely upon their strict legal powers. Thus unfairness may consist in a breach of the rules or in using the rules in a manner which equity would regard as contrary to good faith I would apply the same reasoning to the concept of unfairness in section 459.

. . .

An example of . . . equitable principles in action is *Blisset v Daniel*[45] to which Lord Wilberforce referred *in In re Westbourne Galleries Ltd.*[46] Wood VC held that upon the true construction of the articles, two-thirds of the partners could expel a partner by serving a notice upon him without holding any meeting or giving any reason. But he held that the power must be exercised in good faith. He said, 10 Hare 493, 523, that 'the literal construction of these articles cannot be enforced' and, after citing from the title 'De Societate' in Justinian's Institutes, went on, at pp 523–524:

> It must be plain, that you can neither exercise a power of this description by dissolving the partnership, nor do any other act for purposes contrary to the plain general meaning of the deed, which must be this—that this power is inserted, not for the benefit of any particular parties holding two-thirds of the shares, but for the benefit of the whole society and partnership . . .

[44] [1992] BCLC 213, 227. [45] (1853) 10 Hare 493. [46] [1973] AC 360, 381.

In a quasi-partnership company, [the limits to the exercise of power] will usually be found in the understandings between the members at the time they entered into association. But there may be later promises, by words or conduct, which it would be unfair to allow a member to ignore. Nor is it necessary that such promises should be independently enforceable as a matter of contract. A promise may be binding as a matter of justice and equity although for one reason or another (for example, because in favour of a third party) it would not be enforceable in law.

I do not suggest that exercising rights in breach of some promise or undertaking is the only form of conduct which will be regarded as unfair for the purposes of section 459. For example, there may be some event which puts an end to the basis upon which the parties entered into association with each other, making it unfair that one shareholder should insist upon the continuance of the association. The analogy of contractual frustration suggests itself. The unfairness may arise not from what the parties have positively agreed but from a majority using its legal powers to maintain the association in circumstances to which the minority can reasonably say it did not agree: . . . It is well recognised that in such a case there would be power to wind up the company on the just and equitable ground [47] and it seems to me that, in the absence of a winding up, it could equally be said to come within section 459. But this form of unfairness is also based upon established equitable principles and it does not arise in this case.

In *Re Saul D Harrison & Sons Plc*,[48] I used the term 'legitimate expectation,' borrowed from public law, as a label for the 'correlative right' to which a relationship between company members may give rise in a case when, on equitable principles, it would be regarded as unfair for a majority to exercise a power conferred upon them by the articles to the prejudice of another member. I gave as an example the standard case in which shareholders have entered into association upon the understanding that each of them who has ventured his capital will also participate in the management of the company. In such a case it will usually be considered unjust, inequitable or unfair for a majority to use their voting power to exclude a member from participation in the management without giving him the opportunity to remove his capital upon reasonable terms. The aggrieved member could be said to have had a 'legitimate expectation' that he would be able to participate in the management or withdraw from the company.

It was probably a mistake to use this term, as it usually is when one introduces a new label to describe a concept which is already sufficiently defined in other terms. In saying that it was 'correlative' to the equitable restraint, I meant that it could exist only when equitable principles of the kind I have been describing would make it unfair for a party to exercise rights under the articles. It is a consequence, not a cause, of the equitable restraint. The concept of a legitimate expectation should not be allowed to lead a life of its own, capable of giving rise to equitable restraints in circumstances to which the traditional equitable principles have no application. That is what seems to have happened in this case.

Was Mr Phillips unfair?

. . . To take the shareholdings first, the Court of Appeal said that Mr O'Neill had

[47] See *Virdi v Abbey Leisure Ltd* [1990] BCLC 342.
[48] [1995] 1 BCLC 14, 19.

a legitimate expectation of being allotted more shares when the targets were met. No doubt he did have such an expectation before 4 November and no doubt it was legitimate, or reasonable, in the sense that it reasonably appeared likely to happen. Mr Phillips had agreed in principle, subject to the execution of a suitable document. But this is where I think that the Court of Appeal may have been misled by the expression 'legitimate expectation.' The real question is whether in fairness or equity Mr O'Neill had a right to the shares. On this point, one runs up against what seems to me the insuperable obstacle of the judge's finding that Mr Phillips never agreed to give them. He made no promise on the point. From which it seems to me to follow that there is no basis, consistent with established principles of equity, for a court to hold that Mr Phillips was behaving unfairly in withdrawing from the negotiation. This would not be restraining the exercise of legal rights. It would be imposing upon Mr Phillips an obligation to which he never agreed. Where, as here, parties enter into negotiations with a view to a transfer of shares on professional advice and subject to a condition that they are not to be bound until a formal document has been executed, I do not think it is possible to say that an obligation has arisen in fairness or equity at an earlier stage.

The same reasoning applies to the sharing of profits. The judge found as a fact that Mr Phillips made no unconditional promise about the sharing of profits. He had said informally that he would share the profits equally while Mr O'Neill managed the company and he himself did not have to be involved in day-to-day business. He deliberately retained control of the company and with it, as the judge said, the right to redraw Mr O'Neill's responsibilities. This he did without objection in August 1991. The consequence was that he came back to running the business and Mr O'Neill was no longer managing director. He had made no promise to share the profits equally in such circumstances and it was therefore not inequitable or unfair for him to refuse to carry on doing so. The Court of Appeal seems to have contemplated that Mr Phillips might have been entitled to do what he did if he had given Mr O'Neill notice of his intentions and treated him more politely at the meeting on 4 November 1991. But these matters cannot affect the question of whether a change in the profit-sharing arrangements was a breach of faith.

It follows in my opinion that there was no basis for the Court of Appeal's finding that Mr O'Neill had been driven out of the company. . .

Mr Hollington, who appeared for Mr O'Neill, said that it did not matter whether Mr Phillips had done anything unfair. The fact was that trust and confidence between the parties had broken down. In those circumstances it was obvious that there ought to be a parting of the ways and the unfairness lay in Mr Phillips, who accepted this to be the case, not being willing to allow Mr O'Neill to recover his stake in the company. Even if Mr Phillips was not at fault in causing the breakdown, it would be unfair to leave Mr O'Neill locked into the company as a minority shareholder.

Mr Hollington's submission comes to saying that, in a 'quasi-partnership' company, one partner ought to be entitled at will to require the other partner or partners to buy his shares at a fair value. All he need do is to declare that trust and confidence has broken down. . . The Law Commission Report on Shareholder Remedies to which I have already referred considered whether to recommend the introduction of a statutory remedy 'in situations where there is no fault' (paragraph

3.65) so that members of a quasi-partnership could exit at will. They said, at p 39, para 3.66:

> In our view there are strong economic arguments against allowing shareholders to exit at will. Also, as a matter of principle, such a right would fundamentally contravene the sanctity of the contract binding the members and the company which we considered should guide our approach to shareholder remedies.
>
> The Law Commission plainly did not consider that section 459 already provided a right to exit at will and I do not think so either.

Lord Hoffman went on to find that the relationship of O'Neill to the company was one of employee so that, even had there been unfair prejudice it was not suffered in the capacity as member. Further, a fair offer to buy shares would prevent the grant of a section 459 remedy, although both these latter findings were obiter. Lord Hoffman's decision shows clearly the different approaches of the contractual approach, described by him as the 'legal' approach as opposed to the concessionary (equitable) approach. What is most important about the judgment is the attempt to find some framework or boundaries where it might be possible to formulate where a sensible boundary between the two approaches lies.

In this he is not wholly successful since 'equity', 'fairness' and 'conscience' are vague terms. We are told that the terms of the bargains between the participants may not be upset by the exercise of the 'equitable' power: 'one useful cross-check in a case like this is to ask whether the exercise of the power in question would be contrary to what the parties, by words or conduct, have actually agreed. Would it conflict with the promises which they appear to have exchanged.' However, whenever the courts have stepped in to prevent alteration of articles, have used their section 459 powers or prevented voting by a member in a particular way they have inevitably run counter to the 'bargain' since the applicant would not be seeking the aid of the court if she could achieve the desired result by using the voting power that they have by virtue of the 'contract'. Lord Hoffman's formulation must be seen as narrowing the discretion previously exercised by favouring a more contractual approach and leaving the situations which constitute unfairness in doubt.

A. Winding Up Orders

Section 122(1)(g) of the Insolvency Act 1986 provides that a company may be wound up by the court if the court is of the opinion that it is just and equitable that the company should be wound up. This is qualified by section 125(2) of the Insolvency Act 1986 that the company should not be wound up if some other remedy is available to the petitioners, and the court is of the opinion that they are acting unreasonably in seeking to have the company wound up instead of pursuing that other remedy. This proviso is likely to be of much greater importance in the light of the wide jurisdiction exercised by the courts under section 459 (CA 1985). It is a drastic move to destroy the company completely as a remedy for unfairness. Far better to allow an aggrieved party to buy his way out at a fair valuation. The cases prior to 1980 can only therefore afford guidance about the availability of the winding up remedy now. In the light of section 459, petitioners might be prevented by section 125(2) of the Insolvency Act 1986 from obtaining a winding up order which they could have obtained before a section 459 remedy appeared on the statute book. Nor need the 'alternative remedy' necessarily be a section 459 remedy. In *Re A* Company,[49] the court emphasised that the power to grant a winding up order on the just and equitable ground was discretionary and should certainly be refused where a reasonable offer to buy the petitioner's shares had been refused.

A petition for section 459 relief can be combined with a petition to wind up on the just and equitable ground. It should be noted that unfair prejudice or malpractice need not be alleged in order to show that there is a case for winding up (see, for example, *Re German Date Coffee Co*,[50] where the purpose for which the company was formed was no longer attainable). In *Re R.A. Noble & Son (Clothing) Ltd* [51] the judge held that malpractice need not be shown provided that the conduct of those in control had been the 'substantial cause' of the lack of mutual confidence between the parties. In that case the judge dismissed the petition for s.459 relief and made an order for the winding up of the company on the just and equitable ground.

When a Winding up Order is Likely to be Made

The leading case on 'just and equitable' winding up is Re Westbourne Galleries Ltd [1973] AC 360. In that case the petition was brought by a Mr Ebrahami, who for many years had been an equal partner with Mr Nazar in a business dealing in Persian carpets. In 1958 it was decided to incorporate the business and Ebrahami (E) and Nazar (N), who were both appointed directors, each held 500 shares. Soon after this N's son was made a director and E and N each transferred 100 shares to the son. After this the Nazars held a majority of the votes. In 1965, the relationship between the Nazars and E began to break down. In 1969, the Nazars used their majority to remove E from his directorship. Thereafter he was unable to take any part in the management of the business and he received no money since all payments were made to the participants in the business by way of directors' salaries rather than dividends. The court held that the removal of E had been lawful. Nevertheless, because the company was in essence an incorporated partnership, the Nazars had abused their power and were in breach

[49] [1983] 1 WLR 927. [50] (1882) 20 Ch D 169. [51] [1983] BCLC.

of the good faith partners owed to one another. E was therefore entitled to a winding up order.

This may well now be a situation in which section 59 relief could be granted and thus a winding up order would be refused. Other situations in which the remedy has been granted are where deadlock has been reached because shares were equally divided between two factions at odds with each other: *Re Yenidje Tobacco Co Ltd*[52] and where the whole purpose or substratum of the company had failed. An instance of the latter is *Re German Date Coffee Co*[53] where the company (mercifully?) failed to obtain the patent to make coffee from dates. That activity had been the major purpose for which the company was formed.

In order for a petition to succeed a shareholder must show that he has an interest in the winding up: that is, that there is a probability that the company is solvent and so, after the winding up, there will be assets to be distributed to the shareholders.[54]

B. Squeezing Out

Where, following a takeover offer the bidder holds 90 per cent in value of al the shares in the company, a non-assenting shareholder may, by written notice under section 430A CA 1985, require the offeror to buy the shares. The acquisition is on the terms of the offer unless the court orders otherwise. Within one month of the end of the period of the offer, notice of rights under section 430A must be given to all shareholders who have not accepted the offer.. After the offeror has acquired or contracted to acquire 90 per cent of the shares he may give notice under section 429 CA 1985 entitling and binding him to acquire remaining shares on the terms of the offer. The recipient of such a notice may apply to the court within 6 weeks for an order preventing the acquisition or to obtain different terms of acquisition.

XI. MINORITY RIGHTS AND GROUPS

Apart from the accounting provisions driven by the EC Seventh Directive and tax provisions, companies are treated on almost all issues as separate entities. There are no rights of disclosure although the DTI Review suggests extending the operating and financial review to groups of companies and in practice director's statements to shareholders accompanying the accounts will generally deal with group issues, although a degree of selectivity may be detected.

52 [1916] 2 Ch 426

53 (1882) 20 ChD 169.

54 *Re Expanded Plugs Ltd* [1960] 1 WLR 514.

XII. COMPLEMENTARY AND SUBSTITUTE MECHANISMS

There are a number of remedies available to a liquidator where the company has been mismanaged. These include avoidance of suspect transactions such as unfair preferences and a claim against directors personally to contribute to company funds where there has been 'wrongful trading' (section 214 Insolvency Act 1986. Wrongful trading means trading on after any hope of solvency has gone. This latter is not much used as directors in this situation often have little money. On liquidation all insolvency practitioners must also consider whether the report directors as being 'unfit' and therefore considered for disqualification. Over 1,500 disqualification orders are made annually for various types of misconduct in the operation of companies and a register of disqualified directors is kept. It is a criminal offence to act as a director (or shadow director) if disqualified. There are, of course the general penal provisions against theft, forgery and fraud.

The new Financial Services authority (FSA) has wide powers to supervise the financial services industry and prosecute for offences of market abuse, insider trading and money laundering. It is not possible to discover their sources of information to determine whether minorities gain any protection from this source. The DTI have powers over the non-regulated companies and very few prosecutions under the provisions of Part X of the Companies Act 1985 have ever been brought. This Part enacts sanctions (mostly criminal) for such matters as large loans to directors. The DTI inspectorate and the FSA have wide powers to seize documents and a much contested power to force the self-incrimination of defendants.[55]

XIII. SUMMARY

It could fairly be said that minority shareholders rights provide great fun for academics and some rich pickings for lawyers but ae otherwise a fairly incoherent mess. As noted above, there is no doubt that the court's attitude to minority shareholders is driven by the perception that they have entered into a consensual arrangement of their own free will and have therefore taken the risk of an unfavourable outcome. The courts will therefore be extremely careful to enforce all procedural protections provided in law and in the company statutes but it is very rare to find instances of sympathetic treatment by the courts which go beyond those protections. This is more marked where the decision has been taken by substantial majorities.

The costs of court action are high: statistics published by the Law

[55] See *Saunders v UK* (Case 43/1994/490/572) [1997] BCC 872 (European Court of Human Rights.

Commission show 170 petitions filed under section 456 in 1994–5 (12 months). Of these 113 showed petitioner was a minority shareholder and in 109 cases the relief sought was purchase of the petitioner's shares. Only thirty petitioners had any legal aid. During the period thirty-seven reached settlement, ten were struck out, twenty-eight were dormant and sixty-six ongoing. Only seven reached a full hearing.

The major effect of concentration of share ownership in large companies is to give power to institutional investors, exercised through their fund managers. Usually, any control exercised by these investors is done on an informal basis and will not reach the public view. Such concentration means that these investors have considerable power but also means that individual investors may lose out first to management, then to a majority of shareholders, then to a powerful institutional investor minority. There is no legal recognition of this distinction.

Chapter 10

Copyright Issues and the Information Society

*Charlotte Waelde**

I. ACCESS TO WORKS ON LINE

A. The Right to Information

The right to information, and to some extent its counterpart the right to free speech, is at the core of our society. Any person using the web should be able to access any kind of information and express his opinions. Is this a right limited only by the technology or should these rights be limited as subjective rights within the existing political frameworks?

There has never been an absolute right to information in the UK just as there has never been an absolute right to freedom of expression. Recent developments in the law, including the introduction of the Freedom of Information Act 2000 (fully in force in 2005) the Data Protection Act 1998, and the incorporation of the European Convention on Human Rights by way of the Human Rights Act 1998 into domestic law do mean that the parameters on both access to information and freedom of expression are in a state of flux. Nevertheless, both the right of access to information, and the right to express opinions freely are still tempered by the law of copyright on the one hand, and the laws of defamation and injurious falsehood on the other.

In the UK the law of copyright developed as an encouragement to creators. Because the state has granted rights to authors of creative works to control onward dissemination of a work, so, it is argued, creators are encouraged to create because they are able to obtain an economic return from that creation. However, merely because a work is created, that does not, and never has given a third party the 'right' to access and use that work. Thus a poet might write a poem and lock that poem in a safe. Merely because the law of copyright protects that work, it does not give the right to a third party to access and to reproduce it. However, if the author of the poem chooses to distribute the work, and to use state backed rights to control reproduction, then equally the author must permit a third party to

* Co-Director AHRB Research Centre for Studies in Intellectual Property and Technology Law, University of Edinburgh.

critique the work for specified purposes, such as criticism and review. The law as it historically developed has thus provided a balance between the creator on the one hand, and the user on the other.

In the information society, it would appear that within the political and technical framework the balance between the creator of the work and the user has shifted quite markedly in favour of the creator. This move is evidenced in two particular ways. The first is by the increase in the grant of property rights over creative works in favour of the creator with the consequent ability to control further reproduction. In other words, increased rights to control *use* of a work once disseminated. These moves are evidenced through both political and technical developments. The second is by the expansion and legal protection of technical measures that guard *access* to a work. These are evidenced by the increasing sophistication of the technical measures available to control access to a work disseminated in digital form, and secondly through the political process during which is has been deemed essential to provide legal protection against circumvention of these *access* controls.

These developments have occurred because of the concerns of those who own rights (the right holders) to works of mainly popular culture, such as digitised music and films. These right holders fear, perhaps justifiably, that if works are disseminated in digital form with no controls, it would be impossible to control onward dissemination of perfect copies. The effect, however, spreads to all forms of creative and non-creative works (information) disseminated in digital form.

The problem for the user is twofold. The first is the difficulty in gaining *access* to a work except perhaps under specified terms and conditions or for a payment. The second is in the diminishing rights available to the user of a work to draw on that work, and use it in new creative and informational ways.

1. *The Information Society and the Information Superhighways: Ambiguities and Differences*

Copyright was first put on a statutory basis in England in 1710, with the enactment of the Statute of Anne.[1] The momentum for formal protection arose in large part from publishers, who lobbied for the ability to control reproduction of books prior to distribution to the public. After the advent of the printing press, competitors could relatively easily and cheaply reproduce further copies, with few controls. While accepting the need for State assistance in controlling copying, Parliament considered the right should be granted to publishers and authors, only in return for satisfaction of the

[1] 8 Anne Ch 19 (1710).

public interest.[2] This came in the form of encouraging dissemination of works for: '*The encouragement of* learning'.[3] The 1710 Act gave the '*sole right and liberty of printing books*' to authors and their assigns. This right depended on a book being registered with the Stationers' Company, applied only to published works, and existed only for a period of 14 years. If the author was still alive after this period, the right was returned to him for a further period of 14 years.[4] Over the next 200 years, there were few changes, and those that were made extended the term of copyright, broadened the variety of works protected by copyright, and made provision for the protection of works of foreign authors as required when the UK first became a signatory to the Berne Convention for the Protection of Literary and Artistic Works 1889. In 1911 and 1957 major changes were made to the law of copyright in the UK. The law was revised and brought up to date in the Copyright Designs and Patents Act 1988 (CDPA) which, as subsequently amended, forms the basis of the current UK copyright law. This Act represents a mix of national policies, and provisions arising from regional and international obligations. In recent years, the amendments that have been made almost wholly stem from the EU as the harmonisation programme moves forwards.

Historically, the justifications for the development of the law in the UK have focussed on an economic approach. Property rights are granted in intellectual goods because it is economically efficient. However, theorists have all recognised that limitations on the property right are necessary, in part because of the need to take from what exists in order to create anew.

> If every valuable interest constituted property, then practically any act would result in either a trespass on, or a taking of, someone's property . . . [5]

[2] There are a number of texts which consider the historical development of the law of copyright. For example, M Rose, *Authors and Owners The Invention of Copyright* (Harvard: Harvard University Press, 1993). SM Stewart, *International Copyright and Neighbouring Rights* 2nd edn (London: Butterworths, 1989), part 1 and variously through the individual chapters are both interesting sources.

[3] The preamble to the 1710 Act provides: '*A Bill for the Encouragement of Learning and for Securing the Property of Copies of Books to the rightful owners thereof.*'

[4] Some argue that although it might appear to favour authors over the intermediary, it was in fact intermediary who pushed hard for formal protection and whose interests in being able to exploit the creative works were protected. See, eg, D Vaver 'Intellectual Property Today: Of Myths and Paradoxes' (1990), *Canadian Bar Review*, 69, p 98 at 104. WB Cornish, *Intellectual Property: Patents, Copyright, Trade Marks and Allied Rights*, 4th edn (London: Sweet & Maxwell, 1999) (hereinafter Cornish *Intellectual Property*), ch 9.

[5] RP Merges and RR Nelson, 'On the Complex Economics of Patent Scope' (1990), 90 *Colum L Rev* 839. See also the following, who question the economic analysis behind the grant of increasing property rights in intellectual property products. S Breyer, 'The Uneasy Case for Copyright: A Study of Copyright in Books, Photocopies and Computer Programs' 1970, 84 *Harv L Rev*, 281. KJ Vandevelde, 'The New Property of the Nineteenth Century: The Development of the Modern Concept of Property' (1980), 29 *Buff L Rev*, 325. WJ Gordon, 'Fair Use as Market Failure A Structural and Economic Analysis of the Betamax Case and its Predecessors' (1982) 82 *Colum L Rev*, 1600.

Despite hesitations over increasing property rights in intellectual products, the trend at international and national level has been to increasing property rights. At a meeting[6] organised to examine the position of least developed countries in the global market place, the Director General of WIPO highlighted: 'the growing importance of intellectual property as a key component of wealth creation,' and asserted that: 'In a knowledge-based society, intellectual property will be used as a major source, as a critical tool, for economic growth and economic development.'

The next section will discuss the various instruments that have been negotiated to date, and which clearly exhibit this trend in favour of increased property rights.

2. *Information Society and the Political and Economic Environment: The European Union, the WTO, from a Regional to a World-Wide Approach*

Perhaps the first international move in the direction of increasing property rights in intellectual products for the purposes of facilitating trade came with the negotiation of the TRIPs Agreement in 1994.[7] This agreement was one of the products of the Uruguay round of negotiations on the General Agreement on Tariffs and Trade (GATT).[8] Historically, responsibility for

J Litman, 'The Public Domain' 1990, 39 *Emory LJ*, 965. Id, 'Copyright as a Myth' (1991), *University of Pittsburgh Law Review*, vol 53, 235. WM Landes and R Posner, `An Economic Analysis of Copyright Law' (1989), 18 *J Legal Stud*, 325. 'For copyright law to promote economic efficiency its principal legal doctrines must, at least approximately, maximise the benefits from creating additional works minus both the losses from limiting access and the costs of administering copyright protection', at 326. CA Promo Braga and C Fink, 'The Economic Justification for the Grant of Intellectual Property Rights: Patterns of Convergence and Conflict' (1996), *Chicago Kent Law Review*, vol 72, 439 discussing IP and world trade concluding that although there is conflicting economic evidence to support the benefits: 'As countries introduce the minimum standards of protection required by TRIPs, a gradual strengthening of IPR's on a global scale will ensue', at 461.

[6] WIPO web site <http://www.wipo.org>.

[7] Agreement on Trade-Related Aspects of Intellectual Property Rights 1994 (TRIPs). For an interesting discussion on the politics involved in the negotiation of TRIPs see Drahos, `Global Property Rights in Information: The Story of Trips at the Gatt' (1996), *Prometheus*, vol 13, no 1, 6. In common with others, Drahos points to the interests of the US in negotiating the Treaty. Large US corporations in particular were concerned about loss of profits due to piracy; in addition, there was a general fear over the loss of US international competitiveness. See also Sell, 'Intellectual Property Protection and Antitrust in the Developing World: Crisis, Coercion, and Choice' (1995), *International Organisation*, 49, 2, p 315. Ricketson, `The Future of the Traditional Intellectual Property Conventions in the Brave New World of Trade-Related Intellectual Property Rights', *IIC*, vol 26, no 6 (1995), 872 giving a useful introduction to the gestation of Trips and the inclusion of intellectual property. An interesting note in the text attributed to the Australian commentator Drahos, op cit, `TRIPs grew directly our of US concern with its declining trade position and its desire to protect its intellectual property abroad' (898).

[8] General Agreement on Tariffs and Trade administered by the World Trade Organisation in Geneva.

international copyright protection rested with WIPO, where the focus of protection was the author. The regime for the protection of intellectual property endorsed by TRIPs, and the obligations it places on signatory states, was hailed as a break though in facilitating the international trade of intellectual property.[9]

Once this link between trade and intellectual property rights was established, other Treaties have followed on. On the international front, the World Intellectual Property Organisation (WIPO) Copyright Treaty 1996 (WCT) evidences the same convergence between copyright as a creative right, and the link with trade.

(a) The Political/Regulatory Framework: Increasing Control for Right Holders

(i) The WCT

Because the WCT is a special agreement within the meaning of Article 20 of the Berne Convention,[10] the focus is at least in part on the interests of the author. This is reflected in the preamble to the WCT:

> Desiring to develop and maintain the protection of the rights of authors in their literary and artistic works in a manner as effective and uniform as possible emphasising the outstanding significance of copyright protection as an incentive for literary and artistic creation and recognising the need to maintain a balance between the rights of authors and the large public interest, particularly education, research, and access to information as reflected in the Berne Convention.

However, this focus on the interests of the author is not fully borne out in the Articles where the spotlight is rather on the needs of right holders. The WCT is a relatively brief Treaty, consisting of twenty-two Articles, and nine Agreed Statements. A number of the Articles are merely restatements of the existing law.[11] Thus, Article 2 restates the generally accepted rule that 'copyright protection extends to expression and not to ideas, procedures, methods or operation or mathematical concepts as such'. Other articles were added to clarify the law where there was some doubt about interpretation and inclusion in the existing Treaties. Article 4 provides that

9 An indication that the trade concerns rather than those of authors were uppermost in the drafters minds can be gleaned from the absence of any reference to moral rights in the Treaty. There is an explicit statement that the moral right provisions of the Berne Convention are not included. TRIPs Art 9.1.

'Members shall comply with Articles 1 through 21 of the Berne Convention (1971) and the Appendix thereto. However, Members shall not have rights or obligations under this Agreement in respect of the rights conferred under Article 6 bis of that Convention or of the rights derived therefrom'.

10 WCT Art 1(1).

11 WCT Art 2 concerning the scope of copyright protection.

computer programs are to be protected as literary works.[12] Yet other articles introduce a measure of harmonisation into the laws of contracting States, for instance on the right of rental for computer programs, films, and phonograms.[13]

There are two real advances concerning digital works. These are contained in Article 8 and Articles 11 and 12 concerning the right of communication to the public, and the protection of technical measures designed to control access to and use of creative works, and rights management information respectively.

It is Article 8 that contains the required measure to separate the work which is protected by copyright, from the physical article in or on which it is usually held. Article 8 provides that:

> authors of literary and artistic works shall enjoy the exclusive right of authorizing any communication to the public of their works, by wire or wireless means, including the making available to the public of their works in such a way that members of the public may access these works from a place and at a time individually chosen by them.

Thus there is no requirement under this article that the work be fixed in any tangible form. Rather it is the *communication to the public* and the *making available* of the literary and artistic work that is a right reserved to the author. The effect of these new rights is to give to the author (or other right holder) not only the exclusive right to authorise when a work will be made available over the Internet, but also the exclusive right over every further movement of that work. This, in turn means that the author can licence every further reproduction.

Article 11 which contains the requirements relating to the protection of technological measures provides:

> Contracting Parties shall provide adequate legal protection and effective legal remedies against the circumvention of effective technological measures that are used by authors in connection with the exercise of their rights under this Treaty or the Berne Convention and that restrict acts, in respect of their works, which are not authorized by the authors concerned or permitted by law.

The point of this article is to ensure that where rights holders protect a work against unauthorised reproduction through the use of technology, then it will be unlawful to circumvent that technology to make use of the work. That is unless the action is authorised by the right holder, or the circumvention is permitted by law. Finally, Article 12 of the WCT provides that where a work is disseminated over the Internet in conjunction with

[12] WCT Art 4 stating that computer programs are protected as literary works within Art 2 of the Berne Convention.

[13] WCT Art 7.

information about that work, for instance the name of the author, or the conditions under which the work may be re-used, then it will be unlawful to remove that information. This article is designed in part to maintain the integrity of the information disseminated in conjunction with the work, but perhaps more importantly, a number of the databases being designed by right holders depend on such information being automatically available in conjunction with the work. The process of managing rights (and payment) can become almost automatic so long as that information remains reliable.

(ii) The WPPT

The WIPO Performances and Phonograms Treaty (WPPT) is the second Treaty concerning the information age, negotiated by WIPO at the same time as the WCT. WPPT concerns the rights of performers and producers of phonograms.[14] This Treaty provides that performers and producers of phonograms should have the right to authorise fixation of performances, and the rights to authorise reproduction, distribution, rental and, for the Internet, to make available fixed performances by wire or wireless means. Equitable remuneration is to be paid to both performers, and producers of phonograms, for the direct, or indirect, use of phonograms published for commercial purposes, for broadcasting, or any communication to the public.[15] Protection for performers lasts until the end of a period of 50 years from the end of the year in which the performance was fixed in a phonogram,[16] and for producers of phonograms for 50 years from the end of the year in which the phonogram was published or in which it was made.[17] There are also common provisions concerning technological measure[18] and rights management information.[19] The separation between the two Treaties follows the paths taken by the Berne Convention and the Rome Convention respectively.

(iii) The EU

The EU has been both influenced and been influenced by the developments on the International stage. The EU has been working on a harmonisation programme in the field of copyright and related rights for a number of years. Specifically for the digital agenda, the Commission published an action plan 'Europe's way to the Information Society'[20] in 1994. This was

[14] Because of the wording of the Berne convention, WCT and WPPT, performers of audio-visual works lack any explicit protection in the Treaties. WIPO have indicated that they will be working in this area to try and negotiate formal protection. Measures similar to those provided for performers were introduced into the EC in Council directive 92/100/EEC of 19 Nov 1992 on Rental Right and Lending Right and on Certain Rights Related to Copyright in the Field of Intellectual Property.

[15] WPPT Art 15.

[16] Ibid, 17(1).

[17] Ibid, 17(2).

[18] Ibid, 18.

[19] Ibid, 19.

[20] COM (94) 347 final of 19 July 1994.

followed by a Green Paper on Copyright and Related Rights in the Information Society in 1995,[21] and a Follow up to the Green Paper on Copyright and Related Rights in the Information Society in 1996.[22]

The latest part of this programme is the European Parliament and Council Directive on the harmonisation of certain aspects of Copyright and Related Rights in the Information Society (the Copyright Directive). Its provisions are vitally important as they will be reflected in the laws of the fifteen Member States.[23] The purpose of this directive is said to be twofold.[24] First, it will create harmonised legal protection within the internal market in accordance with the EC Treaty. Secondly, it will resolve the uncertainties surrounding the applicability of existing legislation to electronic media. The Copyright Directive is also intended to be the means by which Member States implement the obligations imposed under the WCT and WPPT.

The Copyright Directive deals with both rights of authors and rights of the producers of phonograms, films and broadcasting organisations.[25] In this it diverges from the Berne Convention and the WCT where the focus is on the author. The international regime for protection of neighbouring right holders, those who have rights in the media through which authors rights are exploited, has been by way of the Rome Convention. The WPPT dealt with phonograms. The provisions of the Copyright Directive are applicable to both the basic author rights, and the neighbouring rights.

The Copyright Directive contains measures for harmonising the reproduction right, including the temporary right of reproduction;[26] introduces the making available and communication to the public rights[27] in conformity with the WCT; harmonises the distribution right;[28] seeks to harmonise a number of exceptions to the right, of reproduction, communication to the public and making available to the public;[29] and imposes obligations concerning technical measures and rights information.[30]

(iv) The Balance in the Copyright Directive

Overall, the trend in the Copyright Directive is to increase rights for authors and right holders. It is perhaps in the recitals that the focus of protection is most clearly visible. The recitals were revised many times during the passage of the Copyright Directive through the legislative process. Even as finally drafted, the Recitals evidence some confusion as to the purpose of the increase in protection of copyright.

Recital 9 makes some play of the traditional justifications:

[21] COM (95) 382 final of 19 July 1995.
[22] COM (96) 568 final of 20 Nov 1996.
[23] And others if, and when, the EU enlarges.
[24] COM 97 628 at 3.
[25] Called 'right holders' in the Copyright Directive.
[26] Copyright Directive Art 2.
[27] Ibid,3.
[28] Ibid, 4.
[29] Ibid, 5.
[30] Ibid, 6 and 7.

Any harmonisation of copyright and related rights must take as a basis a high level of protection, since such rights are crucial to intellectual creation. Their protection helps to ensure the maintenance and development of creativity in the interests of authors, performers, producers, consumers, culture, industry and the public at large. Intellectual property has therefore been recognised as an integral part of property.

There is the clear assumption that there must be a 'high level of protection' as the rights are 'crucial to intellectual creation'. On balance, the recitals exhibit a tendency to favour the investment needed to disseminate products over the Internet, rather than the rights of authors: Recital 10 confirms this:

The investment required to produce products such as phonograms, films or multimedia products, and services such as 'on demand' services, is considerable. Adequate legal protection of intellectual property rights is necessary in order to guarantee the availability of such a reward and provide the opportunity for satisfactory returns on this investment.

Copyright has always been at least partly about the need for the intermediary to obtain a return on the investment made in bringing the product to the market. But the Copyright Directive goes further, and suggests that a high level of protection of intellectual property will foster,

substantial investment in . . . network infrastructure, and lead in turn to growth and increased competitiveness of European industry, both in the area of content provision and information technology and more generally across a wide range of industrial and cultural sectors. This will safeguard employment and encourage new job creation.[31]

It is noticeable that any discussion on moral rights has been entirely absent from the process, moral rights rather being left to the province of national law.[32]

The political moves at both international and regional level in the information society have thus been to increase the rights granted to creators of works to facilitate trade. These moves have been significantly bolstered by the programme that has been enacted to protect technological measures used to guard *access* to those same works which are disseminated over the Internet, and which encompass those works are sufficiently creative to be protected by copyright, and others which merely amount to information.

[31] Ibid, Recital 3.

[32] Recital 19 of the Copyright Directive states: 'The moral rights of right holders should be exercised according to the legislation of the Member States and the provisions of the Berne Convention for the Protection of Literary and Artistic Works, of the WIPO Copyright Treaty and of the WIPO Performances and Phonograms Treaty. Such moral rights remain outside the scope of this Directive.'

(b) The Political/Regulatory Environment: Protecting Technical Controls

There are a number of different types of technological controls used to protect digitised works. One of the most sophisticated is made up of a number of elements[33]. The first is a database which contains information about the work. This may include the name of the author, the copyright owner, the work being protected, and other information necessary to authorise a third party to use that work for a specified purpose. The database may also contain the conditions on which a licence may be granted to use the work.[34] Some systems also incorporate the hardware (eg, the computer, the modem, the printer) in which special semi-conductor chips are implanted. These systems are called by some 'rights management containers',[35] because the container placed around the work (the © chip) automatically performs a number of functions. It can control access to the work protected by copyright. It is capable of encrypting and decrypting the content. The content itself (the work protected by copyright or the information) is useless outside the container because it is encrypted, and only the container has the key.[36] The container can store precise instructions detailing which uses to permit, and which to deny.[37] Because the instructions are in the container, which must be passed through every time the content is accessed, the right holder can maintain complete control over every interaction between the surfer and the content.[38] In time, it is anticipated that these technical controls will incorporate a payment system, so the user can be automatically charged, and pay, for each use of a protected work.[39]

[33] Gervais, `Electronic Rights Management Systems', WIPO/EC/CONF/99/ SPK/10-A Available on the WIPO website (below note 60).

[34] There are currently several initiatives underway to standardise the of information that is required for such a database (metadata). These include the INDECS project sponsored by the EU. The instructions will be implemented by software. The new version of Windows Media 7 apparently contains instructions to limit copying of music files. EMI have launched a number of new products in conjunction with this software. <http://www.bbc.co.uk>.

[35] Stefik, `Trusted Systems', Special Report, *Scientific American* (March 1997), <http://www.sciam.com/0397issue/0397stefik.html>. Pareles, `Trying to get in Tune with the digital Age; Recording Industry Seeks a Standard for Distributing Music on the Web', Northern Light Business Research Centre, *New York Times*, 1 February 1999. Reprinted in *Northern Light* <http://www.nytimes.com/partners/microsites/dec/n1/223/standard.html>.

[36] For an explanation of cryptography see M Hogg, `Secrecy and Signatures Turning the Legal Spotlight on Encryption and Electronic Signatures', in L Edwards and C Waelde (eds), *Law and the Internet: A Framework for Electronic Commerce* (Oxford: Hart Publishing , 2000).

[37] M Gimbel, 'Some thoughts on the implications of Trusted Systems for Intellectual Property Law' (1998), 50 *Stan L Rev*, 1671.

[38] Stefik, `Shifting the Possible: How Trusted Systems and Digital Property Rights Challenge us to Rethink digital Publishing` (1997), *Berkeley Technology Law Journal* , vol 12, issue 1.

[39] For a discussion on payment systems see S Miller, `Payment in an On-Line World', in Edwards and Waelde (eds), op cit.

In tandem with the development of these technical controls, a number of questions have arisen concerning their protection. The first is to what extent they should be protected by law against an act of circumvention. The question concerns the owners of the work and information because, without legal protection against circumvention the controls might be worthless once a work is disseminated on the Internet. The question also concerns users, as a result of the effect the technical measures can have on both access to, and use of, the works behind the fence. A second problem arises because the technical controls do not just control unauthorised dissemination of a work. They also control *access* to that work. Access can then be denied or conditioned on payment: not only for the first time that a work is viewed, but for every time thereafter. Payment could also be required for each and every different act carried out with that work: for instance, viewing on a screen, copying insubstantial parts of a work directly from that work, saving a copy in the hard drive of a computer, or printing out a copy. A third issue then arises. Because the technical controls guard access to a work which is available over the Internet, it is generally on a one to one basis that the interaction between the surfer and the right holder occurs. Therefore, the right holder, can contract on a one to one basis with the surfer. Contractual terms and conditions may accordingly be deployed to govern both *access* to, and *use* of, a work delivered to a user.

(c) Legal Protection of Technical Controls

Because of the concerns of the right holders (as opposed to the users) in relation to unauthorised circumvention of technical controls, a raft of legislative measures have been introduced to protect against circumvention without permission.

(i) The WCT

The WCT provides:

> Contracting Parties shall provide adequate legal protection and effective legal redress against the circumvention of effective technological measures that are used by authors in connection with the exercise of their rights under this Treaty or the Berne Convention and that restrict acts, in respect of their works, which are not authorised by the authors concerned or permitted by law.[40]

In addition, the WCT obliges contracting parties to provide: 'effective legal remedies against the facilitation or removal or alteration of electronic rights management information or to distribute copies of works on which such information has been altered'.[41]

[40] WCT Art 11 Obligations Concerning Technological Measures.

[41] WCT Art 12 Obligations Concerning Rights Management Information. Right management information means information which identifies the works, the author of the work, the

The focus in the WCT is thus on the act of circumvention, and not the technologies which might make circumvention possible. In addition, the test relates to what is not 'permitted by law'. This would suggest that it would be permissible to circumvent a technical control if the purpose was to access materials that lay in the public domain.

(ii) The EU Debate

In 1997, in the Proposal for a Directive on Copyright and Related Rights in the Information Society, it was suggested that protection of technical controls was not to be directed against the circumvention of technological measures as such (the standard adopted in WCT). Rather the focus was to be on preparatory activities such as writing a program that could itself circumvent a technical control. This was seen as fundamental: 'because the real danger for intellectual property rights will not be a single act of circumvention by individuals but preparatory activities to produce devices or offer services to circumvent.'[42] So there was to be a wide ban on the act of circumvention which would in turn allow a wide ban on circumventing technologies. The provisions as implemented in the Copyright Directive are to be found in Article 6. This article obliges Member States to 'provide adequate legal protection against the circumvention of any effective technological measures'.[43] But in addition, Member States are to:

> provide adequate legal protection against the manufacture, import, distribution, sale, rental, advertisement for sale or rental, or possession for commercial purposes of devices, products or components or the provision of services which:
>
> > are promoted, advertised or marketed for the purpose of circumvention of, or have only a limited commercially significant purpose or use other than to circumvent, or are primarily designed, produced, adapted or performed for the purpose of enabling or facilitating the circumvention of, any effective technological measures.

The phrase 'technological measure' is defined as:

> any technology, device or component that, in the normal course of its operation, is designed to prevent or restrict acts, in respect of works or other subject matter,

owner of any right in the work or information about the terms and conditions of use of the work and any number or codes that represent such information when any of these items of information is attached to a copy of a work or appears in connection with the communication of a work to the public.

42 Copyright and related rights in the Information Society–Proposal for a Directive 10 Dec 1997 <http://europa.eu.int/comm/dg15/en/intprop/intprop/1100.htm>.

43 The expression 'technological measures', means 'any technology, device or component that, in the normal course of its operation, is designed to prevent or restrict acts, in respect of works or other subject matter, which are not authorised by the right holder of any copyright or any right related to copyright as provided by law or the sui generis right provided for in Ch III of the European Parliament and Council Directive 96/6/EC.'

which are not authorised by the right holder of any copyright or any right related to copyright as provided by law or the sui generis right provided for [by the Database Directive].

The definition does not refer to *access*, and would appear only to prohibit circumvention and devices that facilitate reproduction of a work where that is not 'authorised by the right holder or as provided by law'. Thus, circumvention of a technological measure in order to gain access to a work that had fallen into the public domain might be permissible, perhaps because the work was no longer protected by copyright. However, that is clearly not the intention, as the Copyright Directive goes on to provide that a technological measure shall be

deemed 'effective' where the use of a protected work of other subject matter is controlled by the right holders through application of an access control or protection process, such as encryption, scrambling or other transformation of the work or other subject matter or a copy control mechanism, which achieves the protection objective.

Thus, the focus here is also on protection against *access* to works, and is not limited to circumvention for infringing purposes.

However, in addition the EU has provided that, in certain circumstances, specified classes of users are to be permitted to make reproductions of works. In so doing, technical protection systems may be circumvented. It is instructive to note that these measures do not extend to gaining *access* to the work, but affect activities that may thereafter take place. The relevant provision[44] states:

Notwithstanding the legal protection provided for in paragraph 1, in the absence of voluntary measures by right holders, including agreements between right holders and other parties concerned, Member States shall take appropriate measures to ensure that right holders make available to the beneficiary of an exceptions or limitation provided for in national law . . . the means of benefiting from that exception or limitation, to the extent necessary to benefit from that exception or limitation, where that beneficiary has legal access to the protected work or other subject matter concerned.

Before a 'beneficiary of protection' (not further defined in the Copyright Directive) may circumvent technical controls in the way provided for in this paragraph, legal access to the work must first be obtained. The prohibition against circumvention thus remains in place where the purpose of circumvention might be to gain *access* to the protected work.

Finally, in line with the obligations imposed under the WCT, the Copyright Directive obliges Member States to provide for adequate legal protection against the removal or alteration of electronic rights manage-

[44] Copyright Directive Art 6 para 4.

ment information that may be contained in the work as disseminated over the Internet:[45] in other words, the information in the database which forms the basis on which rights can be managed and licensed.

The overall effect of these political moves at International and regional level is thus firstly to increase the property rights granted in creative works to right holders by limiting the *use* that may be made of them by third parties; and secondly to buttress the position of right holders over control of *access* to the works by validating and protecting technical measures used to prevent such access without authorisation. The overall implication is that the ability of a person using the web is limited in both *access* and *use* of works by both the political framework and the technical controls.

3. *Which Convergence between the Anglo-Saxon Free Economy vs the Continental Controlled Economy?*

Initiatives taken by WIPO (International) and the EU (Regional) discussed above exhibit a marked degree of convergence in shaping copyright for the information era. Not only have the property rights in creative works been strengthened, but technical controls used to guard access to those works will now be protected by all those States who have (or will) sign the WCT, and those Member States who are current members of the EU. Taken together with the developments occurring in the US, notably in the enactment of the Digital Millennium Copyright Act 1988 that protects technical controls against the act of circumvention it is noticeable how these standards are coming together.

The influence of these measures has been, and will be, profound. The US and Europe between them support the most active entertainment industries, and thus those that are particularly affected by copyright issues on the Internet. The Copyright Directive will affect domestic legislation in fifteen Member States initially, and a number of others in due course should the Community enlarge. The WCT, where the negotiators were influenced strongly by the debate that had already taken place in the US and the EU, will provide the benchmark for many other countries in the protection of creative works. The broad standard for protection at international, regional and individual State level appears to have been set, and that is for increasing protection for creative works. The reason given is to ensure that the Internet will continue to develop apace and to facilitate trade in intellectual products.

The result does, however, seem to be a move away from the traditional idea of balancing private and public interests to an emphasis on private property rights. That in turn leaves open the question as to what rights

[45] Copyright Directive, Art 7.

there might be to access 'public' information, and how that information might thereafter be used.

(a) What Status for Public Data (Definition, Free Access, Market Price, etc)?

Public data is not defined in any of the instruments discussed above. Looking to the traditional theories of copyright in the Anglo-American tradition public data could be defined in two ways. First, it could mean information that exists (facts, data, etc) and which is collected as a function of public bodies, for instance Government departments in pursuit of their statutory functions. Or secondly, public data could mean those elements of existing creative works over which historically the owner of the copyright in the work has not been able to exert control. This is normally defined as 'the public domain'. For the purposes of this discussion, the second meaning will be taken.

In the UK, the public domain is made up of all those elements of creative and non-creative works that are beyond ownership of the right holder, and over which the right holder has historically not been able to exert control. The public domain is thus one expression of the balance that has been struck between absolute property rights in creative works, and the commons. The public domain contains all those works, parts of works, ideas, facts, uncreative material, and other limitations on the property right and upon which authors may draw upon in fashioning new creative works, critiquing existing works, or simply using and enjoying ownership of a work.

Specifically in the UK, those parts beyond ownership of the copyright holder, and over which the owner has been unable to exert control, include works on which copyright protection has expired, unoriginal works (data, facts), ideas, existing works which are used for the purposes of fair dealing, parts of works which are insubstantial and the copying of which does thus not infringe the rights of the existing owner. In addition, the exhaustion doctrine contributes to the public domain. Not by allowing copying from existing works, but by allowing a free flow and movement of works throughout defined territories unhampered by right holder control.

(b) The Price of the Public Domain

One issue that is often discussed in relation to the public domain on the Internet concerns the price of access and use. One body of opinion believes that such access and use should be free. However, even in the non-Internet world access to works protected by copyright and thus to the public domain element of those works has, in the main, never been free in the sense in that at some point, a payment has to be made. If a book is borrowed, the person from whom it is obtained will have already paid the book store for the copy of that book.[46] If a copy of an article from a journal is made, for the purposes of research and private study, the library will already have paid for the copy of the journal. The publisher of a book, may have to deposit a number of copies with the National Library of Scotland and other copyright libraries, and thus make them available to be consulted by others. But the library is already paid for through public funding. In many countries, private copying is funded through an uplift on the price of the blank tape or CD.[47] Exhibition in public galleries is supported through public funding, and an entrance fee may have to be paid. The BBC is funded though the television licence fee. Cable or satellite television depends on subscription charges. An entry fee may be required for a cinema or theatre. Operators of web sites who stream music may have to pay a fee for that service.[48] Those who rent a work are likely to have to pay for the privilege.[49] Whatever payment is made might be immediate, in the sense of having to hand over cash, or further removed, in the sense of being supported by taxes, or spread out over a longer term, as paying the license fee for the BBC in instalments. In each case a payment is required.

However, the requirement that a payment be made for access to and use of parts of a work in the public domain sits uncomfortably with notions of creative authorship and freedom of speech. Certainly payment for access does, in essence, represent a shift in the cost to be paid at some point, but in so doing it appears to become a '*per use*' or '*per idea*' cost rather than a '*per copy*' cost.[50] For a *consumer* of creative works disseminated over this Internet, this may not be seen to be an issue. A consumer tends to want to do little more than to enjoy a work for which a fair price should be paid.

[46] Lessig, 'Code and Other Laws of Cyberspace' (1999), 139. 'Today, when you buy a book, you may do any number of things with it. You can read it once or 100 times. You can lend it to a friend. You can Xerox pages in it or scan it into your computer. You can burn it, use it as a paper weight or you can sell it. You can store it on your shelf and never once open it'.

[47] French Intellectual Property Code Book III Title 1. In the US payment has to be made on all digital home recording devices Audio Home Recording Act 1992 USC 17 Chapter 10. *Recording Industry Ass'n of America Inc. v Diamond Multimedia Sys Inc.* 29 F Supp 2d 624

[48] Digital Performance Right in Sound Recordings Act of 1995 17 USC ss 106(6) and 114 and Digital Millennium Copyright Act 1998. See generally Spaulding *Copyright Protection of Music on the* Move <http://eon.law.harvard.edu/mp3/> *UMG Recordings Inc v MP3.com Inc* US District Court, SDNY (Rakoff J), 4 May 2000, <http://www.nysd.uscourts.gov/courtweb/pdf/00-04756.pdf>.

[49] For the position in the EU see EC Directive on Rental, Lending and Related Rights 92/100 UK law gives rental and lending rights in literary, dramatic, musical and most artistic works, films and sound recordings. CDPA s 18A. Rental is the temporary provision of copies 'for direct or indirect economic or commercial advantage' on terms that they will or may be returned. Thus electronic provision is excluded. WB Cornish, *Intellectual Property*, para 11.28.

[50] See Spoor, 'The Copyright Approach to Copying on the Internet', in PB Hugenholtz (ed), *The Future of Copyright in the Digital Environment* (Dordrecht: Kluwer, 1996), 67.

But perhaps critically for the re-use of a work, whether for freedom of speech, or for the purposes of developing new works, the cost may represent a charge for access to and use of the public domain.

However, it is appreciated that the answer to the conundrum is far from obvious. Free access to surf, and listen to, works on the Internet, would at a stroke, solve the tensions associated with metering and charging for the public domain, and ensure that those elements were freely available for the purposes of freedom of information, freedom of speech, and for re-use in creating new works. But mandating for free access is not viable option. Consider the news and information gathering company, Reuters.[51] That company recently announced the intention to develop the Internet side of their business: to make available information over the Internet, by e-mail and on their web site. If Reuters were obliged to make this information available for all to read, they would not be able to receive a return on their investment.[52] And that will be true of countless other companies. If payment cannot be obtained to view, then it is possible (although not necessarily the case) that information gathering and dissemination will be reduced.[53] As one commentator has noted: 'to suppose that [the uncalculating exchange of ideas] . . . will supplant the need for informational, educational and entertainment material which is generated upon the expectation of a market return is the stuff of dreams.'[54]

The discussion above perhaps gives a flavour of the difficult issues that face those who might wish to gain access to works considered in the public domain, when faced with technological controls guarding access to those works and the demand for a payment in return for access and use of those works.

It would appear that given the new framework that has developed to protect creative works there is no compulsion on the right holder to permit free access to a work, nor free use of those elements in the public domain. Thus, market forces are likely to have the greatest impact in the field of

[51] <http://www.reuters.com>.

[52] One could try and make distinctions in the mode of delivery of the information. For instance, there would be no obligation to give free access to information sent in e-mails—only to information on web sites. But this exercise which seeks to concentrate on technology specific solutions would soon be surpassed by advances in technology, which might render any such distinctions otiose. This writer is not advocating that information in e-mails should be free for all to read. Rather the argument is that if you want to raise distinctions on such things as 'push' or 'pull' technology (one of the differences between e-mails and web sites) then you have to be very sure that the technology will remain the same. Information gatherers might otherwise be tempted to call a web site an e-mail. Technology develops far to fast for technology specific solutions.

[53] Sherwood Edwards, 'The Redundancy of Originality' (1994) *IIC*, vol 25, 658 at 670 arguing that the refusal to grant property rights in facts results in fewer new facts being collected and made available on the market. On the other hand it may lead to wider dissemination of what is already there.

[54] WB Cornish, *Intellectual Property*, para 9-44.

access and use, tempered perhaps only by the threat of the application of competition law to restrictive practices such as excessive pricing or refusal to supply notably where the right holder is in a dominant position.

B. New Informational Works and the Internet

New tools enable the creation of new informational works. What should be the legal regime of these new works? Should one take into account traditional criteria such as originality, intellectual efforts and destination? Should the title in the works belong to the producer rather than to the author? Should one set up a new regime for multimedia works? (Issue of collective works and composite works under the authors' rights systems.)

The discussion above has focussed on the copyright regime in the UK, and drawn on the developments at a regional and International level. What has not yet been mentioned, but which is a development important for the discussion in this section, is the relatively recent legislation introduced at an EU level and implemented in Member States designed to protect compilations of data (databases) (new informational works in the definition above?) and their makers. This is significant for this discussion as both search engines and web pages (discussed below) fall under the definition of a database.

Many databases may be made available over the Internet in electronic form. The legal on-line services provided by the publishers Butterworths (Lexis) and Sweet & Maxwell (Westlaw) being good examples. In addition, as will be argued, a web site consisting of an amalgam of creative works protected by copyright, and information not so protected could itself fall under the definition of a database.

1. Databases: Historical Development

Signatory states to the Berne Convention[55] have been required to accord copyright protection to 'collections' of literary works 'which by reason of the selection and arrangement of their contents constitute intellectual creations'. The TRIPs Agreement[56] provides that 'Compilations of data or other material, whether in machine readable or other form, which by reason of the selection or arrangement of their contents constitute intellectual creations, shall be protected as such.'[57] Attempts were made at the time

[55] Berne Convention Art 2(5).

[56] TRIPs Agreement Art 10(2).

[57] The TRIPs Agreement specifies that the copyright protection for compilations 'shall not extend to the data or material itself', Art 10(2), and that 'copyright protection shall extend to expressions and not to ideas, procedures, methods of operation or mathematical concepts as such' Art 9(2).

of negotiation of the WCT to provide for an International Treaty dealing with the protection of databases. However, it was not possible to do more than agree a broad statement for inclusion in the WCT:[58] 'compilations of data or other material in any form which by reason of the selection or arrangement of their contents are intellectual creations are to be protected as such'; but this 'protection does not extend to the data or the material itself and is without prejudice to any copyright subsisting in the data or material contained in the compilation'.[59] Negotiations are ongoing at WIPO for a treaty specifically on the protection of databases.[60]

2. *Recent Initiatives*

In 1994 there was a move in the EU to increase legal protection accorded to databases: notably, to provide a right against the unauthorised extraction and re-utilisation of the contents of the database. Protection under both the Berne Convention and the TRIPs Agreement was considered to extend to the selection and arrangement of the material, but not to the material in the database itself. A number of cases from member states in the EU yielded inconsistent results as to whether the contents could be protected by copyright. The UK was considered as having such a low requirement of originality, that it was possible to protect contents of at least some databases. In other European states, such protection was not assured because the requirement of originality is higher.[61]

In 1996, the EU enacted the Database Directive.[62] The main justifications for its introduction, included a recognition of the increasing importance of a database as a repository of information, in particular in the electronic era where many are made available on line,[63] together with an acknowledgement that investment, whether in time and effort or financial resources, was needed to compile and maintain a database.[64] This investment should therefore be protected to prevent unconnected parties from

[58] WIPO Copyright Treaty Agreed Statements of the Diplomatic Conference WIPO Doc 226 (E) (1997) Geneva.

[59] WCT Treaty Art 5.

[60] <http://www.wipo.int>.

[61] There was a disparity in protection of databases throughout the member states. In many member states a database was not considered as having sufficient literary merit or originality to warrant protection. For example, Belgium and Luxembourg limited protection of databases to collections of artistic and literary works, but did not afford protection to compilations of facts. Germany and Italy required a collection of facts to be a personal intellectual creation in its own right before protection would be afforded; whereas the UK afforded full copyright protection to compilation of facts so long as the low requirement of skill labour and judgement is expended.

[62] Directive 96/9/EC of 11 Mar on the Legal Protection of Databases; 1996 OJ L77/20. This followed on the action plan set out by the Commission in 1991 COM (90) 584 final 17/1/1991 in which the European Commission proposed to harmonise national laws within the EU on the legal protection of databases.

[63] Database Directive Recitals 9 and 10.

[64] Database Directive Recital 11.

appropriating the contents of the database, and using those contents for their own needs without compensating the original compiler.

Database is defined broadly in the Directive: 'a collection of independent works, data or other materials arranged in a systematic or methodical way and individually accessible by electronic or other means.'[65] Protection under the Database Directive is in two parts: copyright protection is granted for the structure of the database so long as it represents the author's own intellectual creation, a standard drawn from the Berne Convention.[66] A new *sui generis* (database right) right for the contents of the database is enacted in addition. The rights arising by way of copyright in the structure of the database follow the existing rights under the law of copyright. By contrast, the right given under the database right is to the maker of the database, and is to prevent the unauthorised extraction and/or utilisation of the contents of the database.[67] Extraction means the permanent or temporary transfer of all or a substantial part of the contents of a database to another medium by any means or any form.[68] Extraction concentrates on the copying of the contents of a database, even if only temporarily from one form to another. An example would be running a CD ROM on a computer and bringing images on to the screen. By contrast, re-utilisation means making available to the public all or a substantial part of the contents of the database by the distribution of copies by renting, on-line or other forms of transmission. The re-utilisation right thus focuses on the subsequent transmission and distribution of the information, following on the act of extraction. The Database Directive refers only to the extraction and re-utilisation of substantial parts of the database. The taking of insubstantial parts will not infringe this right. However, the repeated and systematic extraction and/or re-utilisation of insubstantial parts, where in conflict with the normal exploitation of the database, and which unreasonably prejudice the legitimate interest of the maker, are then not permitted.[69] The Directive allows a number of exceptions to infringement of the database right. A lawful user may extract insubstantial parts of the contents of a database for any purpose;[70] or a substantial part for the purposes of illustration for teaching and scientific research.[71] Substantial parts may also be extracted

[65] Database Directive Art 1.2 CDPA s 3A.
The focus on the economic interests of the compiler of the database are reminiscent of the philosophies followed by the Chicago Kent school: property rights are required for economic efficiency.

[66] Berne Convention Art 2(5).

[67] Database Directive Art 7. 1. The Copyright and Rights in Database Regulations 1997 SI 1997/3032 (hereafter the Database Regulations) 16.

[68] Database Directive Art 7.2. Database Regulations 12(1).

[69] Database Directive Art 7.5. Database Regulations 16(2).

[70] Database Directive Art 8. Database Regulations 16(1) and 19(1).

[71] Database Regulations 20(1)(b) Database Directive Art 9 (b).

and re-utilised for the purposes of public security or an administrative or judicial procedure.[72] The last two of these provisions are permissive and not mandatory. In the UK, the main exception[73] incorporated into domestic law, is that the database right is not infringed by fair dealing with a substantial part of its contents, if they are extracted (but not re-utilised) for the purpose of illustration for teaching or research, and not for any commercial purpose. The source must be indicated.[74]

Copyright in the structure of the database lasts for 70 years after the death of the author.[75] The database right expires at the end of the period of 15 years from the end of the year in which the database was completed[76]or 15 years from the point at which it was made available to the public.[77] But where there has been a substantial change to the database, including one which results from the accumulation of successive additions, deletions or alterations resulting from substantial new investment, then that is to be considered as a new database and thus qualify for its own protection. A database qualifies for the database right where there has been substantial investment in obtaining verifying or presenting the contents of the database.[78] There is no requirement for originality. Rather, it is the investment that is protected. Hence, the owner or maker of the database and the person who qualifies for the database right is the person who takes the initiative in obtaining, verifying or presenting the contents of a database, and who assumes the risk of investing in the creation of the database.[79]

As a result of the implementation of the Database Directive, there is now quite a complicated structure of protection surrounding databases. A database may consist of a compilation of information some of which is not protected by the law of copyright, and some creative works that are. These creative works will still be protected by copyright. In addition, the database right will subsist in the collection as a whole. If the structure represents the author's intellectual creation, then copyright protection will also attach to that structure.

As suggested, the definition of a database is sufficiently broad to encompass web sites, which can be made up of both creative works, protected by copyright, and works not so protected. A web site is generally made up of a collection of independent works, such as articles protected by literary copyright, and pictures protected by artistic copyright. In addition there is

72 Database Regulations 20(2) and Schedule 1 Database Directive Art 9(c).

73 Databases Regulations 20(b).

74 There are a number of public interest exceptions in Schedule 1 of the Database Regulations.

75 CDPA s 3(1)(d) and 12(2).

76 Database Directive Art 10 Database Regulations 17.

77 Database Directive Art 10(2) Database Regulations 17(2).

78 Database Directive Art 7 Database Regulations 13.

79 Database Directive Art 7(1) Database Regulations 14(1).

likely to be data such as names and addresses, lists of products sold protected by the database right. The material incorporated will be arranged in a systematic way in the form of the presentation of the web site, as well as through the various levels within the site. The contents are individually accessible by electronic means, usually through the technique of hypertext linking. Web sites are thus likely to qualify for the added tier of protection of the database right. Given the expansive definition of a database, it must be questionable as to whether new rights should be introduced for multimedia works. However, that might depend on the outcome of a reference made to the ECJ by the UK Court of Appeal.

The first reported case in the UK on infringement of the database right was heard in the Patents Court on 9 February 2001 and subsequently appealed. In, *British Horseracing Board Ltd and others v William Hill Organisation Limited*[80] the question to be determined related to William Hill's (WH) extraction and re-use of information about horse racing fixtures from a database compiled by the British Horseracing Board (BHB). BHB compiles a database comprising of information supplied by owners, trainers and others connected with the racing industry, including names of horses, details of registered owners, racing colours and pre-race information. The information is licensed to a number of different organisations, including a company called Satellite Information Services who uses the information for specified purposes, including onward transmission to subscribers, among whom is WH. WH used this data in developing a bookmaking business over the Internet, for which there was no authorisation from either BHB or Satellite Information Services. BHB sued WH for unauthorised extraction and re-utilisation of a substantial part of the contents of its database. The court found that there had indeed been both unauthorised extraction and re-utilisation of a substantial part of the contents of BHB's database, and this was so even if WH changed the data used on its website.

The Court of Appeal[81] lifted the injunction granted in the Patents Court but has referred a number of questions to the ECJ. The Court of Appeal broadly endorsed the approach taken by the lower court but was concerned that there had been no definitive ruling to date from the ECJ concerning the interpretation of the directive. This was made all the more pertinent by rulings from courts in two other Member States, Holland and Sweden. In *NV Holdingmaatschappij de Telegraf v Nederlandse Omroep Stichting*,[82] the Court of Appeal of The Hague refused to hold that broadcasting listings were apt to attract database right as there was no evidence of substantial investment in their compilation. In *Fixtures Marketing Limited v AB*

80 [2001] 2 C.M.L.R. 12; [2001] RPC 31.
81 [2001] EWCA Civ 1268; 24059 2001 WL 825162.
82 99/165, 30 Jan 2001.

Svenska Spel[83] the Gotland City Court found that although there had been substantial investment in the production of football fixture lists there was no infringement of the database right. The court considered that the right only encompassed 'reprinting or copying the information in the same or a similar compilation'. In other words, the right did not extend to the underlying information.

The actual questions to be referred to the ECJ by the Court of Appeal have, at the time of writing, yet to be drafted, but it appears that they may be quite wide. One of the most important is likely to concern the 'databaseness' of the compilation. Both the lower court and Court of Appeal referred to the argument made by counsel for WH in this regard. This argument was that what is protected by the database right is the 'database-ness' of the collection of information; that is, that the materials are arranged in a systematic or methodical way, and are individually accessible. Any acts that do not make any use of the arrangement of the contents of the database, nor take advantage of the way in which the maker has rendered the contents individually accessible, cannot infringe the database right. In other words, it is not the *contents* of the database that are protected, but the way in which the database is put together. This is a crucial question concerning the protection of databases. Commentators on the database right have generally been of the view that it is the *contents* that are protected by the new right, and not the *form*. As such, the Directive involves a significant expansion of protection in this area. All manner of works, or parts of works which, for whatever reason, do not attract copyright protection could attract database right if the requirements for investment in making the compilation are met. Equally, works that do attract copyright protection can also acquire database protection if incorporated into that type of product. If the ECJ ultimately decides that it is merely the form that attracts protection, it is hard to see how that would add to existing protection. Copyright already subsists in the structure – or viewed another way, the form—of a database so long as it is original. Equally limiting database right to the *form* would seem to run counter to those Recitals of the Directive that refer to the investment in collating the information. On the other hand, should the ECJ decide that it is merely the form that is protected, the implications for the public domain are positive. The contents of the database would receive no greater protection that already available by way of copyright. The author would merely be prevented from extracting or re-utilising a substantial part of the form.

[83] T 99-99. 11 Apr 2000.

3. *Search Engines*

There are many examples of search engines on the Internet. Currently among the most popular are <http://www.Google.com> and <http://www.askJeeves.com>.

These search engines trawl though web pages on the Internet and compile lists of web pages and their content. Much of what is collated by the search engine is taken from key words (meta tags) from websites. When a search request is made by a surfer the search engine returns relevant information based on that which has been collated. The search engine is thus a collection of facts, data, information and other relevant information collected in such a form that it may be returned to the user in a useful form. The search engine itself may be a software program, and thus currently protected by copyright. However, when considered with the contents, it falls under the definition of a database as discussed above.

Given that the search engine falls under the definition of a database (and note that there is no requirement for originality in the compilation for database protection to attach), then the economic rights fall to the maker of that database, that is, the person who is responsible for the financial investment in compiling the database. The right is thus given to the *maker* to prevent the extraction and re-utilisation of a substantial part of that database for a period of 15 years from its creation. In the case of an internet based search engine (eg. Google.com) the maker will be able to claim that period of 15 years should be extended at least to the extent that the database is continually updated and the investment is considered as a substantial new investment in that database.

Given that the database maker has the right to prevent the extraction and re-utilisation of substantial parts, and the repeated extraction of insubstantial parts, then the maker has the right to charge users for the use of that database. However, such is the business model of this 'new' form of exploitation on the Internet, it is not the user who is charged for using the search engine, but rather those who advertise with the company, or those who buy key-words or advertisements who ensure its financial viability.

Are new rights needed for database makers? In light of the above discussion, the answer must be no. The maker is given all the rights necessary to extract an economic return from users of the database if so required. It is not the lack of a legal basis on which to charge that inhibits the makers from extracting a payment from users, but rather the likelihood that users would not pay turning instead to alternative free search engines. Equally, the maker of the search engine is at liberty to prevent the extraction and re-utilisation of a substantial part of the database, or repeated extraction and re-utilisation of insubstantial parts. Once again, it is not the lack of a legal basis that prevents the maker from exercising these rights, but rather a perception that if such rights were exercised, then the basis on which the business is set up would collapse: it is unlikely, at least at present, that those using search engines would pay to do so.

4. Web Pages

As may be apparent from the preceding discussion, web pages currently receive protection in a number of different ways in the UK. Not only does the law of copyright apply to elements of the website, but a website as a whole is apt to fall under the definition of a database, and thus the database right also applies to protect the site.

5. Copyright

Web sites may contain literary, dramatic, musical and artistic works within their pages, which would be protected by copyright. This would be the case whether those parts of a site were created specifically for and directly as part of a web site, or if they pre-existed the compilation of the website. Sound recordings, moving images (films) may also be incorporated into a web site. A good example of a multi media web site is that of the BBC at <http://www.bbc.co.uk>. This site contains elements which would be protected by copyright, whether as authors copyright (literary, dramatic, musical and artistic works), or as a neighbouring right (sound recordings). These rights would give to the owner of the copyright the right to prevent reproduction unless authorised.

6. Database Right

As well as being protected by the law of copyright a web site, and indeed an individual web page (a multimedia work) is a database within the definition discussed above. Therefore the rights to prevent unauthorised extraction and re-utilisation also apply to the maker of the database (the person responsible for making the investment in the web site).

In analysing the existing protection for a web site, taken individually and as a whole, there seems to be no case for justifying either new or increased protection for the creator and owner of the copyright and/or the maker of the database. Indeed, when the above regime of protection is coupled with the protection of technical measures that control access to a web site, and which could be used to prevent such access except at the behest of either the copyright owner or the database maker, the case is rather the opposite—that there is too much protection for this type of product. Instead of increasing protection, the argument might rather be made for increased *access* and *use* rights in relation to the public domain to ensure that 'legitimate' re-use of information may take place in the interests of freedom of speech and future creation.

7. Hypertext Links

Navigation of web sites, and the web pages which go to make up a web site, is accomplished seamlessly by hypertext links that enable a surfer to move from one web page to another, and from one web site to another. A hypertext link is thus an address of another web site that the surfer can click on, and move to that other site to retrieve that information stored there. Many web sites have hypertext links buried within their structure, or collated in particular sector pointing the reader to other sites that may be of relevance and interest.

In certain circumstances the use of hypertext links has aroused much passion. This is most often the case when the links from one site are directed into the body of the second site, thus by-passing the home page. One early case arose in Scotland: *Shetland Times Ltd v Wills.*[84] *The Shetland News*, an electronic newspaper based in the Shetland Islands,[85] copied the headlines from the *Shetland Times*, a hard copy newspaper also based in the Shetland Islands, which had an electronic version.[86] *The Shetland News* used the headlines to link directly to the story on the *Shetland Times* web pages. The inclusion of the headlines was challenged by the *Shetland Times* as an infringement of copyright in the headlines, and an infringement under the Copyright Designs and Patents Act 1988 as the inclusion of an item in a cable programme service.[87] An interim interdict was granted, but just before the full hearing had begun, the parties reached settlement.

Linking has also been challenged in the US in *Bernstein v JC Penney Inc.*[88] Bernstein argued that JC Penney had infringed his copyright in photographs of Elizabeth Taylor by maintaining a link on their web site through which (via several other links[89]) copies of the photographs could be viewed. The copies were ultimately held on a server maintained by a Swedish University. It appeared that there was a history of difficult relationships between Bernstein and JC Penney. Bernstein had been commissioned to take the photographs for the purpose of advertising Passion Perfume (manufactured by Arden). The agreement had broken down—

[84] 1997 SC 316.

[85] <http://www.shetland-news.co.uk>.

[86] <http://www.shetland-times.co.uk>.

[87] CDPA s 20.

[88] No 98-2958-R (CD CA dismissal 22 Sept (1998). <http://eon.law.harvard.edu/property/metatags/Linking1.html>.

[89] Arden pointed to the links that would need to be followed to reach the Swedish web site: from Penney home page to Taylor Passion part of the Penney site; to biography part of the passion site containing information about Taylor; to work on screen; to the IMDB site; to FTP a link on the IMBD; site that took the user to the Swedish site through which she could access the infringing photographs.

acrimoniously. Bernstein argued that Penney had deliberately designed the site so that visitors would be able to see the two disputed images of Taylor, and thus Penney and Arden would benefit from their use without paying a royalty. The Californian Federal Judge dismissed copyright infringement allegations.

It appears to be the general view of courts in different jurisdictions, and of commentators, that linking could not, of itself, constitute an infringement of copyright.[90] However, a recent case from the US indicates that linking may, in certain circumstances, be unlawful under the provisions of the US Digital Millennium Copyright Act 1998 (DMCA). The case in question is *Universal City Studios Inc v Shawn Reimerdes.*[91] This case had its origins in Norway where a student, Jon Johansen, wrote a program (DeCSS) which could overcome the encryption (CSS) which limited access to Digital Video Discs (DVDs). The purpose of overcoming the control (it was alleged) was to allow DVDs to be run on the Linux operating system, rather than Windows, for which the DVDs were intended. However, once the control mechanism was overcome, the DVDs could be copied at will. The DeCSS program was copied on to web pages belonging to *inter alia*, Eric Corley (alias Emmanuel Goldstein) at <http://www.2600.com>. The major motion picture studios operated with some speed. A case was brought against Eric Corley and others, who the studios accused of violating the anti-circumvention provisions of the DMCA by making details of the DeCSS code available on the web site, and by linking to other web sites containing the same code. This encryption technique, and the legal protection surrounding these controls will be examined in Chapter 4 of this study. However, for this discussion on linking, one of the actions taken by the defendants was to link to sites which contained information about and copies of the DeCSS program. One of the questions to come before the court was whether this technique of linking to sites containing this program was unlawful. The judge in the District court compared the technique of linking to sites containing the program, which itself was unlawful, to the spread of a plague. In these cases, it was not possible to prevent further spread of the disease simply by treating the source. All manifestations had to be controlled. As a result, there are times when linking could be found to

[90] DL Burk, 'Proprietary Rights in Hypertext Linkages' 1998 (2) *The Journal of Information, Law and Technology* (JILT). <http://elj.warwick.ac.uk/jilt/intprop/98_2burk/>. Norderhaug/Oberding, 'Designing a Web of Intellectual Property' (1995), *Computer Networks and ISDN Systems*, 27 (6), 1037, 1042. Lemley, 'Dealing with Operlapping Copyrights on the Internet', 1997, 22 *University of Dayton Law Review*, 548–85, 565.

Hardy, 'Computer RAM 'Copies': Hit or Myth?' (1997), 22 *University of Dayton Law Review*, 449. MA O'Rourke, 'Fencing Cyberspace: Drawing Borders in A Virtual World' (1998), 82 *Minnesota Law Review*, 609.

[91] 111 F Supp 2d 294 (SDNY 2000). Amended final judgement: 111 F Supp. 2d 346 (SDNY 2000).

infringe the terms of the DMCA. The court said that the relevant factors to be taken into account included whether those responsible for the link knew that the offending material is on the linked-to site; that they knew that it is circumvention technology that may not lawfully be offered; and the link is created or maintained for the purpose of disseminating that technology.

On appeal,[92] the main focus of the arguments were directed towards the constitutionality of the DMCA: was the DMCA consistent with freedom of speech as laid down in the First Amendment to the US Constitution? Specifically it was argued that outlawing linking amounted to a content-based restriction on speech, one that if to be upheld 'demand(s) the highest level of scrutiny',[93] but the requirements for which were not present in this case.

On the effect of the DMCA, its application to linking and interaction with the First Amendment, the Appeals Court were not prepared to accept that the 'rigorous' test articulated by the lower court was necessary. That Court did however reject the argument that an *intention* to cause harm was required. Ultimately a choice had to be made between two alternatives:

> either tolerate some impairment of communication in order to permit Congress to prohibit decryption that may lawfully be prevented, or tolerate some decryption in order to avoid some impairment of communication.[94]

These public policy issues were not for the court to decide, but for Congress. For the purposes of the present case, the Appeals Court found that the lower court's injunction including those parts prohibiting linking to sites containing DeCSS were consistent with the First Amendment. Thus the injunction including that part relevant to the prohibition on linking was upheld.

Although this case does not say that linking itself is an infringement of copyright in the US, it does say that linking to websites that contain information on how decrypt controls that surround creative works can result in liability under the DMCA.

Although this is a US case, it may have important implications for those countries that are signatory states to the WCT, and particularly Member States of the EU. As may be apparent from the discussion above on the legal protection of technical controls, the standard of protection chosen in the EU Copyright Directive is similar to that to be found in the US Digital

[92] *Universal City Studios v Eric Corley* US Court of Appeals 2nd Circuit 28 Nov 2001. <http://www.2600.com/news/112801-files/UniversalBrief_3.pdf>.

[93] 'If laws must be struck down when they outlaw advocacy of the "duty, necessity, or propriety of violence" *(Brandenburg v Ohio*, 395 US 444, 447, 89 SCt 1827 (1969)) or the burning of the American flag *(Texas v Johnson,* 491 US 397, 109 SCt 2533 (1989)), mere reference to a computer program alleged to circumvent copyright or access controls clearly may not be enjoined. The First Amendment does not countenance such a prior restraint.' For full details see Amicus Curiae filed by the Harvard Openlaw forum at <http://eon.law.harvard.edu/openlaw/DVD/amicus.html>.

[94] Ibid, n 238.

Millennium Copyright Act 1998. Thus, when these provisions are implemented into national laws of Member States, those who link to sites containing information details of decryption programs may also run foul of the law.

The question then arises as to whether new rights are needed in hypertext links, or to the practice of linking to sites. For example, it might be possible to give to the website owner a veto against others linking to the site. The answer here again has to be no. As has been discussed above, it does seem possible that linking may be found to be an infringement of copyright (at least in Scotland), although that is far from clear. However, a web site designer would simply have to place technical restrictions on deep linking thus requiring the surfer following a link from another site to enter by the home page. It does not seem appropriate to add a further tier of regulation by making the practice of linking unlawful unless permission was given. Such a requirement may inhibit the flow of information, opportunities for free speech and freedom of information together with the chance to link disparate parcels of information to form a coherent whole, all of which the Internet was designed to support.

8. Domain Names

A discussion on domain names leads away from copyright into the realm of trademark law.

A domain name is part of the address of the location of a site on the Internet. For instance harrods.com is the domain name of the London department store, Harrods. The portion of the address taken by 'harrods' is sometimes the part of the address that equates to the registered (or unregistered) trademark of the person seeking to use the domain name: for instance, virgin or caesars-palace. The next part is the top level domain (TLD). .com, .net and .org are all generic Top Level Domains (gTLDs). .uk, .de and .fr are Country Code Top Level Domains (ccTLDs).

Disputes have arisen over ownership of domain names for a number of reasons. The first is because domain names have been treated as trademarks. Thus those who own these marks feel themselves 'entitled' to ownership of the domain name that equates to the mark.

Secondly, they have arisen because trademark law is territorial and the Internet is global. Thus, there may be two or more business in different territories that own the same mark (registered or unregistered) registered or used in relation to the same or similar goods and services. However, on the Internet no two domain names can be identical. Therefore there can only be one microsoft.com; one avnet.co.uk; one marksandspencer.com; one prince.com, or one harrods.com. There may, however, be two or more business in the same country or in different countries equally entitled to the use of a name, but only one name of a particular variation is permitted on the Internet. prince.com is a good example in that it was the subject of a dispute between Prince plc in the UK and Prince Sports Inc. in the US. Prince plc registered the domain name first and was challenged by Prince Sports Inc.[95] The name remains with Prince plc.

Thirdly, there are the cases where Internet participants, with a degree of entrepreneurial spirit, have registered domain names where very often the name is the same as or very similar to the trading name or registered trademark of a company that is well known or famous or which has a reputation. Generally the intent has been to do one of two things. One option might be to offer it to the owner of the registered trademark or trading company in return for some payment. Alternatively, if it is a name that is similar to the well known name, such as porschegirls.com, the intention might be to use the domain name in an effort, not necessarily to confuse, but to draw people to the site. In other words to draw on the magnetism that attaches to the mark. These types of disputes are generally known as 'cybersquatting'.

Finally there are the cases where the owners of well known or famous marks have aggressively pursued policies to prevent other Internet participants from using any rendition of a name that includes or alludes to their registered trademark, in some cases quite unjustifiably. These cases are sometimes termed 'reverse domain name hijacking'.

Two main legal weapons have been used in these battles, the first is the law of registered trademarks, and the second is passing off. National courts in many different territories have been called on to hear disputes concerning domain names. In the UK there have been surprisingly few reported cases, but that is perhaps because disputes tend to be settled out of court. In relation to Cybersquatting cases, the UK courts have had little difficulty in requiring the cybersquatter to return the domain name to the mark holder. In British Telecommunications and Others v One in a Million and Others[96] (One in a Million) a number of domain names including marksandspencer.com, bt.org, britishtelecommunication.net were registered by, among others, One in a Million. The case was decided primarily by looking to the law of passing off, and by some extension of existing principles, the court determined that by registering the domain names the defendants had created instruments of deception. Thus the domain names had to be handed back to the trademark and brand owners. In dealing with the registered trademark aspect, the court seems to have considered that the domain name itself was the trademark, observing that the domain names were registered to take advantage of the distinctive character and reputation of the

[95] *Prince plc v Prince Sports Group Inc.* [1998] FSR 21.
[96] 1999) 4 All ER 476, [1999] RPC 1.

marks, which was both unfair and detrimental. The relevant provision (section 10(3)) of the Trade Marks Act 1994 was therefore infringed. The court made clear its dislike of these practices and it is no doubt that it is the robust dismissal of the defendants arguments that have been relied upon in persuading other *cybersquatters* to give up domain names in appropriate circumstances.

Where the cases have concerned *domain name envy*, the courts have shown more sympathy to the person who has had the initiative to register the domain name first. This is illustrated in the case of *Avnet Inc v Isoact Limited (Avnet)*.[97] Avnet Inc a US company runs a business selling goods by catalogue and in so doing they carry advertisements for different manufacturers.[98] They registered the trademark 'Avnet' in the UK in class 35 for advertising and promotional services. Isoact Limited, by contrast is an Internet Service Provider with a particular interest in aviation. They use the words Aviation Network and Avnet in connection with their interests. Isoact Limited registered the domain name avnet.co.uk and allowed customers to display their own advertisements on their site. Avnet argued that Isoact infringed their registered trademark by using the word 'avnet' in their domain name. Avnet Inc. argued that the sign used by Isoact was identical to their registered mark and used in connection with identical goods and services which would fall foul of section 10(1) UK Trade Marks Act 1994 which prohibits the use of an identical sign with a registered mark for the identical goods and services for which the mark is registered. Therefore, looking to the specification of the goods and services, their registered trademark had been infringed. The court disagreed with Avnet. Judgement was given purely by looking to the terms of what was covered by the registration of the mark 'Avnet'. In substance it was decided that Isoact were not providing advertising and promotional services within class 35 of the trademark Register, but rather provided the services of an Internet Service provider. These activities would (if registered) probably fall within class 42. In other words, the services provided were different. Therefore there was no infringement under section 10(1). Therefore Isoact had a perfect right to keep and use the domain name.

The above cases do tend to illustrate that the UK courts at least have an appreciation of some of the nuances associated with domain names and charges of trademark infringement. However, it is a pity that there seems to be a general assumption, certainly in some cases, that a domain name and a trademark are synonymous. A domain name is merely an address of the location of a computer, although its use in some circumstances can result in

[97] [1998] FSR 16

[98] Jacob J doubted that this activity actually fell within class 35 of the trademark Register and thought the activity was more akin to retail sales, but did not decide the point.

a convergence between the two. Suffice it to say that on a national level, in disputes concerning the cc TLDs domestic courts have, over the years worked out some rules to allow co-existence of the two, and it would appear inappropriate at present to disturb this delicate balance by introducing new rights over domain names.

The position in relation to resolution of disputes concerning domain names registered in one of the gTLDs however differs. In recent years there have been significant changes in this area. The most common method of resolving domain name disputes in these gTLDs is through the Internet Corporation for Assigned Names and Numbers Uniform Dispute Resolution Process (ICANN UDRP) run though a series of accredited arbitrators. The dispute resolution policy is based on ICANN's rules which can be found on the ICANN website. It is not intended at this juncture to analyse the disputes in detail, but it is notable that since the inception of this arbitration process in late 1999, the four dispute resolution providers have between them heard over 4000 cases.

There are a number of commentators who are critical of the process, not only in relation to procedural unfairness,[99] but also in relation to substantive matters such as the lack of a coherent set of principles emerging from the cases; bias in favour of the 'large' trademark owner and away from the small business or individual; and inconsistent judgements arising from substantially similar facts.

It is understood that the UDRP process is under constant review by ICANN. In addition, WIPO is currently working on a programme of consultations aimed at widening the scope of the dispute resolution process to cover areas such as personal names.

What should be the legal regime of domain names? Given the rather fragile framework that has developed to date, both at national and international level, it would be unwise at this juncture to take individual action on a national level. Upsetting the frail construct on a national level may disturb the shaky edifice to the detriment of all the players. It is essential that critical analysis continues of the ICANN UDRP, and of decisions made at national level. As a consequence informed contributions can be made both at national and international (ICANN) level to the debate concerning the use of domain names. However, this is not the time to make radical changes to the legal regime surrounding domain names.

[99] See study by Michael Geist at <http://aix1.uottawa.ca/~geist/geistudrp.pdf>.

II. PROTECTION OF THE AUTHORS

A. *Authors and their Audience*

Should the exclusive rights recognised to the authors on their works be limited to take into account fair use and private copying? The issue of works put by the authors in the public domain (Free software etc).

1. *The Directive on the Information Society and the Digital Millennium Copyright Act*

(a) *Fair Use: The Directive on the Information Society (the Copyright Directive)*

One element of the public domain in the UK has been the fair dealing limitations (the place of private copying will be discussed below). These provisions allow an author to copy a substantial part of an existing work for specified purposes. These are criticism and review, research and private study and news reporting. As a result of the passing of the Copyright Directive, the shape of the existing UK fair dealing limitations will change when the Directive is implemented into national law.

The extent to which fair dealing should apply in the Internet environment has taxed regulators since the first Treaty, the WCT, dealing with dissemination of works over the Internet was negotiated in 1996. The formula from the Berne Convention expressing the circumstances under which the exclusive right of the author to control reproduction of a work may be limited, has been repeated in the WCT.[100] This Treaty permits Contracting Parties to provide: 'limitations of or exceptions to the rights granted to authors of literary and artistic works under [the WCT] in certain special cases that do not conflict with a normal exploitation of that work and do not unreasonably prejudice the legitimate interests of the author.'[101] Perhaps, concerned during negotiations that the Berne Convention might advocate wider exceptions than considered appropriate for the digital age, the WCT exhorts contracting parties when applying the Berne Convention to: 'confine any limitations of or exceptions to rights provided for therein to certain special cases that do not conflict with a normal exploitation of the work and do not unreasonably prejudice the legitimate interests of the author.'[102] But somewhat inconsistently, the WCT Agreed Statements [103] provide that Contracting Parties can: 'carry forward and appropriately extend into the digital environment limitations and exceptions in their national laws which have been considered acceptable under the Berne

[100] Art 10. [101] Art 10(1). [102] Art 10(2).
[103] Agreed Statement Concerning Art 10.

Convention' and to 'permit Contracting Parties to devise new exceptions and limitations that are appropriate in the digital network environment'. So while the Articles of the WCT might seem to suggest that the exceptions to the exclusive right of an author should be limited, the Agreed Statements seem rather to point the other way, that existing limitations and exceptions should be carried through to the Internet, and, if anything, extended.

B. The US

Among the first official documents to deal with the question of fair use for the Internet in the US was a report which came about as a result of an initiative by President Clinton to further the US Administration's goals for the National Information Infrastructure (NII).[104] Principles for government action were described in *NII Agenda for Action*[105] and *GII Agenda for Cooperation.*[106] The aim was 'to develop comprehensive telecommunications and information policies and programs that would promote the development of the NII and best meet the country's needs'. The task force was divided into three groups, one of which was the Working Group on Intellectual Property Rights.[107] The remit of the group was to examine the intellectual property implications of the NII, and make recommendations on any appropriate changes to US intellectual property law and policy.[108] The final report (the NII Report) focused primarily on copyright law and its application and effectiveness in the context of the Internet.[109]

[104] NII refers to the National Information Infrastructure, and is the term used for the Internet in the NII Report.

[105] Information Infrastructure Task Force, National Telecommunications and Information Administration, *National Information Infrastructure: Agenda for Action* (Sept 1993).

[106] Information Infrastructure Task Force, *Global Information Infrastructure: Agenda for Cooperation* (Feb 1995).

[107] Chaired by Assistant Secretary of Commerce and Commissioner of Patents and Trademarks Bruce A. Lehman.

[108] In the course of its work, the Working Group identified issues in other areas, such as defamation and obscenity, which were considered separately by the Information Policy Committee.

[109] The Committee stated 'The 'National Information Infrastructure', as it is discussed in this Report, encompasses digital, interactive services now available, such as the Internet, as well as those contemplated for the future. To make the analyses more concrete, however, the Working Group has, in many instances, evaluated the intellectual property implications of activity on the Internet, the superstructure whose protocols and rules effectively create (or permit the creation of) a 'network of networks'. This reflects neither an endorsement of the Internet nor a derogation of any other existing or proposed network or service that may be available via the NII, but, rather, an acknowledgment that a currently functioning structure lends itself more readily to legal analysis than a hypothetical construct based on future developments' At 8 n 5. The description of current US law in the NII Report has been questioned by some eminent writers. For example:

Boyle 'Intellectual Property Policy OnLine: A Young Person's Guide' (1996), 10 *Harv JL and Tech*, 47. JC Ginsburg 'Putting Cars on the Information Superhighway Authors Exploiters and Copyright in Cyberspace' (1995), 95 *Colum L Rev*, 1466. J Litman, 'The

The NII Report contained no general proposals for limiting or expanding the existing US fair use doctrine in the digital era apart from a recommendation to change some definitions for public libraries.[110] Much of the attention in the US has been directed to the question as to whether, and when, it might be lawful to circumvent a technical control to obtain access to the underlying work in order to exercise fair use. The question was raised in the NII Report, where the Committee opined that: 'if the circumvention device is primarily intended and used for legal purposes, such as fair use, the device would not violate the provision, because a device with such purposes and effects would fall under the "authorized by law" exemption.'[111] This would suggest that circumvention devices could be manufactured which would allow access to works, if the reason for access was to exercise fair use rights. There are suggestions in the NII Report that fair use would be limited in application on the Internet: 'technological means of tracking transactions and licensing will lead to reduced application and scope of the fair use doctrine.'[112] This suggests that because technical controls can track and monitor usage, so such use may be licensed. In other words, fair use is simply a manifestation of market failure, and on the Internet, the means to correct that market failure are available.

Because the debate has caused such controversy a study was carried out into the potential effect technical controls and anti-circumvention rules may have on the exercise of fair use.[113] The House Committee on Commerce on the Digital Millennium Copyright Act of 1998[114] provided that the prohibition against circumvention

> shall not apply to persons who are users of a copyrighted work which is in a particular class of works, if such persons are, or are likely to be adversely affected by virtue of such prohibition in their ability to make noninfringing uses of that particular class of works under this title.[115]

To ascertain whether there were any such 'class of works' which should be exempted from the prohibition against circumvention, the relevant

Exclusive Right to Read' (1994), 13 *Cardozo Arts & Ent LJ*, 29. Samuelson, *Wired* (Jan 1996), at 134. Loundy, 'Revising the Copyright Law for Electronic Publishing' <http://www.leepfrog.com/E-Law/revising-HyperT.html>. Copyright issues raised on the Internet in the US are also considered in depth in Hardy, *Project Looking Forward: Sketching the Future of Copyright in a Networked World* (US Copyright Office, 1998) final report <http://lcweb.loc.gov/copyright/reports>.

110 NII Report, 225. 111 Ibid, 164. 112 Ibid, 82.

113 DMCA ss 1201(a)(2) and 1201(b) were brought into force immediately. Section 1201(a)(1) was the focus of the inquiry.

114 HR Rep No 105-551, (1998), part 2, at 36

115 The full text of the Federal Register release and other related information is available at <http://www.loc.gov/copyright/1201/anticirc.html>.

section of the DMCA (section 1201(a)(1)(A))[116] was not to be brought into force until October 28 2000. During this time the Librarian of Congress was charged with making a determination as to which (if any) classes of works should be exempted.[117] After extensive consultations two classes of works were exempted from the prohibition on circumventing access controls. These are:

- Compilations consisting of lists of websites blocked by filtering software applications.
- Literary works, including computer programs and databases, protected by access control mechanisms that fail to permit access because of malfunction damage or obsoleteness.

During these consultations it had been argued that an exemption should be introduced to permit circumvention of access control measures for the purpose of accessing materials in the public domain, in particular where the use of that work might fall under the head of 'fair use'. However, the Librarian had difficulty with this proposal. The first problem was because the exemption was sought in respect of certain classes of users, or uses for certain purposes. This was beyond the scope of the Librarian's task that was to determine whether to exempt any particular class of works, and not to consider the use to which the work was to be put. Secondly, those who argued for the exemption were unable to demonstrate that they had been unable to engage in such uses because of *access* control measures. The concerns related to use of a work once accessed, rather than to failure to obtain access. In other words, the technological controls that prevent access to the underlying works did not thereby prevent non-infringing uses.

In relation to the second main fear, that access controls would result in a 'pay-per-view' business model, the Librarian pointed out that contributors to the debate had failed to show any hard evidence of the model in operation. There were merely 'speculative and alarmist' fears. What was more, such a pay per use model could be 'use facilitating'.[118] Consumers given the choice between paying $100 for permanent access to a work, and $2 for each individual occasion may prefer the latter. This in turn may make access to the work more widely available, thus enhancing use. 'The record in this proceeding does not reveal that 'pay-per-use' business models have,

[116] USC Title 17 s 1201(a)(1)(A) provides: (1)(A) 'No person shall circumvent a technological measure that effectively controls access to a work protected under this title. The prohibition contained in the preceding sentence shall take effect at the end of the 2-year period beginning on the date of the enactment of this chapter.'

[117] Federal Register, vol 65, no 209, Friday 27 2000. Rules and Regulations 37 CFR Part 201 Exemption to Prohibition on Circumvention of Copyright Protection Systems for Access Control Technologies; Final Rule.

[118] Ibid at 64564.

thus far, created the adverse impacts on the ability of users to make non-infringing uses of copyrighted works that would justify any exemptions from the prohibition on circumvention'. However, it was also hinted that: 'If such adverse impacts occur in the future, they can be addressed in a future rulemaking proceeding.'

There are two interesting points that arise from the results of this study. The first was that the focus was on *access* to works, and not on subsequent *use*. Thus, there is a recognition that these two steps are distinct and require separate consideration. The second point arises in relation to the 'pay-per-view' model highlighted by the Librarian. It is notable that it was argued that this model might facilitate use by *consumers*. Economic argument would suggest that it is correct. If all consumers pay a little, and there is a reduced risk of infringement and piracy, so the costs to the right holder and to the consumer can fall, while at the same time facilitating an increase in the numbers of works available. However, this does not address the position of the *author* whose interests differ from those of the consumer. A pay-per-view business model which in effect requires an author to pay for access to works for the purpose of fair use would not appear to be a model which encourages creativity.

C. The Copyright Directive

As compared with the US, there has been less vocal debate in the UK over the extent to which technical controls might alter fair dealing in relation to works made available over the Internet. There may be a number of reasons for this. One is that, by contrast with the US, the EU has proposed in the Copyright Directive that the fair dealing limitations for Member States be changed. The proposals have been made partly with the intention of harmonising laws of Member States,[119] and partly with the intention of limiting fair dealing on the Internet.[120] Focus has therefore been on these changes, rather than the interaction between fair dealing and technical controls. Another reason may lie in the differences in approach to fair dealing between the Civilian systems and the UK. As the exceptions in the Civilian systems are more specific, and in many cases their exercise may be subject to payment, so they lend themselves much more readily to be operated in conjunction with technological controls on access. The UK, in having broader categories, may be a lone voice in Europe in considering that there may be difficulties for the operation of fair dealing on the Internet.

The proposals for fair dealing in the Copyright Directive have undergone fundamental changes since first introduced. It appears that those involved

[119] Copyright Directive Recital 21. [120] Ibid Recitals 22 and 29.

in the negotiations in the EU may have been influenced by the debate in the US as to the effect that technical controls may have on the operation of fair dealing. In addition, participants in the negotiations for the Copyright Directive have had the opportunity to witness some of the litigation occurring in the US, in particular in relation to Napster and DeCSS. This may have had an effect on the shape of the proposals as they have developed.

D. Fair Dealing in the Copyright Directive: Permitted Reproductions

The Berne Convention three-step formula, permitting exceptions to be made to the exclusive right of authors in the reproduction of a work, has been repeated in the Copyright Directive,[121] but with one telling difference. The Berne Convention (and WCT) refer to rights of authors. By contrast, the Copyright Directive refers to the legitimate interests of authors and *right holders*. This phrase may have been used because the Copyright Directive is an attempt to deal with rights of authors and rights of neighbouring right holders, producers of phonograms, films, and broadcasting organisations. However, use of this terminology may depart from the standards found in other International Treaties. The Rome Convention has specific areas in which rights of phonogram producers might be limited, including for private use, and use solely for the purposes of teaching or scientific research.[122] This article in the Rome Convention was applied to phonogram producers in the TRIPs agreement.[123] What the effect of applying the 'authors' formula' to exceptions for neighbouring right holders will ultimately entail is not at all clear.

The Copyright Directive has extensive provisions relating to fair dealing. These are to be found in Article 5 and provide exceptions to the exclusive rights of reproduction,[124] communication to the public and making available to the public,[125] and distribution.[126] While it was not obvious at some points during the passage of the Copyright Directive, whether the limitations were designed to replace all existing fair dealing provisions in domestic legislation, it has now become clear that is the case.[127] Apart from a few examples,[128] the Copyright Directive is intended to provide a complete code for fair dealing both on the Internet and off.

Article 5.1 of the Copyright Directive exempts from the reproduction right temporary acts of reproduction which are transient or incidental to

121 Copyright Directive Recital 29 and Art 5.4.

122 Rome Convention Art 15.

123 TRIPs Agreement Art 14.6.

124 Copyright Directive Art 2.

125 Ibid Art 3.

126 Ibid Art 4.

127 Ibid Recital 22.

128 Recital 25 provides that: 'Existing national schemes on reprography, where they do exist, do not create major barriers to the Internal Market. Member States should be allowed to provide for an exception in respect of reprography.'

the functioning of the Internet.[129] The purpose of the inclusion of this article was to ensure that Internet Service Providers (ISPs), and others who own and operate equipment that make the Internet function would not be liable for such technological processes as caching, or for copies made on servers as works are transmitted around the Internet. It is not yet clear how the ISP liability provisions will interact with those to be found in the Electronic Commerce Directive, but no doubt will become more so once the necessary implementing measures are drawn up. However, this Article is not the focus of the present discussion. More important are those found in Articles 5.2 and 5.3.

Article 5.2 provides that Member states *may* provide for limitation to the exclusive right of *reproduction* in cases ranging from:

> reproductions on paper or any similar medium, effected by the use of any kind of photographic technique or by some other process having similar effects, with the exception of sheet musical work, provided that the right holders receive fair compensation;

to

> in respect of specific acts of reproduction made by publicly accessible libraries, educational establishments or museums, or by archives, which are not for direct or indirect economic or commercial advantage;

It is noteworthy that implementation by Member States of the measures contained in Article 5.2 is not mandatory. Thus, the Directive is unlikely to bring about the harmonisation of national laws which is one of the reasons for its introduction in the first place.

One important measure found in Article 5.2.b, provides limitations to the reproduction right may be made 'in respect of reproductions on any medium made by a natural person for private use and for ends that are neither directly nor indirectly commercial, on condition that the right holders receive fair compensation. . . .This would appear to be the measure in the Copyright Directive that is closest to the current UK exception for private study for individuals. However, it is hedged with a number of conditions. One is that right holders must receive fair compensation. If this is the measure that is intended to equate to fair dealing for the purposes of research and private study, and the UK Government decides to implement it in domestic law, it changes the current law from a defence to a charge of infringement of copyright for the purposes of private study, to a compulsory

[129] Copyright Directive Art 5.1 states: Temporary acts of reproduction referred to in Art 2 [of the Copyright Directive], which are transient or incidental, which are an integral and essential part of a technological process, whose sole purpose is to enable a transmission in a network between third parties by an intermediary or a lawful use of a work or other subject matter to be made, and which have no independent economic significance, shall be exempted from the right set out in Art 2.

licence for which the right holder must receive compensation. When it was added to the Copyright Directive, it may be that the drafters had in mind the French Code which permits private reproductions of phonograms, for which a charge must be paid by way of a levy on equipment, rather than the UK private study limitation. This would mean that if, for example, a copy of an MP3 file were placed on to the Rio, so that the surfer could listen to that at a more convenient time, the right holder would need to receive fair compensation for that reproduction. This has always been a 'chargeable' reproduction under UK law, as such private copying has not been considered to be fair dealing. By contrast, this 'space shifting' would appear to remain categorised as fair use in the US, so long as the act was carried out by the owner of the original copy.[130] A second point is that it is relevant only to the right of *reproduction*, and not to the communication to the public and making available to the public rights. This would appear to prevent a library making copies of works available on terminals in a library, to be consulted by researchers under this heading.

Much more extensive are the limitations to be found in Article 5.3. This article permits exceptions to be made to the exclusive rights of reproduction and communication to the public and making available to the public. The details are therefore applicable to works placed on servers and disseminated on the Internet, as well as to other forms of reproduction. Article 5.3 provides a list of circumstances for which Member States may provide for limitations to these exclusive rights. These are:

(a) use for the sole purpose of illustration for teaching or scientific research, as long as the source, including the author's name, is indicated, unless this turns out to be impossible and to the extent justified by the non-commercial purpose to be achieved;
(b) uses, for the benefit of people with a disability, which are directly related to the disability and of a non-commercial nature, to the extent required by the specific disability;
(c) reproduction by the press, communication to the public or making available of published articles on current economic, political or religious topics or of broadcast works or other subject matter of the same character, in cases where such use is not expressly reserved, and as long as the source, including the author's name, is indicated, or use of works or other subject matter in connection with the reporting of current events, to the extent justified by the informatory purpose and as long as the source, including the author's name, is indicated, unless this turns out to be impossible;
(d) quotations for purposes such as criticism or review, provided that they relate to

[130] In *UMG Recordings Inc and others v MP3.com Inc* 92 F Supp 2d 349 (SDNY) Rakoff J found that MP3.com had infringed copyright belonging to record companies when they (MP3.com) made a compilation of copies of thousands of songs, and then made those songs available to users of their 'Beam-It' and 'Instant Listening' Services. The copies made by MP3.com did not fall under the head of 'fair use' in the US.

a work or other subject matter which has already been lawfully made available to the public, that, unless this turns out to be impossible, the source, including the author's name, is indicated, and that their use is in accordance with fair practice, and to the extent required by the specific purpose;

(e) use for the purposes of public security or to ensure the proper performance or reporting of administrative, parliamentary or judicial proceedings;

(f) use of political speeches as well as extracts of public lectures or similar works or subject matter to the extent justified by the informatory purpose and provided that the source, including the author's name, is indicated, except where this turns out to be impossible;

(g) use during religious celebrations or official celebrations organised by a public authority;

(h) use of works, such as works of architecture or sculpture, made to be located permanently in public places;

(i) incidental inclusion of a work or other subject matter in other material;

(j) use for the purpose of advertising the public exhibition or sale of artistic works, to the extent necessary to promote the event, excluding any other commercial use;

(k) use for the purpose of caricature, parody or pastiche;

(l) use in connection with the demonstration or repair of equipment;

(m) use of an artistic work in the form of a building or a drawing or plan of a building for the purposes of reconstructing the building;

(n) use by communication or making available, for the purpose of research or private study, to individual members of the public by dedicated terminals on the premises of establishments referred to in paragraph 2(c) of works and other subject matter not subject to purchase or licensing terms which are contained in their collections;

(o) use in certain other cases of minor importance where exceptions or limitations already exist under national law, provided that they only concern analogue uses and do not affect the free circulation of goods and services within the Community, without prejudice to the other exceptions and limitations contained in this Article.

This list is lengthy, but that is because it is designed to replace existing limitations found in domestic laws of Member States. The merging of the UK and the Civilian systems is fascinating. There are clear influences from the French approach, for example in the exception for: 'the purpose of caricature, parody or pastiche'. Equally, there is evidence of the slightly broader UK fair dealing categories. Thus there is a limitation for illustration for teaching and scientific research, one for news reporting, and one for purposes *such as* criticism and review. Each has certain conditions attached, for example that the name of the author and the source must be indicated.

In making a comparison of the new provisions in the Copyright Directive with existing UK law on fair dealing, some points deserve special mention. There is no provision directly equivalent to the UK research and private study exception. However, there is the limitation 'for the sole purpose of illustration for teaching or scientific research'. The word scientific is likely to be broader than appears at first sight, and relate to knowledge in general, and so to as broad categories as our existing limitation. In addition, use for the purpose of illustration for teaching would be permitted. The UK has no such exception at present. There is also the limitation for

> use by communication or making available, for the purpose of research or private study, to individual members of the public by dedicated terminals on the premises of establishments referred to in paragraph 2c of works or other subject matter not subject to purchase or licensing terms which are contained in their collections.[131]

This would appear to be relevant to libraries which may make works available on dedicated terminals within their establishments. However, such use, it would appear, could be limited by contract, although how it might be limited is far from clear.

Member States may make exceptions to both the reproduction right and the making available to the public right for 'quotations for purposes such as criticism or review'. However, this is subject to an important proviso. The quotation must:

> relate to a work or other subject matter which has already been lawfully made available to the public, that, whenever possible, the source, including the author's name, is indicated, and that their use is in accordance with fair practice, and to the extent required by the specific purpose.

The words 'such as' compare favourably with the current UK section, which is limited to 'criticism and review', and might suggest the limitation would be available in a broader range of circumstances. However, the work must have been lawfully made available to the public. In some ways this is no different from current UK law. Works which are confidential or unpublished[132] are not subject to the criticism and review exception, at least not to the same extent as published works. But it does raise the tension as to when a work that has been made available over the Internet has been lawfully made available to the public. If that work sits behind a technical control, has it been made available to the public? If the work has been made available only to a few select recipients, has that been lawfully made available to the public? As a final point on this particular exception, the use of

[131] Art 5.2.n above.

[132] *PCR Ltd v Dow Jones Telerate Ltd* [1998] FSR 170. A number of reports on cocoa crops had been produced by PCR Ltd and distributed to a limited number of subscribers. Dow Jones acquired copies of these reports, and used some of the material in them to produce three articles. The plaintiff alleged breach of confidential information and copyright infringement. The court found that as the journalist was not aware of the confidential nature of the information that claim failed. However, given the reports had been published - albeit to a limited number of people, then the defence of fair dealing was open.

the quotations must be only to the extent 'required by the specific purpose'. Again, seemingly a limitation but perhaps no different from the UK fair dealing exception, where the criticism and review must deal fairly with the work.

The news reporting exception also appears to be as wide as current UK law:

> use of works or other subject matter in connection with the reporting of current events, to the extent justified by the informatory purpose and as long as the source, including the author's name, is indicated, unless this turns out to be impossible.

The wording in the Copyright Directive limits the exception to 'the extent justified by the informatory purpose', but may differ little from current UK law. The article may actually be wider, as it also provides that: 'reproduction by the press, communication to the public or making available of published articles on current economic, political or religious topics or of broadcast works or other subject matter of the same character, in cases where such use is not expressly reserved, and as long as the source, including the author's name, is indicated'. However, reproduction under the Copyright Directive in these circumstances is limited to cases where *such use is not expressly reserved*. This might suggest that if a user of a web site accepts a restriction that refuses permission to reproduce the work for the purposes of news reporting, then the restriction might be valid.

E. Technical Controls and Fair Dealing

The picture becomes much more complex when the fair dealing provisions in the Copyright Directive are considered along with those for technical controls.

As discussed above, Member States are to provide legal protection both in respect of the act of circumvention of a technical control, and the circulation of devices designed to facilitate such circumvention.[133] Technical controls are thus protected to the extent that they control the use of a work, and comprise of an access control limiting access to that work. The arguments that have arisen in relation to access to a work for the purposes of exercising one of the fair dealing limitations in the US apply equally to access to a work under the Copyright Directive. No doubt with these arguments in mind, Article 6.4 of the Copyright Directive appears to be aimed at ensuring those who are entitled to exercise one of the fair dealing limitations can exercise their rights.

Article 6.4 of the Copyright Directive aims at facilitating the exercise of some of the limitations to be found in Article 5, while at the same time

[133] Copyright Directive Art 6.1 and 2.

upholding the integrity of technical controls. The first paragraph of Article 6.4 provides in part that:

> Member States shall take appropriate measures to ensure that right holders make available to the beneficiary of an exceptions or limitation provided for in national law in accordance with article 5.2a, 2c, 2d, 2e, 3a, 3b or 3e the means of benefiting from that exception or limitation, to the extent necessary to benefit from that exception or limitation, where that beneficiary has legal access to the protected work or other subject matter concerned.

A beneficiary of the exception would appear to refer to a third party who wishes to exercise one of the limitations specified. Concentrating on Article 5.3, the limitations referred to are those for the illustration for teaching or scientific research, for the benefit of people with a disability, and for the purposes of public security and parliamentary or judicial proceedings. So despite the fact that the circumvention of technical controls is to be made unlawful, it would appear that those who are entitled (wish) to exercise a limitation for the purposes of *inter alia* illustration for teaching or research, must be able to do so. However, before being able to exercise such a limitation, the beneficiary of protection must have *legal access* to the protected work. So it would appear the help given in respect of exercising the limitation refers to, for example, overcoming controls which would otherwise prevent a copy being made for the purposes of scientific research, such as if the cut and paste functions or the print command on a website were disabled. The help is *not* given in respect of overcoming the access control. So the copyright owner might still refuse access, or condition access on payment. Depending on how the digital controls and business models of intermediaries develop, this limitation might either become unusable because the user cannot afford to pay for access, or develop in the form of a compulsory licence with remuneration payable to the intermediary each time it is exercised.[134] The payment may not be explicitly required to exercise fair dealing, but rather be for access. This is not quite how fair dealing for the purposes of research and private study is currently understood. Certainly, in most cases, a payment for the book or other work must be made at some point. However, if that book is purchased, or a copy obtained from a public library, then no further payment need be made to make a copy of a substantial part for the purposes of research. If works are only released on the Internet, then it would appear that a payment could be required each time this limitation is exercised.

The provision in Article 5.3.n appears to have been designed to avoid

[134] In a previous draft of the directive, a limitation was permitted for the sole purpose of illustration for teaching or scientific research, so long as the right holder received compensation. Although, as currently drafted, the limitation looks different, the effect may well be the same.

this outcome in respect of libraries. Thus, the reproduction, making available and communication to the public rights may be limited in respect of works made available over dedicated terminals in the library, where those works are to be used for the purpose of research or private study. This could mean, for instance, that books made available in electronic form in libraries could be accessed at dedicated terminals. Reproductions that were made would not infringe these rights so long as they were for the purposes of research and private study. However, that in turn is subject to the proviso that the limitation only applies to works '*not subject to purchasing or licensing terms*'. It would appear that a digital publisher could stipulate that no copy be made for the purposes of research and private study, or that a payment is required each time, or that the works should not be made available on these dedicated terminals. As far as payment is concerned, none of the limitations in Article 5.3 specifically state their exercise is conditioned on payment, although, as discussed above, the copyright owner could condition access on such payment. This is in contrast with Article 5.2, where private copying, paper-based copying, and copying in certain institutions is conditioned on the proviso that right holders should receive fair compensation. However, Recital 36 states that '*Member States may provide for fair compensation for right holders also when applying the optional provisions on exceptions which do not require such compensation*'. So, if the UK or any other Member State chooses to implement any of the fair dealing limitations, they may opt for a requirement that a fee be paid for each use. Recital 35 does recognise that in certain circumstances, a payment might not be appropriate, however: 'In certain situations, where the prejudice to the right holder would be minimal, no obligation for payment may arise.'

F. Technical Controls, Fair Dealing, and Licensing

One further question remains as to whether it would be possible, under the Copyright Directive, to limit by contract how fair dealing could be exercised, either at the point of access to the work, or at the point of use. Some of the questions have been discussed above. One further part of the Copyright Directive suggesting that such action might be possible for at least some limitations, is contained in the fourth paragraph of Article 6(4). This paragraph states that the 'first and second subparagraphs [of Article 6.4], shall not apply to works or other subject matter made available to the public on agreed contractual terms in such a way that members of the public may access them from a place and at a time individually chosen by them'. The first and second paragraphs of Article 6.4 place the obligation on Member States to provide the means by which a beneficiary of protection can benefit from a number of the limitations including making reproductions on paper,[135] and for the purpose of illustration for teaching and scientific research.[136] Article 6.4 would appear to imply that works may be made available over the Internet on certain terms and conditions proffered by the owner. If this is the case, and an author agrees to them, for instance by clicking on an 'I agree' icon (a click-wrap licence), then those terms and conditions will govern use of the underlying work by the author. If there is such agreement, then the author will not be able to use any of the exceptions discussed above. Thus, an owner might stipulate that 'no part of the works made available on this web site may be used for the purposes of illustration for teaching or scientific research'. It would appear that these conditions would govern the relationship between the parties.

G. *Fair Dealing and Databases*

Under the Database Directive, certain elements in relation to user rights are entrenched in law. The maker of a database may not prevent a lawful user from extracting and re-using insubstantial parts of that database, whether evaluated qualitatively or quantitatively.[137] This cannot be limited by contract. In addition, Member States had the option under the Database Directive to allow for the extraction of a substantial part of the contents of a database for limited purposes, including extraction for the purposes of illustration for teaching or scientific research.[138]

It appears that this could now be limited under the Copyright Directive. The fourth paragraph of Article 6(4) provides: 'first and second subparagraphs [of Article 6.4], shall not apply to works or other subject matter made available to the public on agreed contractual terms in such a way that members of the public may access them from a place and at a time individually chosen by them', applies also to databases. Article 6.(4) paragraph 5:

[135] Copyright Directive Art 5.2.a.

[136] Ibid 5.3.a.

[137] Database Directive 96/9/EC Recital 49 and Art 8. In the UK, copyright in the structure of a database is not infringed by a person who copies that structure if it is necessary for the purposes of access to and use of the contents. The database right is not infringed by the fair dealing of a substantial part of the contents if they are extracted (but not re-utilised), for the purpose of illustration for teaching or research and not for any commercial purpose. For favourable comment in relation to this element of the Database Directive see Samuelson *Copyright digital Data and Fair Use in digital Networked Environments* <http://www.droit.umontreal.ca/crdp/en/equipes/te.../samuelson.htm>. The other area in which 'user' rights may be said to be entrenched is in relation to computer programs. Broadly Council Directive (EEC) No 9/250 of 14 May 1991 on the Legal Protection of Computer Programs provides that it is not unlawful to copy a program for the purposes of decompilation if it is necessary to find the information necessary to create an independent program which can be operated with the decompiled program or with another program. CDPA s 50B(2)(a) See also further restrictions in s 50B.

[138] Database Directive Art 9.a.

'This paragraph shall apply mutatus mutandis to . . . Directive 96/9/EC of the European Parliament and of the Council of 11 March 1996 on the legal protection of databases.'[139]

Given that web sites and individual web pages fall under the definition of a 'database' regardless of the content, it would appear that it might be possible to limit the fair dealing provisions by contract. Thus, if an owner chose to place restrictions on extraction of information from the database where it was to be used for the purposes of illustration for teaching or research, it may be permissible to do so.

The question at the outset of this section was whether the exclusive rights recognised to the authors on their works should be limited to take into account fair use and private copying? As can be seen from the discussion above, the US has not altered fair use for the information era. The question remains, however, as to how a user can gain access to a work in order to exercise fair use. In the EU extensive changes have been made to the fair dealing regime, measures introduce to ensure the integrity and protection of technical control measures and dissemination subject to contract terms anticipated. Thus, on the one hand it appears to be recognised by regulators that fair dealing and use is an important property limitation/restriction in relation to existing works, designed to encourage the creation of new works: on the other hand, how fair use will be exercised in the information era is far from clear. Restrictions on the exercise of fair use may well mean consequent restrictions on freedom of speech. Once again, the increase in property rights granted to right holders, coupled with the legal protection of technical controls should argue for fair use to be widened in the interests of a democratic society. The effect of the new measures should be carefully monitored to ensure that the development of new works continue apace in the information era.

1. The Balance between Authors' Rights and Copyright?

In this discussion, the term authors' rights will be taken to mean authors' moral rights, and copyright will be taken to mean the owners' economic rights.

Given that copyright law in the UK developed from economic concerns, rather than out of respect for the author, moral rights have historically not played a large role in domestic copyright law where they did not attain any prominence until the Copyright Designs and Patents Act 1988. Prior to this, an author who was concerned about her right of integrity being compromised, or a failure to acknowledge authorship, had to rely on the general

[139] This subparagraph also applies to Council Directive 92/100/EEC of 19 Nov 1992 on rental right and on certain rights related to copyright in the field of intellectual property.

laws of defamation,[140] passing off[141] or injurious falsehood. During the 1970's, the UK was preparing to ratify the Berne Convention, and as a consequence accepted that it would be required to introduce moral rights into domestic law.[142] Four moral rights were introduced in the 1988 Act.[143] These are the right to be identified as author[144] which requires to be asserted before it can be infringed[145] (the right of paternity), the right to object to derogatory treatment of a work[146] (the right of integrity), the right against false attribution of a work,[147] and the right to privacy in private photographs and films.[148] All the rights are inalienable[149] and transmissible on death.[150] However, they may be waived by agreement.[151] The rights to be identified as author of a work (which requires to be asserted before it can be infringed),[152] to object to derogatory treatment of a work, and to privacy in certain photographs and films, subsist so long as copyright subsists in the work.[153] The right against false attribution subsists until twenty years after death.[154] These rights are hedged around by many exceptions. For example, the right to be identified as an author does not apply to a computer program, nor does it apply to anything done by or with the authority of the copyright owner where the copyright originally vested in the author's employer.[155] The right to object to derogatory treatment does not apply to a raft of exceptions, including computer programs, to publication in a newspaper or an encyclopaedia, nor does it apply to anything done by or with the authority of the copyright owner where the copyright vests in the employer, and only then applies when the author has been identified as such.[156]

There have not been many cases on the UK's version of moral rights. One case that does not bode well for those who would seek to rely on the right to object to derogatory treatment is *Tidy v The Trustees of the Natural History Museum*.[157] Tidy had produced a series of cartoons of dinosaurs and given permission to the Natural History Museum to display these. A book was produced which contained reproductions of the cartoons reduced to about one-sixth of the original size.[158] Tidy claimed that the reduction was a distortion of his work, or alternatively it was prejudicial to his honour or reputation, as the public would think that he could not be both-

[140] *Humphreys v Thompson* [1905–1910] Mac CC 148.
[141] *Samuelson v Producers Distributing* [1932] 1 Ch 201.
[142] Whitford Report 1977 Cmnd 6732.
[143] CDPA ss 77–89.
[144] CDPA s 77.
[145] CDPA s 78.
[146] CDPA s 80.
[147] CDPA s 84.
[148] CDPA s 85.
[149] CDPA s 94.
[150] CDPA s 95.
[151] CDPA s 87.
[152] CDPA s 78.
[153] CDPA s 86(1).
[154] CDPA s 86(2).
[155] See generally CDPA s 79.
[156] See generally CDPA ss 81 and 82.
[157] (1995) 37 IPR 501 High Court 29 March 1995 Rattee J. See also *Morrison Leahy Music Ltd v Lightbody Ltd* [1993] EMLR 144 and *Patersfield v Denham* [1999] FSR 168.
[158] 420 mm x 297 mm to 67 mm x 42 mm.

ered to reproduce the drawings specifically for the book. The court found that, in the absence of evidence from the public that the honour and reputation of Tidy would be affected, there could be no infringement. The court thus favoured an objective test.

The moral right of false attribution has fared better. In *Alan Clark v Associated Newspapers*[159] the Evening Standard newspaper carried a regular column in the form of parodies of the diaries of Alan Clark. Although it was clearly stated the author of the parody was a Mr Bradshaw, this was not noticed by a number of readers, who attributed the articles to Mr Clark himself. The court found that a case was made out for false attribution.[160]

Given the very few cases that have come before the courts in the UK, it is hard to predict where the decisions on moral rights may go. It may be that economic, rather than personality concerns influence the courts. In other words, if the market considers, or would consider, that the reputation of the author is devalued by a particular treatment of a work, then the moral right will be infringed.[161]

In the international developments that have occurred to ready copyright for the information society, moral rights have not played a significant role. The WIPO Copyright Treaty does not mention moral rights although there is an obligation in the WIPO Phonograms and Performances Treaty to introduce a regime of moral rights for performers.

The Copyright Directive equally does not mention the question of moral rights, preferring instead to leave this aspect to the domestic laws of Member States.

It is perhaps unsurprising that moral rights have been omitted from the recent initiatives concerning copyright in the information society. As has been discussed above, each of the instruments readying copyright law for the information era has favoured the development of copyright as an economic concern, rather than as one of the author. At their most extreme, moral rights allow an author a perpetual right to exercise some control over the use of a work, and how the work may and may not be exploited in the

159 [1998] 1 WLR 1558; [1998] 1 All ER 959; [1998] RPC 261.

160 Although this could have been a case for passing off. D Vaver, `Moral Rights Yesterday, Today and Tomorrow (2000), *IJLIT*, vol 7, no 3, at 270

161 It may also be that the author considers that her reputation may be sullied with potential future subjects, and thus her market harmed. In the US case *Leibovitz v Paramount Pictures* February 19, 1998, US 2nd Cir CA <http://laws.findlaw.com/2nd/977063.html>, Paramount pictures parodied a photograph Ms Leibovitz had taken of Demi Moore standing naked and pregnant. Paramount pictures argued parody as a defence to the claim of copyright infringement. The defence was accepted. One factor that appeared to concern Ms Leibovitz was the effect that the parody could have on her 'special relationships' with the celebrities whom she makes a living photographing [n 6]. The moral right of integrity might have been successfully pled in droit d'auteur systems, although, even those systems do tend to allow a defence of parody to claims of infringement. French Intellectual Property Code Art L 122–5.

marketplace.[162] The exercise of moral rights can thus impede the finality of contracts, and inhibit the freedom of the holders of the economic rights to deal with the tangible object embodying the work. In essence, they can detract from the ability of those who wish to transform the author's work into another medium, to do so without interference.[163] They are thus inconsistent with the absolute nature of property, and with its alienation. As a consequence, and because economic rights are considered by many to be of paramount importance, in the UK, it has been argued that because every infraction of a moral right impairs another person's freedom to do business, enforcement should be confined to cases of real injury.[164]

Whether international harmonisation of moral rights could ever be achieved on a global scale must be open to doubt. It has been said by a US commentator that:

> It may be a good idea to try to incorporate some droit d'auteur concepts in US copyright law. However, this may be a difficult, if not impossible exercise. In any case, the US and Europe need a common standard for treating commercially exploitable works on the Internet. If Europe wants to be on the same level as the US, it will probably have to be without the author's rights paradigms. The US most likely will not accept them.[165]

These views are consistent with the belief that the economic functions of copyright are paramount.[166]

Returning to the subject of this section: the balance between copyright and moral rights, it can be said drawing on the discussion above that there is no International consensus, and thus no balance between copyright and moral rights in the information era. Rather, and because regulators have considered economic concerns to be paramount, moral rights have been left to Member States in the EU, and for States to comply with international

[162] Hansmann and Santilli 'Authors' and Artists' Moral Rights: A Comparative legal and Economic Analysis' 1997, 26 *J Legal Stud*, 95, p 101.

[163] Some argue that establishing a 'moral right imposes a real economic and political cost on society'. Those who want to use works need to deal with two owners: the moral and economic. Each new use is 'at the mercy of the author'. MA Lemley, 'The Economics of Improvement' (1997), *Texas Law Review*, vol 75, 989, p 1032. Lemley also argues that no parodies or satires would be permitted. But cf French Intellectual Property Code L122–5.

[164] Cornish Intellectual Property, 11–89. For these reasons, in particular the second, 'The introduction of a moral rights regime has been and continues to be fiercely combated mainly by US industries and US industry oriented policy which tend to favour the interests of producers in commercialising the protected work with as few restrictions as possible from residual rights vested in authors.' Drier, 'Copyright issues in a Digital Publishing World', <http://associnst.ox.ac.uk/~icsuinfo/dreier.htm>.

[165] Lehman in colloquium discussions in PB Hugenholtz(ed), *The Future of Copyright in a Digital Environment* (Dordrecht: Kluwer, 1996, 239.

[166] The US in particular has historically been an importer rather than an exporter of authors' works. Thus re-use with as little interference as possible has been of great concern. Hansmann and Santilli 'Authors' and Artists' Moral Rights: A Comparative legal and Economic Analysis' 1997, 26 *J Legal Stud*, 95, p 142.

obligations under the Berne Convention. Some have argued that a strengthened regime of moral rights for the information era would be advantageous, particularly so because digital images are so easy to alter. However, the likelihood of international agreement being attained on the subject is slim.

2. *The Place of Private Copying?*

Private copying has not historically played a role in UK copyright law. Beyond the limits set by the legislature on ownership of property rights in creative works, such as copying for the purposes of fair dealing and permitting an insubstantial part of a work to be copied without infringement, there are no rights for a user of a work protected by copyright to copy that work for the purposes of private enjoyment. This is in contrast to a number of other European Countries where, in return for a levy on blank media, such as a video tape, users are permitted to take copies for purely personal and domestic use.

Right holders fear a regime of private copying, perhaps not unjustifiably. This is because in contrast with copies made on analogue media, making a digital copy produces a perfect copy that can be repeated ad infinitum. Without rules against private copying, or alternative, levies on the media upon which the copy is made, right holders are concerned that the opportunity to reap a reasonable reward from the reproduction would be prejudiced.

In considering the question as to whether private copying should be permitted in the information age, it can be argued that given the increased control that right holders can exert over the dissemination of creative works, notably through the use of technical controls, so the permissions for individuals should be relaxed perhaps to include the right to make a copy of a work for personal and private ends. Technical controls used in conjunction with the dissemination of the work could ensure that further copying would be limited.

Such a 'right' for users would accord well with understanding that a layperson has of copyright. Seldom do those who have not studied the subject understand that private copies may not be made, far less the rationale for such a decision. The user is unlikely to purchase a second copy of a creative work. Permitting private copying would at least ensure that the law is not flouted on a regular basis.

However, it would appear that within the EU private copying is a long way from the reality, or at least what private copying can take place may only so occur where the right holder is remunerated. As discussed in the previous section, every right for the individual user is hedged with the requirement for compensation for the right holder. So while private copying might be built into the legislation, it will be at a price.

H. How to Deal Internationally with the Infringements?

If infringement of copyright occurs on an international basis, the rules relevant to determining when and where redress might be obtained are complex, made all the more so because many of the infringements will be by individuals, rather than by a single entity. One dispute, which has had a high profile in the media illustrates graphically the problems faced by right holders confronted with multiple reproductions of protected works carried out on an individual basis. The dispute concerns Napster, an Internet-based company which distributes software facilitating sharing of MP3 music files on the Internet.[167] Napster makes its proprietary MusicShare software available for surfers to download on to computers linked to the Internet. After downloading the software, a surfer can access the Napster system directly from the home computer. The software on the computer interacts with Napster's software held on Napster's servers. When the surfer, who wants to locate an MP3 file logs on, there is an automatic connection to one of the 150 servers operated by Napster. The surfer enters the name of the artist on the search page. The music files are not located on Napster servers, but held on the computer belonging to another surfer who has downloaded the Napster software. The software provided by Napster indexes the location of music files and matches a request for a particular MP3 file with the location of that same MP3 file on another computer. Once the MP3 file is found, the surfer can download the file directly from the computer on which it is held.[168] Napster states that it does not make any copies of MP3 files on its own servers.

Napster has been sued by record companies,[169] and by several individual musicians and bands.[170] On 26 July 2000, a US court ruled that Napster committed contributory and vicarious copyright infringement, and ordered the site to be closed pending full hearing of the case.[171] The ruling was immediately appealed, and the temporary injunction lifted on 28 July, again pending full hearing of the case.[172] On 12 February 2001, the US 9th Court of Appeals found that the activities of those who used Napster to share music files constituted copyright infringement.[173] As far as Napster

[167] <http://www.napster.com>.

[168] See generally *A&M Records Inc v Napster Inc* ND Calif 239 F 3d 1004.

[169] A&M Records Inc., Arista Records Inc, Mowtown Reocrd Company LP, Capitol Records Inc, Sony Music Entertainment Inc, Warner Bros. Records Inc, and 10 others. It has been estimated that 317,377 individuals, located all over the world, shared songs by one just one band. http://www.napster.com/metallica-notice.htm http://www.qlinks.net/items/qlitem7384.htm172

[170] Metallica and Dr Dre.

[171] *A&M Records Inc v Napster Inc ND Calif.* 239 F 3d 1004.

[172] <http://www.bbc.co.uk>.

[173] *A&M Records et al v Napster Inc.* Case 239 F 3d 1004.

was concerned, the court found that it was liable for contributory copyright infringement because they both knew of the infringing activity and made a material contribution to it. Secondly, Napster were found liable for vicarious copyright infringement because Napster had the ability to supervise the infringing activity, as well as a financial interest in the activity. In Napster's case this test was satisfied because they would at some point in the future be able to gain revenue from exploiting the database containing details of those who used the Napster system. The appeals court remitted the case back to the court of first instance to vary the terms of the original injunction such that the plaintiffs would be required to notify Napster of any material protected by copyright on its system before Napster would require to remove access to those songs. However, Napster was still to monitor the use of the system within its own limits to ensure that users did not gain access to unauthorised material.[174]

After handing down of the amended injunction, there was and continues to be both a war of words, and action between the parties. The RIAA argued that Napster had not disabled access to songs when notified. In return, Napster alleged that RIAA had included in the given details, works in which the copyright was not under control of the RIAA. Napster filed a request for a rehearing and rehearsing of the case[175] but meanwhile closed its service because of the inability to comply with the terms of the injuction. Napster has now been bought by Vivendi. Information on the site states that it hopes to re-open in the Spring with a new fee-paying service.

The storm whipped up by this case is unlikely to die down in the near future. It has prompted much wider questions about the development of the law as it applies to the Internet. In particular it has raised concerns as to whether courts should impede technological progress by requiring that new technologies should be shut down, a move that some consider could have a negative effect on the development of the Internet as a whole. A crucial point arising from the case is that the record companies were able to sue Napster. Had Napster not been liable, the right holders would have been left to sue the individuals who uploaded and downloaded copies of digital musical files onto and from the Internet.[176]

174 The amended order was issued on 5 Mar 2001. C99-05183. MDL No C00-1369MHP.

175 This step in the procedure not only requests the court to reconsider the findings, but also to vary the terms of the second injunction issued to facilitate Napster's compliance with its terms.

176 For a flavour of the difficulties that would be faced by right holders see generally the papers relating to the discussions that have been held at WIPO on Private International Law and Intellectual Property, Lucas, *Private international law aspects of the protection of works and objects of related rights transmitted through digital networks*, Paper GCPIC/1; id, Lucas, *Private international law aspects of the protection of works and of the subject matter of related rights transmitted over digital networks*, Paper WIPO/PIL/01/1. Ginsburg, *Private international law aspects of the protection of works and objects of related rights transmitted through digital networks*, Paper GCPIC/2; id, *Private international law aspects of the protection of*

However, Napster is not the only technology on the Internet that facilitates copying between individuals. Other systems have been developed which allow peer-to-peer networking where users connect their computers directly from one to another, and swap files between them.[177] Such a network does not depend on a centralised indexing system akin to that used by Napster. This means that there does not appear to be any central point which could be attacked by the right holder. Enforcement of rights has thus been seen as one of the greatest challenges for right holders in relation to digital dissemination.

If the copyright owner does wish to sue for multiple infringements over the Internet, then who should be sued? Looking to the way in which the work would travel around the Internet, there are three main events: (1) first, the steps taken to digitise the work and make it available over the Internet by the content provider, whether the work is subsequently held on the individual computer or posted to a web site; (2) second, uploading and storing the work on to the servers belonging to the ISP, although, as discussed above, some ISPs do not store works on their servers, but may merely facilitate finding those works via the Internet; (3) third, downloading at the stage of the surfer.

So the three main contenders to be sued for infringement would appear to be the content provider, the ISP who makes the facilities available and may store the work on servers, and the surfer who reproduces the work on the home computer.

1. The Content Provider

One of the most significant events in the chain is the actions by the content provider, in taking the decision to make the material available over the Internet, and putting it in a form which makes such distribution possible. Where the content provider has digitised a work with the intent of placing it on the Internet, or having it available in a computer for others to access and copy, it is foreseeable that the file will be available world wide, and foreseeable that copies will be downloaded. Conceptually, the content provider may have actually committed only one act of infringement: digitisation. However, these actions have been the ones that have led to other infringements, as the work is reproduced around the Internet, and finally downloaded at the point of the surfer.[178] Despite the fact that the content

works and objects of related rights transmitted through digital networks (2000 update), Paper WIPO/PIL/01/2; Austin, *Private international law and intellectual property rights. A common law overview*, Paper WIPO/PIL/01/5.

[177] ee, eg, <http://www.wego.gnutella.com>.

[178] The actual number of copies downloaded or estimated to be downloaded might be a difficult figure to assess, and may be rough and ready Just because an assessment of damages might

provider may not have made a profit from the infringement, this should not prevent the publisher from obtaining an award of damages.[179]

The publisher might, however, have difficulties in suing the content provider. The content provider may be located in a forum where it is not possible, or practical, to sue. Additionally, the content provider may have few or no resources to meet any monetary order obtained. Any successful action may, in substance, be an empty victory. If an interdict is granted requiring removal of the infringing material from the Internet, the content provider may be able to remove the digitised file from the computer over which control is exerted, but not from computers belonging to other surfers, nor from servers belonging to ISPs. So the publisher may prefer to look elsewhere.

2. *The ISP*

As an alternative to the content provider, the publisher might sue the ISP on whose servers the infringing material is located and thus 'made available' for surfers to download. Some ISPs may, or may not carry copies of works on their servers. Thus an act infringing copyright may have occurred; the reproduction of the work without authorisation, and possibly also the authorisation of infringement of the work by the ISP, in providing the facilities to make further reproductions of the work available. If the work is held on a server, it may be the one single point where the work can be located, before it is replicated around the Internet. So the ISP, who controls the server, might seem an appropriate target. Often (but by no means always) the ISP is located in a place where it is feasible to sue for infringement. The ISP is more likely to have assets which can be used to satisfy a monetary award. And if the remedy sought is an interdict to have the infringing material removed, the ISP could comply with such an order, since the server is under its control.

As a result of the concerns expressed by ISPs that they might become liable for infringing activities although they had no reasonable means of controlling or monitoring the content of the material on their servers, specific rules have now been enacted in a number of jurisdictions which broadly require an ISP to remove such material from their servers when they become aware of its presence, but not to monitor the information. Both the EU and the US have now implemented regimes in this area.

In the EU provisions relative to ISP liability are to be found in the E-

be difficult and may be rough and ready is not a reason for refusing to attempt it. *Chaplin v Hicks* [1911] 2 KB 786; WB Cornish, *Intellectual Property*, para 2.4.

179 In the US, the No Electronic Theft Act 1997 was passed so that criminal sanctions could be imposed on those who distributed software and other works protected by copyright. Previously, if no money exchanged hands, those liable could escape prosecution.

Commerce Directive 2000.[180] The Directive creates a single 'horizontal' liability regime for the breach of any type of substantive law. The horizontal regime chosen by the EU stands in contrast with the US approach in the Digital Millennium Copyright Act[181] which deals with liability of ISPs for copyright infringement only and spells out the precise procedure to be followed in the event that infringing material in found on servers belonging to an ISP.

3. *The EU Approach*

The E-Commerce Directive broadly provides that ISPs will not be liable for the content that is passed through their servers so long as their activities are limited to pure transmission of content (the mere conduit approach).[182] Further, ISPs will not be liable for caching material, provided that the integrity of the cached information and of the technology used by the content providers to protect that information are respected.[183] ISPs will have no liability for hosting information, subject to an obligation '*expeditiously to remove or disable access to information*' where the host service provider has actual knowledge or awareness of facts or circumstances from which illegal activity is apparent.[184] In addition they will have no general obligation to monitor online services.[185] The procedure to be followed to notify the ISP that it carries infringing material is to be left to guidelines to be developed by Member States.

While a number of questions arise in relation to this regime,[186] the intent is perhaps clear. Infringing works should be removed from the Internet, and ISPs will not have liability for damages for hosting infringing works where they are unaware that the material is infringing. They will however be required to comply with an order such as an interdict which may be made to remove the infringing material.[187]

Therefore, in the circumstances where the owner of the copyright has informed the ISP that there is infringing material on the servers and it is removed expeditiously, the ISP will not be liable for damages. If the mater-

[180] E-Commerce Directive (COM (1999) 427) (E-commerce Directive) Arts 13, 14, and 15. This Directive came into force on 17 July 2000 and is due to be transposed into the laws of Member States by 17 Jan 2002. A copy can be found at <http://www.europa.eu.int/eur-lex/en/dat/2000/l_178/l_17820000717en00010016.pdf>.

[181] Digital Millennium Copyright Act 1998 Title IV 17 USC.

[182] E-Commerce Directive, Art 12.192.

[183] Ibid Art 13.194·

[184] Ibid Art 14.196.

[185] Ibid Art 15.198·

[186] Bortloff and Henderson, *Notice and Take Down Agreements in Practice in Europe. Views from the Internet Service Provider and Telecommunications Industries and the Recording Industry*, WIPO Paper 1999 OSP/LIA/3 Available on the WIPO website.

[187] E-commerce Directive Art 14(3).

ial is not removed, then it would be worth considering suing the ISP for damages.

4. *The US Approach*

The provisions in the US are similar to, although more prescriptive than, the procedures to be found in the E-Commerce directive. The Online Copyright Infringement Liability Limitation Act[188] limits the remedies a copyright owner may seek from an ISP for copyright infringement under certain circumstances. Four acts are covered: (1) transmitting, routing, and providing connections to infringing material (the 'mere conduit' limitation); (2) system caching; (3) storing infringing material at the direction of a user (the 'hosting' limitation); or (4) linking or referring users to infringing material (the 'linking' limitation).

In relation to the 'hosting' limitation, so long as a specific procedure is followed both by the copyright owner and by the ISP, then the ISP will not be liable for hosting infringing material.[189] The copyright owner must notify the ISP in a prescribed form that it is hosting infringing material.[190] The ISP must remove this, notify the person who placed the material there (the content provider) that it has been removed: allow the content provider 10 days to state why the information should not be removed, and replace the information if the content provider so states.[191] The copyright owner must then go to court to obtain the material's permanent removal.[192]

So if the publisher seeks damages for the loss that is suffered from having had a work distributed over the Internet, the ISP may not be the person to pursue, unless the ISP knows that material is infringing and has not removed it. If, on the other hand, the remedy sought is removal of the material from the server, and the ISP is in a place subject to US or EU jurisdiction, then the publisher is likely to achieve its objective. This does not, however, solve the problem of the one-to-one copying where no copies are held by the ISP. If this is the case, the publisher may have no alternative but to sue individual surfers.

[188] Incorporated as Title II of the DMCA.

[189] In *A&M Records et al v Napster Inc.* No C-99-5183 MHP (ND Cal 5 May 2000) Napster was found not to qualify under the safe harbour provisions of the DMCA.

[190] DMCA s 512. See generally Oktay and Wrenn, '*A Look Back at the Notice - Takedown Provisions of the US Digital Millennium Copyright Act One Year After Enactment*' WIPO Paper 1999 OSP/LIA/2 Available on the WIPO website.

[191] One of the most contentious aspects of the procedure is that it allows those who do not like some content, to inform the ISP that it infringes copyright. If the ISP then wants to take advantage of the 'safe harbour' provisions, as most do, then the ISP will immediately take down the allegedly infringing material. This totally ignores any fair use that might be pled as a defence, and put the onus rather on the content provider to be proactive. Apparently, the practical experience of ISPs is that once material is taken down, it stays down. Oktay and Wrenn, op cit.

[192] DMCA s 512.

4. The Surfer

A final alternative might be to sue the end user, the surfer. Surfers make both temporary and permanent reproductions of a work, for instance by bringing a copy of a work on to the screen of a computer (a temporary reproduction) and making a copy of that work in the hard drive of the computer (a permanent reproduction). It is at the point of the surfer where the actual act of reproduction takes place that damages the publisher.

Whether acting at the final downloading stage, or uploading works available for others, the most telling difficulty for the publisher is that there will be as many defendants as there are surfers who have downloaded the work, as each reproduction will be made by a different person. Thus the publisher may have to chase all the individual cases separately. [193] The cost of pursuing individual surfers for individual acts of infringement is likely far to exceed any return in damages. Bad publicity might also flow from chasing individual surfers. Where the pursuer is a large entity, such as one of the collecting societies representing its members, it is possible that the negative publicity likely to attach to surfers being sued would outweigh any commercial considerations in pursuing such an action. On the other hand, in some circumstances, intermediaries might feel that chasing individuals may provide just the lesson to others that is required as a deterrent.

I. The Rules on Jurisdiction and Choice of Law

Whoever the publisher or right holder decides to sue, the appropriate jurisdiction and choice of law must be ascertained. It is not intended at this juncture to go into these rules in depth. However, which rules are relevant will generally depend on the location of the defendant. As an example, if the defendant is located in the EU or EFTA country then the Brussels Convention[194] will apply to determine jurisdiction (the Brussels

[193] There are questions over the extent of an implied licence for surfers to make at least temporary reproductions on their computers that occur during the normal course of browsing. Although an implied licence should have no place where the owner of the copyright has not given permission for the work to be placed on the Internet, it is difficult for the surfer to distinguish between those works that infringe and those that do not. Although a surfer in the UK would not be able to rely on an innocent infringement defence, given that such a defence applies only where an infringer has no reason to know that copyright subsists in the work, nonetheless, the court might be moved to award minimal damages. The costs of pursuing individual surfers for individual acts of infringement is likely to far exceed any return in damages.

[194] The Brussels Convention on Jurisdiction and the Enforcement of Judgements in Civil and Commercial Matters 72/454, 1972 OJ (L299) 32. (the Brussels Convention). The Brussels Convention applies in courts of contracting States of the EU where the defendant is domiciled in a Contracting State. The Brussels Convention has been implemented in the UK by way of the Civil Jurisdiction and Judgements Act 1982. The Lugano Convention on Jurisdiction and Enforcement of Judgements in Civil and Commercial Matters Convention 88/592, 1988 OJ

Regulation[195] will replace the Convention in March 2002). The main ground of jurisdiction to be found in the Brussels Convention and the Brussels Regulation is the domicile of the defendant in Article 2.

> Persons domiciled in a Contracting State shall, whatever their nationality, be sued in the courts of that state.

This ground of jurisdiction would allow the publisher to consolidate a number of claims arising in various territories in the one action, assuming that it is the same defendant responsible for the infringements. The right holder would also have an option of suing under Article 5(3) of the Brussels Convention or the Brussels Regulation:

> In matters relating to tort, delict or quasi delict, in the courts for the place where the harmful event occurred.

This, in copyright terms is likely to be where the reproduction of the work protected by copyright was made. Where there are many defendants, the copyright owner would have to sue each individually in the appropriate jurisdiction.

The law to be applied will also have to be determined. The Berne Convention provides:

> The extent of protection, as well as the means of redress afforded to the author to protect his rights shall be governed exclusively by the laws of the country where protection is claimed.

This is generally considered to be the country 'for which' protection is claimed against infringing acts occurring there.[196] The infringement would be where the reproduction was made (whether on the server, or on the individual computer of the surfer). Thus there may be many different laws to

(L319) 9 extends the Brussels Convention to EFTA States. One of the main aims of these Conventions was to ensure that a judgement granted in one contracting state would be recognised and enforced in another with the minimum possible of formalities. One of the main mechanisms was to harmonise rules on jurisdiction. See generally A Anton with P Beaumont, *Private International Law*, 2nd edn (Edinburgh: W Green, 1990), 154. The Civil Jurisdiction and Judgements Act 1982 Schedule 1 contains rules for the United Kingdom, schedule 4 which only applies when Schedule 1 rules do not, and Scottish rules on jurisdiction Schedule 8 which only applies when neither Schedule 1 nor schedule 4 applies. The Brussels Convention was replaced within the EU by the Brussels Regulation. Council Regulation on jurisdiction and the Recognition and Enforcement of Judgements in Civil and Commercial Matters COM (2000) 689 final. For a flavour of the debate that has surrounded this instrument, particularly as it will affect consumer contracts concluded over the Internet, see generally *Electronic Commerce: Jurisdiction and Applicable Law*' 4–5 Nov 1999, Position papers submitted to the European Commission <http://europa.eu.int/comm/scic/conferences/991104/contributions.pdf>.

[195] Council Regulation No 44/2001 of 22 Dec 2000 of 2001 L12/1.

[196] JC Ginsburg, *Private International Law Aspects of the Protection of Works and Objects of Related Rights Transmitted through Digital Networks*, WIPO paper, Nov 1998 (available as GCPIC/2 paper on the WIPO website).

be applied either in the one action where the one defendant is sued but reproductions are made in a number of different territories, or in many different actions, where different defendants are sued in different territories, each responsible for his or her own action.

If the defendant is not domiciled in the EU/EFTA, then local laws will determine jurisdiction. As an example, in the UK. the Civil Jurisdiction and Judgements Act 1982 looks to the domicile of the defendant as the main basis for jurisdiction, failing which jurisdiction can also be found in the territory where the harm occurred.

Further problems may arise when it comes to recognising and enforcing a judgement. While the Brussels Convention (and the Brussels Regulation) are both designed to streamline the rules on jurisdiction and thus to make recognition of a judgment almost automatic, nonetheless difficulties may arise where what is being sought is the enforcement of a judgment in a territory in which the act complained of may not be an infringement of copyright.

Because of these difficulties, it might be thought that re-vamping the rules on jurisdiction and choice of law would be the most obvious route to follow. To this end a number of suggestions have been made designed to rework the rules on infringement over the Internet. WIPO has convened several meetings of committees of experts from various countries to consider the problems posed and to suggest possible solutions.[197] In the course of these discussions, many have focussed on the desire to localise both jurisdiction and infringement in one place thus both minimising the need to resort to different jurisdictions, and cutting down on the numbers of laws that may be applied to an infringement action. Among other suggestions has been that the relevant jurisdiction and law to be applied should be that of the location of the server, where the server is located in a country which adheres to the Berne Convention, the TRIPs agreement and/or the WCT. The difficulty with such an approach is twofold. The first is that it would encourage the location of servers in copyright havens. The second is that it would necessarily negate the territorial nature of copyright. Instead of infringements being judged by the standards of the country in which the infringement occurs, the infringement would be judged by the standards of a different country. This once again may have the consequence of making domestic courts reluctant to enforce judgements handed down by courts in other countries where those are based on an infringement in another country where in fact no infringement may have occurred in the territory where it was sought to enforce. These difficulties prompt the more fundamental question. Should copyright law be amended in this way? Copyright has always been a bundle of national rights: there is no such thing as interna-

[197] See the papers cited at n 176 above.

tional copyright law. To change the rules concerning jurisdiction and choice of law would be to change the face of copyright beyond all recognition. No longer would copyright law be a territorial right. In cyberspace, there would be one law of copyright. The discussion above concerning the differing attitudes to moral rights between the continental legal system and the Anglo Saxon system where divergencies run deepest, suggest that there is no easy answer.

With the development of technical controls utilising both hardware and software coupled with legal rules against the circumvention of those controls; the development of the practice of licensing works on a one to one basis; the increasing ability to 'zone' cyberspace into geographical regions; the liability placed on ISPs to remove works that infringe copyright, the question is raised as to whether the rules on infringement should be revamped? Copyright owners, on a national and international basis have an array of means available to them which would firstly permit control over dissemination, and secondly have works that infringe copyright removed from the Internet. Admittedly, there will always be some infringements that occur on an international basis that will be hard to stop. But the increasing activity of international watchdogs such as the International Federation of Phonograpic Industries may do more to stall infringements than would changing the territorial nature of copyright law.

J. Specific Issues

Traditional ways of exploiting works are changing; the new technologies also generate new forms of businesses. Publishers, journalists and performers are directly affected by the technological evolution. Should their status and regime be related to the ones they had in the past or should one adopt new laws to take into account the new technical environment of the information society?

1. On-line Publishing

As has been explained above, there are 'new' laws that have been negotiated to protect copyright in the digital environment. The rights of making available to the public and communication to the public to be found in both the WCT and the Copyright Directive being prime examples. In addition, many new forms of technology are appearing almost daily. One such development is the e-book reader. Books can be digitised, transmitted over the Internet, and downloaded onto the e-book to be read by the user. These e-books can be protected by technical protection measures to prevent copying and onward dissemination of the text. The technical measures that control copying can (and are) in turn be protected against circumvention. It is also understood that it is possible to set the technology up such that the work that is copied on to the e-book may only be available to the reader for a limited period of time. After this set period of time (say a week) the text will no longer be available. Thus the work is 'lent' to the user. In addition, there are many new business models emerging by means of which publishers can disseminate works over the Internet. One example is the book *Riding the Bullet* by the author Stephen King. The author permitted users to download the book, chapter by chapter for a 'voluntary' payment. If he did not receive sufficient such payments, he would not then finish the book. It is understood that he did not.

It is true that certain problems have arisen for publishers, but these rather stem from existing contracts with their authors rather than from the absence of sufficient rights and controls in the digital environment. One example emanates from the US: *Random House v Rosetta Books*[198]. RosettaBooks acquired the electronic-publishing rights to a number of book titles, including works by William Styron, Kurt Vonnegut and Robert Parker. On 27 February 2001, Random House, Inc, filed suit against Rosetta Books[199]. The suit alleges that Random House owns exclusive electronic rights to the titles and that Rosetta is infringing Random House's rights by publishing them electronically. Random House argues that the rights it received from the authors during a period over twenty years previously to 'print, publish and sell in book form' should now be interpreted to include e-books. So the nub of the issue concerns contract interpretation. The stakes are however very high. If the court decides in favour of Random Books, then that company will have the right to exploit a 'new' market in digitising its existing stock of books. Both the authors and RosettaBooks will lose the chance to earn extra income from digital exploitation. If, on the other hand, RosettaBooks wins, then the value of the stock that Random House holds could fall dramatically if and when the consuming public determines that it prefers e-books to hard copies. It is also unlikely to be just RosettaBooks and Random House who will be affected by the outcome of the case. Contracts used in the publishing industry tend to be similar as between publishers. It is said that the outcome could therefore affect the electronic rights to hundreds of thousands of books industry-wide, and thus determine the shape of the e-publishing business in the future.[200] On 11 July 2001, District Judge Stein refused Random House application for an injunction prohibiting the digitisation of the books on the grounds that the contract did not include e-publishing rights. It is understood that the case will now go to full trial.

[198] Most of the legal documents have been collated at <http://www.rosettabooks.com/pages/legal.html.

[199] In the Federal Court in the Southern District of New York.

[200] <http://www.rosettabooks.com/pages/legal.html>.

Despite these seeming setbacks for publishers (but not for the author), there appears to be no good reason at present to introduce yet more rights for on-line publishers. What appears to be more important is for the on-line publishers to work out a successful business model that can ensure that they receive a reasonable return on their investment in the digital era. But that is a question for the free market rather than the legislature.

2. *The Journalists*

In terms of their economic interests, journalists are in a similar position to on-line publishers. Journalists wish to obtain a fair return for their work, and not have their work exploited where they have not agreed to such exploitation. The exploitation of economic rights of journalists has arisen again in the US where in *New York Times Co v Tasini* the Supreme Court ruled that a group of newspaper and magazine publishers infringed the copyright of freelance contributors by making their articles accessible without permission in electronic databases after publication. The case turned on the interpretation of Title 17 USC section 201(c) which provides that: 'Copyright in each separate contribution to a collective work is distinct from copyright in the collective work as a whole, and vests initially in the author of the contribution. In the absence of an express transfer of the copyright or of any rights under it, the owner of copyright in the collective work is presumed to have acquired only the privilege of reproducing and distributing the contribution as part of that particular collective work, any revision of that collective work, and any later collective work in the same series'. The court found that this section did not authorise the copying in question (from hard copy newspaper to on-line newspaper) because the databases in which the articles were held reproduced and distributed the articles standing alone, and not in their original context. Thus the publishers had first to seek permission from the authors. The fact that the publishers argued that if the case was decided in favour of the authors this would have devastating consequences for the dissemination of digital works by 'punching gaping holes in the electronic record of history' had no bearing on the question to be decided. 'Speculation about future harms is no basis for this Court to shrink authorial rights created by Congress'. It is understood that new contracts with freelance authors allow for digitisation and incorporation into databases. However, older contracts which did not contain this provision are affected. As a result of this case a number of electronic newspapers will apparently remove large parts of their archived material from their electronic databases[201].

A similar conclusion should result in the UK given similar facts, but by

[201] <http://www.nytimes.com/2001/06/26/technology/26BIZC.html>.

a different route Many journalists are self employed, and licence their work to a newspaper for a specific edition, or for a specific purpose. Thus, if the work was pace on the Internet without permission, that would infringe the copyright belonging to the journalist. No doubt current contracts with journalists permit the digitisation and storage of their work on the Internet.

Moral rights of journalists (and other journalists) are, however, a different matter and require specific consideration. As has been explained above, the UK has only a weak regime of moral right protection for authors. This means, that it may be difficult to object to changes made to his or her work if she considered the changes derogatory.

It is very simple on the Internet to make alterations to digitised material, whether in the form of text, pictures or photographs. Clearly a journalist is right to be concerned about the integrity of a work and thus to protect their reputation against the publisher, and in the eyes of the public. Thus it would be useful if moral rights were strengthened for journalists (and other authors) permitting objection to alterations to work giving the chance to ensure their personal integrity in the marketplace was not sullied. This would have the additional benefit of maintaining the integrity of the work for the benefit of the public.

3. The Holders of Neighbouring Rights

Under the copyright regime in the UK and taking into account the amendments that will be made for the digital era, in common with on-line publishers discussed above, it would appear that neighbouring right holders have sufficient rights and that no new ones are necessary in order to exploit these rights in the digital environment.

III. THE FINANCIAL FLOWS

A. Remuneration of the Authors

The authors are entitled to a fair remuneration. But does the worldwide exploitation of their works justify a remuneration that appears out of proportion with the remuneration paid to the other categories of citizens?

The remuneration paid to authors, often through either royalties or lump sum payments for publishing in the non-Internet world is not, in the capitalist system, regulated. Rather the sum paid is a result of negotiation, whether individual or collective, and driven by market forces. Thus, it is perfectly possible for a single author to reap millions from a publication (for example JKL Rowling author of the Harry Potter books), or nothing if the book fails to find a market.

A major question in relation to digital dissemination is whether these competitive pressures will work in the same, or a similar fashion, particularly given the power of the right holders to control access to creative and non-creative works. In relation to this matter, it should be noted that it is not necessarily the author who will benefit from increased control over digital dissemination. Often the author will assign copyright to the publisher, who then stands in the shoes of the author in relation to economic return. The question of the remuneration of authors lies at the interface between the author and the publisher.

Market forces may work to keep prices reasonable. It is in the interests of publishers and authors to have their work accessed, and in order to reach as wide an audience as possible, so the price of access to the work may be kept reasonable. In addition, competition in the marketplace for creative works disseminated over the Internet will mean that prices will be kept low. Such competition may come not only from competitors in the market place, but also from works made available through public funding, such as libraries, and Government information services. So long as these are kept free, and other copyright owners and database makers are competing with these services, so those in the private market place will be forced to keep prices low.

In addition, because the Internet offers wide distribution, and holds out the possibility of charging for many and varied uses, these factors could combine to ensure that many people will each pay a little towards the costs of producing creative works, rather than more being paid by fewer participants in a limited market. Some economists go further[202] and argue that, because there is substitutability across works protected by copyright, so demand curves would be flat. This in turn would force content providers to push access costs back towards marginal costs.[203] Price discrimination might be possible:

> Expanded control may increase the private cost of reading, viewing and listening to authors' expression to such an extent that, in some cases and for some people access becomes prohibitively expensive. [But] digital technology may make possible highly refined price discrimination that could, in theory, alleviate this problem.[204]

However, whether competitive pressures will work in this way is questionable. It is those works that are valuable for authorship which will ultimately prove to be the most lucrative for publishers who will able to charge at

[202] Harvard Law Review Association, 'Clarifying the Copyright Misuse Defence: The Role of Antitrust Standards and First Amendment Values '1991, 104 *Harv L Rev*, 1289. 'The fact that copyright prevents . . . works from being copied does not mean that . . . authors and composers enjoy market power.'

[203] WW Fisher, 'Reconstructing the Fair Use Doctrine' 1988, 101 Harv L Rev 1659. The degrees of market power enjoyed by copyright holders vary considerably.

[204] NW Netanel, *Copyright and a Democratic Civil Society*, 106 *Yale L J*, 283 at 295

prices totally unrelated to economic incentive (whether this in turn is passed on to the author is another question). One example might be the journal 'Nature' published by Macmillan publishers. This journal is essential reading for researchers and teachers in the Science and Medicine professions. An individual subscription costs around £400 per journal. A site licence for a University for one year can cost up to £8000 depending on the numbers of staff and students within that University[205]. If the University decides to take the electronic subscription (which includes one hard copy) and to drop all other hard copy subscriptions (around ten), the price to the University has doubled, although for that year access to the publication within the University may be significantly enhanced. The licence, however, only lasts for one year. If at the end of that year the University finds that it can no longer afford the price of access, which could be significantly increased by the publisher, not only does it not have access to the electronic version, but neither does it have the hard copies that used to adorn the shelves. The library can, of course, refuse to take an on-line subscription. However, in these circumstances, the benefits of the digital age are denied to just that interest group that copyright is designed to support. Price discrimination in these circumstances may be possible allowing the library to be charged what it can afford, but here it leaves the uncomfortable feeling that the producer is exploiting the de facto dominant position that it holds in relation to that particular digitised product.

The question then would be whether competition law might come in to regulate the prices charged by on-line publishers, if it was felt that such prices were excessive. Where works are not rendered exclusive by virtue of their being under the control of one entity, then the refusal to supply is unlikely to cause problems. For instance if the question is whether a recording of a particular piece of classical music will not be supplied by one record publisher, then a recording of the same piece of music may be obtained from another. Alternatively, a recording of a different piece of music might be chosen. In other words, there is cross elasticity in the market for the particular work. However, where refusal to supply could become problematic is when the information, perhaps factual information is both created and held by one entity, and that entity refuses to supply that information to a third party. In *British Horseracing Board Ltd and others v William Hill Organisation Limited*[206] the information that William Hill sought to use may not have been created by the British Horseracing Board, but that was the central repository for it. The question of refusal to supply did not in this case arise, but if it had, then competition law may have been called upon to

[205] Information received from electronic licensing division of the main library at the University of Edinburgh.

[206] 9 Feb 2001.

provide an appropriate remedy for the bookmakers because of the difficulties of obtaining that information elsewhere.

The refusal to supply works protected by copyright did arise and was considered by competition law authorities in the EC in the judgement of the European Court of Justice in *Magill.*[207] In this case, the court had to tackle the question of the refusal to licence listings of forthcoming television programmes protected by copyright. Three TV broadcasting companies, RTE, BBC and ITP, refused to licence the information contained in their television listings for publication in a comprehensive TV guide which Magill wished to develop for the newer market. On appeal to the Court of First Instance in Europe, that court found that the TV companies were in a dominant position on the market for TV listings by virtue of their factual monopoly over information on which the programmes were based. The refusal to supply in such circumstances was an abuse under Article 86 of the Treaty of Rome[208]. The remedy was to license the listings at an appropriate rate.[209]

On appeal, the ECJ found that the exclusive right of reproduction is part of the author's rights. Thus, a refusal to grant a licence even by a firm in a dominant position cannot in itself constitute abuse of a dominant position. However, in exceptional circumstances, the exercise of an exclusive right may amount to abusive conduct. In *Magill*, three factors made these exceptional circumstances:

- there was no actual or potential substitute for a weekly guide offering listings for the coming week
- there was no objective justification for the refusal to supply
- the TV companies reserved to themselves the secondary market for listings by excluding competition and denying access to the necessary basic information. They had a de facto monopoly on one market consisting of an essential facility[210]

However, there may be limitations to the supply of copyright works that can be demanded. First, the work in *Magill* consisted of fact-based information. Because of the low level of originality required to attract copyright protection, these listings were protected by copyright. Where works under consideration exhibit a greater degree of originality, a court may be more

[207] *RTE and ITP v EC Commission* [1995] 4 CMLR 718, [1995] FSR 530.

[208] Now Art 82 of the Consolidated version of the Treaty establishing the European Community.

[209] During the course of judgment by the Court of First Instance, that court discussed the *'essential function'* of copyright, which is to protect the moral rights in the work and ensure a reward for creative effort while respecting the aims of Art 86. Case [1991] ECR 11-485.

[210] For a discussion on the potential implications see S Anderman, *EC Competition Law and Intellectual Property Rights. The Regulation of Innovation* (Oxford: Clarendon Press, 1998), 211.

circumspect about granting compulsory licences.[211] In addition, where fact-based information is not in question, there may be products that can be substituted for the work under consideration. The second possibly limiting factor is that by exercising copyright in this manner, the television companies prevented a new market from being exploited. Magill wanted to sell weekly listings of television programmes, rather than limit the dissemination of the information to daily listings. Finally, the power exercised over the listings by the television companies was ancillary to broadcasting[212] which was their main activity. Where the copyright owner engages in its primary market area, the exploitation of creative works, then the courts may be far less willing to require supply of those works against the wishes of the owner, as that is exactly the type of monopoly that copyright is designed to give.

To keep in step with these guidelines, some database makers may adjust their behaviour so that they do not refuse to supply substantial parts of the contents of the database: particularly where the information is fact-based. But how much more useful the ruling is, is not clear. In particular, for authors seeking random access, wishing to copy insubstantial parts of works, glean ideas, or exercise one of the fair dealing limitations, competition law may not prove to be so useful.

There is now a developing public sense that concentration in the publishing market, coupled with power over digital dissemination of creative works might just operate against the public interest in respect of the price of the public access to those works. Concerns were raised in the UK over the recent merger of Harcourt General, Inc (Harcourt) with Reed Elsevier plc (RE). That matter was referred to the Office of Fair Trading under the merger provisions of the Fair Trading Act 1973. While the competition commission agreed to the merger going ahead, specific concerns were raised during the course of their investigation relating to the science, technical and medical (STM) group. In their investigation of the STM market, the commission identified three potential public interest concerns. These were:

(a) arrangements for providing customers with access to electronic versions of STM journals;
(b) arrangements under which other access mechanisms would be able to establish links with RE's and Harcourt's electronic platforms; and
(c) the pricing of annual subscriptions to STM journals.

As a result of these findings, the competition commissioner has asked inter-

211 Anderman, *EC Competition Law and Intellectual Property Rights. The Regulation of Innovation.*
212 WB Cornish, *Intellectual Property*, para 18–16.

ested parties to comment on whether a further investigation should take place on these three specific issues.

This is one example of a small part of the electronic marketplace. In an era when there are a number of mergers occurring within the publishing and entertainment industries, questions must arise as to the extent of competition in the marketplace, and hence whether the competitive pressures are in fact in place to exert a downward pressure on prices.

1. *Lump Sum or Royalties?*

Drawing on the discussion above, it does not seem appropriate that the way in which remuneration is obtained from Internet dissemination should be regulated. If, however, those returns become excessive, then competition law controls might be required as a counterbalance to the lack of competition in the marketplace.

2. *New Kinds of Contracts?*

If there are to be new types of contracts for exploitation of works in the digital era pertaining to revenue flows, then these should be negotiated between the participants in the industry. Right holders, as suggested above, have sufficient rights to be able to exploit their works. How they do that should be up to negotiation within the industry once a suitable business model has been found.

3. *Compulsory Licences?*

As has been discussed earlier in this paper (Fair dealing and the Copyright Directive), the Copyright Directive provides for certain conditions under which a Member States may provide that limitation to the reproduction right may be made. This includes 'in respect of reproductions on any medium made by a natural person for private use and for ends that are neither directly nor indirectly commercial, on condition that the right holders receive fair compensation'. Article 5.2.6 Copyright Directive.

If member States choose to implement this limitation to the right of reproduction, this would appear to act as a compulsory licence: a user may make a copy for the purposes specified. However, it is on the condition that the right holders receive fair compensation. It is also noteworthy that it operates in relation to the right of reproduction only, and not the making available and communication to the public rights.

Should other compulsory licences be added? To the extent that it is considered that 'fair dealing' and like exceptions/limitations fall under the head of a compulsory licence, these have been discussed .

The difficulty with increasing the numbers of compulsory licenses is that it runs counter to the nature of copyright—in that copyright grants to the author the exclusive right to reproduce a work, albeit that the right is limited. In addition, those circumstances in which a compulsory licence could be required would need to comply with the three-step test to be found in the Berne Convention, itself the subject of much debate during the negotiation of the WIPO Copyright Treaty.

On the other hand, increasing those circumstances in which a user has the benefit of a compulsory licence may do much to counter the trend in recent legislation to focus on the needs of the right-holder, rather than on the user.

4. *Collecting Societies (Role, Organisation, Status and Repertoire, One Single Collecting Society on the Internet?)*

It is a matter of some debate as to whether collecting societies have a role in relation to Internet dissemination. In the analogue environment, collecting societies have worked well where it has been difficult, if not impossible for authors and right holders to manage their rights in a diverse marketplace. Equally they have provided a good service for users of works who have been able to approach a single organisation for permission to use a work in a given situation, rather than needing to seek out many copyright owners, who may be widely scattered.

However, on the Internet, it becomes much easier for individual authors, and other right holders, such as publishers to manage their own rights. For example, in the UK, the Copyright Licensing Agency (CLA) manages the rights of authors and publishers in relation to reproductions of their texts. However, the CLA do not have a mandate from their members (the authors and publishers) to manage digital rights. Instead, these rights tend to be managed by publishers who have been entering the on-line market. For instance, Sweet & Maxwell offers the legal database, Westlaw, and Butterworths offers the legal database, Lexis. Both of these publishers take licences or assignations of the digitisation rights in a number of works belonging to other publishers and authors. So it appears that the publishers are now acting as a type of collecting society in relation to their offerings in these databases.

There are other examples where it is clear that authors would prefer to manage their own digital rights, rather than to have these managed on their behalf by a collecting society. During the debate surrounding the Napster case, a number of artists came out in support of that file-sharing system because it gave them an opportunity to find their own market, unhampered by the licensing conditions negotiated on their behalf either by the music companies or by other collecting organisations.

With the development of technological management protection systems, authors should be able to manage their own works with ease, and thus have to rely less on the intervention of collecting societies on their behalf.

In sum, it would not appear to be an appropriate time to regulate for the establishment of any form of collecting society to manage digital rights. The market is in a state of flux. It is preferable to wait and see what develops in response to these changing market conditions. In the event that new forms of collecting societies do develop, and they end up in a dominant position, and that position is abused, then competition law may need to be used to shape behaviour.

B. Technical Means of Collecting the Royalties

As discussed above, new forms of digital payments systems are currently being developed. If successful, it would appear that these may the most appropriate mechanisms for collecting royalties as critically, they allow for micro-payments to be made. Such small sums would seem to be eminently suited to the requirements of digital delivery of entertainment products, for instance, the right to listen to a work for a particular period of time or number of times.

1. What Control Systems?

As discussed above new forms of digital management protection systems are being developed with consist of *inter alia* information designed to allow the exploitation of creative works over the Internet. These systems incorporate means by which copying and other uses of a work can be prevented where those uses have not been authorised by the right holder.

(a) Who Should Pay, to Whom, and How?

Technical means are already being developed whereby users of works disseminated over the Internet can pay for access to and use of those works by means of 'digital cash'. Several studies have indicated that these methods will allow 'micro charging'. Thus a user can pay a small sum simply to listen to a work. If a copy were to be made, a higher sum could be charged, reflecting the use made of the work in question. It would seem wholly appropriate that these types of charging mechanisms were developed and used in connection with digital dissemination.

(b) Should one put Levies on the Media and/or the Hardware?

One suggestion that has started to emerge in some literature is that of an imposition of a 'royalty' on the purchase of hardware (such as a computer and modem) or levied by way of access providers.[213] Such 'royalties' would be collected by collecting societies and then distributed to their members. In this case, it would be all right holders whose work was distributed on the Internet. The imposition of a royalty or levy on blank recording media is used in a number of European countries[214] but has so far been resisted in the UK. Broadly, the levy is designed to cover private copying of audio and audio visual works, very little taping of which, it is said, could be justified as fair dealing for the purposes of research and private study as that exemption does not cover sound recording and film copyright.[215] Thus for those countries which do permit private copying, the economic interests of the authors and right holders are protected by way of the imposition of the royalty or levy on the recording media that makes such copying possible, such as the video or cassette tape. However, the debate over such levy is far from settled. Those who oppose the levy argue that these media are used for many purposes other than copying of protected material, and that the levy represents little more than a special interest tax.[216] Those who are in favour of it see it as representing no more than the return to which the right holder and author is entitled.

However, in its potential application to the Internet, a number of factors should be borne in mind. First, in those countries where the levy applies, because it is put on to a formal footing, so private copying is permitted, or at least tolerated. If a levy were to be imposed on the hardware that makes up the Internet, then, by analogy, so private copying should be tolerated. It is not at all clear, and perhaps unlikely that private copying would be in the contemplation of those who push this line of thought. Rather, it appears that the levy would be to compensate those who lost revenue through the unauthorised and unremunerated copying using such facilities as those provided by Napster. There would thus be no direct benefit for those who paid the levy. Secondly, it is notable that one of the advantages that right holders take from the Internet is that individual licences can, where appropriate be entered into. They are unlikely to want to give up the potential of such control, and indeed individualised payment for specific uses in return for a blanket fee that may bear no relation to underlying use[217]. Thirdly, the

[213] See, eg, WW Fisher, *Digital Music: Problems and Possibilities* <http://www.law.harvard.edu/Academic_Affairs/coursepages/tfisher/Music.html>. Fisher considers the matter of tax and royalty systems, but then seems to dismiss it.

[214] For instance Germany, Austria, and France. W Kreile (1992) 23 *IIC* 449.

[215] CDPA s 29(1) Cornish, *Intellectual Property*, para 13–19.

[216] See generally G Davies, *Copyright and the Public Interest* (Germany: Max Planck Institute, 1994).

[217] Note PE Geller, 'Conflicts of Law in Cyberspace: International Copyright in a Digitally Networked World', in PB Hugenholtz (ed), *The Future of Copyright in a Digital Environment* (Dordrecht: Kluwer, 1996), 27, who argues that there is no role for compulsory licences in relation to the Internet because it is possible to licence individually. There is thus no econom-

ability for individual right holder control is significantly increased by the introduction of protection against the circumvention of technical devices used to protect access to a work. Certainly, unauthorised copying goes on and will no doubt continue. But, in the absence of the right to make private copies because a levy is imposed, what that levy would in fact amount to would be a tax on every purchaser of hardware designed to compensate right holders for those who continued to make private copies but with no additional benefit to themselves.

In light of the extensive framework that has been put into place to allow right holders to disseminate works over the Internet, and to have control over payment for and use of those works, it does not seem equitable that a compulsory levy be placed on those who use the Internet for perfectly legitimate purposes.[218]

ically justifiable reason for recourse to compulsory royalty rates since there need be no absence of agreement as required by the Berne Convention Art 11*bis* 2. Legal licences would therefore contravene normal modes of network exploitation. At 45.

[218] As it is, purchasers of computers will be paying an uplift in price to meet the needs of rights holders. Marks and Turnbull, 'Technical Protection Measures: The Intersection of Technology, Law and Commercial Licences' [2000] *EIPR*, 198 who discuss the initiatives taken by right holders and equipment manufacturers in developing copy protection systems for hardware. It will ultimately be the consumer who pays for these developments.

Chapter 11

The Legal Effect of Collective Agreements: A UK Perspective

*Douglas Brodie**

I. THE LEGAL STATUS OF COLLECTIVE AGREEMENTS

In the UK statute creates a conclusive presumption that collective agreements are not intended by the parties to be legally enforceable unless a number of specified conditions are met.[1] These conditions are that the agreement is in writing, and contains a provision which (however expressed) states that the parties intend that the agreement shall be a legally enforceable contract. How explicit must that intention be? It seems clear that it would not be legitimate to infer an intention from the nature of the agreement or its wording in general. The intention of the legislature was to avoid argument 'as to the inferences that could be legitimately drawn from the language used in collective agreements, and to the industrial relations functions of collective agreements'.[2] There must be a provision which expresses that intention. On the other hand, the use of the term 'however expressed' shows that any form of wording indicating a desire for legal enforcement would suffice:

> unless a collective agreement contains a statement in terms that show, at least, that the parties have directed their minds to the question of legal enforceability and have decided in favour of legal enforceability, there is . . . no sufficient statement of intention.[3]

However, in practice, it is very rare for a collective agreement to be legally enforceable between the collective parties. As a result, the main way in which collective agreements derive legal effect is through incorporation into the individual employment contract. It is important to stress that lack of legal enforceability at collective level is not a barrier to incorporation at individual level. In *Marley v Forward Trust Group* the collective agreement

* University of Edinburgh
1 Section 179, Trade Union and Labour Relations (Consolidation) Act 1992.
2 *NCB v NUM* [1988] IRLR 439, at 449.
3 Ibid.

provided that 'This agreement is binding in honour only and it is not intended to give rise to any legal obligation.'[4] The Court of Appeal held, unequivocally, that such a clause did not prevent appropriate terms from being incorporated into individual employment contracts.

II. COLLECTIVE AGREEMENTS AND EMPLOYMENT CONTRACTS

A. Incorporation

In the UK the matter of incorporation of collectively agreed terms is a two-stage process. First, there must be an intention to incorporate the term. Secondly, the term must be apt for incorporation (see below). Clearly, the easiest way to demonstrate the existence of an intention to incorporate is for the employment contract to make express reference to the collective agreement. Historically, where express incorporation was absent, matters were somewhat problematic. In 1940 the great Labour Lawyer Otto Kahn-Freund addressed the relationship between individual employment contracts and collective agreements and noted that 'English law has not so far taken cognizance of the normative function of collective industrial rules'.[5] He continued, 'it will then be necessary to reflect upon the ways in which the normative function of collective agreements can be made legally effective.[6] In the absence of express incorporation Kahn-Freund's solution was to deem that the employment had been concluded upon the terms of the 'collective bargain'.[7] There was no suggestion, at this stage, of how this result might be achieved in terms of legal mechanism. In 1943, however, Kahn-Freund expressed the view that a collective bargain could be regarded as custom and the appropriate terms implicitly incorporated:

> terms of employment can . . . become usages which, like commercial customs in mercantile law, become the lex contractus for individual contracts . . . The collective agreement is the embodiment of a custom, pre-determining the content of contracts of employment, unless contradicted by the express terms of those contracts.[8]

Kahn-Freund may have been saying no more than that collectively agreed terms could constitute a custom and hence be incorporated on the basis that the conventional contractual tests for binding custom had been satisfied.[9] If that was the case then there is nothing exceptional about his views but it is clear that he was saying more than that. Kahn-Freund believed that 'the

[4] [1986] ICR 891.

[5] Kahn-Freund (1941) *MLR*, 225, at 226.

[6] Ibid.

[7] Ibid.

[8] Kahn-Freund (1943) *MLR*, 112, at 117

[9] The standard formulation is contained in *Sagar v Ridehalgh* [1931] 1 Ch 310 at 338 and requires that the custom be reasonable, certain and notorious.

terms of a collective agreement are likely to be "crystallised custom" and as such automatically implied in the relevant contracts of employment.'[10] Even more boldly he states that

> the parties are, in the absence of an express term to the contrary, deemed implicitly to have incorporated the substance of the prevailing usages or customs, [and this] remains the principal link between collective agreements and contracts of employment.[11]

This view was put forward with complete confidence yet without discussion of the case law on binding custom.[12] Underpinning this stance was the view there was good reason to favour ready incorporation on policy grounds: 'the principal social function of the agreement as a code is the maintenance of wages and other standards in the interests of the workers.'[13] Collective bargaining seeks to 'convert formal into factual freedom of contract as between employer and workman, by raising the latter to a level of equality of bargaining power'.[14] The foregoing aim would be thwarted if incorporation was not facilitated.

It is worthy of note that Kahn-Freund does not appear to have ever addressed the concept of crystallised custom at any length. He returned to the topic in later writings but did not greatly elaborate on previous discussion. He appears to have been content to have found a device to bridge the gap between collective decision-making and individual rights and duties. Crystallised custom was a convenient veil behind which one could hide the automatic incorporation of the collective bargain.[15] Such an expansive use of custom brought it into the realms of legal fiction. Valuable as such reasoning can be, on policy grounds, one might argue that it will always be vulnerable to challenge to the extent it is not soundly grounded in pre-existing legal principle. Thus where one sought to incorporate but could not satisfy the general contractual rules on binding custom there was always the danger that reliance on crystallised custom would not lead to incorporation.

[10] Kahn-Freund, *Labour and the Law*, 2nd edn, 172.

[11] P Davies and M Freedland (ed), *Kahn-Freund's Labour and the Law*, 3rd edn (London: Stevens, 1983), 172

[12] *Hart v Riversdale Mill Co* [1928] 1 KB 176 and *Sagar v Ridehalgh* [1931] 1 Ch 301 are referred to in the text of *Labour and the Law* without discussion.

[13] Kahn-Freund, *Labour and the Law*, 2nd edn (London: Stevens, 1977), 132.

[14] Kahn-Freund 1943 *MLR*,112, at 117.

[15] The 1930s case of *Maclea v Essex Line* [1933] 45 Lloyds LR 254 at 257 may be an instance of 'crystallised custom'. There the plaintiff was employed 'upon the terms and conditions of the National Maritime Board as they were from time to time revised . . .', such an arrangement being found to be one 'perfectly familiar' to people in the shipping industry. The main evidence in *Maclea* amounting to mere assertions of this familiarity by two witnesses from the shipping industry.

B. Incorporation by Custom

In *Hamilton v Futura Floors Ltd*[16] it was sought, without success, to incorporate a term contained in an agreement between an employers' association and a trade union. At the time the employment contract was entered into, in 1982, the employer was not a member of the association and the judge concluded that incorporation was inappropriate even though the association represented 'most, but not all, of the major employers engaged in the . . . trade in Scotland'.[17] On the Kahn-Freund theory the lack of membership would not have been a barrier to incorporation as long as the agreement was actually applied in that trade:

> it does not matter whether the worker is a member of a union party to the agreement or whether the employer is or has at any time been a member of a 'contracting' association. What does matter is whether the terms of the agreement are in fact applied in the industry and district. The wages scales and other 'Codes' it contains can easily become `crystallised custom.'[18]

The court, however, noted the absence of evidence as to custom and refused to incorporate. In 1983 the employer joined the association but, not surprisingly, it was held that this did not lead to a variation in the employment contract. The issue arose again in the context of a debate as to relevancy in *Littlejohn v Clyde Port Authority.*[19] The pursuer alleged that he had been made redundant and sought to recover compensation under a scheme which had been negotiated between the employer and the relevant trade unions. He did not possess a written contract of employment and the statutory written statement made no mention of the scheme. However, Mr Littlejohn averred that it was

> custom and practice that employees of the defenders were compensated in terms of said agreement or one of its revisals . . . Accordingly by implication the said scheme became a term of the employment of all the employees of the defenders.

The case was allowed to go to proof. Lord Osborne acknowledged that

> the pursuer's averments . . . make it clear that his contention is that in all cases of redundancy which occurred before his, compensation was paid in terms of the compensation scheme and its revisals. That seems to me to be a potentially sound basis for an implication.

The pursuer in *Littlejohn* appeared to have learned from *Hamilton* and sought to prove that the mooted custom genuinely existed.

The cases of *Littlejohn* and *Hamilton* demonstrate that the UK courts

16 [1990] IRLR 478.

17 Ibid, at 480.

18 Kahn-Freund, in AD Flanders and HA Clegg (ed), *The System of Industrial Relations in Great Britain* (Oxford: Basil Blackwell, 1964), 58.

19 (1995) GWD 31-1611.

have not adopted an approach of 'automatic incorporation'. They make clear that if the basis of incorporation is custom then that custom must be established. The cases do not, however, deal with how difficult or otherwise it will be to establish the existence of a custom in the context of incorporation of a collective agreement. Such questions were recently considered by the EAT in *Henry v London General Transport Services.*[20] The tribunal below had held that in relation to the incorporation into a contract of employment of a term by way of a custom and practice, the custom and practice so relied on must be reasonable, certain, and notorious. They also held that strict proof is required of the custom and practice and that the burden of such proof is upon the party seeking to rely on the consequential incorporation of the term into the contract. The EAT agreed that the criteria which had to be satisfied before a custom could be incorporated were that the custom was 'reasonable certain and notorious'. However, they did not accept that these criteria had to be proved strictly:

> It is plain that courts and tribunals should not lightly find a custom to exist, but a requirement that the three ingredients of reasonableness, certainty and notoriety are proved on the conventional balance of probabilities is in our judgment a sufficient bar to ensure that customs will not too lightly be taken to be present.

Having said that it may be argued that the criteria are in themselves strict. Davies and Freedland have observed that were the courts to apply to collective agreements

> the sorts of tests that the general principles of the law of contract impose as the criteria for binding customs; . . . these rather exacting requirements would be unlikely to be met in any given case.[21]

Before leaving the case of *Henry* it is worth noting that the term which was sought to be incorporated was that

> a change in the staff's terms and conditions in respect of which the T&GWU had reached agreement with the employer, which had been notified to the staff and which that union bona fide believed (and so informed the employer) had attracted the support of the majority of the staff affected, would, without more, thereafter become a term or condition of the employment of all the staff so affected, whether members of the union or not.

It is also noteworthy that the EAT observed that

> given the large number of staff concerned, the occasional commercial need for a speedy decision on changes in employment rights and practices and the consequential difficulty in conducting individual negotiations and given also the settled history of the union's negotiating role over a number of years, it would be hard to describe such a term as unreasonable.

[20] [2001] IRLR 132.

[21] Davies and Freedland, op cit, 168.

C. Incorporation by Implication

It is also possible that incorporation of a collective agreement may take place if that is implicit in the contract of employment that was entered into. After all, on general contractual principles, to the extent that the parties have not expressly set out the terms of their bargain, the court will fill in the gaps based on what they regard as the implicit intention of the parties. In *Alexander v Standard Telephones Ltd (No 2)* it was said that before incorporation could take place on this basis there had to be `the extraction of a recognisable contractual intent as between the individual employee and his employer'.[22] The difficulty that arises is to determine the circumstances in which an intention to incorporate can be inferred given that `the mere existence of collective agreements which are relevant to the employee and his employment does not include a contractual intent . . . '.[23] Certainly it has been suggested judicially that the process of inference may be an arduous one since 'very often the evidence will not be sufficient to establish such an intent in a manner which satisfies accepted contractual criteria and satisfies ordinary criteria of certainty'.[24]

How then can one surmount the hurdle of establishing the existence of an implicit intent to incorporate? The Courts have found this issue a somewhat difficult one. It might have been thought that the fact of contracting against a background of a particular collective agreement or collective bargaining machinery would be taking as evidence of an intention to incorporate. This would help 'convert formal into factual freedom of contract as between employer and workman'. However, it is doubtful whether evidence of that nature would be of much assistance since the courts have taken the view that 'there is no necessity to infer an intention to incorporate since collective agreements have a function and value of their own which exists wholly independently of any individual contract of employment'.[25] The case law suggests that a variety of other factors are likely to be relevant. It has been suggested that the intent of the collective parties was relevant:

> it is clear that no-one involved in the April 1991 talks which led to the agreement . . . believed that the agreement was binding upon individuals; and no-one intended that that should be the case.[26]

The relevant intent must surely be that of the parties to the contract of employment and it would seem that other views are irrelevant.[27] Some of

[22] *Alexander v Standard Telephones (No 2)* [1991] IRLR 286, at 292.
[23] Ibid. [24] Ibid. [25] Ibid.
[26] *Lee v GEC* [1993] IRLR 383, at 391.
[27] The intent of the collective parties would be relevant to a case, in Scotland, where the employee was raising the action on the basis of Jus Quaesitum Tertio. In such a case the pursuer sues on the basis of the collective agreement not the contract of employment. See Hunter (1975) *JR*,47.

the recent case law also suggests that the content and character of the collective agreement is relevant.[28] Certainly, it has always been the case that, where the parties intend to incorporate terms from a collective agreement, it is not every term that is incorporated but only those which are appropriate to the individual employment relationship:

> all this applies only to those collective terms which are capable and intended to be terms of the contracts of employment, and as terms of those contracts to give rise to rights and obligations which can be enforced through the remedies of the law of contract.[29]

The novelty in the approach in the more recent cases was that if a term was apt for incorporation that would go towards inferring an intention to incorporate. Third, the proportion of the collective agreement which relates to individual obligations may be relevant:

> where none of the other clauses of the collective agreement are apt to be incorporated into the individual employment contract, it would require some cogent indication in clause 6 that it was to have a different character and, be incorporated.[30]

It is highly questionable how much can be read into the overall content of an agreement. Many agreements deal with both collective and individual matters and the question must be what is the function of the term in dispute. Indeed, a particular term may have both a collective and an individual dimension.

The conduct of the contracting parties may also be relevant. Thus if an employer has been in the practice of paying wages in accordance with a collective agreement that may allow an inference to be made that the term(s) as to wages is to be incorporated:

> where the relevant subject-matter is one of present day-to-day relevance to the employer and employee, as for example wage rates and hours of work, the continuing relationship between employer and employee, the former paying wages and providing work, the latter working and accepting wages, provides a basis for inferring such a contractual intent.[31]

However, the difficulty with this approach is that it somewhat atomised. It does not allow one to say that, because some parts of an agreement are adhered to in practice, an implicit intention exists to incorporate the agreement as a whole. This might pose a problem in a situation like redundancy given the weight placed on 'day-to-day relevance': where, as in the case of redundancy, the situation does not have daily implications but only arises occasionally the inference will be more difficult to sustain'.[32]

[28] For instance, Lee, above n 26, at 391.
[29] Kahn- Freund, *Labour and the Law*, 1st edn (London: Stevens, 1972), 149.
[30] Alexander, above n.22 , at 293.
[31] Ibid, 292 .
[32] Ibid.

III. *JUS QUAESITUM TERTIO*

In Scotland the doctrine of *jus quaesitum tertio* provides a further possible basis for incorporation. However, a number of obstacles arise. In particular, one must remember that, by virtue of section 179, most collective agreements will be unenforceable between the collective parties. Does it then follow that it would be incompetent for an employee to sue on the collective agreement? The case of *Love v Amalgamated Society of Lithographic Printers* is directly in point.[33] There, the wife of an insane trade union member sued for certain benefits allegedly due to her under the contract of membership contained in the union rules. It was objected that section 4 of the Trade Union Act 1871 (now repealed) was an insuperable bar to the action; section 4 provided that certain agreements entered into by trade unions were not directly enforceable in the courts. However, it was said that 'it is plain that it was not the intention of the statute to exclude the jurisdiction of a court in the case of a claim made by a third party against a trade union'. The court went on to allow the claim on the basis of *jus quaesitum tertio*. *Love* is of interest because a third party was allowed to enforce a contract which was unenforceable between the two contracting parties. However, matters may be more problematic in the case of a collective agreement since the Court of Appeal have held that where a collective agreement is not a legally enforceable contract there is no contract at all.[34] Even if one disregards the foregoing difficulty other difficulties also exist:

> It is an accepted rule that to bring the doctrine into operation both contracting parties must have intended the tertius to sue . . . it will rarely be the case—especially if a collective agreement is negotiated in London on a national basis—that both contracting parties would intend to confer on employees a right to sue as tertii in Scotland while their English counterparts had no such right.[35]

One might also note that while 'collective agreements frequently impose obligations on employees, the doctrine of *jus quaesitum tertio* does not extend to the imposing of duties on tertii'.[36]

A. Agency

It seems clear that it would be possible for the terms of a collective agreement to be incorporated into an individual employment contract on the basis that in entering into the collective bargain the trade union acted as the

[33] 1912, 2 SLT 50.
[34] *Montresso Shipping Co v ITWF* [1982] ICR 675.
[35] Scottish Law Commission, Memorandum No 38, Constitution and Proof of Voluntary Obligations, 45.
[36] Ibid at 46.

agent of the employee. It is equally clear that to offer the concept of agency as a generally applicable rationale for incorporation in the UK would be erroneous. The courts have not been sympathetic to arguments, which treat the union as an agent for its members. For instance, the EAT has denied that membership of a union, per se, creates a relationship of general agency whereby a trade union was entitled to bargain with the employer on the member's behalf.[37] The EAT went on to remark that

> there is no reason at all why, in a particular case, union representatives should not be the agents of an employee to make a contract, or to receive a notice, or otherwise effect a binding transaction on his behalf. But that agency so to do does not stem from the mere fact that they are union representatives and that he is a member of the union; it must be supported in the particular case by the creation of some specific agency, and that can arise only if the evidence supports the conclusion that there was such an agency.[38]

There are, of course, a number of sound reasons which explain why more use has not been made of agency principles in this context. One problem is that of contractual capacity given that a number of employees will be under the age of 18 and lack full capacity. The main problem, however, is the question of the authority of trade unions to act as agents of their members. When entering into collective agreements trade unions are normally regarded as acting as principals not agents. Even if a union is regarded as having the power of a general agent to bind its members in dealings with the employer what is the position of those who have not joined the union, those who have left the union and those who join the union after the agreement is concluded? In the case of new employees they will be readily assumed to have accepted employment on the same terms as existing employees (though this does not arise through the operation of agency law).[39] Ultimately the concept of agency is perhaps most apposite where 'the number of workers involved is small, the matters in dispute are personal to them and the issues are localised to a single employer'.[40] A court may on occasion be prepared to regard the union as having a certain implied authority to bind its members through the collective bargaining process. In *Mordecei v Jacob Beatus Ltd* the tribunal remarked that

> in these days such a matter as this [a flexibility agreement] which is very commonly included in agreements between management and unions, probably was within the implied authority of the union to negotiate on behalf of their membership.[41]

[37] *Burton Group v Smith* [1977] IRLR 351.

[38] Ibid at 353.

[39] *Mordecei v Jacob Beatus Ltd* [1975] 170.

[40] B A Hepple and P O'Higgins, *Employment Law*, 4th edn (London: Sweet & Maxwell, 1981), 127.

[41] *Mordecei*, above n 39, at 171.

It must also be said that should an adjudicator not wish to incorporate he may borrow the language of agency to further this aim. The rigidity of the agency doctrine when applied in the industrial relations context can be played on here. A possible instance of this occurring is *Singh v BSC* where the respondents failed to produce any documents

> which stated specifically either that [the union] had been appointed the sole negotiating agency for the applicant . . . or that the applicant's contract of employment could be varied without his consent by agreement reached between the respondents and [the union].[42]

B. *Appropriateness for Incorporation*

Even where an intention to incorporate the terms of a particular collective bargain is established, the courts will only give legal effect to those terms which are appropriate for incorporation into the individual employment contract. This is the case even where a collective agreement is expressly incorporated.[43] For instance, in *NCB v NUM* the employees' contracts stated that they were 'regulated by and subject to National . . . Agreements for the time being in force'. In 1946 an agreement had been entered into which established a conciliation scheme under which the NUM was given exclusive recognition. Two mineworkers contended that under their contracts of employment they were entitled to insist that the NCB negotiate with the NUM. This contention was rejected and it was held that the reference in the contracts to collective agreements 'is to those National Agreements that contain substantive provisions regarding wages or conditions of service'.[44] Cases dealing with the appropriateness or aptness of terms for incorporation have more often arisen in situations where the collectively agreed terms were implicitly incorporated. Should the rules on aptness be applied in the same way in both cases? One might take the view that because a source of terms has been expressly referred to in the contract then these terms should have binding effect. There may, of course, be difficulties caused by vagueness of wording and the like. Nevertheless, it has been contended that, 'in linguistic terms any collective obligation is capable of individuation'.[45] There are, however, competing considerations. Take the 1946 agreement referred to above:

> In the procedures laid down . . . no part is played by any individual mineworker. The machinery is designed to be invoked and operated either by the NCB or by the NUM with the co-operation of the other. It simply does not lend itself to enforceability at the suit of an individual mineworker.[46]

[42] [1974] IRLR 131 at 135. [43] Alexander, above n 22, at 292.
[44] *NCB v NUM* [1986] IRLR 439, at 454.
[45] Davies and Freedland, op cit, 292.
[46] *NCB*, above, n. 44, at 454.

Furthermore collective agreements are normally unenforceable as between the collective parties given the statutory presumption to this effect. It is submitted that to allow an individual to enforce a scheme such as the one in the NCB case would be to circumvent legislative policy. Thus where a clause is of a type which is collective in nature I would argue that it normally should not be given legal effect through the medium of the individual employment contract. This is irrespective of whether there are express words of incorporation, unless the wording clearly indicates that the parties intended incorporation of particular parts of the collective agreement.

The fact that it is only the appropriate terms of a collective agreement which are incorporated gives judges a significant amount of discretion and the cases do not reveal an articulated set of principles. The courts tend to be no more forthcoming than to furnish statements along the lines that a term apt for incorporation is one not 'outside the ambit of the employer/employee relationship . . .'[47] Determining that ambit can be difficult and is not a value free exercise. The case of *City and Hackney Health Authority v NUPE*[48] is of interest because the term at issue was very much on the divide between individual and collective obligations. There a provision of the Whitley Council agreement for hospital ancillary staff provided that

> full-time union officers shall be permitted to visit the workplace in the performance of their union duties and for the purpose of seeing that the council's agreements are observed . . .[49]

Lord Justice Oliver stated that

> there is at least an arguable case for saying that the existence and maintenance of trade union facilities at a hospital is a condition of service which can be treated as incorporated . . .[50]

Perhaps the essence of the difficulty is caused by the fact that, in truth, the term has both a collective and individual aspect.

Collective agreements (or parts thereof) that deal with redundancy have tended to pose particular problems for the UK courts. Clauses dealing with redundancy pay clearly fall within the ambit of the employment relationship. For instance, in *Lee v GEC* it was common ground in the case that redundancy pay was pay in the normal sense of that word.[51] In *Alexander (No 2)* the litigation concerned the part of the collective agreement in question

[47] *Tadd v Daily Telegraph* [1983] IRLR 320, at 328. In *Alexander v Standard Telephones*[1990] IRLR 55 at 59 the distinction was drawn between 'terms in a collective agreement which are designed and intended to govern the relationship between the employer and the union, and those designed and intended to benefit individual employees . . . '

[48] [1985] IRLR 252.

[49] Ibid at 253.

[50] Ibid at 255.

[51] [1993] IRLR 383.

which set out a redundancy procedure; clause 15.5.1. providing that: `In the event of compulsory redundancy selection will be made on the basis of service within the group . . .'[52] Clause 15.5.2. stated that

> If in the event of compulsory redundancy, the balance of skills is jeopardised it will be redressed by operators moving voluntarily into the required shift or areas. Failing the necessary number of volunteers . . . the company will direct operators to the required areas to be retrained if necessary.[53]

In relation to clause 15.5.1. it was held that it was `not sufficiently cogently worded to give rise to an inference of incorporation into individual contracts of employment'.[54] This seems very much arguable. The wording of the clause seems clear enough and it would not be difficult to argue that individual rights are conferred on the basis of seniority. Indeed at interlocutory stage it had been held that

> the plaintiffs have an arguable case that the provisions in the collective agreements which provide for LIFO are part of their contracts of employment. They have the effect of benefiting employees who have been with the defendant for a long time and put at risk those that have not.[55]

With regard to clause 15.5.2. it was held that it `is expressed as an obligation of the company towards employees in general and therefore is not appropriate as a term of any individual contract of employment'.[56] Again the reasoning seems less than overwhelmingly persuasive. Terms of collective agreements will frequently be expressed as obligations of the company towards employees in general. The issue is whether the content of the clause is meant to regulate the individual employment relationship(s). If that is the case then incorporation should take place provided that the wording is sufficiently certain. Here individual employees would appear to have a right to retraining in the event of redeployment.

It may be that there is a reluctance to incorporate terms contained in redundancy agreements; particularly if the term is procedural or at least is contained in a procedural agreement.[57] Certainly the outcome of such cases seems particularly difficult to predict. One recalls the 1978 decision in *BL(UK)Ltd v McQuilken*[58] where a redundancy agreement was held to be inappropriate for incorporation on the grounds that the `agreement was a long-term plan, dealing with policy rather than the rights of individual employees'.[59] The key clause provided that the

[52] *Alexander*, ibid, n 22, at 291.

[53] Ibid at 291.

[54] Ibid at 294.

[55] *Alexander v Standard Telephones* [1990] IRLR 55 at 59.

[56] *Alexander*, above, n 22, at 294.

[57] Such an approach can be traced back to the decision of the Privy Council in the case of *Young v Canadian Railway* [1931] AC 83.

[58] [1978] IRLR 245.

[59] Ibid at 246.

employees . . . would be interviewed by a member of the personnel department with the object of establishing a list of employees who wished to take up the option of (a) retraining or (b) redundancy.[60]

It would seem that it would not have been difficult to have held that the employee had a contractual right to elect for either retraining or redundancy. One might argue that the effect of the decision is to re-write the bargain for the purpose of increasing managerial prerogative.

IV. SUMMARY

It would be an unusual occurrence to find a collective agreement in the UK that was legally enforceable between the collective parties. Contracts of employment in the UK do, however, frequently contain terms that are derived from collective agreements. Incorporation will take place (subject to the question of the aptness of the term) where the employment contract contains an express clause to that effect. Demonstrating that incorporation has taken place implicitly or by custom may be no easy task. It may be that, at present, the courts are displaying something of a reluctance to give normative effect to collectively agreed terms. This may be duc, at least to some extent, to a return to traditional contractual principles, and as a corollary, a distaste for legal fictions such as crystallised custom. Nonetheless it is tempting to speculate whether the perpetual evolution of the common law has been influenced by legislative policy towards collective bargaining. In the UK, during the 1980s and 1990s, the traditional consensus as to the value of collective bargaining was lost and it became dangerous to assume that a court would do anything other than apply the common law in a traditional way . The question of which terms are appropriate for incorporation is also not without controversy. It may be that, on occasion, the real reason for not failing to incorporate is a desire to protect managerial prerogative.

[60] Ibid at 245.

PART FIVE: CRIMINAL PROCEDURE

Chapter 12

Prosecutorial Discretion and its Limits— The Scottish Approach

*Joëlle Godard**

I. INTRODUCTION

Scottish lawyers are generally proud of the perceived effectiveness and fairness of their criminal justice system and this is true for their system of public prosecution. According to Lord Moncrieff 'a more efficient and a more satisfactory mode of conducting criminal affairs does not exist in any country in the world'.[1] There is no better platform than the International Academy of Comparative Law for challenging such a statement.

The system of public prosecution in Scotland is well established (see II below) and is considered to operate properly but in recent times it has undergone, and continues to undergo, some of the most profound changes in its long history. The Scotland Act 1998, and the establishment of a Scottish Parliament,[2] have paved the way for more searching scrutiny of the policy and decisions of the Lord Advocate than ever before. This led to the publication of a prosecution code in June 2001[3] (annex 1). The code sets out the range of options available to procurators fiscal in dealing with reports of crime and the criteria for making decisions (see III below).

The needs of victims and witnesses and demands for greater openness and accountability have also led to the publication in October 2001of two reports[4] into the investigation, legal proceedings and family liaison

* University of Edinburgh.

[1] Alex Robertson, 1887 15 Rettie (J) 1, *per* Lord Justice-Clerk Moncrieff.

[2] The Scottish Parliament and its Executive, first elected in May 1999, and assuming full powers in July 1999, has taken over the responsibilities previously enjoyed by the Scottish Office in relation to criminal justice. The legislative and executive responsibility for the machinery of criminal justice is now entirely in devolved hands.

[3] <http://www.crownoffice.gov.uk/publications/CO_Pcode.pdf>.

[4] The two inquiry reports were laid before Parliament on 24 Oct 2001: 'Report of the Inquiry into the Liaison Arrangements Between the Police, the Prosecutor Fiscal Service and the Crown Office and the Family of the Deceased Surjit Singh Chhokar in Connection with the Murder of Surjit Surjit Sing Chhokar and the Related Prosecutions', by Dr Raj Jandoo, Advocate; and 'The Report of an Inquiry into Crown Decision-Making in the Case of the Murder of Surjit Singh Chhokar', by The Rt Hon Sir Anthony Campbell.

arrangements in the case of the murder of Surjit Singh Chhokar.[5] These reports, which have shown some system failure, are unprecedented. Never before has an individual prosecution decision been open up to such scrutiny. The Lord Advocate, Colin Boyd, has assured the Scottish Parliament of his will to follow their recommendations. The Scottish Parliament's Justice Committee, 'Justice 2 Committee', is also conducting an inquiry into the Crown Office and Procurator Fiscal Service[6] and reviews of the management and prosecution of High Court cases and of summary court business have also been announced. We also have to mention the incorporation of the ECHR and the Lockerbie trial which were unprecedented events in the Scottish legal system.

The prosecution office, which used to be called 'the silent service',[7] has increasingly found itself in the spotlight in relation to the effectiveness of the prosecution system in the discharge of justice. It has now to adapt. According to the Crown Office and Procurator Fiscal Service Strategic Plan 2000–2003, the department should be seen to be more open and accountable.

II. PROSECUTION SERVICE

A. Origins

The long history and traditions of the prosecution system in Scotland continue to play an important part in its present administration.

According to William Reid[8]:

> the institution of the procurator fiscal was imported into Scotland from the Continent and more particularly France around 1560 when French influence was at its height. It was adapted and utilised first in the trading burghs which were relatively amenable to innovation and quite rapidly thereafter the office became established in the sheriffdoms and other territorial jurisdictions.

It was the Sheriff who had investigative powers and gradually, between the sixteenth and eighteenth centuries, the Procurator Fiscal developed the role of prosecutor.

The prosecution of crime in Scotland is a public function. The Crown's

[5] A thirty-two year old Sikh was stabbed to death during an attack by three men who were charged with murder. The failure to obtain a conviction for murder has been attributed to the fact that all three men did not stand trial together: at each trial the accused before the court blamed another not before the court.

[6] This enquiry aims to examine in broad scope whether the Crown Office and PFS is equipped to meet the needs of a modern justice system.

[7] S Moody, 'The Silent Service Speaks', in *Scots Law Times* (1992), 293–5.

[8] W Reid, 'The origins of the office of Procurator Fiscal in Scotland', 1965 Judicial Review, 154–60.

right was clearly established by the Act of 1587, cap 77, whether the victims chose to prosecute or not but the party injured had still the right to prosecute. Gradually, the right of private parties to institute proceedings became subordinate to the prosecutor's leave and Scotland moved towards a system of public prosecution which arose from the involvement of the Lord Advocate as public prosecutor[9].

B. Present Structure

There is a national prosecution service in Scotland, termed the 'Crown Office and Procurator Fiscal Service', headed by the Lord Advocate

The Lord Advocate has responsibility for prosecuting the most serious criminal cases in the High Court along with his deputy, the Solicitor General, and members of the Scottish Bar appointed as Advocates Depute. The Lord Advocate and the Solicitor General are the Scottish Law Officers and they are both members of the Scottish Executive. They and the advocates depute are known collectively as Crown counsel.

The responsibility for prosecuting all other less serious cases is also in the hands of the Lord Advocate and this function is devolved to local prosecutors, known as procurators fiscals. The prosecutors fiscal are qualified lawyers, usually solicitors, trained in criminal law and employed as civil servants. The Fiscal Service was established as a department of state under the Sheriff Courts and Legal Officers (Scotland) Act 1927. There is a network of 48 Procurator Fiscal offices across Scotland. They are grouped into six regions, coinciding with the Sheriffdoms (annex 2).

C. Procedure

The Procurator Fiscal receives reports of crime from the police and reporting agencies. The decision whether criminal proceedings should be commence rests, in the majority of cases, with the Procurator Fiscal whether or not any person has been arrested or 'charged' by the police[10]. Unlike in England, where the police are still responsible for charging the accused, it is the Procurator Fiscal in Scotland who decides what charges will be brought and can modify or drop some charges in return for a guilty plea (a 'plea-bargain'). The prosecutor in Scotland has a wide discretion as to prosecute or to divert cases to alternative measures (see IV below). Where criminal proceedings are taken, the Procurator Fiscal will decide in what forum. The accused has no say in the matter and may not demand that his case be heard before a jury.

[9] WG Normand, 'The Public Prosecutor in Scotland' (1938) 54 *LQR*, 345–57.

[10] *A Guide to the Crown Office and Procurator Fiscal Service* (Crown Office, 2001), 6.

If the crime is serious, solemn proceedings will be started which means that the case will be heard by a jury in the Sheriff Court or in the High Court (for the most serious crimes). If the case is less serious, a Sheriff can sit without a jury (summary proceedings) or the case can be heard by the District Court. For details on different stages of prosecution, see annex 3.

D. Staff Problem, Numbers, and Experience

While the total number of cases received annually by the Prosecution Service has remained steady at around 285,000, the number of cases requiring prosecution on indictment, both in the Sheriff Court and the High Court, has increased. The creation of the new Parliament has also generated an increase of work with requests to give evidence to parliamentary committees.

According to a study commissioned by the Crown Office,[11] it appears that work related pressure is having a serious impact on the wellbeing of many staff and on levels of job satisfaction across the organisation. The general public became aware of this problem with the resignation of a senior procurator fiscal, David Hingston, who wrote in a daily newspaper:[12]

> The Procurator Fiscal service is not working anymore. There are too few people trying to do too much work and the victims are justice and the Scottish public . . . The entire service is totally depressed and extremely stressed . . . There are not enough fiscals to do the work and as a result mistakes are made. And with every mistake made by a fiscal, justice suffers.

The Crown Office has recognized the need to strengthen resources[13] and has been actively recruiting staff in recent times[14] with a 22 per cent increase in staffing. The problem of retention of staff is also a problem that must be addressed. That raises the issue regarding the experience levels of deputes because there is an inevitable delay between being recruited and becoming an effective resource.

The current profile of legal staff experience levels as at 31 Oct 2001 is:

[11] *Success Through People*, vol 1, issue (1 Nov 2001).

[12] Reported in *The Scotsman* (30 Oct 2001).

[13] In the previous comprehensive spending review, the service received £22.5 million over three years. In the budget consequentials that was strengthened by a further £6 million over three years, in recognition of the increasing burden of drugs prosecutions. Our baseline has gone up from just over £47 million in 1997 to £61 million in 2001

[14] Since Nov 1998, 62.3 members of legal staff have been appointed—representing an increase in total legal staff numbers (excluding trainees) of 22 per cent. Numbers of legal staff in the supervisory grade of Principal Depute have increased by 32 per cent over the same period, from 55.9 to 74.2.

	Crown Office	PF Service	Total
Under 1 year	0	29	29
1–2 years	0	29	29
2–3 years	0	37	37
3–4 years	1	10	11
4–5 years	1	13	14
5–6 years	6	12	18
6–8 years	5	17	22
8–10 years	7	18	25
10 years +	23	157	180
Total 365			

III. CRITERIA FOR PROSECUTION

In Scotland the master of the instance in all prosecutions for the public interest is the Lord Advocate. It is for him to decide when and against whom to launch prosecution and upon what charges. It is for him to decide in which court they shall be prosecuted. It is for him to decide what pleas of guilt he will accept and it is for him to decide when to withdrawn or abandon proceedings. Not only so, even when a verdict of guilt has been returned and recorded it still lies with the Lord Advocate whether to move the court to pronounce sentence and without that motion no sentence can be pronounced or imposed.[15]

Lord Cameron's summary of the public prosecutor's powers encapsulate the prosecutor's role for starting prosecution (section 1) and once the prosecution is started (section 2) but his Lordship gives no indications of the controls on the exercise of prosecutorial discretion (section 3).

A. *Criteria for Starting Prosecution*

In making their decisions, the prosecution service act independently of the police, the victim, or of any other party. The High Court of Justiciary has specifically acknowledged:[16]

The Lord Advocate in this country is the recognised prosecutor in the public interest. It is for him, in the exercise of his responsible office, to decide whether he will prosecute in the public interest and at the public expense, and under our constitutional practice this decision is a matter for him and for him alone. No one can compel him to give his reasons . . . the decision whether or not to prosecute is exclusively within his jurisdiction.

[15] *Boyle v HM Advocate* 1976, JC 32—Lord Camreon.
[16] *McBain v Crichton* 1961, JC 26—Lord Justice-General Clyde.

Prosecutors could generally decide not to prosecute even in the most serious cases such as rape or were not required to report to or consult any higher authority[17] and Peter Duff mentions some cases which led him to conclude that 'it is possible to get away with murder in Scotland as long as the Lord Advocate sympathises with your motives'.[18]

It is to avoid this lack of accountability and to 'provide an improved understanding of the decision making process as well as an indication of its complexity'[19] that the Prosecution Code set out the criteria for decision making:

In considering the action to be taken in relation to reports of crime the prosecutor must take account of both legal and public interest considerations.[20]

1. *Legal Considerations*

Legal considerations include domestic law, European law and international law. Since devolution the European Convention on Human Rights has been particularly significant.

(a) Domestic Law

In considering cases the Procurator Fiscal must first decide whether the conduct complained of constitutes a crime known to the law of Scotland and whether there is any legal bar to prosecution (for example, a statutory time limit might already have expired when the case is reported to the fiscal; or the Scottish courts might not have jurisdiction over the offence).

(b) International and European Law

The Human Rights Act 1998 and the Scotland Act 1998 require Scottish prosecutors to act in a way which is compatible with the European Convention on Human Rights. The Scotland Act 1998 also makes it clear that the Scottish Executive must act compatibly with the United Kingdom's international obligations in general.[21]

Between 20 May 1999 and 1 September 2001, 1157 'devolution issues' (ECHR challenges taken in terms of the Scotland Act 1998) were intimated to the Lord Advocate. Of these 1157 challenges, 1097 (or 94.8 per cent) were decided in favour of the Crown, some after a hearing before the Judicial Committee of the Privy Council.

[17] In cases of homicide the Procurator Fiscal must report to Crown Counsel and, with complaints against the police there is a requirement to report in certain circumstances.

[18] P Duff, 'The Prosecution Service: Independence and Accountability', in P Duff and N Hutton (ed), *Criminal Justice in Scotland* (Aldershot: Ashgate, 1999)

[19] Crown Office and Procurator Fiscal Service—Prosecution Code (2001), 1.

[20] Ibid, 3.

[21] Ibid.

It is also important to note that since 2 October 2001 it has been possible, by virtue of the Human Rights Act 1998, for accused persons and appellants to rely upon Convention rights arguments in criminal proceedings.

2. *Evidential Considerations*

Evidential considerations take account of both the quantity and the quality of the available evidence.

(a) Sufficiency of Evidence

Sufficiency is a technical, legal measure of the evidence. A prosecution will proceed only when there is sufficient admissible and corroborated evidence in law. Scottish criminal procedure requires that there must be evidence from at least two sources to prove each of the essential elements of the crime and also to prove that the particular accused person was the one who committed that crime.

'If, after a full inquiry, the procurator fiscal is satisfied that the evidence is insufficient, he cannot then proceed with a prosecution.'[22] Insufficiency of evidence accounts for a substantial proportion of all 'no proceedings' cases (25 per cent) in the period from October 2000 to September 2001).

The sufficiency of the evidence is determined independently of its quality. If there is a sufficiency of evidence the prosecutor will authorise prosecution even if there are reservations about the quality of that evidence, because the quality of the evidence is a matter for the jury to determine. The question is whether there is evidence from two independent sources which, if accepted by the jury, could prove the essential facts. If there is not, the accused has no case to answer and the trial judge would withdraw the case from the jury and acquit the accused. If there is a sufficiency of evidence the case will be determined by the jury who will decide, taking into account the quality of the evidence, whether the Crown has proved guilt beyond reasonable doubt.

(b) Quality of Evidence

The quality of the evidence is simply a measure of the ability of the evidence to persuade a jury beyond reasonable doubt of the guilt of the accused on the charge. It takes into account consideration of the credibility (honesty) and reliability (accuracy) of the evidence.[23]

Assuming that there is sufficient admissible, reliable and credible

[22] Ibid, 4.

[23] The Report of an Inquiry into Crown Decision-Making in the Case of the Murder of Surjit Singh Chhokar, above n 4, ch 13.

evidence of a crime committed by the accused, the prosecutor must consider what action is required in the public interest.

(c) Public Interest

Public interest considerations often include an assessment of a range of competing interests. The factors that require to be taken into account will vary according to the circumstances of each case. Factors taken into account include:[24]

(i) The nature and gravity of the offence
(ii) The impact of the offence on the victim and other witnesses
(iii) The age, background and personal circumstances of the accused
(iv) The age and personal circumstances of the victim and other witnesses
(v) The attitude of the victim
(vi) The motive for the crime
(vii) The age of the offence
(viii) Mitigating circumstances
(ix) The effect of prosecution on the accused
(x) The risk of further offending
(xi) The availability of a more appropriate civil remedy
(xii) Powers of the court
(xiii) Public concern

B. Once the Prosecution is Started

Special requirements are applicable to the Scottish prosecutor.

1. Time Limits

It is a virtue of Scottish criminal procedure that the Crown must bring a case against an accused to trial within strict time limits. This protection has been enjoyed in Scotland since the Criminal Procedure Act 1701.

The trial of a person fully committed in custody must begin within 110 days of committal.[25] If it does not he must be liberated forthwith and cannot be charged again with that offence. In certain limited circumstances a judge may extend the time. Fault on the part of the prosecutor is specifically excluded as a circumstance for granting an extension of time.[26] This '110-day rule' was described in the Department's annual report 1998–9, as one of the most rigorous time limits in the world.

[24] Submission of the Crown Office and Procurator Fiscal Service to the Scottish Parliament (Justice 2 Committee) 19 Nov 2001.
[25] Criminal Procedure (Scotland) Act 1995 s 65(4).
[26] Ibid, s 65(7).

If the accused is on bail he cannot be tried on indictment unless the trial begins within a period of twelve months of his first appearance on petition.[27] If the trial does not begin within this period he will be 'for ever free from all question or process for that offence'.

It is relevant in the context of these general remarks about the Prosecutorial Discretion and its limits to draw attention to consequence of time limits. The urgency to have a case prepared and to commence the trial leaves little time for consideration of papers. The Crown is under time constraints. In order to meet the deadlines, Crown counsel and fiscals might have to drop cases so that they can divert their resources to dealing with the serious cases that come under the rule. Adjournment rates of solemn cases in the High Court was around 25 per cent and during the year 2000 it was often as high as 40 per cent with a similar caseload.[28] Two recent cases in which delays by the fiscal service resulted in the cases being time-barred attracted media attention and it was suggested in Parliament to extend the 110–day rule to 150 days.[29]

2. *Charges and Choice of Court*

Where prosecution is the chosen option, the prosecutor determines the court and the charges. As 'the master of the instance', the prosecutors exercise their discretionary powers in their quasi-judicial role.

(a) The Choice of Court

According to the Departmental guidance:[30]

> The choice of court will, in the first instance, be determined by considerations of jurisdiction. If there remains a choice of court, the Procurator Fiscal will have regard to the gravity of the offence, the offender's record and the likely penalty. The practical test to be applied in determining whether the trial is to take place according to solemn or summary procedure is to consider whether, having regard to the gravity of the offence, an adequate sentence can be imposed by a summary court in the event of conviction.

The choice of court and the form of procedure gives him an indirect control over the nature of the sentence imposed. With the 'two strikes' policy,[31] 'if an accused was being prosecuted for a second offence, the

[27] Ibid, s 65(1).

[28] The Report of an Inquiry into the Murder of Surjit Singh Chhokar, above n 4, ch 15.

[29] Gordon Jackson: Scottish Parliament Official Report—7 Nov 2001, col.3687.

[30] Submission of the Crown Office and Procurator Fiscal Service to the Scottish Parliament (Justice 2 Committee) 19 Nov 2001.

[31] Crime and Punishment Act (1997), a High Court has to impose a life sentence on those convicted of certain serious offences if they had a previous High Court conviction for a similar offence.

prosecution could determine whether he faced an automatic life sentence, by prosecuting in the High Court, or a maximum of five years, by prosecuting in the Sheriff Court.'[32]

(b) The Charges

The prosecutor possesses wide discretion in deciding whether to modify or drop some charges in return for a guilty plea (a 'plea-bargain').[33] He is not bound by the terms of the charge with which the police have formerly cautioned and charged an accused person. This gives him a lot of scope for negotiation with the accused. Apart from direction by the Lord Advocate, he cannot be obliged to change the terms of the charge by any person. This negotiation, which does not involve the judge, can take place at any time up to the leading of evidence at a trial or even during the trial which may be adjourned for this purpose at the request of the parties.

C. Challenge of the Prosecutor's Decision

The prosecution service is accountable solely to Parliament through the Lord Advocate. The independence of the prosecutor is often shown as an essential feature of the criminal justice system but, 'the shield of independence must not be used to hide prosecutors from reasonable scrutiny'.[34]

What are the options for individuals to challenge a decision to prosecute, not to prosecute or to question the charges?

A decision not to prosecute in a particular case may be challenged by the victim applying to the High Court for permission to bring a private prosecution (see VI below) but this is rarely granted. A decision to bring a prosecution may be open to challenge, for example, on the ground that the prosecutor has previously renounced the right to prosecute.[35] In addition, the courts have the power to disallow proceedings in the case of oppressive conduct by the prosecutor but the courts are reluctant to exercise this power to interfere with the discretion of the prosecutor.[36] The review of prosecution decisions by the courts is not impossible but extremely difficult and such challenges will rarely succeed.

Lord McCluskey, while Solicitor-General, commented that:[37]

[32] Duff , 'The Prosecution Service: Independence and Accountability', at 123.

[33] Sheriff Sheehan prefers to refer to 'plea adjustment' or 'plea negotiation'.

[34] B Smith, Scottish Public Prosecution, Policy and Practice: Issues of Independence and Accountability, in *Judicial Review* (1999), at 146.

[35] C Gane and C Stoddart, *Criminal Procedure in Scotland—Cases and Materials* (1994), 34.

[36] Ibid, 53.

[37] Lord McCluskey, 'The Prosecutors Discretion', 1980 *International Journal of Med Law* 1, 5, pp 8–9 quoted in J Fionda, *Public Prosecutors and Discretion: A Comparative Study* (Oxford: Oxford University Press, 1995), at 89.

when the system accords the public prosecutor with a discretion it must also create machinery for guarding against its abuse, whether corruptly or misguidedly. Answerability to Parliament is not the only possibility; the courts or the Ombudsman could provide the check.

Let us examine these two options:

Any judicial review would undermine the independence and function of public prosecution.

Lord Justice-General Clyde stated:[38]

It is utterly inconsistent with such a system that the courts should examine, as it was suggested that it would be proper or competent for us to do, the reasons which have affected the Lord Advocate in deciding how to exercise his discretion, and it would be still more absurd for this court to proceed to review that soundness.

Any review of prosecutors' decisions by the Ombudsman is prohibited by the Parliamentary Commissioner Act 1967 so the introduction of this form of remedy would require a change in the law. In certain limited circumstances, a Scottish appeal may provide for redress through the Ombudsman.

Since the current dispute centered on the Crown Office delay in examining new evidence, some years after the accused's original appeal, it was argued that 'the work done by the Crown Office after (the) appeal was done on behalf of the Scottish Office –that is to say acting as an agent of the Scottish Office.[39]

For individuals, the current provision for accountability of the Lord Advocate through Parliament is inadequate and ineffective. However, following the death of Steven Dekker, in a car accident on 19 September 1998, the Scottish Campaign Against Irresponsible Drivers ('SCID') suggested that 'the considerations and decisions taken in investigating and prosecuting road traffic deaths by the criminal justice system is cost and resource driven'. In connection with Mr and Mrs Dekker's Petition on the road death of their son the Lord Advocate's predecessor wrote at length to the Convenor of the Justice and Home Affairs Committee to explain why it could not be said that such cases were 'downgraded' for budgetary reasons.

In the *Chhokar* case (see note 4), Lord McCluskey addressing the jury, criticized the Crown's decision not to prosecute the three accused together. His comments and the response by the Lord Advocate at the time received widespread publicity. The Chhokar Family Justice Campaign and the general public concern led to the publication of two reports into the Crown Decision-Making on this case.

These two cases show that the Crown Office and Procurator Fiscal

38 *McBain v Crichton*, 1961 JC 25, *per* Lord Justice-General Clyde, at 29.

39 P Hill, 'Another Weapon in the Armoury' (1995) *NLJ*, 1620.

Service are facing the challenge of an increased scrutiny from Parliament. The publication of the Prosecution Code might encourage more challenges from individuals.

IV. DIVERSION FROM PROSECUTION

If there is sufficient evidence to justify proceedings, prosecution will be the preferred option. 'That means that alternatives to prosecution should be excluded before prosecution itself is considered.'[40]

A. Alternatives to Prosecution Include:

Fixed financial penalties, in the form of a conditional offer of a fixed penalty. These are issued in a wide range of Road Traffic offences depending upon the seriousness of the offence and sometimes the previous criminal record of the accused.

Warning letters: if the Procurator Fiscal decides the case merits action short of prosecution or an administrative penalty, he may warn the accused. Warning may be given in person but the majority are conveyed by letter.

Diversion: in certain cases, the Fiscal may decide to divert the matter from prosecution (psychiatric disposal or social work for example).

Conditional offers of fixed penalty ('Fiscal Fines'). Section 302 of the Criminal Procedure (Scotland) Act 1995 gives the Procurator Fiscal the power to make a conditional offer of a fixed penalty in relation to any offence in respect of which an alleged offender could competently be tried before a district court. A range of penalties of £25, £50, £75, or £100 is available and fixed installment payments of between £5 and £20 per fortnight may be offered.

B. Guidelines Regarding the Use of Fiscal Fines

Procurators Fiscal are provided with detailed and extensive guidelines regarding the use of fiscal fines, to ensure that they are employed consistently, and appropriately in the public interest.[41]

The Lord Advocate has directed that a fiscal fine must not be issued:

[40] Submission of the Crown Office and Prosecutor Fiscal Service to Justice Committee, 19 Nov 2001, 8.

[41] Ibid,12.

- Where the offence is possession of a class A drug, or where the offence of obstruction relates to a Class A drug and involves violence or is a contravention of section 23(4) (b) or (c) of the Misuse of Drugs Act 1971;
- Where the offence under the Vehicles Excise and Registration Act 1994 involves a claim for back duty, or involves forgery;
- Were the case involves overtones of sexual behaviour or racial motivation;
- Where the accused is under the age of 16 years;
- Where a non-police agency, empowered by statute to offer a fixed penalty has done so but the accused has failed to take up the offer, and
- Where there is information to suggest that the accused suffers from a mental disorder.

In addition, it may be *inappropriate* to offer a fiscal fine where:

- the case merits a disposal other than or in addition to a fine (e.g. forfeiture, destruction of an animal; compensation; disqualification of any kind);
- the offence was committed when the accused was on bail;
- the accused had previously been offered a fiscal fine but has not accepted the offer or where it is known that he has previously accepted an offer but failed to complete payments;
- there are good reasons for believing that the fine will not be paid;
- the accused has recent and analogous previous convictions, it would not normally be appropriate to offer a fiscal fine;
- the accused resides outwith Scotland—although a fiscal fine may be offered as long as he has a fixed address in Scotland or for:

A breach of the peace involving:

- Persistent alarming behaviour to the public or any individual
- A major disturbance
- Brandishing of firearms, knives or other similar weapons
- Intimidation of witnesses

Crimes of dishonesty other than the most trivial, and those in circumstances that disclose breach of trust or embezzlement;

Contraventions of the Civic Government (Scotland) Act 1982:

- Section 57 (in or on a building etc with intent to commit theft)
- Section 58 (convicted thief in possession)
- Section 52 (offences involving indecent photographs of children)
- Section 51 (publication of obscene material)
- Schedule 2, para 19 (sex shops)

Assault where:

- The injury is not minor
- The assault occurred in prison
- The victim is a child or particularly vulnerable It was associated with dishonest intent or intent to pervert the course of justice
- The victim is a police officer

Certain tachograph offences

Certain offence under the Licensing (Scotland) Act 1976

Other specified reason—there will be cases where a monetary penalty (ie a fine) is the appropriate disposal but the particular circumstances of the offence are such that a prosecution in court is in the public interest.

Fiscal fines are not intended for use in relation to serious or persistent offending.

C. Controversy

There is a public and media concern that the Crown may operate a policy in relation to diversion of prosecution which might be cost or resource driven. This was denied in Parliament:[42]

> Budgetary considerations form no part of decision making in the public interest in the way that has been suggested. We consider it is right to consider costs to the taxpayer and to prioritise resource allocation in favour of the investigation and prosecution of serious crime, but we are sorry to see that the myth of the 'no pro' quota persists. We are concerned with the efficient and effective use of our resources in the public interest, not 'prosecution by numbers.

As far as diversion from prosecution is concerned, according to Bill Aitken, a member of the Scottish Parliament,[43]

> When the system of diversion was introduced, it was supposed to be used for first offenders with one offence. There are now cases in Glasgow of people with previous convictions who have previously been offered a diversion being offered further diversions. That cannot be gainsaid; there is clear evidence that it happens. It is totally inappropriate. Everybody is entitled to a chance, but how many chances are people now getting? They are getting warning letters from fiscals, conditional offers and they are being diverted. The system is not working.

V. REGULATORY PROSECUTIONS

In Scotland, a few statutory offences may be prosecuted by a public body—

[42] Submission of the Crown Office and Prosecutor Fiscal Service to Justice Committee, 13.
[43] Official Report, 24 May 2001, col 962.

for instance, Customs and Excise or an education authority—but in practice, such proceedings are normally undertaken by the public prosecutor, who also receives occasional reports from other agencies such as the Television Licence Records Office and Health and Safety at Work Inspectorate. Thus, there is no problem of inconsistent prosecution policies.

VI. RELATION OF PROSECUTOR TO VICTIM

Compared to France, victims in Scotland are not in a strong position. In recent years, there has been a growth of public interest in victims in Britain but they have no kind of official standing in the process.

A. Victim's Influence on Proceedings

1. Starting Prosecution

There is a deep-seated distrust in Scotland of the concept of a private individual having the right to mount a criminal prosecution against a fellow citizen. The task of prosecution is seen as a job within the exclusive domain of the state.

The right to private prosecutions was abolished in summary cases (Criminal Justice (Scotland) Act 1995, section 63) and in solemn cases such proceedings it is necessary to apply for the Lord Advocate's permission to bring the case. The Lord Advocate's control over private prosecution is not absolute. The private prosecutor may apply to the supreme criminal Court in Scotland to ordain the Lord Advocate to give his concourse or to authorise the private prosecution.[44] There have only been two instances last century where the necessary permission has been granted.

The police have never prosecuted in Scotland as they did in England for many years.

2. For Plea Adjustment

According to the Lord Advocate,[45]

> if a procurator fiscal has a dozen cases with which to deal, there is little prospect of a discussion about plea adjustment with a victim in a summary case. When more serious cases such as sexual offences are being dealt with in the High Court, a genuine attempt is made to discuss the possible acceptance of a plea. However, the views of the victim will not and could not be decisive in such a situation. Part of the

44 *J and P Coats Ltd v Brown*, 1909, 6 Adams's Reports 19.

45 Scottish Parliament—Justice 1 and 2 Joint Committee, Official Report, 19 Sept 2001, col. 107 and 108.

consideration in serious sexual offences, in particular when children are involved, is whether it is better to accept a plea and to avoid the trauma for a witness giving evidence. That is the type of thing that might be gauged from a face-to-face interview. We are always conscious of the victims, in particular in serious cases, and we attempt to discuss the matter with them. That is not always possible or effective, because the victim does not always agree with our decision, but an effort is made.

3. Consultation on the Appropriate Sentence

A few years ago, Lord McCluskey invited the views of the victim before sentencing an accused in the High Court. On appeal, this approach was not met with approval.

B. Victim's Representation

The prosecutor is not the lawyer for the victim. The prosecutor's role is to prosecute independently in the public interest. As mentioned by a prosecutor[46]

> there is a relationship with the victim and with other witnesses, and there are duties associated with that. However, the relationship and duties are by no means the same as those in a solicitor–client relationship.

The procurator fiscal acts in the interests of the general public, rather than that of individuals.

The victim is Scotland is not represented in court.

C. Information, Support and Assistance

A study was commissioned last year by the Lord Advocate and the Justice Minister to examine a proposal by the Lord Advocate for a more integrated and comprehensive service to ensure that victims and witnesses in cases referred to Procurators Fiscal receive appropriate information, support and assistance.

Victim liaison office (VLO) for victims and next of kin in general have been established in Aberdeen and Hamilton and by Spring 2002 each Procurator Fiscal Regions should be have one.

In his report on the *Chhokar* case,[47] Dr Raj Jandoo stressed that 'needless and avoidable distress was caused to the family'. Serious failures in liaison with relative by the police and the Crown Office and Procurator Fiscal Service were established and the Lord Advocate publicly apologised to the family for the prosecution service's failure to liaise appropriately with them.

[46] Dr Alastair Brown from the Crown Office—Scottish Parliament, 18 Dec 2001.
[47] Above n 4, s 2.7.

VII. PROSECUTING POLICE OFFICERS

The Regional Procurators Fiscal have a duty to investigate all complaints which are made against police officers where the complaint alleges that a crime may have been committed by a police officer in the course of his duty. In the first instance most complaints are made direct to police forces. Where it may reasonably be inferred that a constable has committed a criminal offence in the course of duty the complaint must be referred by the Assistant Chief Constable to the Regional Procurator Fiscal. Further enquiries are directed and controlled by the fiscal personally or by staff acting on his behalf.

If the Regional Procurator Fiscal considers there is any substance in the complaint against the police, he will submit a full report of the evidence to Crown Office along with his assessment of the merits of the case and his recommendation. All reports submitted to Crown Office are considered personally by a Law Officer (the Lord Advocate or the Solicitor General) who takes the decision to prosecute or not. The decision must be communicated to the Regional Procurator Fiscal who is responsible for informing the complainer, the police and the Procurator Fiscal of the district concerned. The majority of reports do not lead to criminal proceedings being taken against a police officer.

The Procurator Fiscal has responsibility for the investigation and any subsequent prosecution. It is normally the role of the police to gather evidence and this can give rise to the impression that 'the police are investigating themselves'. In fact, the police undertake enquiries on behalf of the procurator fiscal who retains primacy at all times. The Lord Advocate's authority to investigate and prosecute all crime has been in existence long before the creation of any police force. The relationship between the Crown and the police is regulated by statute.[48]

The need to improve the general understanding of the independence of the Crown Office and Procurator Fiscal in investigating allegations of crime committed by a police officer was highlighted in the report 'A fair cop? Her Majesty's Inspectorate of Constabulary Report on the Police Complaints System' published in 2000.

In July 2001, the Justice Minister, Jim Wallace, announced the creation of a new independent body dealing with complaints against the police in Scotland. 'Although it has been shown that the vast majority of police

[48] Section 17 of the Police (Scotland) Act 1967 requires the police to make reports to the appropriate prosecutor. Section 12 of the Criminal Procedure (Scotland) Act 1995 provides that the Lord Advocate may, from time to time, issue instructions to a chief constable with regard to the reporting, for consideration of the question of prosecution, of offences alleged to have been committed within the area of such chief constable, and it shall be the duty of a chief constable to whom such instruction is issued to secure compliance.

complaints are dealt with fairly and impartially, we believe more independence in the system is needed to remove the doubt which still exists in the minds of some people.'[49]

The Minister underlined that the Procurator Fiscal Service will retain responsibility for the prosecution and the investigation of criminal allegations against the police. 'The same laws should apply to the police and the general public, and it would be wholly inappropriate to create a two-tier prosecution service.'

What might change is the possibility for those who were dissatisfied with the progress or the conduct of their complaint to appeal to the Ombudsman who could order new investigations, investigate the handling of complaints and carry out the 'random-testing' of the handling of complaints. The other option would be for the Independent Police Complaints body to have responsibility for handling all complaints in the first instance. It could either refer them to the police for investigation, supervise investigations into only the most serious complaints, supervise all investigations or undertake its own investigations into serious or all complaints.

[49] <http://www.scotland.gov.uk/news/2001/07/se1640.asp>.

United Kingdom National Committee for Comparative Law

Every four years the International Academy of Comparative Law convenes an International Congress devoted to examining current problems facing all legal systems. The XV Congress was held under the auspices of the United Kingdom National Committee of Comparative Law in partnership with the Faculty of Law of the University of Bristol and with the support of the British Institute of International and Comparative Law. The listed titles are a product of the Congress.

Volume 19 *(2nd ed.)*

UK LAW FOR THE MILLENNIUM

Building on the first edition this volume contains the complete collection of the *United Kingdom National Reports* which were presented at the XV International Congress of Comparative Law at the University of Bristol in the summer of 1998. These Reports provide expert, scholarly and reflective accounts of the state of the law of the United Kingdom in the approach to the Third Millennium. It provides an invaluable repository of learning on a wide range of issues of continuing topicality and importance.

Edited by John Bridge

ISBN 0 904281 15 9
Priced at £25.00

Volume 20

COMPARATIVE LAW FACING THE 21ST CENTURY

This companion volume, containing the *General Reports* which were presented to the XV Congress held in Bristol in 1998, extends the debate and provides a wide-ranging body of comparative analysis covering *inter alia* legal history, civil law and procedure, agrarian law, commercial law, constitutional law, human rights, administrative law and tax law which is not to be found elsewhere.

Edited by John Bridge

ISBN 0 904281 16 7
Priced at £45.00

Volume 15

UNITED KINGDOM LAW IN THE MID 1990s

Volume 1 of UK Law in the Mid 1990s addresses public law issues, principally of a constitutional character. Topics considered include the legitimacy of the constitutional judge and theories of interpretation, developing trends in parliamentarianism, the legal framework of foreign policy, subsidiarity as a principle of constitutional law, freedom of religion, agriculture and the environment, the legal condition of refugees in the United Kingdom, terrorism in its legal, political, domestic and international senses and state sponsored varieties, and the collective rights of employees in the public sector.

Volume 2 spans an important range of procedural subjects with an emphasis on techniques adopted by lawyers, the courts and the legislature to improve the quality and efficiency of the legal process, which is not only instructive in relation to the law in England and Wales, in Ireland and Scotland but provides an admirable basis for comparison. Emphasising the importance of comparison and of comparative methodology, consideration is also given to procedural questions, of prescription, jurisdiction, mass actions and testimony.

Edited by J.W. Bridge, E.K. Banakas,
J.P. Gardner & D.L. Carey Miller

ISBN 0 904 281 05 1 (vol 1)
ISBN 0 904281 10 8 (vol 2)
Priced at £35.00

UNITED KINGDOM NATIONAL COMMITTEE FOR COMPARATIVE LAW SERIES

THE BRITISH INSTITUTE OF INTERNATIONAL AND COMPARATIVE LAW
in association with
THE UNITED KINGDOM NATIONAL COMMITTEE OF COMPARATIVE LAW

Order Form

Please send me (__________) copy(s) of the following United Kingdom National Committee for Comparative Law books:-

____

______________________________ [____ Copy(s) @ £ ______]

____

______________________________ [____ Copy(s) @ £ ______]

*P&P @ £ __________ (UK)/£ __________ *(Overseas)* for the first book and £ __________ *(Overseas for every subsequent book)*

Price: £ __________

***P&P** - *UK £3.53 1st book, £1.18 each additional book (inc. VAT) Europe £4.00 1st book, £1.00 each additional book*

Members 25% Discount: £ __________

TOTAL: £ __________

Please make cheques payable to "BIICL" and return with this order form to:

Orders Department,
British Institute of International and Comparative Law,
Charles Clore House, 17 Russell Square, London WC1B 5JP
Fax no.: +44(0)20 7862 5152 *e-mail: info@biicl.org*

Address for delivery:

____

____

____

______________________________ Post Code ______________

Credit Card Payments:-

Name: ____

Card No. : ____

Card Type: ____

Expiry Date: ________ / ________ / ________

Signature: ____